FREE MOVEMENT IN EUROPEAN
COMMUNITY LAW

FREE MOVEMENT
IN
EUROPEAN
COMMUNITY
LAW

F. BURROWS

C.M.G., M.A. (Cantab.),
OF GRAY'S INN, BARRISTER

Formerly the Legal Adviser in the
Office of Her Majesty's Permanent Representative
to the European Communities, Brussels.

CLARENDON PRESS · OXFORD

1987

Oxford University Press, Walton Street, Oxford OX2 6DP
Oxford New York Toronto
Delhi Bombay Calcutta Madras Karachi
Petaling Jaya Singapore Hong Kong Tokyo
Nairobi Dar es Salaam Cape Town
Melbourne Auckland
and associated companies in
Beirut Berlin Ibadan Nicosia

Oxford is a trade mark of Oxford University Press

Published in the United States
by Oxford University Press, New York

British Library Cataloguing in Publication Data
Burrows, F.
Free movement in European Community law.
1. European Economic Community countries
2. European communities
I. Title
341'.094 [LAW]
ISBN 0-19-825492-X

Typeset by Joshua Associates Limited
Printed in Great Britain
at the University Printing House, Oxford
by David Stanford
Printer to the University

Preface

WHEN I first began to study European Community law, at about the time when the United Kingdom became a member of the Community, I gained the initial and no doubt shallow impression that here was a branch of law which was exciting, dynamic, intriguing, perplexing, and sometimes chaotic (in that order). It seemed to me that there was a need, shared by practitioners and students alike, for a book devoted solely to the basic freedoms upon which the substantive law of the European Community was so largely based, and to which so much of the litigation in the European Court had been devoted. This is such a book. Its preparation has, I hope, brought me to a deeper understanding of the subject. Today I can express the more confident and mature opinion that this field of law is exciting, dynamic, intriguing, perplexing, and sometimes chaotic (in that order).

Assiduous readers of literature on Community law will no doubt recognize Chapter 3 (State Monopolies) as an expanded version of my article on the same subject in volume 3 of the *Yearbook of European Law* (1984).

I am deeply indebted to all those who have offered encouragement, and to the successive secretaries who have with unfailing patience prepared the typescript. In particular I should like to thank my colleague Joanne Foakes for having prepared the index.

To the best of my information, belief, and understanding the law is stated as it was on 1 January 1985.

24 January 1985   F.B.

Contents

PART III CAPITAL

PART IV TERRITORIAL APPLICATION

PART V GENERAL EXCEPTIONS

Table of Cases

EUROPEAN COURT OF JUSTICE: LIST OF CASES
(IN ALPHABETICAL ORDER)

NATIONAL COURTS: UNITED KINGDOM

Table of Community Treaties

Table of Community Acts

Table of International Agreements

Abbreviations

Act of Accession	Act concerning the Conditions of Accession and the Adjustment to the Treaties, annexed to the Treaty, signed in Brussels on 22 January 1972, whereby Denmark, Ireland, and the United Kingdom of Great Britain and Northern Ireland became members of the EEC and EURATOM
AMLR	*Anglo-American Law Review*
Article 1 (etc.) EEC	Article 1 (etc.) of the Treaty establishing the European Economic Community
BK/L	Letter from the Allied Kommandatura, Berlin
Commission	Commission of the European Communities, established by Article 9 of the Merger Treaty
CAP	Common Agricultural Policy
CCT	Common Customs Tariff
CMLR	*Common Market Law Reports*
CML Rev.	*Common Market Law Review*
Council	Council of the European Communities established by Article 1 of the Merger Treaty
Court	The Court of Justice of the European Communities, unless otherwise stated
Crim. LR	*Criminal Law Review*
ECLR	*European Competition Law Review*
ECR	*European Court Reports* (official reports in English of the Court of Justice of the European Communites)
ECSC	European Coal and Steel Community
ECSC Treaty	Treaty establishing the European Coal and Steel Community
EEC	European Economic Community
EEC Treaty	Treaty establishing the European Economic Community
EFTA	European Free Trade Association
EL. Rev.	European Law Review
European Parliament	The Assembly referred to in Article 20 of the ECSC Treaty, Article 137 of the EEC Treaty, and Article 107 of the EURATOM Treaty
EUA	European Units of Account
EURATOM	European Atomic Energy Community
EURATOM Treaty	Treaty establishing the European Atomic Energy Community

GATT	General Agreement on Tariffs and Trade
Germany	The Federal Republic of Germany
Greek Act of Accession	Act concerning the Conditions of Accession and the Adjustment to the Treaties, annexed to the Treaty, signed in Brussels on 28 May 1979, whereby the Hellenic Republic became a member of the EEC and EURATOM
Ireland	The Republic of Ireland
ICLQ	*International and Comparative Law Quarterly*
JWTL	*Journal of World Trade Law*
KB	King's Bench Division
LIEI	*Legal Issues of European Integration*
LQR	*Law Quarterly Review*
Merger Treaty	Treaty establishing a single council and a single commission of the European Communities, signed in Brussels on 8 April 1965
NATO	North Atlantic Treaty Organization
New LJ	*New Law Journal*
OJ	*Official Journal of the European Communities*
Rec.	Recommendation
Reg.	Regulation of the Council of the European Communities, unless otherwise stated
RSC	Rules of the Supreme Court
RTDE	*Revue Trimestrielle de Droit Européenne*
SI	Statutory Instrument
TS	Treaty Series, published by HM Stationery Office
UNTS	United Nations Treaty Series
VAT	Value Added Tax, also referred to as 'turnover tax'
WLR	*Weekly Law Reports*
YEL	*Yearbook of European Law*

Bibliography

W. J. Ganshof van der Meersch, M. Waelbroeck *et al.*, *Droit des Communautés européennes* (Brussels, 1969).

T. C. Hartley, *The Foundations of European Community Law* (Oxford, 1981).

P. J. G. Kapteyn and P. Verhoren van Themaat, *Introduction to the Law of the European Communities* (London, 1973).

A. Parry and S. Hardy, *EEC Law* (London, 1981).

K. R. Simmonds (general editor), *Encyclopedia of European Community Law* (looseleaf, with regular supplements, London, 1973–).

D. Wyatt and A. Dashwood, *The Substantive Law of the EEC* (London, 1980).

PART I

GOODS

I

The Customs Union

THE task of the Community is to establish a common market (Article 1 EEC). The pillar on which a common market is built is a customs union, and Article 9 EEC provides for this. The first basic concept of a customs union is that goods produced in one of the member states should be able to circulate freely in all member states without the payment of customs duties.[1] The second is that goods produced outside the Community are subject, if imported into any member state, to payment of the appropriate customs duty, in accordance with a tariff which is common to all member states. The third is that once goods are imported into a member state, and allowed to circulate freely in that state, they may also circulate freely in all other member states, without the payment of any further customs duties. These three concepts are heralded in Article 9 EEC and developed in Articles 10–29. The establishment of the customs union is thus a fundamental feature of the system for free movement of goods throughout the Community.

According to Article 9, the customs union must involve the prohibition as between all member states of all customs duties on imports and exports and of all charges having equivalent effect. Article 12 prohibits all new duties and charges of that kind.[2] Articles 13–17 made transitional arrangements for the original member states leading towards these objectives. The arrangements have been completed, and are now largely of historical interest, although they did give rise to some judgments of the Court during the transitional period. The Court's interpretation of them therefore gives some insight into concepts which they share with the more permanent Articles. Articles 18–29 required the gradual setting up of the Common Customs Tariff for products from third countries. Article 9(2) ensures that the rules for the elimination of customs duties and equivalent charges between member states apply to products from third countries which are in free circulation. This rule was applied, for example, in *Hansen*.[3] Article 10 establishes how third-country goods get into free circulation.

---

[1] This includes freedom of transit when goods move from one member state to another via a third member state: Case 266/81, *Società Italiana per l'Oleodotto Transalpino (SIOT)* v. *Ministero delle Finanze* [1983] *ECR* 731.

[2] On the meaning of 'new', see Case 10/61, *Commission* v. *Italy* [1962] *ECR* 1.

[3] Case 148/77 [1978] *ECR* 1787. Once in free circulation, the products enjoy free movement in other respects as well: Case 119/78, *Peureux* [1979] *ECR* 975.

In relation to the customs union, there were transitional arrangements for Denmark, the Republic of Ireland, and the United Kingdom in the Act of Accession. These too are now spent. Similar provisions are to be found in Articles 24–34 of the Greek Act of Accession. They create several transitional periods, the last of which expires at the end of 1985.

THE MEANING OF 'GOODS'

Article 9 EEC refers to 'goods', a term with which we are familiar, and which has been given varying meanings in different United Kingdom statutes, although usually only with an indication that the expression 'includes' certain things (see for example s. 62 of the Sale of Goods Act 1893). Yet here we are faced with the familiar problem which arises when a multilingual treaty uses a term which has perhaps slightly different meanings in each of the languages, or which is legally defined in different ways in the private laws of the contracting states. The English, French, Danish, Dutch, German, Greek, Irish, and Italian texts of the EEC Treaty are equally authentic (Article 248 EEC, Article 160 Act of Accession, Article 152 Greek Act of Accession). There is therefore no reason to prefer the technical meaning of the expression 'goods' in any one member state to that in any other. Indeed, the meaning given to the word 'goods' in s. 20 of the Monopolies and Restrictive Practices (Inquiry and Control Act) 1948, where buildings and structures are included, would seem to be singularly inappropriate if applied to a treaty provision relating to free movement. Moreover, this linguistic problem arises in even more acute form when there is a need to consider the meaning, for example, of 'ordre public' or 'public policy' in Article 36 EEC and elsewhere. How then should it be resolved for Community purposes?

In the case of many earlier treaties, international tribunals have resorted to various methods of interpretation. One very useful test, which has frequently been applied, is to ask what meanings the word or phrase in question has in the various texts, and then to consider what essential principles can be deduced from them, and from other sources such as the *travaux préparatoires*. In this way a single common meaning can be distilled from the various ingredients. More general rules are now contained in Articles 31–3 of the Vienna Convention on the Law of Treaties of 23 May 1969.[4]

The European Court did not, however, reveal that it had resorted to any of these methods of interpretation in *Export Tax on Art Treasures: Commission v. Italy*.[5] That case was concerned with Italian legislation, designed to

[4] TS No. 58 (1980) Cmnd. 7964.
[5] Case 7/68 [1968] *ECR* 423. However, in Case 30/77, *R. v. Bouchereau* [1977] *ECR* 1999, at p. 2010, the Court used a method very similar to the ones prescribed in Articles 31–3 of the Vienna Convention.

discourage the export from Italy of art treasures and other items which formed part of the cultural heritage (Law No. 1089 of 1 June 1939). In some cases the law simply prohibited any export, and in others the exporter was required to pay a tax, calculated in increasing stages and with reference to the market value of the object. This tax was challenged by the Commission on the grounds that it had equivalent effect to a customs duty on export, and was therefore contrary to Article 16 EEC. Article 36 EEC provides an exception to the prohibition in Article 34 EEC of quantitative restrictions on exports and measures of equivalent effect. But the difficulty facing the defendants was that Article 36 relates only to Articles 30–4, and there is no corresponding clause to provide an escape from Article 16. The Italian government nevertheless referred to Article 36, and sought to argue that, since that article provided a special rule, the tax should be considered only in the light of that rule. It also maintained that items of artistic, historical or ethnographic interest were not merchandise in the ordinary sense, and that they were therefore not subject to the provisions of the Treaty relating to goods. The Court dismissed the argument and said:

Under Article 9 of the Treaty the Community is based on a customs union 'which shall cover all trade in goods'. By goods, within the meaning of that provision, there must be understood products which can be valued in money and which are capable, as such, of forming the subject of commercial transactions. The articles covered by the Italian law whatever may be the characteristics which distinguish them from other types of merchandise, nevertheless resemble the latter, inasmuch as they can be valued in money and so be the subject of commercial transactions.[6]

Coal and steel

It will be noted that this definition is wide enough to cover coal and steel, which fall within the provisions of the ECSC Treaty, and the nuclear materials with which the Euratom Treaty deals. It follows that these products are in principle also within the scope of the EEC Treaty. In order to avoid any conflict between the Treaties, Article 232 EEC provides that the EEC Treaty shall not affect the provisions of the ECSC Treaty or derogate from the Euratom Treaty. Despite the curious drafting of this Article, which at first sight seems to draw a distinction between not affect-ing and not derogating from, no difference of meaning seems to have been intended. The golden rule, therefore, when dealing with coal, steel, or nuclear products, is to see whether the ECSC or the Euratom Treaties contain any relevant provisions. If there are any, they prevail. Otherwise the EEC Treaty applies.

[6] Case 7/68, *Export Tax on Art Treasures: Commission* v. *Italy* [1968] *ECR* 423, p. 428. In Case 7/78, *R.* v. *Thompson, Johnson and Woodiwiss* [1978] *ECR* 2247, the court held, however, that coins which are legal tender, or which circulate freely in a member state, are to be treated as means of payment, falling for example within Article 106 EEC, rather than as goods. Other coins may be goods.

Article 4 ECSC prohibits within the Community all import and export duties, or charges having equivalent effect, as well as quantitative restrictions on the movement of coal and steel products. In this respect there is no significant difference between the EEC and ECSC Treaties. Article 72 ECSC, however, does not provide for a common customs tariff for coal and steel. It allows the Council, acting unanimously on a proposal from the High Authority[7] to fix minimum rates below which member states must not lower their customs duties on coal and steel as against third countries, and maximum rates which they must not exceed. The Article provides that, within any such limits, 'each Government shall determine its tariffs according to its own national procedure'.

If the matter rested there, a situation could therefore arise in which coal and steel was imported from outside the Community into one member state, which imposed a low import duty, and was then re-exported to another, which had a higher tariff with regard to non-Community countries. Once those products were in free circulation in the first member state, the second could not impose customs duties on them, because to do so would contravene Article 16 EEC; and in that way the second member state's external tariff might be undermined. In view of the unstable situation which could result from such practices, it is not surprising that steps have been taken to align the customs duties imposed by the member states on ECSC products, notwithstanding the latitude allowed to them by Article 72 ECSC. The first step in this process has usually been a decision of the representatives of the member states meeting within the Council. This is a procedure which is followed when the Council as such has no power under the relevant treaty to legislate, and its members, when assembled for Council business, take the opportunity of each other's presence to reach an agreement, which is in effect an intergovernmental agreement, although it is normally described as a 'decision'. In English the terminology is confusing because it is not a 'decision' of the legislative variety referred to in Article 189 EEC. The latter is called in German an 'entscheidung' whereas the former is a 'beschluss'. The next step has been for the Commission to make a recommendation under Article 74 ECSC.[8] Such recommendations are binding, by virtue of Article 14 ECSC, as to the aims to be pursued, although each member state is left free to choose the appropriate method for achieving those aims.[9] After the member states have taken appropriate action[10] the Community publishes the rates so fixed by incorporating them in the current Council regulation establishing the Common

---

[7] Now the Commission, by virtue of Article 9 of the Merger Treaty.
[8] See, e.g., Rec. 1905/78 of 28 July 1978, *OJ* 1978, L217/5.
[9] Cf. Directives under Article 189 EEC.
[10] See, e.g., the Customs Duties (ECSC) (No. 2) Order 1977, SI 1977/2041.

Customs Tariff.[11] However, the regulation records in the preamble that coal and steel products are included for information purposes, and in order to make the Schedule of Customs Duties easier to understand.[12] The practice is still to refer to coal and steel duties as 'the ECSC unified tariff', rather than the Common Customs Tariff. The former expression is defined in Article 31 of the Act of Accession. As a result of this whole process, the alignment of customs duties for ECSC products has largely been achieved.

The special rules in the ECSC Treaty which are relevant to the customs union are to be found in Article 71 (in general reserving to member states the conduct of their commercial policy towards third countries), Article 72 (referred to above), Article 73 (dealing with the administration of imports and export licences for trade with third countries, and providing for some degree of supervision by the Commission), Article 74 (enabling the Commission to make recommendations to counter the adverse effects of dumping,[13] of low pricing e.g. by monopolistic cartels outside the Community, and of unusually high imports into the Community which threaten serious injury to production in the common market of like or directly competing products,[14] and Article 75 (dealing with commercial agreements made by member states and the recommendations about them which the Commission is empowered to make).

Nuclear materials

The position with regard to nuclear materials is simpler. Special rules in the Euratom Treaty, which prevail over the EEC Treaty, are to be found in Articles 93–5. They provide a procedure and a timetable for achieving a customs union for the various nuclear products covered by the Treaty. The abolition of customs duties in intra-Community trade in these goods was as a result achieved before it was for products which fell only under the EEC Treaty. Nuclear materials were at the outset incorporated in the Common Customs Tariff which was prepared for EEC purposes. Since they now form part of that tariff, the duties can be altered or suspended in accordance with Article 28 EEC, a contingency not provided for by the Euratom Treaty.

The new member states, ECSC and Euratom

Articles 32 and 36 of the Treaty of Accession also contain special rules

[11] See, e.g., Council Regulation (EEC) No. 3000/80 of 28 October 1980, *OJ* 1980, L315/1, in particular ch. 27 (coal) and ch. 73 (steel).

[12] Ibid., last preambular paragraph.

[13] See, e.g., Rec. 1535/78 of 21 June 1978 (*OJ* 1978, L183/1), Rec. 1704/78 of 19 July 1978 (*OJ* 1978, L195/17), Rec. 1715/78 of 20 July 1978 (*OJ* 1978, L198/1), and Rec. 3140/78 of 29 Dec. 1978 (*OJ* 1978, L372/1).

[14] See, e.g., Rec. 330/77 of 15 Apr. 1977 (*OJ* 1977, L114/15), Rec. 282/78 of 9 Mar. 1978 (*OJ* 1978, L73/37) and Rec. 451/78 of 3 May 1978 (*OJ* 1978, L141/22).

concerning ECSC and Euratom products. Article 32(2) (a) of the Act of Accession required customs duties on imports of coal to be abolished between member states from the date of accession (1 January 1973). Article 32(2) (b) required the abolition of customs duties on imports of nuclear materials from 1 January 1974. Article 36(2) (a) and (b) provided similarly for charges having equivalent effect to customs duties on imports. These are all exceptions to the timetable relating to goods generally. Article 32 of the Greek Act of Accession deals with ECSC tariffs, but that Act contains no special rules for nuclear products.

CUSTOMS DUTIES, EQUIVALENT CHARGES, AND INTERNAL TAXATION

Articles 9 and 12 EEC prohibit the introduction of any new customs duties on imports or exports, or any charges of equivalent effect, and provide for the establishment of a customs union in which such duties and charges are prohibited. In order to understand the nature of these basic provisions it is necessary to consider the nature of a customs duty. It might be thought that this need is not removed by the fact that charges of equivalent effect are also eschewed, because it is difficult to ascertain whether a charge is of equivalent effect without first knowing the standard against which its equivalence is to be tested. However, the European Court has not found it necessary to give much guidance on the meaning of 'customs duty'. In so far as its judgments give any guidance at all, they do so largely by defining 'equivalent effect', from which it is possible by a reverse process of reasoning to infer the sense in which a customs duty is to be understood.

A customs duty is not defined in the Treaty. It may in a general sense be understood to be a charge levied in respect of goods on the occasion of their crossing a frontier, whether by import or export. This is not adequate, however, by way of a definition because it would also cover, for example, the excise duty which the ordinary traveller from France would have to pay if he landed at Dover with a quantity of Scotch whisky in excess of the duty-free allowance.[15] The duty is payable on the occasion of the entry of the goods into the United Kingdom, because section 5(a) of the Alcoholic Liquor Duties Act 1979,[16] imposes an excise duty on spirits imported into the United Kingdom. Section 5(b) of the Act, however, requires the same duty to be paid on spirits distilled in the United Kingdom. Herein lies the key to the difference between a customs import duty and an excise duty.

---

[15] Travellers' exemptions from turnover tax (VAT) and excise duties (the 'duty-free allowances') are set out in Dir. 169/69 (*OJ* 1969, L133/6), as amended by Dir. 230/72 (*OJ* 1972, L139/28), Dir. 82/77 (*OJ* 1977, L023/50), Dir. 800/77 (*OJ* 1977, L336/21), Dir. 1032/78 (*OJ* 1978, L366/28), Dir. 1033/78 (*OJ* 1978, L366/31), and Dir. 933/81 (*OJ* 1981, L338/24).

[16] C. 4.

The duty on the imported whisky is an excise, and not a customs, duty because the same amount is payable in respect of both home and imported products. It is a revenue-producing duty, imposed without discrimination on the grounds of the origin of the goods.[17] A customs duty, on the other hand, is essentially one which is imposed exclusively on goods crossing the frontier. It may be levied either to protect home-produced goods or simply as a means of raising revenue. Article 17(1) EEC may thus be understood to indicate that the latter kind of customs duty is subject just as much to the rules contained in Articles 9 and 15(1) as is the former kind. But the reason why both are caught is because both are in substance customs duties.

The direction in which the goods cross the frontier, however, may possibly be relevant. In the case of charges made exclusively on exported goods, the Court appeared at one stage to have created an exceptional rule. In *Demag*[18] it considered that a special turnover tax, levied only on exported goods, could not constitute a charge having an equivalent effect to a customs duty on export. Germany had introduced the tax in order to reduce its surplus balance of payments. The objective may at the time have been thought to be laudable. Nevertheless it is difficult to follow the logic of the distinction drawn by the Court between levies on imports and levies on exports. Indeed, it is not easy to reconcile the judgment in *Demag* either with the language of Article 12, which draws no distinction between imports and exports, or with the Court's later decisions in *Hulst*,[19] which in principle seems to have been correctly decided. In that case the Court ruled as follows:

An internal levy may have equivalent effect to a customs duty on export if it falls more heavily on export sales than on sales inside the country, or where the levy is intended to fund activities tending to make the home market more profitable than exports or in any other way to place the product intended for the home market at an advantage compared with the product intended for export.

It may be asked whether it is possible to have a fiscal duty which is levied only on imported products.[20] It clearly is not if there are identical or similar home-produced goods, because that would infringe Article 95. But if there is no home-produced equivalent it is permissible,[21] although as a matter of form, the national law ought to impose the duty on the product without appearing to draw any distinction between home-produced goods and goods produced elsewhere.

---

[17] See Case 7/67, *Wöhrmann* [1968] *ECR* 177, p. 184, Case 13/70 *Cinzano* v. *Hauptzollamt Saarbrücken* [1970] *ECR* 1089, p. 1096, and Case 32/80, *Officier van Justitie* v. *Kortmann* [1981] *ECR* 251.
[18] Case 27/74 [1974] *ECR* 1037.
[19] Case 51/74 [1975] *ECR* 79. See also case 7/68, *Commission* v. *Italy* [1968] *ECR* 423.
[20] See Article 17(3) EEC.
[21] Case 27/67, *Fink—Frucht* [1968] *ECR* 223.

Thus, in its judgment in *Commission* v. *France*,[22] the European Court
indicated that even a charge on a product from another member state,
when there is no domestic equivalent, does not amount to a charge
equivalent to a customs duty, but is to be regarded as internal taxation to
which Article 95 applies 'if it relates to a general system of internal dues
applied systematically to categories of products in accordance with objective criteria irrespective of the origin of the products'.[23] The facts in that
case were that France introduced in 1976 a tax on sales of photocopying
and other reproductive machines, and also a levy on the publication of
books. The proceeds were to go to a fund to subsidize the publication of
quality works, and the purchase of French and foreign books by libraries.
The French government maintained that the scheme helped to compensate authors and publishers for their loss of earnings through the wide-
spread use of reprography. The Commission claimed that, because French
production of reprographic machines was extremely small, the levy fell
almost exclusively on imported goods, and therefore contravened Article
12 EEC (and also Article 113 in so far as it applied to equipment from non-
member countries). The French defence was that the charges were neither
customs duties nor their equivalent, and that they were in accordance with
Article 95. The Commission's claim was dismissed. In its reasoning the
Court appears to have followed its usual practice in cases where a levy is
not actually called a customs duty, of concentrating on whether it is nevertheless of equivalent effect. It summarized its past jurisprudence in the
following terms:

Well-established case law of the Court is to the effect that the prohibition laid
down by Articles 9, 12 and 13 of the Treaty in regard to charges having equivalent
effect covers any charge exacted at the time of or on account of importation which,
being borne specifically by an imported product to the exclusion of the similar
domestic product, has the result of altering the cost price of the imported product
thereby producing the same restrictive effect on the free movement of goods as a
customs duty.

The essential feature of a charge having an effect equivalent to a customs duty
which distinguishes it from an internal tax therefore resides in the fact that the
former is borne solely by an imported product as such whilst the latter is borne
both by imported and domestic products.[24]

The second paragraph quoted above must, however, be qualified in the
exceptional case—to which reference has already been made—where there
are no equivalent domestic goods.

---

[22] Case 90/79 [1981] *ECR* 283.
[23] Ibid., p. 19, which appears to qualify what the Court said in Joined Cases 2 and 3/69
Diamentarbeiders [1969] *ECR* 211, p. 221, and Case 24/68, *Commission* v. *Italy* [1969] *ECR* 193,
p. 200. See also Case 78/76, *Steinike* [1977] *ECR* 595, p. 613.
[24] Ibid., p. 19. See also Case 142/77, *Statens Kontrol* v. *Larsen and Fleming* [1978] *ECR* 1543.

In a number of other cases the European Court has had the opportunity to consider the meaning and scope of 'charges having equivalent effect', and it is in this way that it has developed and refined the rules in Articles 9 and 12 EEC. Thus in *Fratelli Cucchi*[25] it had to consider Italian surcharges and special surcharges on sugar, the proceeds of which were intended to be used as part of government aid to the Italian sugarbeet producers and processors. Apart from the question of the compatibility of the aid with Articles 92 and 93 EEC, there was the issue as to whether the surcharges were equivalent to customs duties. They were levied on home-produced and imported sugar alike, and were therefore arguably a permissible internal tax, falling within Article 95 and not Article 9. As the Court pointed out, they could not fall to be dealt with under both Articles. The Court appears at first to have taken the view that if the levies in question had the sole purpose of financing activities for the specific advantage of the taxed domestic product so as to make good, wholly or in part, the fiscal charge imposed on that product, they should be regarded as equivalent to customs duties.[26] The ruling ('dispositif') given to the national court which had referred the question under Article 177 was slightly different, in that it suggested that the charges imposed on the domestic product would have to be made good in full out of the proceeds of the surcharge before the latter could be regarded as equivalent to a customs duty.[27] Nevertheless, it seems clear that if a levy is made on imported goods, it is not a complete answer for the member state imposing the levy to say that the same charge is made on home-produced goods.[28] It is necessary to consider how the proceeds of the levy are used and to ask whether, while appearing to be a non-discriminatory tax, it is in reality merely a device for imposing the equivalent of a customs duty. Nor is it sufficient to say that scales of tax are the same for home products and imported ones, if in fact they lead to heavier taxation of the latter.[29]

On the general question as to whether a charge should be regarded as part of a general internal tax, and thus subject only to Article 95, or as the equivalent of a customs duty, and therefore caught by Articles 9 and 12, the Court has given some general guidance in *Denkavit* v. *France*.[30] It said:

It is, however, appropriate to emphasize that, in order to relate to a general system of internal dues, the charge to which an imported product is subject must impose

---

[25] Case 77/76 [1977] *ECR* 987.

[26] Ibid., p. 1005, repeating the view expressed in Case 78/76, *Steinike* [1977] *ECR* 595.

[27] Case 77/76, *Fratelli Cucchi* [1977] *ECR* 987, p. 1010. The same discrepancy appears in Case 105/76, *Interzuccheri* [1977] *ECR* 1029. See also Case 222/78, *Beneventi* [1979] *ECR* 1163.

[28] See also Case 77/72, *Capolongo* v. *Maya* [1973] *ECR* 611, Case 94/74, *IGAV* v. *ENCC* [1975] *ECR* 699, and Case 7/67, *Wöhrmann* [1968] *ECR* 177.

[29] Case 127/75, *Bobie Getränkevertrieb* [1976] *ECR* 1079.

[30] Case 132/78 [1979] *ECR* 1923. Articles 95 and 12 cannot both apply to the same situation: Case 57/65, *Lütticke* [1966] *ECR* 205, Case 77/76, *Fratelli Cucchi* [1977] *ECR* 987.

the same duty on national products and identical imported products at the same marketing stage and that the chargeable event giving rise to the duty must also be identical in the case of both products. It is therefore not sufficient that the objective of the charge imposed on imported products is to compensate for a charge imposed on similar domestic products—or which has been imposed on those products or a product from which they are derived—at a production or marketing stage prior to that at which the imported products are taxed. To exempt a charge levied at the frontier from the classification of a charge having equivalent effect when it is not imposed on similar national products or is imposed on them at different marketing stages or, again, on the basis of a different chargeable event giving rise to duty, because that charge aims to compensate for a domestic fiscal charge applying to the same products—apart from the fact that this would not take into account fiscal charges which had been imposed on imported products in the originating Member State—would make the prohibition on charges having an effect equivalent to customs duties empty and meaningless.[31]

An earlier case of charges having equivalent effect was *Commission* v. *Luxembourg and Belgium*[32] (the gingerbread case). It arose over levies made on the import into Belgium and Luxembourg of gingerbread, created before the Treaty entered into force (on 1 January 1958), and in 1960 and 1961 progressively increased and extended to similar products. In considering whether these levies infringed Articles 9 and 12, the Court first emphasized the essential nature of the prohibition which they imposed, from which it followed that any exception must be clearly stated and narrowly interpreted. Charges of equivalent effect, being an extension of, and not exceptions to, the rule meant all measures which were not customs duties in the classic form (a concept which the Court did not explain or define) but which would lead to the same discriminatory or protective results as customs duties. The Court said:

It follows from all these factors that a charge having equivalent effect within the meaning of Articles 9 and 12, whatever it is called and whatever its mode of application, may be regarded as a duty imposed unilaterally either at the time of importation or subsequently, and which, if imposed specifically upon a product imported from a Member State to the exclusion of a similar domestic product, has, by altering its price, the same effect upon the free movement of products as a customs duty.[33]

Judged by this standard, the unilateral increases in duty which were made after the entry into force of the Treaty, and their extension to other products, could not be reconciled with Article 12. They could not be justified under Article 95 because they were not imposed on similar domestic products. The defendants' argument that they were justifiable because

[31] Case 132/78, *Denkavit* v. *France* [1979] *ECR* 1923, pp. 1934-5.
[32] Joined Cases 2 and 3/62 [1962] *ECR* 425.
[33] Ibid., p. 432. See also Case 10/65, *Waldemar Deutschmann* [1965] *ECR* 469.

they prevented price undercutting by the imported articles was dismissed on the ground that it ignored the competition rules in the Treaty,[34] and would lead to an absurd situation which was diametrically opposed to that intended by the Treaty.

It will be noted that in defining equivalent measures the Court, in the passage quoted above, referred only to unilaterally imposed duties, thus excluding any measure which might result from the application of a Community procedure. One such procedure, which was available during the transitional period, is referred to in Article 26. It also appears that, even after the end of the transitional period, it would be open to the Commission, acting under Article 115, to authorize a member state to introduce a protective customs duty against another member state if the provisions of that Article were satisfied. It may be thought, however, that the Commission would be reluctant to take such a step if the problem could be solved by other means.

The distinction between unilateral national measures and those which are taken in pursuance of a Community procedure is important in various contexts. Actions which would appear difficult to justify under the EEC Treaty if taken by member states on their own initiative seem less so when taken by agreement, and in furtherance of a community objective. This can be illustrated by the attitude of the Court in *Bauhuis* v. *Netherlands*,[35] which concerned the requirement in Article 16 EEC that member states must abolish customs duties on export, and charges having equivalent effect. The Dutch government imposed charges for certain veterinary and public health inspections which had to be carried out on bovine animals, swine, and other animals destined for export. Some of the charges were only sufficient to cover inspections made in pursuance of Council Directive 64/432/EEC. Others were not covered by the Directive, and the inspections in those cases were governed solely by provisions of national law, although they were designed to ensure that the exported goods would meet the standards imposed by the importing countries. The Advocate General considered that both sets of charges contravened Article 16. So far as concerned the cases covered by the Directive, he relied on the judgment of the Court in *Cadsky*,[36] in which the Court had ruled that it was irrelevant that the fee was payable in connection with the application of Community regulations. In *Bauhuis*, however, the Court drew a distinction between those inspections which were made under the Directive and those which were not. Charges for the former were held to be permissible, provided that they did not exceed the actual cost of the inspection and did not infringe Article 95. The Court's reasoning seems to have been that, although the charges were

---

[34] Articles 85–94.
[35] Case 46/76 [1977] *ECR* 5.
[36] Case 63/74 [1975] *ECR* 281.

not harmonized on a Community basis, both the inspections and the objective of the Directive were to eliminate the need for multiple national inspections at the frontier. Seen in that light, they assisted rather than hindered free movement. On the other hand, the Court condemned charges for inspections not covered by the Directive for two reasons: first, because the inspections were carried out unilaterally and were in no way connected with any Community rules, and secondly because the inspections for exported animals were different from those on animals for the home market.[37]

The Court went even further in *Commission* v. *Netherlands*.[38] In that case some of the inspections were not carried out at the frontier, and the charges were not levied at that time. However, as has already been seen, the criterion is not the time at which the charges are payable, but rather the event which makes them payable. Thus a true excise duty can be levied at the time a frontier is crossed, and a charge can amount to a customs duty even if levied before or after such an occasion. What matters is whether the reason for the payment is that a frontier has been, or will be, crossed.[39] Since the charge was made because the goods were to be exported, it was thus necessary to consider whether they amounted to a customs duty or its equivalent. The Court answered that question by upholding the legality of Dutch charges for phyto-sanitary inspections before export, which were made, not in pursuance of Community rules, but in accordance with the International Plant Protection Convention of 6 December 1951, by which all member states were bound. The Court's reasoning was that the Dutch measures were not adopted unilaterally for purely national reasons, that they did not hinder trade but, on the contrary, removed obstacles which would otherwise arise through use by the importing states of Article 36 EEC, and that provided the fees did not exceed the cost of the inspections they were not equivalent to customs duties.

There are, however, limits to the extent to which secondary Community legislation may authorize exceptions to basic principles. In *Ramel* v. *Receveur des Douanes*,[40] the Court declared Article 31(2) of Regulation 816/70 to be incompatible with Article 13 EEC, in so far as it authorized member states to levy charges equivalent to customs duties in intra-Community trade. The case can be distinguished from *Bauhuis*[41] and *Commission* v. *Netherlands*,[42] in that in those cases free movement could on one view be

---

[37] See also Case 132/80, *United Foods* v. *Belgium* [1981] *ECR* 995, holding a levy for health inspection of imported fish to contravene Articles 9, 12, and 13.

[38] Case 89/76 [1977] *ECR* 1355.

[39] Joined Cases 2 and 3/62, *Commission* v. *Luxembourg and Belgium* [1962] *ECR* 425; Case 78/76, *Steinike* [1977] *ECR* 595.

[40] Joined Cases 80 and 81/77 (1978] *ECR* 927.

[41] Case 46/76 (1977] *ECR* 5.

[42] Case 89/76 [1977] *ECR* 1355.

taken to have been assisted, whereas in *Ramel* the French import duty on Italian wine could in no sense have been said to have that effect.

The Court added, in *Germany* v. *Commission*,[43] and repeated in *Diamentarbeiders*,[44] a refinement to its definition of charges having equivalent effect, by holding that the smallness of the charge was immaterial. A closer examination of the latter case reveals features which are not altogether easy to reconcile with *Commission* v. *France*.[45] It concerned a Belgian law requiring compulsory contributions to a social fund for diamond workers, which were levied on all persons importing unworked diamonds. In the course of its judgment, the Court concluded that the prohibition in the Treaty of customs duties and equivalent charges was absolute in nature, and that its object was to ensure the free movement of goods across frontiers. Thus the objective was not simply to remove barriers which were designed to protect the products of the importing country and to shield them from competition. When prohibiting customs duties the Treaty did not, as the Court pointed out, distinguish between those goods which competed with local products and those which did not. From this it might be inferred that charges cannot be levied on imported goods even when there is no local equivalent. As has been stated above, the Court considered in *Commission* v. *France* that the French government could in effect, and as part of a general scheme of taxation, make charges on imported goods when there was no local equivalent. One difference between the two cases was that, in the earlier one, the charges specifically referred to the importing of goods as the event which gave rise to the charge, whereas, in the later case, the qualifying event was not specifically related to import. It seems possible, therefore, that by making a particular levy relate to some event unconnected with the crossing of a frontier, e.g. the supply of uncut diamonds to a diamond-cutter, a member state could avoid infringing Articles 9 or 12, even if all uncut diamonds were imported and the tax therefore fell exclusively on imported goods. If the latter is the case it would also seem necessary, in order to avoid infringing the principle established in *Cucchi*,[46] to ensure that the proceeds were not devoted wholly, or perhaps even in part, to creating a benefit for the producers of a domestic product. In that respect it will be noted that in *Diamentarbeiders*[47] the monies were indeed used for social purposes. It will be interesting to see whether the Court on some future occasion will seek to explain the interrelation of these cases. On the other hand, it may be that *Commission* v. *France*[48] simply represents a modification of the Court's earlier thinking;

[43] Joined Cases 52 and 55/65 [1966] *ECR* 159.
[44] Joined Cases 2 and 3/69 [1969] *ECR* 211.
[45] Case 90/79 [1981] 3 *CMLR* 1.
[46] Case 77/76 [1977] *ECR* 987.
[47] Joined Cases 2 and 3/69 [1969] *ECR* 211.
[48] Case 90/79 [1981] 3 *CMLR* 1.

and if that is so, the Court may in future prefer not to draw attention to *Diamentarbeiders*.

For a charge to be equivalent to a customs duty it need not necessarily be levied by the central government. It can be charged by what the Court described as 'an agency governed by public law': *Capolongo* v. *Maya*.[49] The body in question was an Italian corporation incorporated under public law, consisting of producers of paper and cellulose and enterprises using cellulose. The Court's reference to an agency governed by public law does not provide a precise test for a common law country like the United Kingdom. Nevertheless, the principle could extend to nationalized bodies in the United Kingdom which provide a public service, and whose activities are governed by statute. To what extent the rule in this case does apply to such bodies can only be clarified by the Court itself. In such cases the distinction between charges for services rendered (e.g. in transporting goods) and other charges would probably be crucial.

Charges for services rendered

The levying of a charge in the event of goods crossing a frontier does not infringe Articles 9, 12, or 16 when the charge can genuinely be said to represent payment for a service rendered. The logic is simple. The payment is exacted, not because goods cross a frontier, but because a service is given. Examples might be charges for the use of a ferry, bridge, or tunnel which crossed a frontier; and it would be immaterial whether the facility was provided by some governmental or local authority or by persons in the private sector. In *Commission* v. *Italy*[50] the Court mentioned, in relation to charges made by a member state, the possibility of a proportional[51] payment for a service rendered, which would be permissible provided that it could not lead to the circumvention of Articles 9, 12, 13, and 16. The Court proceeded to reject, however, the argument that, because it enabled exporters to have precise statistics on the movement of goods and the state of the market, a 'statistical levy' on exported goods was consideration for a service rendered. The statistical information was, in the Court's view, beneficial to the economy as a whole and to administrative authorities, and any benefit to exporters was too general and too difficult to assess for it to be regarded as consideration for the levy.

The notion of payment for services rendered has given rise to a line of cases. An investigation of whether a quantitative restriction (which was legitimate at the time) applied or whether the goods could be admitted to the German market, was held not to be a service rendered so as to justify a

---

[49] Case 77/72 [1973] *ECR* 611.
[50] Case 24/68 [1969] *ECR* 193.
[51] Proportionality was also mentioned in Joined Cases 2 and 3/69, *Diamentarbeiders* [1969] *ECR* 211, Case 39/73, *REWE* [1973] *ECR* 1039, and Case 132/78, *Denkavit* v. *France* [1979] *ECR* 1923.

frontier charge: *Germany* v. *Commission*.[52] Nor was a statistical levy (*Commission* v. *Italy*[53]); nor a duty for administrative services rendered by customs officers in connection with imported goods (*Commission* v. *Italy*[54]); nor a charge for inspecting beef crossing a frontier (even if permitted by Article 36 EEC) and for giving a certificate that the meat was free of disease and of good quality (*Marimex*[55]); nor an unloading charge payable only in respect of imported goods to the customs office at the port of Trieste and devoted to the provision and maintenance of port installations (*Variola*[56]); nor a charge for the phyto-sanitary inspection of apples at the German frontier (*Rewe*[57]); nor charges for veterinary and public health examinations at the frontier which are administrative operations carried out by the state, and intended to ensure public health in the interest of the public rather than that of the importer (*Simmenthal*[58]); nor a charge on the export of fruit and vegetables to cover the cost of exercising quality control at the frontier (*Cadsky*[59]); nor storage charges levied on imported goods when submitted for completion of customs formalities at a special store.[60] Transit charges are prohibited, but not charges for transport or other services connected with transit: *SIOT* v. *Ministero delle Finanze*.[61]

Internal taxation

Internal taxation has to some extent been dealt with earlier in this chapter, because it is impossible to consider customs duties and their equivalent without examining how to distinguish them from taxation falling solely within Article 95.[62] We have seen that to escape Articles 9 and 12, and to be judged instead under Article 95, a national charge must relate to a general system of taxation based on objective criteria, irrespective of the origin of the goods in question;[63] that the chargeable event must be the same in the

---

[52] Joined Cases 52 and 55/65 [1966] *ECR* 159.   [53] See above.
[54] Case 8/70 [1970] *ECR* 961; and see Case 84/71, *Marimex* [1972] *ECR* 89, Case 39/82, *Donner* v. *Netherlands* [1983] *ECR* 19, and Case 133/82, *Commission* v. *Luxembourg* [1983] *ECR* 1669.
[55] Case 29/72 [1972] *ECR* 1309. See also Case 87/75, *Bresciani* [1976] *ECR* 129, Case 21/75, *Schroeder* [1975] *ECR* 905, and Case 314/82, *Commission* v. *Belgium*, judgment of 20/3/84. But see Case 30/79, *Land of Berlin* v. *Wigei* [1980] *ECR* 151, concerning such charges at the external frontiers of the Community; and Case 88/82, *Amministrazione delle Finanze* v. *Armando and Ottavio Leonelli* [1984] 2 *CMLR* 362.
[56] Case 34/73 [1973] *ECR* 981. See also Case 266/81, *SIOT* [1983] *ECR* 731.
[57] Case 39/73 [1973] *ECR* 1039. See also Case 158/82, *Commission* v. *Denmark* [1984] 3 *CMLR* 658.
[58] Case 35/76 [1976] *ECR* 1871; and see Case 70/77, *Simmental* [1978] *ECR* 1453, and Case 1/83 *IFG* v. *Freistaat Bayern*.
[59] Case 63/74 [1975] *ECR* 281. But see Case 46/76, *Bauhuis* v. *Netherlands* [1977] *ECR* 5.
[60] Case 132/82, *Commission* v. *Belgium* [1983] *ECR* 1649; Case 133/82, *Commission* v. *Luxembourg* [1983] *ECR* 1669.
[61] Case 266/81 [1983] *ECR* 731.
[62] For the meaning of 'taxation' in Article 95, see Case 4/81, *Hauptzollamt Flensburg* v. *Andresen* [1982] *ECR* 2835.
[63] Case 90/79, *Commission* v. *France* [1981] *ECR* 283. See also Case 319/81, *Commission* v. *Italy* [1983] 2 *CMLR* 517.

case of national products and imported ones;[64] and that the tax cannot be
imposed only on imported products, leaving the equivalent domestic ones
untaxed.[65]

Once it has been decided that Article 95 applies, rather than Articles 9 or
12, it may be necessary to consider what, for the purposes of Article 95(1), is
an indirect internal taxation of the product concerned. Does it include
taxation of its components, or of the raw materials from which it was made,
or of the services through which it was made? Looking at the question from
a different point of view, when is the taxation so remotely removed from the
end-product that it cannot reasonably be said to amount even to an indirect
taxation of that product? According to the Court in *Molkerei—Zentrale* v.
Paderborn[66] indirect taxation includes all taxation imposed at earlier stages
of manufacture and marketing. It also includes taxation of raw materials
and of semi-finished goods which go to make up the final goods: *Commission* v. *Italy*.[67] A similar question of indirectness arises in connection
with Article 95(2), which prohibits the taxation of the products of other
states if it is of such a nature as to afford indirect protection to other
products. The common situation would be where a member state sought to
tax, for example, oranges, which it did not grow, at a higher rate than
apples, which it did produce. This could well infringe Article 92(2),
because the test seems to be whether the imported product is taxed more
highly than a domestic one which is capable of being substituted for it in
normal usage, and may therefore be in competition with it: *Finck—Frucht*.[68]

That the need to ensure free competition underlies Article 95 can be
seen from *Stier*,[69] where it was held that Article 95 does not prevent
member states from imposing taxes on imported goods originating in other
member states when there is no similar domestic product capable of being
protected. In that case, Germany taxed lemons imported from Italy. It is
distinguishable from the hypothetical example given above about the
oranges and apples. The latter are both dessert fruit, even though not
everybody might find them equally palatable. Germany, on the other hand,
produces no fruit which is capable of being substituted for lemons.

The question of what are 'similar domestic products' for the purposes of
Article 95(1) cannot always be answered simply. The question arose in a
number of infraction cases against France, Italy, Denmark, Ireland, and the

[64] Case 132/78, *Denkavit* v. *France* [1979] *ECR* 1923.
[65] Joined Cases 2 and 3/62, *Commission* v. *Belgium and Luxembourg* [1962] *ECR* 425. But see Case
15/81, *Gaston Schul Douane Expéditeur BV* v. *Inspecteur der Invoerrechten en Accijnzen, Roosendaal* [1982]
ECR 1409 for a different rule in respect of certain VAT payments.
[66] Case 28/67 [1968] *ECR* 143.
[67] Case 45/64 [1965] *ECR* 857. A tax on transport is also an indirect tax on the goods carried:
Case 20/76, *Schöttle* [1977] *ECR* 247.
[68] Case 27/67 [1968] *ECR* 223.
[69] Case 31/67 [1968] *ECR* 235.

UK, along with other issues concerning the scope of Article 95 as a whole. They all related to alcoholic drinks, and the reasoning in the Court's decisions was very similar in all of them.

In *Commission* v. *France*[70] the Court declared France to be in breach of Article 95 as regards imported products, by applying discriminatory taxation on spirits. France taxed geneva, and other spirits distilled from cereals (mainly imported), more heavily than spirits obtained from wine and fruit (mainly home-produced). One issue was whether the two categories were similar products. The Court declined to answer the question, holding that it was unnecessary to do so because it was impossible to deny the protective nature of the French tax system, and this contravened Article 95(2).[71]

Commission v. *Italy*[72] concerned the taxation which bore more heavily on spirits distilled from cereals and sugarcane than spirits obtained from wine and marc. This tax too was held to contravene Article 95(2) without the need to consider whether they were similar products for the purposes of Article 95(1).

Similar conclusions were reached, for much the same reasons, in *Commission* v. *Denmark*,[73] where Danish taxation was less severe on consumers of aquavit (schnapps) than on those who preferred other spirits. The Court summed up the effect of Article 95(1) and (2) as follows:

The above-mentioned provisions supplement, within the system of the Treaty, the provisions on the abolition of customs duties and charges having equivalent effect. Their aim is to ensure free movement of goods between the Member States in normal conditions of competition by the elimination of all forms of protection which result from the application of internal taxation which discriminates against products from other Member States. As the Commission has correctly stated, Article 95 must guarantee the complete neutrality of internal taxation as regards competition between domestic products and imported products.[74]

The Court described 'similar' products as needing to be interpreted flexibly. The criterion was not whether they were strictly identical in nature, but whether they were given similar or comparable use. It also said:

The function of the second paragraph of Article 95 is to cover, in addition, all forms of indirect tax protection in the case of products which, without being similar within the meaning of the first paragraph, are nevertheless in competition, even partial, indirect or potential, with certain products of the importing country.[75]

---

[70] Case 168/78 [1980] *ECR* 347.

[71] Ibid., p. 369.

[72] Case 169/78 [1980] *ECR* 385. See also Case 16/69, *Commission* v. *Italy* [1969] *ECR* 377. But see Case 46/80, *Vinal* v. *Orbat* [1981] *ECR* 77, and Case 26/80, *Schneider—Import* v. *Hauptzollamt Mainz* [1980] *ECR* 3469.

[73] Case 171/78 [1980] *ECR* 447.

[74] Ibid., p. 462.   [75] Ibid., p. 463.

The question of similarity or comparability of alcoholic drinks raised difficulties because, although all the drinks were distilled in the form of spirits, there were differences not only in the raw materials used but also in the widely different tastes of consumers in the various member states. The solution adopted by the Court seems therefore to have been to say that they were all either similar products or, in cases where the similarity was doubtful or contested, covered by Article 95(2) on account of their being in 'partial or potential competition'.[76]

Commission v. *Ireland*[77] was a little different, in that it was common ground that Ireland deferred payment of duty on certain home-produced drinks but demanded immediate payment in the case of the same products when imported from other member states. This discrimination was held to infringe Article 95.

In *Commission* v. *United Kingdom*,[78] the Court found itself in some difficulty. The complaint was that the United Kingdom tax on wine was heavier than it was on beer, and the Commission alleged that, because these two products were in competition with one another, Article 95 was being infringed. The Court found that there was a degree of substitution of one drink for the other, and that they competed with each other, but that there were also great differences between the two. For the latter reason it was difficult to make comparisons from the tax point of view, although the Court tended to favour testing the relevant tax burden by reference to alcoholic strength. The Court then ordered[79] the parties to re-examine the matter and report back to the Court—possibly in the hope that they would be able to settle their differences, thus avoiding the need to pursue the litigation. Having failed to settle their dispute, the parties reported back to the Court, which held, on the facts available to it, that, whichever of the suggested standards of comparison was adopted, the United Kingdom's tax system had the effect of subjecting wine imported from other member states to an additional tax burden, so as to afford protection to domestic beer production. The United Kingdom had therefore failed to fulfil its obligations under Article 95.[80]

Article 95(1) refers to taxation in excess of that imposed directly or indirectly on similar domestic products. What is excessive needs to be tested, not only with reference to the respective rates of the two taxes, but also after taking into account the advantages and exceptions which each tax

---

[76] Ibid., p. 465. In Case 216/81, *Cogis* [1982] *ECR* 2701, the Court equated whisky with other spirits for the purposes of Article 95.

[77] Case 55/79 [1980] *ECR* 481.

[78] Case 170/78 [1980] *ECR* 417 (first judgment).

[79] Ibid.

[80] Case 170/78 [1983] *ECR* 2265 (second judgment). See also Case 112/84 (pending), *M. Humblot* v. *Directeur des services fiscaux, Vesoul*, concerning a special French tax on vehicles of more than 16 CV, such vehicles not being manufactured in France.

carries with it: *Schöttle*.[81] Moreover, a flat-rate tax calculated on the value of goods, which is the same for both imported goods and those produced at home, is excessive if it is levied on the imported product at a later stage of its processing, when its value will naturally be higher: *Commission* v. *Belgium*,[82] where local timber was taxed on its value standing or felled, whereas imported timber was taxed on its value in the semi-processed condition in which it arrived.

If a tax contravenes Article 95, it is for the national court, and not the European Court, to decide in accordance with national laws whether this affects the legality of the tax as a whole or only that part of it which is excessive: *Molkerei*.[83]

It is tempting to assume after reading the text of Article 95 that it is concerned only with products imported from other member states, the object being to ensure that they are not unfairly taxed. The temptation is strengthened by the fact that Articles 96–8 contain special rules about exports. It is quite consistent with such an assumption that the European Court ruled in *Peureux*[84] that Article 95 does not prohibit a member state from imposing on a domestic product internal taxation in excess of that imposed on similar products imported from other member states. However, the Court appears to take the view that Article 95 applies to taxes on exports as well as imports. *Statens Kontrol* v. *Larsen*[85] arose out of a Danish tax on consumers of precious metals. It had to be paid by every undertaking which manufactured, imported, or dealt in articles of precious metal. The questions referred by the national court under Article 177 concerned such articles which were for export. Although the facts are not entirely clear from the report, one of the questions asked was whether it was relevant that the precious metal was supplied to the Danish manufacturer by a foreign customer and then re-exported by him as a finished product. It may be, therefore, that the case was concerned with raw materials which were imported from a member state, transformed into finished articles and taxed as such, and then re-exported. The Court in fact seems to have dealt with the case on that basis. After referring to Articles 95–8, it said:

It therefore seems necessary to interpret Article 95 as meaning that the rule against discrimination which forms the basis of that provision also applies when the export of a product constitutes, within the context of a system of internal taxation, the chargeable event giving rise to a fiscal charge.

It would in fact be incompatible with the system of the tax provisions laid down

---

[81] Case 20/76 [1977] *ECR* 247. See also Case 17/81, *Pabst* [1983] 3 *CMLR* 11; Case 38/82 *Hauptzollamt Flensburg* v. *Hansen* [1984] 3 *CMLR* 1.

[82] Case 77/69 [1970] *ECR* 237.

[83] Case 28/67 [1968] *ECR* 143, p. 154; and Case 34/67, *Lück* [1968] *ECR* 245. See also Case 68/79, *Just* [1980] *ECR* 501, and Case 4/81, *HZA Flensburg* v. *Andresen* [1981] *ECR* 2835.

[84] Case 86/78 [1979] *ECR* 897.

[85] Case 142/77 [1978] *ECR* 1543.

in the Treaty to acknowledge that Member States, in the absence of an express prohibition laid down in the Treaty, are free to apply in a discriminatory manner a system of internal taxation to products intended for export to other Member States.[86]

It is not entirely clear what view the Court would take in a case which did not in any way concern imports, even in the shape of the raw materials from which goods were made and exported. Clarification at some future date would be welcome.

Direct effect of provisions concerning intra-Community trade

At an early stage in the development of the community, and while the gradual elimination of customs duties was proceeding, the Court in *Van Gend en Loos*[87] held Article 12 to have direct effect. The Court has since been inconsistent in its use of the words 'direct effect' and 'directly applicable' (the language of Article 189) when describing certain provisions of some Articles of the EEC Treaty and of some directives. One or two writers have sought to draw a distinction between the two.[88] However, the phrase 'direct effect' will hereafter be used to describe the situation where, as in *Van Gend en Loos*, a provision is held to have direct effect as law in the member states, and to create rights for individuals which the national courts must protect, with the usual assistance from the European Court under the Article 177 procedure, notwithstanding any constitutional or other national law to the contrary. The choice of terminology has been made simply for the purpose of convenience and consistency. It does not represent any attempt to reconcile the Court's decisions on the direct effect of directives with the provisions of Article 189. Nor is it intended to imply support of or opposition to those who maintain that some provisions of regulations do not have direct effect, notwithstanding that Article.[89]

In *Diamentarbeiders* v. *Brachfield*[90] the Court held Articles 9 and 12 to have direct effect, and in *Eunomia di Porro*[91] it held Article 16 to have like effect. In *SACE*[92] it held the obligation in Commission Directive 68/31,[93] to eliminate the Italian duty charged on imported goods for administrative services, taken in conjunction with Articles 9 and 13(2) EEC, to have like effect. In that case the Directive, addressed to the Italian government, supplied a timetable for the progressive abolition of the duties in question,

---

[86] Ibid., p. 1558.

[87] Case 26/62 [1963] *ECR* 1.

[88] J. A. Winter, [1972] 9 *CML Rev.*, 425; A. J. Easson, [1979] *ICLQ*, 319; G. Bebr, [1970] 19 *ICLQ*, 257.

[89] E.g., the Advocate General in Case 131/79, *Santillo* [1980] *ECR* 1585.

[90] Joined Cases 2 and 3/69 [1969] *ECR* 211, p. 223.

[91] Case 18/71 [1971] *ECR* 811.

[92] Case 33/70 [1970] *ECR* 1213; and see Cases 77/72, *Capolongo* v. *Maya* [1973] *ECR* 611, and 94/74, *IGAV* v. *ENCC* [1975] *ECR* 699.

[93] *OJ* 1968, L12/8.

in accordance with the requirements of Article 13(2). Articles 9 and 13(2) read together involved, at the latest by the end of the transitional period, a prohibition on exacting charges having an equivalent effect to customs duties on imports. The Court described the prohibition thus:

It lends itself, by its very nature, to producing direct effects in the legal relations between Member States and their subjects.

If, therefore, an importer or exporter is faced with a charge which conflicts with Articles 9, 12, or 16, he may either refuse to pay and then defend himself in the national courts against any action arising out of that refusal, or pay up and then sue for repayment, or take whatever other remedy may be open to him in the courts to enforce his rights or obtain redress for their infringement. The safest course in the UK would be to pay in accordance with section 127 of the Customs and Excise Management Act 1979,[94] or to seek deferment.[95] Section 127(1) (b) enables the importer not later than three months after the date of the payment to apply to the High Court or, in Scotland, to the Court of Session for a declaration as to the amount of duty, if any, properly payable on the goods.[96]

In *Otto Reichelt* v. *Hauptzollamt Berlin-Sud*,[97] the Court held that, in the absence of Community legislation, a national court may apply the national law concerning claims for repayment of customs duties paid in excess of the amount due. It also ruled that the conditions for repayment must be the same as those which apply when there has been an overpayment of a national charge.

An individual who considers that he is being taxed in contravention of Article 95 also has a right of action in the Courts. The European Court held in *Lütticke*[98] that the first paragraph of Article 95 had direct effect but, because of the third paragraph of the Article, only as from the beginning of the second transitional stage (1 January 1962). The second paragraph of Article 95 was held to have direct effect in *Finck—Frucht*.[99]

The *Molkerei* case[100] shows that it is for the national court to determine whether an excessive tax, contravening Article 95, is invalid in whole or only in part. This measure of discretion left to the national law extends, in the interests of legal certainty, to the imposition of reasonable limitation

---

[94] C. 2.

[95] Under the Customs Duties (Deferred Payment) Regulations 1976, SI 1976 No. 1223, Reg. 4, as amended by the Customs Duties (Deferred Payment) (Amendment) Regulations 1978, SI 1978, No. 1725, Reg. 6.

[96] If his payment has been deferred, the period runs from the date of grant of deferment: Reg. 8 of the 1976 Regulations (see above), as amended by Reg. 9 of the 1978 Regulations (see above), and as interpreted in accordance with sections 17(2) (a) and 23(2) of the Interpretation Act 1978 (c. 30).

[97] Case 113/81 [1982] *ECR* 1957.

[98] Case 57/65 [1966] *ECR* 205; reaffirmed in, e.g., Case 28/67, *Molkerei* [1968] *ECR* 143.

[99] Case 27/67 [1968] *ECR* 223.

[100] Case 28/67 [1968] *ECR* 143.

periods for the commencement of legal actions.[101] The discretion extends even further, as can be seen from *Just*,[102] which arose over Danish excise duties on alcoholic beverages. Without in any way qualifying the rule that Article 95(1) and (2) have direct effect, the Court laid down the principles by which national courts must be guided when entertaining claims based on that Article. The remedy must be no less favourable than it would be in a similar action of a domestic nature. In no circumstances can the remedy be circumscribed in such a way as to make it impossible in practice to exercise the rights which the national courts are bound to protect. That said, however, it is open to the national court to impose conditions, designed to avoid the unjust enrichment of the plaintiff. The Court said:

> It should be specified in this connexion that the protection of rights guaranteed in the matter by Community law does not require an order for the recovery of charges improperly made to be granted in conditions which would involve the unjust enrichment of those entitled. There is nothing therefore, from the point of view of Community law, to prevent national courts from taking account in accordance with their national law of the fact that it has been possible for charges unduly levied to be incorporated in the prices of the undertaking liable for the charge and to be passed on to the purchasers. It is equally compatible with the principles of Community law for courts before which claims for recovery of repayments are brought to take into consideration, in accordance with their national law, the damage which an importer may have suffered because the effect of the dis-criminatory or protective tax provisions was to restrict the volume of imports from other Member States.[103]

If any provision of Community law has direct effect, that effect is secured by section 2(1) of the European Communities Act 1972.[104] Section 2(4) of the Act provides that any enactment passed or to be passed, other than one contained in Part I of the Act, shall not only be construed but also shall have effect subject, inter alia, to the provisions of section 2(1).

THE COMMON CUSTOMS TARIFF

Articles 18–29 EEC contain transitional provisions for setting up the Common Customs Tariff (CCT).[105] Article 23(3) required it to be applied in its entirety by the end of the transitional period at the latest. However, by resorting to Articles 15(2), 24, and 235 the timetable was accelerated. The tariff was fixed in Regulation 950/68[106] and its Annex. It entered into force

---

[101] Case 33/76, *Rewe-Zentralfinanz* [1976] *ECR* 1989, and Case 45/76, *Comet* [1976] *ECR* 2043.
[102] Case 68/79 [1980] *ECR* 501.
[103] Ibid., p. 523.
[104] C. 68.
[105] Articles 39–41 of the Act of Accession, and Articles 24–34 of the Greek Act of Accession, contain corresponding provisions for the new member states.
[106] *OJ* 1968, L172/1.

on 1 July 1968. The Annex is amended and consolidated each year.[107] The CCT establishes the appropriate rate of customs duty (which may be zero) for all goods produced outside the community and imported into a member state.[108] Section 1 of the current Annex contains rules for the interpretation of the nomenclature of the CCT. These are particularly important since the CCT is regarded as exhaustive, and it is therefore necessary to find an appropriate heading somewhere for any import from a third country, and to decide which is the more appropriate in the event of two or more appearing to cover the Articles in question.[109]

In spite of these rules, litigation does arise from time to time. Thus, to quote only one of many stimulating intellectual examples, a German court was required to decide whether porcelain Christmas angels with candles (made in Taiwan) were 'articles for Christmas festivities' or 'porcelain or china statuettes or other ornaments'.[110] In considering such questions the Court has evolved certain principles of interpretation. In *Bakels*[111] it noted that all member states were parties to the Convention on the Nomenclature for the Classification of Goods in Customs Tariffs of 15 December 1950,[112] which obliged each contracting party to conform to the nomenclature when establishing its customs tariff. The CCT annexed to Regulation 950/68 was based on that convention. The convention provided for the setting up of the Customs Co-operation Council, which issued Explanatory Notes, and whose Nomenclature Committee gave Classification Opinions. The Explanatory Notes dealt with categories of goods, and the Opinions with the exact classification of specific products. The Court considered that, in the absence of Community guidance, the Explanatory Notes were authoritative, and a means of interpretation which could not be ignored by Community institutions.[113] Resort to them was a useful way of securing a uniform interpretation of the CCT.

In *Osram*[114] the Court appears to have drawn a distinction between, on the one hand, the general rules of interpretation which appear in Section 1 of the CCT and which are based on the work of the Customs Co-operation Council, and, on the other, the Commission's Explanatory Notes. The latter, while important, could not in the Court's view modify the CCT, nor

[107] See, e.g, Reg. 3400/84, *OJ* 1984, L320/1, which entered into force on 1 Jan. 1985.

[108] It does not, however, apply to unlawfully imported goods such as narcotics: Case 50/80, *Horvath* [1981] *ECR* 385.

[109] An exception is that narcotic drugs illegally imported for illicit use do not attract customs duty, whether or not they are found by the authorities and destroyed: Case 221/81, *Wilfrid Wolf* v. *HZA Düsseldorf* [1983] 2 *CMLR* 170.

[110] The German Court thought the latter and the European Court did not demur: Case 248/80, *Glunz* [1982] *ECR* 197.

[111] Case 14/70 [1970] *ECR* 1001.

[112] Cmnd. 1070, TS No. 29 (1960), as subsequently amended.

[113] This view was repeated in Case 35/75, *Matisa* [1975] *ECR* 1210.

[114] Case 183/73 [1973] *ECR* 477.

those rules of interpretation which were an integral part of it. The distinction is logical because it is for the Council and not the Commission to legislate in these matters, although the former could of course delegate powers to the latter under Article 155 EEC.

The Council has the power under Article 28 EEC to effect, by unanimous decision and at any time, any autonomous alteration or suspension of duties in the CCT. Since the end of the transitional period it has also, under the same Article, been able to decide, by qualified majority on a proposal from the Commission, to make limited changes in such duties for limited periods (not exceeding 20 per cent of the rate in the case of any one duty, and for not more than six months with the possibility of an extension for one further period of six months). The Council fixes autonomous duties when it proceeds independently, whereas duties resulting from some international obligation owed by the Community to one or more third countries are described as 'conventional duties'. The two types are listed separately in the CCT. When fixing conventional duties, the Council acts under Article 113. Decisions of the Council under that Article can all be taken by qualified majority.

The legislative powers conferred by Articles 28 and 113 include the right to insert authoritative Notes or Additional Notes into the CCT. Thus, for example, Regulation (EEC) No. 1/71 of 17 December 1971 inserted an Additional Note in accordance with a classification opinion issued by the Customs Co-operation Council which, in effect, said that photocopiers were photographic cameras (14 per cent duty) rather than office machines (7.2 per cent duty). In *Nederlandse Spoorwegen*[115] the Court held that this Additional Note, which had been established in accordance with Article 28 EEC, had the same binding effect as the text to which it referred, and took effect either as an authentic interpretation or as a supplementary provision. The same case illustrates the interrelation between the General Agreement on Tariffs and Trade (GATT) and the Community's own legal order. The Dutch court asked for a ruling on whether an obligation on the Netherlands under GATT (which according to Dutch constitutional law had legally binding force) should prevail over a Council regulation. The European Court took the view that it was in accordance with Article XXIV of GATT for the CCT to replace the national customs tariffs of the member states. It went on to say:

Similarly, since so far as fulfilment of the commitments provided for by GATT is concerned, the Community has replaced the Member States, the mandatory effect, in law, of these commitments must be determined by reference to the relevant provisions in the Community legal system and not to those which gave them their previous force under the national legal systems.[116]

---

[115] Case 38/75 [1975] *ECR* 1439.   [116] Ibid., p. 1450.

The Court also took the opportunity, however, to point out that the Community has replaced the member states in commitments arising out of the GATT and the Convention on the Nomenclature for the Classification of Goods in Customs Tariffs, and is bound by those commitments.

The origin of goods

Article 9(2) EEC speaks with deceptively simple, although ambiguous, language of 'products originating in Member States' and 'products coming from third countries'. For the purpose of applying the CCT it is essential to know with certainty into which of those categories any particular consignment is placed. If goods made in Germany are taken through Switzerland to Italy, then in a sense they satisfy both descriptions; yet this interpretation would produce a nonsensical situation, since the Italian authorities must decide whether or not to apply the CCT, and for this reason goods cannot be treated as falling into both categories. In fact the phrase 'coming from'[117] has with little difficulty been accepted as meaning 'originating in' and thus, in the example given, customs duties must not be charged on entry into Italy. Certainty over the origin of goods may also be needed if third countries require an exporting member state to give an appropriate certificate.

Clarity which is lacking in the Treaty has therefore been supplied by Regulation (EEC) No. 802/68 on the common definition of the concept of the origin of goods.[118] This regulation also deals with the increasingly common situation where goods consist of components made and assembled in more than one country. The principle adopted is that products are deemed to have originated in the country in which 'the last substantial process or operation that was economically justified was performed, having been carried out in an undertaking equipped for the purpose, and resulting in the manufacture of a new product or representing an important stage of manufacture'.[119] Products taken from the sea are considered to originate in the flag state of the ship which harvested them.[120] Supplementary provisions can be adopted by the Commission, acting with the help of a committee and in accordance with a management procedure, both of which are established by Articles 12–14 of the regulation. One important omission is that the Council found it impossible in 1968 to define the concept of origin in respect of petroleum products. Article 3 of the regulation excludes them, but says that their origin will be defined later—a promise so far unfulfilled.

---

[117] 'en provenance de' in the French text of Article 9(2).
[118] *OJ* 1968, L1148/1, as supplemented and amended.
[119] Art. 5 of Reg. 802/68. There must have been a 'significant qualitative change': Case 49/76, *Uberseehandel* v. *Handelskammer* [1977] *ECR* 41.
[120] Ibid., Art. 4.

EXCEPTIONS TO THE COMMON CUSTOMS TARIFF

Once it has been decided that goods originate in a third country, they become subject to the CCT unless some exceptional treatment is justified. One such exception is to be found in Article 25 EEC which, unlike Article 26, is still fully effective after the end of the transitional period. It deals with the situation where production within the Community of certain classes of goods is insufficient to meet the demands of a member state and the latter traditionally relies to a considerable extent on imports from third countries. The Council may, by qualified majority on a proposal from the Commission, allow that member state to import from outside the Community certain quotas of those goods at a reduced duty or duty-free. In the case of some products the Commission may fix similar tariff quotas. In Article 25(1) and (2) the products are classified according to whether they fall into List B, C, D, E, or G. In spite of the slipshod drafting of Article 19(5), which says that the lists of tariff headings referred to in that Article and in Article 20 (with no mention of Article 25) are set out in Annex I to the Treaty, there is little doubt that Article 25(1) and (2) refer to the same lists. Article 25(3) allows the Commission to authorize any member state wholly or partly to suspend the collection of customs duties or to grant similar tariff quotas in the case of products listed in Annex II to the Treaty, provided this would not result in serious disturbance of the market.

Trade with third countries

A more important exception is to be found in Article 2 of the Second ACP–EEC Convention signed in Lomé on 31 October 1979[121] which requires special customs treatment for products originating in the African, Caribbean, and Pacific states. The general principle is one of freedom from customs duties and charges of equivalent effect. Similar provisions appear in Article 3 of the Council Decision 1186/80 of 16 December 1980 on the association of the overseas countries and territories with the European Economic Community.[122] There are also customs provisions in agreements with the members of the European Free Trade Association (EFTA). Agreements have been made with countries ranging from Finland to Liberia, and Israel to Iceland. Thus the practitioner, wanting to check the appropriate customs duty, would run the risk of misleading his clients if he looked only at the CCT. The 'conventional' duties listed in it, which are based on the worldwide agreements concluded within the framework of the GATT, are not the only duties which are regulated by Community agreements.

[121] TS 3 (1983), Cmnd. 8761.
[122] *OJ* 1980, L361/1, amended by Dec. 559/81, *OJ* 1981, L203/49.

Direct effect in trade with third countries

There is little doubt that, in the current state of international relations, an international organization such as the EEC can conclude treaties by which it will be bound in international law. There is no doubt that, if it chooses to do so, Article 228(2) EEC will make them binding in Community law upon the institutions of the Community and on member states. Through the machinery of Articles 169, 170, and 173 the obligations under Article 228(2) can be enforced by action in the European Court. Moreover, any individual who is capable of writing a letter to the Commission may be able, in a deserving case, to secure the launching of an action by the Commission under Article 169 against any member state, and at virtually no cost to himself. No doubt the Commission would form an independent view on the merits of his allegations and on the prospects of securing compliance with the Treaty by some simpler and quicker means than the launching of litigation. It could also take into account any dispute with the other party to the Treaty as to the meaning of the relevant treaty provisions, and consider whether it would be more appropriate for the Community to exhaust the normal machinery for the settlement of that dispute before resorting to unilateral enforcement of the Community's interpretation. But at the end of the day, and when any such dispute had been resolved, there would be no lack of machinery within the Community to enforce its obligations.

A more difficult question is whether any provision of an agreement between the Community and a third country is capable of having direct effect in the sense described earlier in this chapter. In principle there would seem little justification for according such an effect. To do so might not be so startling to those countries in the EEC where treaties automatically become part of the local law as it would be to those, like the United Kingdom, which require an Act of Parliament for that purpose. But it would be inconsistent with the true nature of the rule of direct effect. The doctrine of direct effect is no more than a creature of Community law, as expounded by the European Court. It is a rule of adjectival Community law which forms no part of customary international law. Thus, when the Community makes a treaty, it is not entitled to expect the other party to allow individuals to enforce the agreement through actions in the latter's courts. There can thus be no expectation of reciprocity if the Community should decide to do so itself. Nor can the Community force the third country to accept rulings of the courts of the member states or of the European Court in suits brought by individuals. The situation could be analysed in the same way as the European Court has done with regard to interrelationship between Community law and national law. Community law binds the member states, and at least so much of it as has direct effect applies within those states. But when it does so, it does not become part of national law. It retains its character as Community law, applying alongside with, and prevailing over, national law. Its terms fall to be interpreted through canons of construction of Community law and not those of the law of the member states. All this was established long ago in *Van Gend en Loos*.[123] When the Community enters upon the international stage and makes a treaty, its international legal obligations thereunder clearly bind the Community. It would be consistent with *Van Gend en Loos* to regard those obligations as applying as law within the Community. It would be equally consistent to accept that they do not lose their character as international legal obligations, and that they fall to be interpreted in accordance with rules of international law, of which, as has been said, the rule of direct effect forms no part. Finally, assuming that the Community had the capacity under the EEC Treaty to incur those international duties, the latter must, by analogy with *Van Gend en Loos* and as a general principle of international law, prevail over rules of Community law.

It is necessary, however, to consider how the European Court has dealt with these questions. In *Haegeman* v. *Belgium*[124] the Court had occasion to consider the Agreement of Association between the EEC and Greece, signed on 9 July 1961.[125] The case turned primarily on the question whether the agreement was an act of one of the institutions of the Community, so as to give rise to a right to refer questions of interpretation to the European Court under Article 177 EEC. The Court held that the Agreement was an act of one of the institutions, having been concluded in accordance with Article 228. The Court considered that it had jurisdiction under Article 177 because:

The provisions of the agreement, from the coming into force thereof, form an integral part of Community law.[126]

The Court then proceeded to interpret certain Articles in the Agreement, including Article 6 which said that the association established between the Community and Greece:

shall be based on a customs union which, save as otherwise provided in the Agreement, shall cover all trade in goods and shall involve the prohibition between Member States of the Community and Greece of customs duties on imports and exports and of all charges having equivalent effect, and the adoption by Greece of the Common Customs Tariff of the Community in its relations with third countries.

The Court in fact held that the countervailing charge imposed on Greek wines when imported into Belgium and Luxembourg constituted a levy within the meaning of Protocol 12 of the Association Agreement, and not a

---

[123] Case 26/62 [1963] *ECR* 1; and also Case 6/74, *Costa* v. *ENEL* [1964] *ECR* 585.
[124] Case 181/73 [1974] *ECR* 449.
[125] *OJ* 1963, No. 26.
[126] Ibid., p. 460.

customs duty or charge having equivalent effect. The Court was not asked whether the provisions of the agreement, or any of them, had direct effect. It is tempting to conclude that, since the questions referred to the Court arose out of an action by the firm of Haegeman, and since the Court cast no doubt on the firm's right to bring it, the Court was implicitly accepting the direct effect of the provisions of the agreement on which the plaintiff was relying. However, this is too simplistic a view. The national court was entitled to ask questions concerning, inter alia, the interpretation of acts of the institutions of the Community if it considered a decision on those questions necessary to enable it to give judgment. It was not for the European Court to query the relevance of the questions, or to ask for what reason they were relevant. For all the European Court knew, the relevance might have been because of some rule in the constitutional law of the member state in question, or it might have been for some quite different reason that the question was asked. The European Court, quite properly, did not ask the reason. The facts are that the Court was not asked about direct effect, it does not appear to have heard argument on the subject, and it made no pronouncement about it. The Court's statement that the agreement formed 'an integral part of Community law' is not surprising if taken to mean that it became an integral part of the law applying within the Community. It *is* surprising if taken to mean that it became an integral part of the law of the Community and as such needed to be interpreted in accordance with Community law rather than international law. The language used by the Court leaves a degree of uncertainty, but it would for the above reasons be going too far to regard it as authority for the proposition that international agreements, even of a special kind such as Association Agreements, have, or are capable of having, direct effect.

Bresciani[127] took matters a step further. It concerned the Yaoundé Convention of 20 July 1963, one of the forerunners of the Second Lomé Convention already mentioned. The question was whether it was lawful for Italy to levy charges for public health inspections, made at the frontier, of raw cowhides imported from France and Senegal (a state associated with the Community under the Convention). The two Yaoundé Conventions each prohibited customs duties on imports and charges having equivalent effect. One question asked by the referring court was whether Article 2(1) of the Second Convention (in similar terms to Article 13(2) EEC) had 'immediate effect so as to confer on Community "citizens" an individual right, which the national courts must protect, not to pay to a Member State a charge having equivalent effect to a customs duty'. In short, did Article 2(1) have direct effect? By way of an answer, the Court referred to the special historical relationship between the Yaoundé countries and the four member states of whom they were formerly dependencies. It also

[127] Case 87/75 [1976] *ECR* 29.

mentioned the lack of reciprocity in the Convention, in that the Community abolished customs duties and their equivalent, while the associated states were allowed to retain customs duties, or even introduce new ones, if this contributed to their development needs or industrialization requirements, or was simply needed as a budget contribution. The Court held that Article 2(1) of the Convention conferred on those subject to Community law the right, which the national courts of the Community must protect, not to pay to a member state a charge equivalent to a customs duty. The Court gave two reasons. First, the imbalance between the obligations of the two sides to the Treaty did not prevent the Community from according direct effect to some of its provisions. Secondly, it said that, since Article 2(1) of the Convention referred expressly to Article 13 EEC, the Community undertook towards the associated states the same obligation as the member states had assumed towards each other. Neither of these reasons is altogether convincing. The second almost seems to be asserting that an international obligation which is in similar terms to an internal Community obligation must be intended to be interpreted and applied in the same way. Apart from new shades of meaning which may be imported by the addition of an equally authentic text in a non-Community language, there is usually nothing in the agreements with third countries to show that they wish to import, and be bound by, Community methods of interpretation and application.[128]

It is unfortunate that balanced arguments were not advanced to the Court. Indeed no arguments against direct effect were presented. The Italian government stated no views, in writing or orally, and the plaintiff and the Commission simply asserted that the provisions in question had direct effect. Advocate General Trabucchi did mention that it might seem contradictory and perhaps counter-productive to apply to international agreements the Community concept of directly applicable law (which he appears to have equated with direct effect). However, the point was not fully argued. He did nevertheless give perhaps the best rationale for the decision which the Court eventually took. He said:

However, the present case is concerned with international conventions which have features of their own. In the first place, it is possible, on a considered view of the position, to state that they are the perfect continuation of the system which was originally laid down in the Treaty establishing the EEC. As the essential purpose of the system of association with the developing countries was to further their interests, the said conventions are not based strictly on the principle of reciprocity. The obligations assumed, on the one hand, by the Community and by its Member States and, on the other, by the associated States, are not the same. The conventions are mainly concerned with privileges granted by the Community and its Member States to the associated countries in order to help their development.[129]

---

[128] See also the Advocate General in Case 51/75, *EMI* v. *CBS* [1976] *ECR* 811, p. 861.
[129] Case 87/75, *Bresciani* [1976] *ECR* 129, pp. 148 and 149.

Polydor v. *Harlequin*[130] presented an opportunity for clarification. It was about quantitative restrictions, rather than customs duties, but it raised the same sort of question. Did Article 14(2) of the agreement between the Community and Portugal of 22 July 1972[131] have direct effect? The Court did not answer the question directly. It ruled that the enforcement of the copyright in question in a member state did not conflict with Article 14(2), and that there was therefore no need to decide the question of direct effect. The Court did, however, give a word of warning about assuming that because Articles 14(2) and 23 of the Agreement were similar to Articles 30 and 36 of the EEC Treaty they must have the same meaning and effect as has been accorded to the latter by the Court. It said:

However, such similarity of terms is not a sufficient reason for transposing to the provisions of the Agreement the above-mentioned case-law, which determines in the context of the Community the relationship between the protection of industrial and commercial property rights and the rules on the free movement of goods.[132]

Later it said:

It is apparent from an examination of the Agreement that although it makes provision for the unconditional abolition of certain restrictions on trade between the Community and Portugal, such as quantitative restrictions and measures having equivalent effect, they do not have the same purpose as the EEC Treaty, inasmuch as the latter, as has been stated above, seeks to create a single market reproducing as closely as possible the conditions of a domestic market.

It follows that in the context of the Agreement restrictions on trade in goods may be considered to be justified on the ground of the protection of industrial and commercial property in a situation in which their justification would not be possible within the Community.[133]

The unsatisfactory situation left by *Bresciani* was again examined in *Kupferberg*.[134] In that case, full argument was addressed to the Court by several member states[135] (as well as by the Commission and the parties) on the question of direct effect, but the judgment was as unsatisfactory as that in *Bresciani*. In spite of the argument advanced by the member states, and the opinion of the Advocate General, to the contrary, the Court held that Article 21 of the Agreement between the Community and Portugal of 22 July 1972 was 'directly applicable and capable of conferring on individual traders rights which the Court must protect'.[136] In support of this ruling,

[130] Case 270/80 [1982] *ECR* 329.

[131] Concluded and adopted by the Community by Reg. 2844/72, *OJ* 1972, L301/166.

[132] Case 270/80, *Polydor* v. *Harlequin* [1982] *ECR* 329, p. 348.

[133] Ibid., p. 349.

[134] Case 104/81 [1982] *ECR* 3641. On the possible direct effect of the GATT, see Cases 21–4/72, *International Fruit Co.* v. *Produktschap* etc. [1972] *ECR* 1219, and Case 9/73, *Schlüter* v. *Lörrach* [1973] *ECR* 1135.

[135] Denmark, Germany, France, and the United Kingdom.

[136] Case 104/81 *HZA Mainz* v. *Kupferberg* [1982] *ECR* 3641, p. 3670.

the Court first referred to the need for uniformity of application of the Agreement throughout the Community.[137] It went on to develop various arguments, which were summed up by the Court itself in the following passage:

It follows from all the foregoing considerations that neither the nature nor the structure of the Agreement concluded with Portugal may prevent a trader from relying on the provisions of the said Agreement before a court in the Community.[138]

The Court then immediately proceeded to examine whether the provision in question was unconditional, and sufficiently precise to have direct effect. In other words, the Court said there was nothing in the Agreement to prevent its being given direct effect, and then applied the rules of Community law on direct effect.

The arguments adduced by the Court in support of this finding are unconvincing. Where an international agreement requires uniform application throughout the Community, this need can be satisfied by resort to more orthodox means such as Community regulations and directives. Moreover, it does not follow from the fact that the Agreement does not prevent the application of the Community's internal rules of direct effect that such application is either appropriate or desirable or in the Community's interests. Whether it is so is a question which the Council and the Commission, as the legislative and negotiating organs of the Community, are best able to judge in the light of the terms of the agreement in question and the degree of reciprocity in matters of enforcement which the other party is willing to accord.

An even more unsatisfactory aspect of this judgment is to be found in the following passage:

The mere fact that the contracting parties have established a special institutional framework for consultations and negotiations *inter se* in relation to the implementation of the agreement is not in itself sufficient to exclude all judicial application of that agreement. The fact that a court of one of the parties applies to a specific case before it a provision of the agreement involving an unconditional and precise obligation and therefore not requiring any prior intervention on the part of the joint committee does not adversely affect the powers that the agreement confers on that committee.[139]

It is possible to interpret that passage as indicating that even if, in the case of a dispute between the Community and the other party to the Agreement, the Agreement contains its own conciliation machinery and its wheels are

---

[137] Ibid., p. 3662.
[138] Ibid., p. 3665.
[139] Ibid., p. 3664.

turning, it is possible for the same issues which have arisen in the conciliation procedure to be the subject of a reference for a preliminary ruling under Article 177. It is doubtful whether such contemporaneous proceedings before the Court will always be helpful to the Community's interests. *A fortiori* a reference to the Court could be unhelpful if arbitral or judicial proceedings under the Agreement were pending. In connection with the latter, it is fair to point out, however, that the Court's dictum refers only to 'consultations and negotiations', which, while aptly describing an essential part of any conciliation procedure, do not seem to refer to arbitral or judicial proceedings.

Small quantities of non-commercial goods

Yet another set of exceptions to the CCT is contained in Regulation (EEC) No. 1544/69 of 23 July 1969 on the tariff applicable to goods contained in travellers' personal luggage, as subsequently amended.[140] This regulation grants certain limited exemptions from the CCT for goods contained in the personal luggage of travellers coming from third countries. The exemptions apply irrespective of the nationality of the traveller or his residence, or of the origin of the goods. However, he must have spent sufficient time in a third country to enable him to purchase the goods in question. It is insufficient, therefore, for the traveller to have been on a cruise ship which made no more than a token call at a third-country port: *REWE*.[141] That case also dealt with certain exemptions from turnover tax and excise duty, but this aspect is beyond the scope of this chapter.

The principle underlying this sort of exception to the CCT is that the efforts involved in assessing and collecting the duty on non-commercial importations of small quantities of goods by large numbers of travellers would be out of all proportion to the amount at stake. What amounts to a non-commercial importation is defined in Regulation (EEC) No. 2780/78[142] as an importation of goods for personal or family use by the consignee or, in the case of travellers, imported goods intended as gifts. The same principle has given rise to other small exceptions, such as those in Regulation (EEC) No. 3060/78 of 19 December 1978, providing exemption from import duties for goods in small consignments of a non-commercial character from third countries.[143]

---

[140] *OJ* 1969, L191/1, as last amended by Reg. 3313/81, *OJ* 1981, L334/1, and as extended to agricultural levies and other import charges under the Common Agricultural Policy by Reg. 1818/75, *OJ* 1975, L185/3.

[141] Case 158/80 [1981] *ECR* 1805.

[142] *OJ* 1978, L333/7, amending Reg. 950/68, *OJ* 1968, L172/1.

[143] *OJ* 1978, L366/1, as amended by Reg. 3313/81, *OJ* 1981, L334/1.

GOODS IN FREE CIRCULATION

When goods originating in a third country are imported into a member state, any customs duties or charges having equivalent effect have been levied, and import formalities have been completed, they are considered in accordance with Article 10(1) EEC to be in free circulation. They can then be sent to other member states free of all similar duties and charges.[144] The only exception in Article 10(1) is where such goods have benefited from a total or partial drawback of the duties. This refers to the case where the duties or charges are paid on import into a member state and then a refund is made by the customs authorities when the goods are exported.

In order to assist the free circulation of goods, the Council adopted various provisions dealing with customs procedures. They were consolidated in Regulation 222/77 of 13 December 1976.[145] The main objective is to avoid a succession of national customs procedures in connection with the carriage of goods. Ideally, goods from outside the Community ought to go through customs procedures when they first enter the Community, and then go to their ultimate destination within the Community without going through unnecessary and time-consuming procedures every time they cross a frontier between two member states. With these aims in view, the Regulation contains rules about documentation and procedures, which differ according to whether the goods are in 'external Community transit' or 'internal Community transit'. These phrases are not particularly illuminating, but they are defined in Article 1. Broadly speaking, the former refers to goods originating outside the Community and not in free circulation, and the latter to goods which either originate in a member state or are in free circulation in accordance with Article 10 EEC. The Regulation was supplemented by Commission Regulation 223/77 of 22 December 1976.[146]

FURTHER READING

J. Amphoux, 'Customs Legislation in the EEC', (1972) 6 *JWTL* 133.

G. Bebr, 'Directly Applicable Provisions of Community Law: the Development of a Community Concept', (1970) 19 *ICLQ* 257.

L. J. van der Burg, 'The Customs Tariff and Customs Legislation in the European Communities', (1970) *CMLR* 184.

A. J. Easson, 'The "Direct Effect" of EEC Directives', (1979) *ICLQ* 319.

I. Forrester, 'EEC Customs Law: Rules of Origin and Preferential Duty Treatment', (1980) 5 *EL Rev.* 167, 257.

---

[144] Free also from quantitative restrictions and equivalent measures: see Case 119/78, *Peureux* [1979] *ECR* 975.

[145] *OJ* 1977, L38/1, amended by Reg. 983/79, *OJ* 1979, L123/1, and Reg. 3813/81, *OJ* 1981, L383/28.

[146] *OJ* 1977, L38/20.

E. Mennens, 'The Common Customs Tariff of the European Economic Community', (1967) 1 *JWTL* 73.

J. Steiner, 'Direct Applicability in EEC Law—a Chameleon Concept', (1982) 98 *LQR* 229.

B. J. M. Terra, 'Introduction to Customs Law', (1981) 2 *LIEI* 77.

J. A. Winter, 'Direct Applicability and Direct Effect: Two Distinct and Different Concepts in Community Law', (1972) 9 *CML Rev.* 425.

II

Quantitative Restrictions and Equivalent Measures

IT IS logical that Title I of the EEC Treaty should contain two chapters, each dealing with closely related provisions designed to ensure the free movement of goods within the Common Market. Chapter I deals with the customs union, and chapter II with the elimination of quantitative restrictions between member states. There are marked similarities between the schemes adopted in the two chapters for the elimination of the barriers with which they deal. Thus Article 30 contains a general prohibition in trade between member states of restrictions on imports and of all measures having equivalent effect. Article 31 prohibits any new quantitative restrictions or equivalent measures. Articles 32–3 contain transitional provisions for the dismantling of quantitative restrictions already in existence when the Treaty came into force.[1] Under Article 35 this process could be (and was) accelerated.[2] Article 34 prohibits quantitative restrictions on exports and equivalent measures. All these provisions have their counterparts, in the field of customs duties, in Articles 9 and 12–16. The most important difference between the two chapters is to be found in Article 36, which has no equivalent in the customs chapter and which allows certain important derogations from the rules of free movement and from Article 30 in particular. These will be considered in some detail later in this chapter.

DEVELOPMENT OF THE NOTION OF QUANTITATIVE RESTRICTIONS AND EQUIVALENT MEASURES

Quantitative restrictions

A simple example of a quantitative restriction would be where a state, wishing to restrict imports in order to control its balance of payments or to protect its own industries, prohibits the import of goods in excess of certain quotas. The scheme might be implemented by a licensing system whereby individual importers would be permitted to import certain quantities of goods, measured by value, weight, number, or some other quantitative test. In that way the authorities of the importing state would divide the import

---

[1] These are now only of historical interest, and so are the corresponding provisions in the Act of Accession. However, Articles 35 et seq. of the Greek Act of Accession allow some transitional arrangements, the last of which expires on 31 Dec. 1985.

[2] Decisions of 12 May 1960 (*OJ* 1960, 1217) and 15 May 1962 (*OJ* 1962, 1284).

quota allocated to the exporting country amongst individual prospective importers, until the total quota was exhausted. This classic form of protectionism was obviously inconsistent with the free trade which must exist witin the boundaries of a common market.

Article 30 clearly prohibits any measure restricting the amount of any commodity which may be imported from another member state. There could never have been much doubt that it also prohibits a total ban. The greatest possible restriction of a quantitative kind is to fix permissible imports at zero. The European Court has accordingly held that a total ban is a quantitative restriction.[3]

Notwithstanding Article 30, member states have on occasion sought to maintain quantitative restrictions, usually on the grounds that they are needed in order to support national organizations of the agricultural market. The Court has repeatedly held that, after the expiry of any relevant transitional period, the operation of a national market organization can no longer prevent full effect being given to the provisions of the Treaty relating to the elimination of quantitative restrictions.[4]

The definition of equivalent measures

The exercise by the Commission of its powers under Article 33(7) EEC, and the jurisprudence of the Court, soon showed that from the legal point of view the most interesting words in Article 30 were those prohibiting 'all measures having equivalent effect'. Article 33(7) enabled the Commission to issue directives establishing the procedure and timetable for the abolition, as between the member states, of measures having 'an effect equivalent to quotas', which were in existence when the Treaty entered into force. Although only transitional in nature, this power enabled the Commission to tackle the problem of defining what was equivalent to a quota, and it did not require great mental agility for the Commission to use that power so as to define what was the equivalent of a quantitative restriction. The Commission accordingly issued Directive 70/50 of 22 December 1969.[5] Article 2(1) required the abolition of measures, unless equally applicable to domestic or imported goods, which hindered imports, e.g. by making them more difficult or costly than the domestic equivalent. Article 2(2) covered 'measures which make imports or the disposal, at any marketing stage, of imported products subject to a condition—other than a formality[6]—which is required in respect of imported products only, or a

---

[3] Case 2/73, *Geddo* v. *Ente Nazionale Risi* [1973] *ECR* 865, p. 879, where the Court referred to 'measures which amount to a total or partial restraint of imports'; Case 34/79, *R.* v. *Henn and Darby* [1979] *ECR* 3795, p. 3812.
   [4] Case 48/74, *Charmasson* [1974] *ECR* 1383; Case 231/78, *Commission* v. *United Kingdom* [1979] *ECR* 1447; Case 118/78, *Meijer* v. *Department of Trade etc.* [1979] *ECR* 1387; Case 232/78, *Commission* v. *France* [1979] *ECR* 2729.   [5] *OJ* 1970, L13/29.
   [6] But see Cases 51–4/71 *International Fruit Company* v. *Produktschap* [1971] *ECR* 1107.

condition differing from that required for domestic producers and more difficult to satisfy.[7] Article 2(3) listed nineteen examples of the measures covered by the directive. The main thread running through the list was that there were to be no measures which discriminated against the imported product, e.g.[8] through price regulation, through marketing rules,[9] through encouraging, requiring, or giving preference to the purchase of domestic products only, or through confining names which were not indicative of origin or source to domestic products only.[10] Article 3 was based on the principle that rules on shape, size, composition, labelling, and so on were not to be maintained where their restrictive effect exceeded the effects intrinsic to trade rules. Put another way, such measures were not allowed if their restrictive effects on free movement infringed the rule of proportionality, and if the same legitimate objective could be achieved by other means which were less of a hindrance to trade.[11] The preamble to the Directive also defined what, for the purposes of Article 30, were to be regarded as 'measures'. In addition to instruments having legislative effect, the word was said to cover 'administrative practices,[12] and all instruments issuing from a public authority, including recommendations'. In this context, 'administrative practices' meant those which were regularly followed by a public authority, and 'recommendations' meant instruments issued by such an authority which, while not legally binding on the addressees, caused them to act in a certain way. In *Vriend*[13] the Court confirmed that Article 30 applies to national rules which a member state implements directly 'or through the intermediary of bodies established or approved by an official authority'.

The classic case on measures equivalent to quantitative restrictions was *Procureur du Roi* v. *Dassonville*.[14] It may still be regarded as the high-water mark in the Court's pronouncements on what are the measures prohibited by Article 30 EEC. Some Scotch whisky had got into France. It was then imported into Belgium without the importer having a certificate of origin

---

[7] Referred to in Case 4/75, *Rewe* [1975] *ECR* 843.

[8] For another example see Case 95/81, *Commission* v. *Italy* [1982] *ECR* 2187 (where importers from other member states were required to provide a security or bank guarantee of 5 per cent of the value of goods when payment was made in advance).

[9] In Case 59/82, *Schutzverband* v. *Weinbetrieb* [1983] *ECR* 1217, a minimum alcohol content prescribed for imported vermouth, which did not apply to the domestic product, was held to be prohibited by Article 30.

[10] See Case 12/74, *Commission* v. *Germany* [1975] *ECR* 181.

[11] See Case 104/75, *de Peijper* [1976] *ECR* 613; Case 261/81, *Walter Rau* v. *De Smedt* [1982] *ECR* 3961; Case 94/82 *Groothandel—Import—Export* [1983] *ECR* 947; and Case 16/83, *Karl Prantl* (judgment of 13/3/84).

[12] e.g. customs delays: Case 42/82, *Commission* v. *France* [1983] *ECR* 1013, and Case 42/82 R, *Commission* v. *France* [1982] *ECR* 841, in which interim measures were prescribed.

[13] Case 94/79 [1980] *ECR* 327, p. 340. See also Case 249/81, *Commission* v. *Ireland* [1982] *ECR* 4005, in which the Irish government's 'Buy Irish' campaign, conducted through the Irish Goods Council, was held to infringe Article 30: see n. 24 below.   [14] Case 8/74 [1974] *ECR* 837.

from the British customs authorities. This infringed Belgian law, and a prosecution ensued, followed by a reference under Article 177 to determine whether the Belgian law conflicted with the Treaty. The European Court found that the importers could have got such a certificate, but only with considerable difficulty. On the other hand, a person importing directly from the UK could easily have obtained the necessary certificate. The Court held that this sort of requirement that indirect importers should obtain a certificate of authenticity, which was more difficult for them to obtain than in the case of a direct import, was equivalent to a quantitative restriction and therefore prohibited.[15] The logic of this decision is easy to understand. Once goods are on the market, their movements across frontiers between member states ought not to be impeded. The Court went on however to say, in its well-known *obiter dictum*:

All trading rules enacted by Member States which are capable of hindering, directly or indirectly, actually or potentially, intra-Community trade are to be considered as measures having an effect equivalent to quantitative restrictions.[16]

The extreme width of that criterion can be appreciated if one considers the case of a national rule which in fact has had no effect on intra-Community trade, at least on the facts in issue,[17] but which in theory is potentially capable of indirectly hindering such trade.

The *dictum* was reaffirmed in very similar terms in *REWE*,[18] and in *Simmenthal*,[19] where the Court said of Article 30 (and similar provisions in Regulations concerning the common organization of the market in beef and veal):

To come within the prohibition contained in these provisions it is enough for the measures in question to be capable of acting as a direct or indirect, real or potential hindrance to imports between Member States.[20]

The hindrance in *REWE* had been the phyto-sanitary inspection of imported apples. In *Simmenthal* it was that meat imported into Italy for human consumption had to be submitted to veterinary and public health inspections. All this meant delay; and therefore transport costs were increased because the vehicles were kept waiting while the inspections were carried out. These hindrances were held to be equivalent to quantitative restrictions. It might be asked how they could be so regarded if in fact

---

[15] See also Case 41/76, *Donckerwolcke* [1976] *ECR* 1921; Case 52/77, *Cayrol* v. *Rivoira* [1977] *ECR* 2261; Case 179/78, *Procureur* v. *Rivoira* [1979] *ECR* 1147.

[16] Case 8/74 [1974] *ECR* 837, p. 852. Compare the earlier definition in Case 2/73, *Geddo* v. *Ente Nazionale Risi* [1973] *ECR* 865, p. 879.

[17] See, e.g., Case 12/74, *Commission* v. *Germany* [1975] *ECR* 181, p. 198.

[18] Case 4/75 [1975] *ECR* 843, p. 858.   [19] Case 35/76 [1976] *ECR* 1871.

[20] Ibid., p. 1884. The test has been confirmed in a number of cases, e.g. Case 190/73 *Van Haaster* [1974] *ECR* 1123, concerning products coming under a common organization of the market; Case 82/77, *Openbaar* v. *Van Tiggele* [1978] *ECR* 25, p. 39.

there were no restrictions in law or in practice on the quantity of apples or meat which could be imported. In response it might be argued that a refusal to admit any unhealthy food, discovered as a result of the inspections, would restrict the quantities imported (although Article 36 would then be relevant). One could also envisage the case where an exporter had only a limited fleet of vehicles at his disposal, so that delaying them at the frontier would restrict the overall quantities he could convey. However, if one applies the test in *Dassonville* and *Simmenthal*, it seems that a plaintiff who seeks to rely on Article 30 need not adduce any evidence of that kind, nor seek to demonstrate any actual restriction of a quantitative nature. Apparently all he has to show is that he has been hindered by this kind of compulsory procedure to his detriment, or even that he might be hindered by it on some future occasion, so that he can fairly say that the measure is capable of hindering him. The plaintiff would do well to consider, however, to what extent the wide ambit attributed to Article 30 in these two cases may subsequently have been restricted by later decisions of the Court. He should also of course consider whether any defence is open to the defendant under Article 36—an aspect which will be considered later in this chapter.

One small, but perhaps significant, modification of the *dicta* in the *Dassonville* and *Simmenthal* cases was introduced by the Court in *NV GB–INNO–BM* v. *ATAB*.[21] The Court began, in answer to two questions about Articles 3(f), 5, and 86, by stating a general proposition:

First, the single market system which the Treaty seeks to create excludes any national system of regulation hindering directly or indirectly, actually or potentially, trade within the Community.[22]

Applying that principle, the Court ruled that Article 86 prohibits any abuse by one or more undertakings of a dominant position, even if such abuse is encouraged by a national legislative provision. The Belgian law in question fixed maximum and minimum prices for tobacco. In reaching its conclusion, the Court also expressed the view that a national measure which facilitated abuse of a dominant position will generally be incompatible with Articles 30–4. In answer to a question about the interpretation of Article 30, the Court defined its scope in the following terms:

For the purpose of this prohibition it is sufficient that the measures in question are likely to hinder, directly or indirectly, actually or potentially, imports between Member States.[23]

In this formulation, the idea that a restriction only had to be capable of

---

[21] Case 13/77 [1977] *ECR* 2115.

[22] Ibid., p. 2144.

[23] Ibid., p. 2147. See also Case 104/75, *de Peijper* [1976] *ECR* 613, p. 635; Case 95/81, *Commission* v. *Italy* [1982] *ECR* 2187.

hindering imports to fall within the prohibition was thus not repeated. Instead, it has now become a question of whether there is a likelihood that imports will be hindered, rather than a mere possibility. Unfortunately, the retention of the words 'actually or potentially' is still capable of causing misunderstanding. One way of interpreting the Court's ruling would be to say that Article 30 prohibits measures which would hinder imports, directly or indirectly, or would be likely to do so. However, it is questionable whether the case can be relied on as authority for the proposition that a mere capability of hindering imports is insufficient to infringe Article 30.

Far from showing any tendency in more recent cases to restrict the *Dassonville* principle, the Court has given some indication of a desire to keep the ambit of Article 30 as wide as possible. An illustration of this is in *Commission* v. *Ireland*,[24] where the Court had to consider the compatibility with Article 30 of a 'Buy Irish' advertising campaign conducted by the Irish government, which involved the use of a 'Guaranteed Irish' symbol and the establishment of a system for investigating complaints about Irish goods. The Irish government argued that 'measures' in Article 30 referred only to binding measures emanating from a public authority. The Court rejected the argument and found that the Irish government had introduced, and assisted in the prosecution of, a national practice the potential effect of which on imports was comparable to binding government measures.

Licensing and monitoring

For a variety of reasons, member states have sought to maintain systems whereby goods in certain categories could only be imported (or exported) upon the grant of appropriate licences. Where such a system resulted in the refusal to allow an import from another member state, there could be no doubt that such refusal was an infringement of Article 30. But the object of these systems has not always been to restrict trade. Sometimes the objective has been simply to monitor the trade flow. Let us suppose that the national authorities institute a licensing system, but that in fact, for many defined categories of goods, they grant exemption from the requirement to obtain a licence, and, even in those cases where one is still required, they always grant a licence on request. Would this infringe Article 30? Such a question was referred under Article 177 in *International Fruit Company* v. *Produktschap Groenten en Fruit*.[25] The Court drew a sharp distinction between intra-Community trade and trade with third countries, and gave a different answer in relation to each. So far as concerned intra-Community trade, to which Article 30 is confined, the Court did not expressly deal with

---

[24] Case 249/81. See also Case 82/77, *van Tiggele* [1978] *ECR* 25, p. 40, and Case 130/80 *Keldermann* [1981] *ECR* 527, p. 537, to the effect that a national measure does not escape the prohibition in Article 30 even though the competent authority has power to make exceptions and the power is freely applied to imported products.

[25] Joined Cases 51–4/71 [1971] *ECR* 1107.

the situation where exemptions were granted by the national authorities. It may have implied, however, that this would not infringe Article 30. It condemned only the application to intra-Community trade of a licensing law, and application does not, *ex hypothesi*, include cases where there is an exemption from such application. However, where the law was applied, and licences were required, Article 30 was infringed. The Court said, after referring to Articles 30 and 34(1):

Consequently, apart from the exceptions for which provision is made by Community law itself those provisions preclude the application to intra-Community trade of a national provision which requires, even purely as a formality, import or export licences or any other similar procedure.[26]

Prior to 1983 the UK maintained a licensing system for the import of UHT milk, a condition for the granting of a licence being that the milk should be packed on premises within the UK. Repacking of milk imported in foreign cartons of course meant opening the latter, and as a result the milk had to be re-treated. The economic effect of this was to exclude imported UHT milk from the United Kingdom market. In *Commission* v. *UK*[27] the Court held this to be incompatible with Article 30. Although the particular licensing scheme was not saved by Article 36, this did not necessarily mean however that a licensing system could in no case be justified under Article 36. This aspect of the judgment will be considered later in this chapter, in connection with the provisions of Article 36 relating to public health.

Price fixing

On several occasions the Court has had occasion to consider the compatibility of national price-fixing rules with Community law. In *Galli*[28] several questions were put to the Court in order to test the validity of an Italian law regulating domestic prices. The question related primarily to whether the Italian rules interfered with the Community's own pricing system, as fixed in accordance with the Common Agricultural Policy by Regulations 120/67/EEC and 136/66/EEC on cereals, fats, and oils. The Court devoted most of its attention to that aspect, and decided that in sectors covered by a common organization of the market, especially when it was based on a common price system, member states could no longer take unilateral national action affecting the Community's machinery of price formation.[29] Since the latter controlled prices at production and wholesale stages, this

---

[26] Ibid., p. 1116.
[27] Case 124/81 [1983] *ECR* 203. See also the second judgment in Case 40/82, *Commission* v. *United Kingdom* (judgment of 31/1/84).
[28] Case 31/74 [1975] *ECR* 47.
[29] See also Case 101/79, *Gaetano Toffoli* v. *Regione Veneto* [1979] *ECR* 3302.

left member states free to control retail prices.[30] In the 'dispositif' the Court did not mention Article 30, but it did so earlier in the judgment, and in answer to the question whether the Italian ban on sales at unauthorized prices, and the duty imposed on an importer to report his prices, were equivalent to quantitative restrictions. Referring, inter alia, to Article 30 the Court described the Community purpose as being the creation of a single market through the removal of all obstacles to the free movement of goods. It then repeated the familiar words taken from *Dassonville*,[31] indicating that it was necessary to exclude any national system of regulation which impeded directly or indirectly, actually or potentially, trade within the Community. The Court did not give any further guidance on how that general principle was to be interpreted in relation to a national price-fixing system which was confined to retail prices and was therefore not excluded by the particular rules of the Common Agricultural Policy. It took the opportunity to do so, however, in *Tasca*.[32] The case was about maximum retail and wholesale prices of sugar, fixed by the Italian government. Again there was a Community pricing system. With regard to Article 30 the Court said:

Although a maximum price applicable without distinction[33] to domestic and imported products does not in itself constitute a measure having an effect equivalent to a quantitative restriction, it may have such an effect, however, when it is fixed at a level such that the sale of imported products becomes, if not impossible, more difficult than that of domestic products. A maximum price, in any event in so far as it applies to imported products, constitutes therefore a measure having an effect equivalent to a quantitative restriction, especially when it is fixed at such a low level that, having regard to the general situation of imported products compared to that of domestic products, dealers wishing to import the product in question into the Member State concerned can do so only at a loss.[34]

It is interesting to speculate whether the same judicial hand wrote the two sentences quoted above. Each read in isolation creates a rather different impression. One can only note that it was the second sentence which was reproduced in the 'dispositif'. It is not possible to draw any further conclusion from *SADAM*,[35] which was decided on the same date as *Tasca*. In *SADAM* the Court resorted to the practice of reproducing *in extenso* the words it had used earlier on the same day.[36]

Openbaar v. *van Tiggele*[37] took the matter further, in dealing with

---

[30] See also Cases 95 and 96/79, *Kefer and Delmelle* [1980] ECR 103; [1982] 2 *CMLR* 77, and the cases cited on p. 86 of that report.

[31] Case 8/74 [1974] ECR 837, p. 852.   [32] Case 65/75 [1976] ECR 291.

[33] Price fixing which distinguished between imports and domestic products was, by contrast, held to infringe Article 30 in Case 181/82, *Roussel* v. *Netherlands*, judgment of 29/11/83.

[34] Ibid., p. 308.   [35] Joined Cases 88–90/75 [1976] ECR 323.

[36] See also Case 78/82, *Commission* v. *Italy* [1983] ECR 1955.

[37] Case 82/77 [1978] ECR 25.

minimum retail prices. Underlying the Court's judgment there seems to have been the thought that competition by importers was good, and that a government ought not to achieve for its own manufacturers a result which the latter could not secure for themselves because they would thereby infringe Article 85. There may also have been the thought that dumping was bad, a thought no doubt inspired by the transitional provisions in Article 97. In issue was the control by the government of the Netherlands of the minimum retail price of gin and other spirits. The starting-point in the reasoning of the Court was that national price controls, applied without distinction to domestic products and imported ones, could not in general amount to a quantitative restriction. Thus, a uniform prohibition against selling below the purchase price paid by the retailer could not restrict imports and was acceptable. So too was a non-discriminatory rule fixing the minimum profit margin by a specific amount and not as a percentage of the cost price, when the margin was an insignificant part of the total price. Nevertheless, fixed minimum retail prices, as distinguished from fixed profit margins, could adversely affect imports. This would be so even although applied alike to imports and home products, if they prevented an importer's lower cost prices from being reflected in the retail selling price. The moral for a government wishing to ensure that higher retail prices were charged than would prevail as a result of the operation of normal market forces would appear to be to fix the minimum profit margin, and not the minimum retail price. Even then there may be pitfalls in deciding what is, and what is not, a margin which constitutes 'a relatively insignificant part of the final retail price'.[38] Moreover, as the Court indicated, it is not a safe defence (to a claim that Article 30 is being infringed) to say that exemptions are freely given to importers, because the administrative formalities needed to gain such exemptions may themselves be equivalent to quantitative restrictions.[39]

The national controls considered in *Joseph Danis*[40] were of a more familiar kind. They were designed to control inflation, which by that time had become a matter of major concern to a number of member states. They applied equally to home producers and importers. Proposed increases in prices had to be notified to a governmental authority, could not enter into force for two months thereafter, and could be delayed even longer. In short, there was a kind of price freeze. The UK government submitted observations, maintaining that the struggle against inflation required the adoption of a variety of measures which might include a requirement for price increases to be notified in advance. It also drew attention to the fundamental objectives of the Treaty set out in Article 2 ('a harmonious

---

[38] Ibid., p. 40.
[39] Ibid.
[40] Joined Cases 16–20/79 [1979] *ECR* 3327.

development of economic activities, a continuous and balanced expansion, an increase in stability, an accelerated raising of the standard of living and closer relations between the States belonging to it'). It further noted that the products in question were not imported, but included imported raw materials—like a high proportion of products manufactured in all member states. In the event the Court's judgment made no mention of Article 2. It followed the line already taken in cases such as *Tasca*[41] and *SADAM*.[42] The Court said:

> Whilst rules imposing a price freeze which are applicable equally to national products and to imported products do not amount in themselves to a measure having an effect equivalent to a quantitative restriction, they may in fact produce such an effect when prices are at such a level that the marketing of imported products becomes either impossible or more difficult than the marketing of national products. That is especially the case where national rules, while preventing the increased prices of imported products from being passed on in sale prices, freeze prices at a level so low that—taking into account the general situation of imported products in relation to that of national products—traders wishing to import the products in question into the Member State concerned can do so only at a loss or, having regard to the level at which prices for national products are frozen, are impelled to give preference to the latter products.[43]

National controls of maximum and minimum prices were again considered by the Court in *Commission* v. *France*,[44] in connection with French rules on the retail pricing of tobacco. In that case the Court held that, although France could lawfully apply measures of a general nature intended to control the increase of prices, it was contrary to Article 30 (and Article 37) to extend to imported manufactured tobacco the application of provisions relating to the fixing by compulsory powers of the price of manufactured tobacco which France had reserved to itself within the scope of the provisions organizing the public tobacco monopoly.[45] The French government had contravened Article 30, inasmuch as its selective intervention as regards tobacco prices restricted the freedom to import tobacco from other member states.[46]

Exports

Although in practice most attention has been focused on restrictions on imports, quantitative restrictions on exports are also prohibited between member states—by Article 34 EEC. That Article was interpreted by the Court in *Procureur de la République* v. *Bouhelier*.[47] The task of a French

---

[41] Case 65/75 [1976] *ECR* 291.
[42] Joined Cases 88–90/75 [1976] *ECR* 323.
[43] Joined Cases 16–20/79 [1979] *ECR* 3327, p. 3339.
[44] Case 90/82 [1983] *ECR* 2011.
[45] Ibid., p. 2031.
[46] Ibid.   [47] Case 53/76 [1977] *ECR* 197.

public utility institution called Cetehor was to examine the quality of all
lever escapement watches and watch movements earmarked for export.
The exporter was allowed only two options for export—to get an export
licence, or to obtain a standards certificate from Cetehor which was issued
without charge. The national rules imposing these requirements were held
to be contrary to Article 34, regardless of their purpose.[48] The Court,
however, confined its decision to the situation where the national restrictions were imposed only in relation to products for export and did not
apply to products to be marketed within the member state. It described this
as leading to arbitrary discrimination between the two types of products
which constituted an obstacle to intra-Community trade.

In *Groenveld*[49] the Court held that a prohibition against stocking or
processing horse-meat did not infringe Article 34 if it did not discriminate
between exports and products marketed at home. It went on to define the
scope of Article 34, and in *Oebel*[50] it repeated its conclusions in the following terms:

Article 34 concerns national measures which have as their specific object or effect
the restriction of patterns of exports and thereby the establishment of a difference
in treatment between the domestic trade of a Member State and its export trade, in
such a way as to provide a particular advantage for national production or for the
domestic market of the State in question.[51]

The Court used the same formulation in *Syndicat National* v. *Groupement
d'Intérêt*.[52]

State aids and fiscal provisions

If a member state grants a state aid to its own producers but not to competitors from other member states, it might be argued that this denial of a
benefit to foreign competitors should be regarded as the equivalent of a
quantitative restriction, falling within the wide definition given to that
concept in *Dassonville*.[53] The argument might have some force if all state

---

[48] Ibid., p. 205. In Case 29/82, *Van Luipen* [1983] 2 *CMLR* 681, Dutch rules prohibiting the export of fruit and vegetables by anyone not affiliated to the national control body were held to contravene Article 34. See also Case 94/79, *Vriend* [1980] *ECR* 327, and Case 173/83, *Commission* v. *France*. Likewise quality controls may be imposed on domestic products, which make no distinction according to whether they are intended for the domestic market or for export: Case 237/82, *Jongeneel Kaas BV, Bodegraven* v. *State of the Netherlands Stichting Centraal Orgaan Zuivelcontrole* (judgment of 7/2/84).
[49] Case 15/79 [1979] *ECR* 3409.
[50] Case 155/80 [1981] *ECR* 1993. See also Case 286/81, *Oosthoek's Uitgeversmaatschappij* [1982] *ECR* 4575, p. 4587.
[51] Case 155/80 [1981] *ECR* 1993, p. 2009. See also Joined Cases 141–3/81, *Holdijk* [1982] *ECR* 1299, where the Court held that Community law does not prevent the retention or adoption of national rules for the protection of calves in pens, which apply without distinction to calves intended for the national market and to calves intended for export.
[52] Case 172/82 [1983] *ECR* 555. See also Case 218/82, *Commission* v. *Council* [1984] *ECR* 4063.
[53] Case 8/74 [1974] *ECR* 837.

aids were prohibited by the EEC Treaty, but that is not the case. Although Articles 92–4 impose Community controls over state aids because they are capable of distorting competition and adversely affecting trade between member states, not all state aids are prohibited. Indeed, Article 92(2) requires some aids to be considered as compatible with the common market. Article 92(3) permits others to be so regarded. Article 93(2) gives the Council wide powers to permit aids. It would scarcely be consistent with those provisions to conclude that an aid which Article 92 or 93 expressly permits was to be regarded as prohibited by another Article of the Treaty. In view of this, and of the fact that Articles 92–4 contain an elaborate system for the handling of state aids at Community level, it is logical that Article 30 should not be interpreted as prohibiting state aids.

Similarly, fiscal discrimination against imported goods should be dealt with under Article 95 and not Article 30, since otherwise inconsistencies between the application of the two Articles might arise.

It is not surprising, therefore, that the Court held in *Iannelli* v. *Meroni*[54] that Article 30 did not cover these matters. It said:

However wide the field of application of Article 30 may be, it nevertheless does not include obstacles to trade covered by other provisions of the Treaty. . . . Thus obstacles which are of a fiscal nature or have equivalent effect and are covered by Articles 9 to 16 and 95 of the Treaty do not fall within the prohibition in Article 30.

Similarly the fact that a system of aids provided by the State or by means of State resources may, simply because it benefits certain national undertakings or products, hinder, at least indirectly, the importation of similar or competing products coming from other Member States is not in itself sufficient to put an aid as such on the same footing as a measure having an effect equivalent to a quantitative restriction within the meaning of Article 30.[55]

However, the fact that a government scheme includes some measures which may amount to state aid does not take the scheme as a whole outside the ambit of Article 30. In *Commission* v. *Ireland*[56] the Irish government's 'Buy Irish' campaign was held to infringe Article 30, because, although a substantial part of the campaign was financed by contributions from the Irish Government to the Irish Goods Council, which may have amounted to a state aid, it also contained other initiatives. These amounted to an integrated government programme for promoting domestic products through a free information service, exhibition facilities, a complaints procedure in respect of products bearing the 'Guaranteed Irish' symbol, and the organization of publicity for Irish goods. Even after the campaign was modified, at the request of the Commission, it still retained an advertising campaign and the use of the 'Guaranteed Irish' symbol. In

[54] Case 74/76 [1977] *ECR* 557.
[55] Ibid., p. 574. See also Case 2/73, *Geddo* [1973] *ECR* 865, p. 879.
[56] Case 249/81 [1982] *ECR* 4005.

practice these had no significant success, but nevertheless the Court said it could not overlook the fact that they were part of a government scheme designed to substitute domestic products for imported products. Nor was the fact that the scheme was implemented through the Irish Goods Council any defence.[57]

The relevance of discrimination

Before any discussion of discrimination can usefully begin, it is necessary to define the sense in which the term is being used. For the purposes of Articles 30 or 34 EEC, it could perhaps best be described as arising when national requirements treat imports worse than home products, or exports worse than goods marketed internally. It may take one of two forms. First, it may be embodied in national rules which expressly distinguish between intra-Community trade and domestic trade, and which put the former at a disadvantage. Examples of this kind which have been held to be quantitative restrictions or their equivalent are referred to in *Commission* v. *United Kingdom*,[58] *Commission* v. *France*,[59] *Bouhelier*,[60] *Commission* v. *Italy*,[61] and *United Foods etc.* v. *Belgium*.[62] Secondly, discrimination may occur when national rules by their terms apply equally to all goods originating in the Community or in free circulation, but the effect in practice of those rules is to put goods imported from, or exported to, other member states into a less favourable position than similar goods produced or marketed at home. Examples of this class which have been held to contravene Articles 30 or 34 are to be found in *Tasca*,[63] *SADAM*,[64] *Openbaar* v. *van Tiggele*,[65] *Joseph Danis*,[66] *Commission* v. *France*,[67] *Commission* v. *Italy*,[68] and *Commission* v. *Belgium*.[69]

Moreover, discrimination has usually existed, actually or potentially, even in those cases where the Court has not specifically drawn attention to it. Thus, in *Pigs Marketing Board* v. *Redmond*,[70] the producers in Northern

---

[57] But see Case 222/82 *Apple and Pear Development Council* v. *Lewis* [1983] *ECR* 4083, where an advertising campaign for Cox and Bramley apples and Conference pears (typical English varieties), conducted by a body set up by Statutory Instrument and financed by charges levied on growers, was held not to infringe Article 30. The Council had neither disparaged foreign products, nor advised consumers to purchase domestic products solely by reason of their national origin.

[58] Case 231/78 [1979] *ECR* 1447.

[59] Case 232/78 [1979] *ECR* 2729.

[60] Case 53/76 [1977] *ECR* 197.

[61] Case 95/81 [1982] *ECR* 2187.

[62] Case 132/80 [1981] *ECR* 995.

[63] Case 65/75 [1976] *ECR* 291.

[64] Joined Cases 88–90/75 [1976] *ECR* 323.

[65] Case 82/77 [1978] *ECR* 25.

[66] Joined Cases 16–20/79 [1979] *ECR* 3327.

[67] Case 152/78 [1980] *ECR* 2299.

[68] Case 193/80 [1981] *ECR* 3019, p. 3034.

[69] Case 155/82 [1983] *ECR* 531.

[70] Case 83/78 [1978] *ECR* 2347.

Ireland were required not to sell 'bacon pigs' except to or through the agency of the Pigs Marketing Board. The Court held this to contravene Articles 30 and 34. The Advocate General seems to have considered that there was at least a potential discrimination against exports. He suggested that the Board might be inclined to protect the processing industry in Northern Ireland by restricting exports of the raw materials, i.e. bacon pigs. In *de Peijper*[71] the United Kingdom Government argued that the disputed Dutch measures were not equivalent to a quantitative restriction because they were applied without any distinction to domestic and imported products, and did not in fact make the sale of the latter more diffi-cult than that of the former. The measures required all persons who marketed certain pharmaceutical products in the Netherlands to produce documents to prove that the particular items had been manufactured in the approved way. There was thus no open discrimination between drugs on account of their origin. In practice, however, it was more difficult, and in some cases impossible, for the importer into the Netherlands to obtain the necessary documents from the manufacturer in any other member state, who could not be compelled by Dutch law to cooperate. In the case in point, the manufacturers and their representative in the Netherlands had indeed refused to cooperate with the importer. The Dutch requirements thus had the effect of putting importers at a disadvantage, compared with sellers of similar drugs manufactured in the Netherlands. The Court referred to this situation as creating an obstacle contravening Article 30, and went on to say:

Rules of [sic] practices which result in imports being channelled in such a way that only certain traders can effect these imports, whereas others are prevented from doing so, constitute such an obstacle to imports.[72]

Again, in *Herbert Gilli and Paul Andres*,[73] concerning German apple vinegar, the Court found that the principal effect of provisions prohibiting the marketing in Italy of products containing acetic acid other than that derived from wine was to protect domestic production.[74] In *Fietje*,[75] the Dutch requirement that certain spirits be labelled 'Likeur' in fact imposed an additional burden on importers of spirits which had already been labelled in a different way.

Although discrimination can thus be found to have existed in these cases, either actually or at least potentially, there remains the question whether it must always exist before there can be any contravention of Articles 30 or 34. Neither of those Articles mentions discrimination, in

---

[71] Case 104/75 [1976] *ECR* 613.
[72] Ibid., p. 635.
[73] Case 788/79 [1980] *ECR* 2071; and see Case 193/80, *Commission* v. *Italy*.
[74] Case 788/79 [1980] *ECR* 2071, p. 2079.
[75] Case 27/80 [1980] *ECR* 3839; [1981] 3 *CMLR* 722.

contrast to Article 36, which makes the absence of arbitrary discrimination an essential condition to be satisfied before there can be any defence under that Article. A textual comparison of Articles 30 and 34 on the one hand and Article 36 on the other might lead to the conclusion that discrimination is not an essential part of the offence, but that its absence is a required element of each of the special defences in Article 36. Some support might be gained for this view in *Rewe-Zentral AG* v. *Bundesmonopolverwaltung für Branntwein* (the 'Cassis de Dijon' case).[76] Taken literally, and out of its context, this view could be inferred from the well-known dictum:

There is therefore no valid reason why, provided that they have been lawfully produced and marketed in one of the Member States, alcoholic beverages should not be introduced into any other Member State . . .[77]

On that basis it might be thought to infringe Article 30 for a member state to prohibit the sale, for example, of any car which did not have a speedo-meter calibrated in both miles per hour and kilometres per hour (thus restricting both foreign and home manufacturers). On the same line of reasoning the member state's only escape would be to try to establish some special defence based on Article 36, or perhaps some reason for saying that its conduct fell outside the scope of Article 30 because it was acting in the defence of the consumer.[78]

The Court gave more direct support in *Eyssen*.[79] Although eventually excusing the Netherlands, under Article 36, for prohibiting the addition of nisin to home-produced or imported cheese, the Court regarded the prohibition as equivalent to a quantitative restriction. It said:

In view of this disparity of rules it cannot be disputed that the prohibition by certain Member States of the marketing on their territory of processed cheese containing added nisin is of such a nature as to affect imports of that product from other Member States where, conversely, the addition of nisin is wholly or partially permitted and that it for that reason constitutes a measure having an effect equivalent to a quantitative restriction.[80]

Advocate General Warner's opinion was more specific with regard to discrimination. He took the following view:

Thus Article 30 does not merely forbid discrimination against goods from other Member States. It can apply even where there is no such discrimination.[81]

[76] Case 120/78 [1979] *ECR* 649.
[77] Ibid., p. 664. The Commission appears to hold this view: see its letter to all member states, reproduced in *OJ* C 256/2, 3 Oct. 1980.
[78] Case 120/78, *Rewe-Zentral AG* v. *Bundesmonopolverwaltung für Branntwein* [1979] *ECR* 649, p. 662, where the Court referred to 'requirements relating in particular to the effectiveness of fiscal supervision, the protection of public health, the fairness of commercial transactions and the defence of the consumer'.
[79] Case 53/80 [1981] *ECR* 409; [1982] 2 *CMLR* 20.
[80] Ibid., p. 33.   [81] Ibid., p. 27.

The *Eyssen* case is however inconsistent with the Court's judgment in *Blesgen* v. *Belgium*[82] in which the Court, less than one month later, ruled as follows:

The concept in Article 30 of the EEC Treaty of measures having an effect equivalent to quantitative restrictions on imports is to be understood as meaning that the prohibition laid down by that provision does not cover a national measure applicable without distinction to domestic and imported products which prohibits the consumption, sale or offering even without charge of spirituous beverages of a certain alcoholic strength for consumption on the premises in all places open to the public as well as the stocking of such drinks on premises to which consumers are admitted or in other parts of the establishment or in the dwelling appurtenant thereto, in so far as the latter prohibition is complementary to the prohibition of consumption on the premises.[83]

The role of discrimination is perhaps best seen in *Commission* v. *Ireland*.[84] In that case certain souvenir jewellery had to be marked 'foreign' when imported into Ireland. The Irish government said this was justified in the interests of consumer protection and the fairness of commercial transactions. The Court held however that the Irish measures could not be regarded as outside the scope of Article 30. This was because they were discriminatory, and it had been made clear in *Gilli and Andres*[85] that discrimination prevented any reliance on those grounds. Nor, in the Court's view, could the Irish Government rely on Article 36 because the same grounds were not listed in that Article.

Having thus in the first eleven paragraphs of its Decision disposed of any defence based on the exceptions referred to in the 'Cassis de Dijon' case or Article 36, the Court turned its attention to the application of Article 30 to the facts. After reciting in paragraph 12 an Irish argument to the effect that there was in fact no discrimination, and in paragraph 13 the Commission's contention that there was, the Court said in paragraph 14:

It is therefore necessary to consider whether the contested measures are indeed discriminatory or whether they constitute discrimination in appearance only.[86]

If discrimination was not an essential part of the offence created by Article 30 it is difficult to see why, at that stage in its judgment, the Court should have considered it 'necessary' to consider that aspect any further. In fact it decided that there was discrimination, and therefore a breach of Article 30. In paragraphs 17 and 18 it said:

Thus by granting souvenirs imported from other Member States access to the domestic market solely on condition that they bear a statement of origin, whilst no

[82] Case 75/81 [1982] *ECR* 1211.
[83] Ibid., p. 1230.
[84] Case 113/80 [1981] *ECR* 1625.
[85] Case 788/79 [1980] *ECR* 2071, p. 2078.
[86] Case 113/80 [1981] *ECR* 1625, p. 1640.

such statement is required in the case of domestic products, the provisions contained in the Sale Order and the Importation Order indisputably constitute a discriminatory measure.

The conclusion to be drawn therefore is that by requiring all souvenirs and articles of jewellery imported from other Member States which are covered by the Sale Order and the Importation Order to bear an indication of origin or the word 'foreign', the Irish rules constitute a measure having equivalent effect within the meaning of Article 30 of the EEC Treaty. Ireland has consequently failed to fulfil its obligations under the article.[87]

There seems therefore to be reasonable ground for thinking that discrimination is just as much an essential part of the prohibitions in Articles 30 and 34 as its absence is for one of the special defences in Article 36 and 'Cassis de Dijon'. If this view is correct the United Kingdom government could not, for example, be criticized, and it would not have the burden of establishing one of those special defences, if it prohibited without discrimination the building of any shops, offices, or factories in the middle of Hyde Park—even if that action was, in the language of *Dassonville*,[88] capable, at least potentially and indirectly, of hindering intra-Community trade (because foreign goods could not be sold in the Park and goods could not be made there for export).

EXCEPTIONS TO THE RULE AGAINST QUANTITATIVE RESTRICTIONS

Furtherance of a Community policy

To answer the question whether it is permissible to maintain the equivalent of a quantitative restriction, within the wide definition in *Dassonville*,[89] in order to promote a Community policy it is convenient first to consider the case of *Donckerwolcke* v. *Procureur de la République*.[90] Goods, coming from third states but having acquired the benefit of Article 30 by getting into free circulation in another member state, were subjected to French customs rules requiring declarations of true origin and also requiring import licences. The French objective was to detect any deflections of trade, for which a remedy under Article 115 EEC might be available. Even after the expiry of the transitional period that Article continues to apply.[91] The Commission has power to authorize certain exceptional protective measures to be taken by member states in order to ensure that the common commercial policy (i.e. measures taken by the Community under Article

---

[87] Ibid., p. 1641.
[88] Case 8/74 [1974] *ECR* 837.
[89] Ibid., p. 852.
[90] Case 41/76 [1976] *ECR* 1921.
[91] For an example of its application, see *OJ* C84/2 of 3 Apr. 1982.

113 as part of the Community's external relations) are not obstructed by deflection of trade. For this purpose the Commission needs the facts, and a member state is entitled to collect them. So much the Court acknowledged, although it pointed out that, in collecting information concerning the origin of goods, a member state can only demand that an importer should give whatever information he has, or could reasonably be expected to have, and that a member state cannot impose disproportionate penalties for failure to do so. On the other hand, the Court found that an import licensing scheme went altogther beyond what was permissible, and infringed Article 30, even if it was used only as an interim measure while the possibility of the application of Article 115 was being considered. Thus the Court, by allowing member states in these circumstances to 'hinder' importers (actually or potentially) by requiring information on origin, was again illustrating how action may exceptionally be allowed to infringe one of the basic freedoms, provided it is taken in pursuance of an agreed Community policy.[92] This case should be contrasted with *Commission* v. *Ireland*,[93] where a demand for indications of origin was held to infringe Article 30, when made in order to pursue an objective of national policy.

An interesting question is whether it is open to the Council to adopt a regulation or other Community act which would allow the equivalent of a quantitative restriction, prima facie in infringement of Article 30, but in order to achieve some other Community objective. On the particular facts it was only necessary for the Court to decide in *Ramel*[94] that Article 31 of Regulation 816/70 was invalid to the extent that it authorized charges equivalent to customs duties. But that Article purported to allow member states to 'take measures that may limit imports from another Member State'. The language was wide enough to embrace the equivalent of quantitative restrictions. If the latter had in fact been instituted, rather than customs charges, and had then been challenged in the same way, it is difficult to see on what basis the Court could have distinguished between customs duties and quantitative restrictions. In each instance the measure would have been prima facie contrary to a basic treaty rule of free movement, even though the Council thought it was pursuing the objective of removing difficulties in the Common Agricultural Policy. Part of the reasoning of the Court was that, by virtue of Article 38(2) EEC, an exception could only be made to Article 13 if an express power to make that exception could be found in Articles 29 to 46—which it could not. It is also the case that Articles 39 to 46 do not specifically allow any exception to Article 30. It would seem that on this line of reasoning the Council has no power, in the field of agriculture, to authorize derogations from Article 30.

---

[92] An example in the customs field is Case 46/76, *Bauhuis* [1977] *ECR* 5.
[93] Case 113/80 [1981] *ECR* 1625.
[94] Joined Cases 80 and 81/77 [1978] *ECR* 927.

It is however not certain that the Court would apply in relation to Article 30 the same principles as it has applied in relation to Article 13. It is possible to detect a tendency on the part of the Court to distinguish between the various fields of application of the Treaty, and to interpret them independently of each other. Thus, for example, in *Iannelli* v. *Meroni*[95] the Court said:

However wide the field of application of Article 30 may be, it nevertheless does not include obstacles to trade covered by other provisions of the Treaty.

In fact, since the legal consequences of the application or of a possible infringement of these various provisions have to be determined having regard to their particular purpose in the context of all the objectives of the Treaty, they may be of a different kind and this implies that their respective fields of application must be distinguished, except in those cases which may fall simultaneously within the field of application of two or more provisions of Community law.

Thus obstacles which are of a fiscal nature or have equivalent effect and are covered by Articles 9 to 16 and 95 of the Treaty do not fall within the prohibition in Article 30.[96]

It could be argued on the basis of *Donckerwolcke*[97] that if a member state is entitled unilaterally to introduce monitoring measures in order to achieve a Community policy, even though they may hinder the flow of goods, then *a fortiori* the Council must have a similar power. There is therefore no reason why the Council should not act in such a way as to hinder free movement, by way of exception to Article 30, in the exercise of any of its powers conferred by other Articles of the Treaty. The Council has, for example, authorized the United Kingdom to retain its Milk Marketing Boards even though they might otherwise have been open to criticism based on Article 34 EEC.[98] In this instance the Council may be taken to have considered itself in a stronger position than a member state acting unilaterally, because the European Court, responding to a reference under Article 177 from the resident magistrate in Armagh, had already struck down Northern Ireland's Pig Marketing Board in *Northern Ireland Pigs Marketing Board* v. *Redmond*[99] on the grounds that its activities were incompatible with Article 34. There are two reasons why the Council may have felt able to take this action (although these cannot be verified because the records of the Council's deliberations are not published). First, as has been seen in Chapter I,[100] it is sometimes easier to justify action if taken collectively by a Community institution than if taken unilaterally by a member state. Secondly, the Council was acting in furtherance of a

[95] Case 74/76 [1977] *ECR* 557.
[96] Ibid., p. 574.
[97] Case 41/76 [1976] *ECR* 1921.
[98] Reg. 1421/78, *OJ* 1978, L171/12; Reg. 1422/78, *OJ* 1978, L171/14.
[99] Case 83/78 [1978] *ECR* 2347.
[100] In connection with Case 46/76, *Bauhuis* [1977] *ECR* 5.

Community policy, as recorded in the preamble to the Regulation. The Community's intervention system for milk and milk products was proving costly. The cost to the Community was being reduced in the UK because the Boards were helping to channel the predominant quantity of milk into direct human consumption. The Community and its funds therefore benefited, even though the Boards had the exclusive right to purchase milk from producers.

Strong though these arguments may be, the Court has not yet had an opportunity to consider them, and until it does so there must remain an element of doubt as to the extent to which the Council could, in further-ance of a Community policy, authorize action which would infringe Article 30, as interpreted by the Court. What is clear is that there is no escape from the full rigour of Article 30 in order to pursue a purely national objective: *Commission* v. *Ireland*.[101]

'Cassis de Dijon'

In view of the very wide definition of measures equivalent to quantitative restrictions, which the Court gave in *Dassonville*[102] and to a large extent repeated in the subsequent cases reviewed earlier in this chapter, it is not surprising that the Court should sooner or later accept the need to restrict the effect of that definition in some way. It did so not by revising its defini-tion but by achieving the same result in a different way. The method chosen was to declare that there were certain exceptions to the rule in Article 30, in addition to those created by Article 36. The word 'exceptions' is used advisedly. It is the word used by the Court itself in *Commission* v. *Ireland*[103] to describe the principles it had created in the line of cases to which it referred. At the head of that line is *Rewe-Zentral AG* v. *Bundesmono-polverwaltung für Branntwein*[104] ('*Rewe*' for short), which is more commonly known as the 'Cassis de Dijon' case.

The facts of *Rewe* were fairly simple. 'Cassis de Dijon' was a French liqueur. The Germans prevented it from being marketed in Germany because its wine-spirit content was too low. The plaintiff attacked this under Article 30 EEC, and the Germans sought to justify their law because it was needed on three grounds—for the protection of public health, the protection of the consumer against fraud, and the suppression of unfair competition. Advocate General Caportorti appears to have accepted that, on the well-established jurisprudence of the Court, the German law was caught by the prohibition in Article 30. He dealt with the German defence by considering whether it came within the ambit of Article 36. Although the

---

[101] Case 113/80 [1981] *ECR* 1625.
[102] Case 8/74 [1974] *ECR* 837.
[103] Case 113/80 [1981] *ECR* 1625, p. 1639.
[104] Case 120/78 [1979] *ECR* 649.

first ground fell within the scope of Article 36, which specifically mentions the protection of the health of humans, he found it difficult to accept that the exclusion of weak liqueurs and the admission of strong ones was in the interests of public health. He considered that the protection of consumers against fraud was legitimate, on the basis of Article 36, because it was covered by the concept of public policy, but he questioned whether that was the motive behind the German restriction, and in any case he found it disproportionate. He did not regard the suppression of unfair competition as falling within public policy, the only possibly relevant exception mentioned in Article 36. Thus the Advocate General regarded the facts as falling prima facie within the scope of Article 30, thought that the only possible escape was through Article 36, and that the latter did not apply in view of the particular facts.

The Court did not analyse the situation in the same way. Nowhere in its judgment did it mention Article 36. It ruled as follows:

> The concept of 'measures having an effect equivalent to quantitative restrictions on imports' contained in Article 30 of the EEC Treaty is to be understood to mean that the fixing of a minimum alcohol content for alcoholic beverages intended for human consumption by the legislation of a Member State also falls within the prohibition laid down in that provision where the importation of alcoholic beverages lawfully produced and marketed in another Member State is concerned.[105]

Before reaching that conclusion the Court, after dismissing Article 37 as irrelevant, held that in the absence of common rules on the production and marketing of alcohol it would be for the member states to regulate those matters on their own territories. But there were limits on their power to do so. The Court said:

> Obstacles to movement within the Community resulting from disparities between the national laws relating to the marketing of the products in question must be accepted in so far as those provisions may be recognized as being necessary in order to satisfy mandatory requirements relating in particular to the effectiveness of fiscal supervision, the protection of public health, the fairness of commercial transactions and the defence of the consumer.[106]

The Court then proceeded to dismiss the German claims to be protecting public health, protecting the consumer against unfair practices, and ensuring the fairness of commercial transactions. Fiscal supervision was not in issue in the case. In this way, while dismissing German arguments on the facts, the Court clearly identified these four possible escape routes from the rule in Article 30. Those who were already familir with Article 30,

---

[105] Ibid., p. 665.
[106] Ibid., p. 662. See also Case 193/80, *Commission* v. *Italy* [1981] *ECR* 3019, p. 3034, and Case 6/81, *Industrie Diensten* v. *Beele* [1982] *ECR* 707.

as previously interpreted by the Court, and who read this latest judgment together with the opinion of the Advocate General in the case, could be forgiven for having thought that the Court's four escape routes must have been based upon an extended interpretation of Article 36.

This, at any rate, appears to have been the understanding of the Irish government, as revealed in its defence in *Commission* v. *Ireland*.[107] Here the issue concerned Irish laws prohibiting the import of certain kinds of souvenir jewellery unless stamped with an indication of origin or the word 'foreign'. There were no such requirements in the case of similar articles produced in Ireland. The Irish government apparently took the view that the public were entitled to assume that a replica of a shamrock, for example, was made in Ireland unless they were warned to the contrary. The Irish government maintained that their restrictions were justified under Article 36 on the ground of consumer protection, and on the ground of maintaining fairness in commercial transactions between producers. The Court held, however, that the Irish government was mistaken in relying on Article 36. That Article constituted a derogation from the basic rule of free movement, and the exceptions listed in it could not be extended. Those exceptions did not include protection of consumers or fairness of commercial transactions. Although however, they were not exceptions falling within Article 36 they were, in the Court's judgment, exceptions to the requirements arising under Article 30. In reaching that conclusion the Court did not of course rely on any specific treaty provisions other than those in Article 36. Nor could it be expected to admit that its often repeated interpretation in *Dassonville*[108] of the scope of Article 30 was mistaken. So it took the line that the fairness of commercial transactions and the defence of the consumer, inter alia, were exceptions to Article 30.[109] As authority for that proposition it cited its own judgments in *Rewe*,[110] *Gilli and Andres*,[111] and *Keldermann*.[112] However, as the Court pointed out, the exceptions listed in those cases only extended to national rules which applied without discrimination to both domestic and imported products. Since there was such discrimination in the Irish case the exceptions could not apply.

The 'Cassis de Dijon' case,[113] as interpreted by *Commission* v. *Ireland*,[114]

---

[107] Case 113/80 [1981] *ECR* 1625. On origin marking, see also Case 207/83, *Commission* v. *United Kingdom* (pending).

[108] Case 8/74 [1974] *ECR* 837.

[109] On the scope of this exception, see Case 6/81, *BV Industrie* v. *Beele* [1982] *ECR* 707; Case 220/81, *Procureur du Roi* v. *Robertson* [1982] *ECR* 2349 (hallmarks); Case 261/81, *Rau* v. *De Smedt* [1982] *ECR* 3961 (requirement that margarine be packaged in cubic form); Case 302/82, *Commission* v. *France*, pending (origin marking of textiles).

[110] Case 120/78 [1979] *ECR* 649.

[111] Case 788/79 [1980] *ECR* 2071.

[112] Case 130/80 [1981] *ECR* 527.

[113] Case 120/78 [1979] *ECR* 649.

[114] Case 113/80 [1981] *ECR* 1625.

was an important case which marked a significant reduction of the rigours of *Dassonville*.[115] It firmly established that, when there was no relevant Community regime,[116] non-discriminatory national rules which were necessary for one of four reasons—i.e. fiscal supervision, the protection of public health, the fairness of commercial transactions, and the defence of the consumer—could be enforced by way of exception to Article 30.

It is curious that when creating these judicial exceptions the Court should have included one, but only one, of the exceptions listed in Article 36 ('the protection of public health', which must presumably be equated with 'the protection of health and life of humans'). As a defence under Article 36 the protection of health is subject to two qualifications. Measures taken on this ground must not constitute (*i*) a means of arbitrary discrimination or (*ii*) a disguised restriction on trade between member states. As an exception to Article 30 under the 'Cassis de Dijon' principle the Court has so far mentioned only the first of these two restrictions, i.e. that the measures must be non-discriminatory. If a member state relies on public health grounds in the future it is difficult however to see how the Court could disregard the second condition. It is specifically mentioned in Article 36 and, as was seen in *Commission* v. *Ireland*,[117] the Court claims no power to amend that Article. But does this mean that the Court will hold that the other escape routes mentioned in 'Cassis de Dijon' are also subject to the second qualification, i.e. that they must not be a disguised restriction on trade between member states? If the Court does so, will it not for all practical purposes simply have added fiscal supervision, the fairness of commercial transactions, and the defence of the consumer to the list of exceptions already in Article 36? If it does not do so, on what principle will it draw a distinction between those three grounds and the ground of public health?

The exception concerning the defence of the consumer was further considered by the Court in *Robertson*,[118] which concerned national rules on the hallmarking of silver-plated articles. The Court held that Article 30 does not prevent a member state from applying national rules which prevent the sale of such articles unless they are stamped with the nationally approved hallmark, or a hallmark which has been approved by another member state and which contains equivalent information in a form which is intelligible to the consumer in the member state of importation. Similarly, Article 30 does not exclude national rules which, without affecting the imported product, are intended to improve the quality of the domestic

---

[115] Case 8/74 [1974] *ECR* 837.

[116] If there is a Community regime there is no room for national rules on the same subject—see, e.g., Case 35/76 *Simmenthal* [1976] *ECR* 1871.

[117] Case 113/80 [1981] *ECR* 1625.

[118] Case 220/81 [1982] *ECR* 2349. See also Case 286/81, *Oosthoek's Uitgeversmaatschappij* [1982] *ECR* 4575.

product, or rules on the mandatory use of names, signs, or control documents, provided no distinction is made between products intended for domestic consumption and those intended for export: *Jongeneel Kaas BV, Bodegraven* v. *State of the Netherlands and Stichting Centraal Orgaan Zuivelcontrole*.[119]

There is one further aspect of the 'Cassis de Dijon' case[120] which should be mentioned. The judgment contains one sentence which, taken out of its context, is capable of being misconstrued in a way which would undermine the value of the exceptions contained in Article 36. The sentence reads:

> There is therefore no valid reason why, provided that they have been lawfully produced and marketed in one of the Member States, alcoholic beverages should not be introduced into any other Member State; the sale of such products may not be subject to a legal prohibition on the marketing of beverages with an alcohol content lower than the limit set by the national rules.[121]

The first half of this sentence might be taken as an indication that, if one member state sees no reason to prevent the marketing of a product in its territory, it is not open to other member states to prevent or restrict its importation on one of the grounds specified in Article 36, e.g. the protection of public health. That this is an incorrect interpretation is illustrated by the *Sandoz* case.[122] In that case certain foodstuffs with added vitamins were lawfully marketed in one member state, but restricted in another (the Netherlands). With certain important provisos designed to ensure that free movement of goods is only restricted on genuine health grounds, the Court held that national legislation prohibiting, in the absence of prior authorization, the marketing of such products was not prevented by Community law.[123]

Article 36

This Article reads:

> The provisions of Articles 30 to 34 shall not preclude prohibitions or restrictions on imports, exports or goods in transit justified on grounds of public morality, public policy or public security; the protection of health and life of humans, animals or plants; the protection of national treasures possessing artistic, historic or archaeological value; or the protection of industrial and commercial property. Such prohibitions or restrictions shall not, however, constitute a means of arbitrary discrimination or a disguised restriction on trade between Member States.

The incorporation in this text of the word 'justified' shows that the existence of considerations of public morality, public policy, etc., and still

[119] Case 237/82, judgment of 7/2/84.
[120] Case 120/78 [1979] *ECR* 649.
[121] Ibid., p. 664.
[122] Case 174/82 [1983] *ECR* 2445.
[123] See also Case 97/83, CMC *Melkunie BV* judgment of 6/6/84.

less a mere assertion by a member state that they exist, are not in themselves sufficient to allow national measures to be taken contrary to Articles
30 to 34.[124] What is justified falls to be determined in the last resort by the
European Court.[125] The Court has given guidance in a variety of situations.
The general trend of its decisions has been to interpret strictly the grounds
mentioned in the Article, as can be seen, for example, in *Bauhuis*.[126] It
summed up its attitude towards the Article in *Commission* v. *Italy*[127] in the
following terms:

It must be recalled that in accordance with the settled case-law of the Court,
Article 36 must be strictly interpreted and the exceptions which it lists may not be
extended to cases other than those which have been exhaustively laid down and,
furthermore, that Article 36 refers to matters of a non-economic nature.[128]

The Court has further held that, even if measures fall within one of such
restrictive interpretations, they will still not be regarded as justified if they
offend against the principle of proportionality. This means that the restrictions on free movement must be no more than are reasonably required in
order to achieve the permitted objective. An alternative way of putting the
same point is to say that measures will not be justified under Article 36 if
such objective could be obtained by other measures which would be less
restrictive of intra-Community trade and which a member state could
reasonably be expected to take. This view of proportionality can be found
in *de Peijper*:[129]

Health and the life of humans rank first among the property or interests protected
by Article 36 and it is for the Member States, within the limits imposed by the
Treaty, to decide what degree of protection they intend to assure and in particular
how strict the checks to be carried out are to be.
   Nevertheless it emerges from Article 36 that national rules or practices which do
restrict imports of pharmaceutical products or are capable of doing so are only
compatible with the Treaty to the extent to which they are necessary for the
effective protection of health and life of humans.
   National rules or practices do not fall within the exception specified in Article 36
if the health and life of humans can as effectively be protected by measures which
do not restrict intra-Community trade so much.[130]

---

[124] See Case 40/82, *Commission* v. *United Kingdom* [1982] *ECR* 2793, concerning imports of
poultry meat.
[125] In the absence of any Community act on the subject, e.g. under Article 235 (EEC). In Case
35/76, *Simmenthal* [1976] *ECR* 1871, p. 1885, the Court equated 'justified' with 'necessary'.
[126] Case 46/76 [1977] *ECR* 5, p. 15. See also Case 13/79, *Eggers* v. *Freie Hansestadt Bremen* [1978]
ECR 1935, at p. 1956; Case 7/61, *Commission* v. *Italy* [1961] *ECR* 317.
[127] Case 95/81 [1982] *ECR* 2187.   [128] Ibid., p. 2204.
[129] Case 104/75 [1976] *ECR* 613.
[130] Ibid., p. 635. See also Case 155/82, *Commission* v. *Belgium* [1983] *ECR* 531, where the Court
held that by restricting the right to apply for authorization to market pesticides and other products
to persons established in Belgium, Article 30 was infringed, even though the restriction was
designed to enable public health legislation to be enforced.

A further general limitation is that when the Community adopts rules designed to protect public policy, public health, and the other matters mentioned in Article 36, those rules are prima facie exhaustive and so, unless they specifically provide otherwise,[131] there is no longer any room for national measures under Article 36. If the Community rules take the form of a harmonization directive under Article 100, national rules cannot go beyond what is permitted by, or necessary to give effect to, the directive. In *Denkavit* v. *Minister für Ernährung*[132] the Court said:

Consequently when, in application of Article 100 of the Treaty, Community directives provide for the harmonization of the measures necessary to guarantee the protection of animal and human health and when they establish procedures to check that they are observed, recourse to Article 36 is no longer justified and the appropriate checks must be carried out and the protective measures adopted within the framework outlined by the harmonizing directive.[133]

Sometimes, however, the first stage of a Community regime leaves room for some additional national rules, as was the case in *Ministère Public* v. *Grunert*.[134]

Yet another restriction on national measures, even in cases which fall within the categories referred to in the first sentence of Article 36, is contained in its second sentence.[135] If a measure is in principle justified on grounds of public morality, public policy, or public security it will cease to be so once it is established that it offends against the second sentence of Article 36 by being a means of arbitrary discrimination or a disguised restriction on trade between member states.[136] In *Commission* v. *France*,[137] laws restricting the advertising of alcoholic drinks were enacted in the interests of public health. But they operated in a way which put products imported from other member states at a disadvantage compared to national products. Advertising of some drinks was restricted, whereas others equally harmful in the event of excessive consumption were unrestricted. This amounted to arbitrary discrimination.

The inclusion in the second sentence of Article 36 of the word 'arbitrary' is not without significance. Thus, if genuinely based on, say, health grounds, a national measure may discriminate against imports, but may not do so in an arbitrary way. An insight into the distinction between

---

[131] E.g., as in Article 11 of Dir. 118/71 on health problems affecting trade in fresh poultry-meat, *OJ* 1971, L55/23.

[132] Case 251/78 [1979] *ECR* 3369.

[133] Ibid., p. 3388. See also Case 148/78, *Ratti* [1979] *ECR* 1629, p. 1644.

[134] Case 88/79 [1980] *ECR* 1827.

[135] On the relationship between the first and second sentences of Article 36, see Advocate General Warner in Case 34/79, *R.* v. *Henn and Darby* [1979] *ECR* 3795, p. 3826.

[136] See Case 40/82, *Commission* v. *United Kingdom* [1982] *ECR* 2793.

[137] Case 152/78 [1980] *ECR* 2299; see also Joined Cases 314–16/81 and 83/82, *Procureur de la République* v. *Waterkeyn* [1982] *ECR* 4337.

discrimination and arbitrary discrimination can be obtained from *Rewe–Zentralfinanz* v. *Landwirtschaftskammer*.[138] In that case Directive 466/69[139] on the control of San José Scale insects was held by its own terms not to preclude additional or stricter national provisions designed to prevent the spread of this harmful organism. A phyto-sanitary inspection of imported fruit at the frontier was therefore in principle justified under Article 36, even though it was discriminatory in the sense that fruit produced in the Federal Republic of Germany was not subjected to a similar inspection when dispatched within that country. However there were some German measures to prevent the spread of the disease from domestic sources. Owners of plants had certain duties to report to the competent authorities, and when a risk was thought to exist, control measures were taken. The Court indicated that, although domestic products and imported ones might thus be treated differently, there would be no arbitrary discrimination if effective measures were taken to prevent the distribution of contaminated domestic products, and if experience showed that there was a risk of the disease being spread if imported products were not inspected.

Public morality

This exception was examined by the European Court in a reference under Article 177 by the House of Lords in *R.* v. *Henn and Darby*.[140] The defendants were charged with fraudulently evading the prohibition of the importation of indecent or obscene articles contrary to section 42 of the Customs Consolidation Act, 1876 and section 304 of the Customs and Excise Act, 1952. The articles were in a lorry load of pornographic films and magazines, produced in Denmark and shipped from Rotterdam. They depicted the commission of a number of sexual crimes. The European Court reached the inescapable conclusion that a law prohibiting the importation of pornography constituted a quantitative restriction within the meaning of Article 30. The question, for the purposes of Article 36, was what was the scope of 'public morality'. The concept defies objective definition. At best it represents a collective, but nevertheless subjective, viewpoint. It varies from time to time, from country to country, and indeed from locality to locality, as can be seen from the fact that the laws in different parts of the UK are not entirely the same. No Community standard exists. In these circumstances it is not surprising that the Court held that a member state may, in principle, lawfully prohibit imports of articles which are of an indecent or obscene character as understood by its domestic laws. Moreover, the Court decided that if there is no lawful trade in such goods within the member state, enforcement of the national prohibition cannot

---

[138] Case 4/75 [1975] *ECR* 843. See also Case 78/70, *Deutsche Grammophon* [1971] *ECR* 487.
[139] *OJ* 1969, L.323/5.
[140] Case 34/79 [1979] *ECR* 3795.

constitute a means of arbitrary discrimination or a disguised restriction on trade contrary to the second sentence of Article 36.

Public policy

Here we are immediately faced with a seemingly irreconcilable linguistic difference between the terms used in each of the equally authentic texts of the EEC Treaty. The original six member states may have had a comfortable feeling that they knew what was meant by 'ordre public', 'öffentlichen Ordnung', 'ordine pubblico', and 'openbare orde', and that they all meant more or less the same thing. Whatever they may have thought at that time, nobody could now imagine that 'ordre public' means exactly the same thing to a French judge as 'public policy' means to an English one. Nor is there any reason to assume that a technical meaning ascribed to a phrase by the domestic law of one party to a treaty, drafted in several equally authentic languages, is to be preferred to the meaning it has in the law of another. Nor is such technical meaning necessarily relevant in an international context. Articles 31 to 33 of the Vienna Convention on the Law of Treaties of 23 May 1969[141] established certain rules. Generally speaking, a treaty is to be interpreted in good faith in accordance with the ordinary meaning to be given to its terms in their context, and in the light of the object and purpose of the treaty: Article 31(1). In the last resort the meaning which best reconciles the texts, having regard to the object and purpose of the treaty, is to be adopted: Article 33(4). The parties may subsequently agree an interpretation: Article 31(3)(*a*).

The emphasis in the Vienna Convention on the object and purpose of the treaty is generally in line with the method of interpretation chosen by the Court in *R. v. Bouchereau*,[142] when called upon to consider the meaning of 'measure', as used in Directive 221/64,[143] and its equivalent in the other Community languages. It said:

The different language versions of a Community text must be given a uniform interpretation and hence in the case of divergence between the versions the provision in question must be interpreted by reference to the purpose and general scheme of the rules of which it forms a part.[144]

In the EEC context the parties have reached some measure of agreement on the scope of public policy, for the purposes of Article 56, in Article 3 of Directive 221/64.[145] That Article, however, relates only to the particular context of Article 56, and is of little assistance in connection with Article 36. In the case of the latter it is necessary at present to rely on judicial interpretation.

[141] TS No. 58 (1980) Cmnd. 7964.
[142] Case 30/77 [1977] *ECR* 1999.
[143] *OJ*, Special Edition, 1963–4, p. 117.
[144] p. 2010.   [145] *OJ*, Special Edition, 1963–4, p. 117.

The Court has understandably shrunk from defining public policy. In *Commission* v. *Federal Republic of Germany*[146] the German Government sought to defend its reservation of the names 'Sekt' and 'Weinbrand' for German wines on the grounds of public policy, because of the need to protect producers against unfair competition and consumers against deception regarding the origin of wines. The Court took the view that 'independently of any definition of the concept of public policy' such a derogation from Articles 30 to 34 was only permissible if it was necessary to protect the producer and consumer from fraudulent commercial practices.[147] The Court thus declined to give a comprehensive definition, restrictively interpreted public policy by introducing the concept of what was necessary, and in so doing applied the principle of proportionality to which reference has already been made.

In *R.* v. *Thompson, Johnson and Woodiwiss*[148] certain enterprising gentlemen decided to take advantage of the fact that the value of the silver content of pre-1947 coins exceeded their face value. The plan was to smuggle such coins out, to be melted down in Germany, and to smuggle krugerrands into the United Kingdom. When subsequently prosecuted for offences against the Export of Goods (Control) Order 1970 and section 304(*b*) of the Customs and Excise Act 1952 they pleaded Articles 30 and 34 EEC. The Court held that the transfer of those silver coins which were still legal tender, and krugerrands which circulated freely, were to be treated as monetary transfers. Therefore while Articles 67–73 or 104–9 might be relevant, Articles 30–7 were not. But those silver coins which were no longer legal tender could not be regarded as a means of payment and were to be treated as goods falling within Articles 30–7. It was therefore necessary to consider whether in their case Article 36 applied. The Court held:

A ban on the export from a Member State of silver alloy coins, which have been but are no longer legal tender in that State and the melting down or destruction whereof on national territory is forbidden, which has been adopted with a view to preventing such melting down or destruction in another Member State, is justified on grounds of public policy within the meaning of Article 36 of the Treaty.[149]

By way of explanation it said:

A ban on exporting such coins with a view to preventing their being melted down or destroyed in another Member State is justified on grounds of public policy within the meaning of Article 36 of the Treaty, because it stems from the need to protect the right to mint coinage which is traditionally regarded as involving the fundamental interests of the State.[150]

[146] Case 12/74 [1975] *ECR* 181.
[147] Ibid., p. 199.
[148] Case 7/78 [1978] *ECR* 2247.
[149] Ibid., p. 2276.
[150] Ibid., p. 2275.

This gives a clue to the sort of matters which can be regarded as falling within public policy. The test seems to be not what the particular member state regards as public policy, but what states in general consider to involve their fundamental interests. Another clue lies in the Court's brief statement in *Commission* v. *Italy*,[151] in answer to Italy's plea that its action was justified on grounds of public policy, that 'Article 36 refers to matters of a non-economic nature'.[152]

Public security

If the Court is disinclined to define public policy, for the purposes of Article 36, it can be expected to be equally reluctant to define public security. In practice, the latter concept appears until recently to have been largely ignored by litigants, possibly because they felt no need to stray beyond the more familiar field of 'ordre public'. This omission has, however, now been repaired in *Campus Oil Limited and Others* v. *the Minister for Industry and Energy, Ireland, and Others*.[153]

In that case the proceedings arose out of an order made by the Irish Minister requiring any person who imported various petroleum products to purchase a proportion of his requirements from an Irish refinery, at a price to be determined by the Minister. The Court had no difficulty in holding that this had a restrictive effect on imports within the meaning of Article 30. The Irish Government, however, contended that it could rely on the exception of public security, in accordance with Article 36. They argued that Ireland's heavy dependence for its oil supplies on imports from other countries and the importance of oil for the life of the country made it indispensable to maintain a refining capacity on the national territory, and thus to enable the national authorities to conclude long term delivery contracts with the oil producing countries. The United Kingdom submitted observations, arguing that Article 36 covered the fundamental interests of the state such as the maintenance of essential public services or the effective functioning of the life of the state. It maintained, however, that the article could not be relied upon in support of measures which were designed predominantly to attain economic objectives.[154] The Commission argued that the Irish order was inadequate and ineffective for the purpose of securing supplies to the Irish market, and that it was disproportionate in that it required all importers to buy petroleum products at prices determined by the competent minister.

The Court first concluded that recourse to Article 36 was no longer justified if Community rules provided for the necessary measures to ensure

---

[151] Case 95/81 [1982] *ECR* 2187.
[152] Ibid., p. 2204.
[153] Case 72/83 [1984] 3 *CMLR* 544.
[154] See Case 95/81, *Commission* v. *Italy* [1982] *ECR* 2187, above.

protection of a member state's public security. However, after reviewing the Community measures already taken to deal with the maintenance of petroleum products in the event of a crisis, the Court concluded that those measures did not give the member states an unconditional assurance that supplies would in any event be maintained at least at a level sufficient to meeting its minimum needs. For that reason the possibility of recourse to Article 36 could not be excluded. The Court then indicated that petroleum products were of fundamental importance for a country's existence since not only its economy but above all its institutions, its essential public services, and the survival of its inhabitants depended upon them. For that reason an interruption of supplies could seriously affect the public security which Article 36 allows member states to protect.

Nevertheless, the Court did not leave member states entirely free to decide for themselves what measures were justified on grounds of public security. National measures must be justified by objective circumstances corresponding to the needs of public security. Lastly, the Court indicated that since Article 36 was an exception to a fundamental principle of the Treaty, measures taken under it must not be disproportionate. The Court accordingly ruled that a member state which is totally or almost totally dependent on imports for its supplies of petroleum may rely on grounds of public security for the purpose of requiring importers to purchase some of their requirements from a national refinery, if the production of the refinery cannot be freely disposed of at competitive prices. The quantities of petroleum covered by such a system must not however exceed the maximum supply requirements without which public security of the state concerned, or the level of production necessary to keep the refinery's production capacity available in the event of a crisis, would be affected.

Protection of health and life of humans, animals, or plants

This is a subject of particular concern to governments, and some progress has been made at Community level towards the adoption of comprehensive Community rules for the protection of public health. In a common market an ideal situation would be one in which all health hazards had been identified, and common rules had been agreed for dealing with all of them. In that way producers of goods could work to one standard, in the secure knowledge that those goods would be freely marketable throughout the Community. Examples of progress towards this goal can be seen, to quote only a few, in directives dealing with dangerous substances[155] and with

[155] See Dir. 548/67, *OJ* 1967, L196/1, on the approximation of laws relating to the classification and packaging of dangerous substances, as subsequently amended, e.g. by Dir. 831/79, *OJ* 1979, L259/10; Dir. 769/76, *OJ* 1976, L262/201, relating to restrictions on the marketing and use of certain dangerous substances and preparations.

animals and meat which cross frontiers.[156] However, Community schemes by no means cover the whole field, and there is therefore still room for national measures.

In the Court's approach to the problem it is possible to discern three strands of thought, which occasionally pull in different directions. First, because Article 36 allows exceptions to the cardinal principle of free movement, it must be interpreted restrictively. Secondly, in matters of public health, particularly so far as humans are concerned, it is better in cases of doubt to err on the side of allowing safety measures. Thirdly, member states ought to trust each other's safety checks, although they need not necessarily rely upon safety precautions taken in third countries.

The first of these concepts has been illustrated earlier in this chapter, when considering proportionality and arbitrary discrimination. Indeed, some of the cases on public health have already been reviewed under those headings.

The second idea of playing safe where public health is concerned can be seen in *Officier van Justitie* v. *Kaasfabriek Eyssen*.[157] Dutch rules prohibited the addition of the antibiotic nisin to processed cheese destined for the home market. Some member states allowed the use of this additive, as did the Dutch for exports. The existence and extent of any health risk was not established but studies were continuing, for example, in the World Health Organization. Directive 54/64[158] left it to national laws to deal with nisin. The Court held that, in view of the uncertainties in the various member states about the levels of nisin which should be allowed, the Dutch prohibition was not a means of arbitrary discrimination or a disguised restriction on trade. Another example of reluctance to upset national safety measures is *Blesgen* v. *Belgium*,[159] concerning a national prohibition on selling alcoholic drinks which were over a certain strength in public places.

The third thought, that in a common market the member states ought to trust each other's safety checks, underlies the Court's judgment in *Commission* v. *Germany*.[160] Germany prohibited the import, even from member states, of meat products unless they were manufactured in an establishment approved by German authorities and situated in the country in which the animals were slaughtered. It was agreed by both parties that this was equivalent to a quantitative restriction, and the case turned on Article 36 and whether the German measures were necessary to protect human

---

[156] See Dir. 118/71, *OJ* 1971, L55/23, on health problems affecting trade in fresh poultry-meat; Dir. 462/72, *OJ* 1972, L302/28 on health and veterinary inspection problems upon importation of bovine animals and swine and fresh meat from third countries.
[157] Case 53/80 [1981] *ECR* 409. See also Case 108/80, *Ministère Public* v. *Kugelmann* [1981] *ECR* 433.
[158] *OJ*, Special Edition, 1963–4, p. 99.
[159] Case 75/81 [1982] *ECR* 317; and see Case 94/83, *Albert Heijn*, judgment of 19/9/84.
[160] Case 153/78 [1979] *ECR* 2555.

health. The Court held that they were not. It was all right to insist that animals were slaughtered within the Community, but it was immaterial in which member state. Moreover, since the German authorities could ask for certification that the meat in the product came from a slaughterhouse approved by a member state in accordance with the Community procedure established by Directive 433/64,[161] it was unnecessary to counter the health risks by insisting that the meat and the product came from one and the same member state. Nor did the crossing of a frontier *ipso facto* affect the health risk. The Court concluded:

Thus the requirement constitutes both an obstacle to the free movement of meat products which is superfluous and in any event disproportionate to its objective, and discrimination against meat-processing establishments which import their raw material from another Member State in comparison with their competitors who obtain supplies of fresh meat from slaughterhouses in their own country. Accordingly, the disputed provision is incompatible with Article 30 of the Treaty and is not covered by the exemption in Article 36.[162]

Similarly, in *Biologische Producten*[163] the Court held that, even where national measures under Article 36 are still permissible, unnecessary chemical analyses and tests cannot be demanded, when these have already been carried out in the exporting member state and the results are available for the asking. On the other hand, a monitoring procedure may be justified under Article 36, even if fees are collected in the process. Such fees may however be equivalent to customs duties, but will not be so if similar fees are charged in respect of domestic products: *Officier van Justitie* v. *Kortmann*.[164]

In *Commission* v. *United Kingdom*,[165] the Court followed the same line of reasoning as in *Commission* v. *Germany*[166] in holding that the UK licensing system for the import of UHT milk (which the UK sought to defend on health grounds) was not saved by Article 36 because it was disproportionate, in that the same result of protecting animal health could be achieved by relying on declarations signed by importers, accompanied if necessary by appropriate certificates.[167] So far as human health was concerned, the Court was satisfied that the controls in the member states for the protection of safe UHT milk were very similar, and that the end-product was of similar quality from the point of view of health. The Court continued:

Under those circumstances, the United Kingdom, in its concern to protect the

---

[161] *OJ*, Special Edition, 1963–4, p. 185.   [162] Ibid., p. 2567.

[163] Case 272/80 [1981] *ECR* 3277. But see Case 202/82, *Commission* v. *France*, judgment of 21/2/84.   [164] Case 32/80 [1981] *ECR* 251.

[165] Case 124/81 [1983] *ECR* 203. See also the second judgment, of 31/1/84, in Case 40/82, *Commission* v. *United Kingdom*.

[166] Case 153/78 [1979] *ECR* 2555.   [167] See also Case 74/82, *Commission* v. *Ireland*.

health of humans, could ensure safeguards equivalent to those which it has prescribed for its domestic production of UHT milk without having recourse to the measures adopted, which amount to a total prohibition of imports. To that end, the United Kingdom would be entitled to lay down the objective conditions which it considers ought to be observed as regards the quality of the milk before treatment and as regards the methods of treating and packing UHT milk of whatever origin offered for sale on its territory. The United Kingdom could also stipulate that imported UHT milk must satisfy the requirements thus laid down, whilst however taking care not to go beyond that which is strictly necessary for the protection of the health of the consumer. It would be able to ensure that such requirements are satisfied by requesting importers to produce certificates issued for that purpose by the competent authorities of the exporting Member States.[168]

A compromise between the second and third strands of thought (play safe in health matters, but trust each other) is to be found in the *Sandoz* case.[169] That case concerned a member state's ban on the sale of food and drinks containing added vitamins unless its national authority gave a specific authorization. The Court accepted that vitamins taken in excessive quantities can be harmful, and that scientific opinion was divided about the limits of safety. It held that this requirement for specific authorization did not infringe Article 30, but that authorizations must be given when this was consistent with the protection of public health. In other words, a member state was not bound to accept the judgment of other member states as to what was safe for human consumption in an area in which opinions were divided.

Protection of national treasures

Article 36 refers to the protection of national treasures possessing artistic, historical, or archaeological value. This is usually relevant in the context of export controls. For example, Italian Law No. 1089 of 1 June 1939, on the protection of articles of artistic or historical interest, imposed an absolute prohibition on export in certain circumstances, gave the state a right to purchase in other instances, and imposed a progressive tax in the case of those exports which were permitted. The prohibition on export was not challenged by the Commission, and subsequent litigation in the European Court focused on the tax aspect.[170]

The Export of Goods (Control) Order 1981[171] contains a general prohibition, to which there are certain exceptions, against the unlicensed export to any destination of any goods manufactured or produced more than fifty years before the date of exportation.[172]

---

[168] Case 124/81, paragraphs 28 and 29.
[169] Case 174/82 [1983] *ECR* 2445.
[170] Case 7/68, *Commission* v. *Italy* [1968] *ECR* 423; Case 18/71, *Eunomia di Porro* [1971] *ECR* 811; Case 48/71, *Commission* v. *Italy* [1972] *ECR* 527.
[171] SI 1981, No. 1641.   [172] Ibid., Articles 2, 3(*a*) and Schedule 1, Part I, Group B.

Protection of industrial and commercial property

Industrial and commercial property is not defined in the EEC Treaty, although its protection is referred to in Article 36. Article 1(2) of the Paris Convention for the Protection of Industrial Property of 20 March 1883, as revised at Stockholm on 14 July 1967,[173] reads:

The protection of industrial property has as its object patents, utility models, industrial designs, trade marks, service marks, trade names, indications of source or appellations of origin, and the repression of unfair competition.[174]

The same conference in Stockholm also drew up the text of the convention establishing the World Intellectual Property Organization.[175] Article 2 of that convention shows an overlap between industrial property and intellectual property, because the latter is said to include:

the rights relating to:
   literary, artistic, and scientific works,
   performances of performing artists, phonograms, and broadcasts,
   inventions in all fields of human endeavour,
   scientific discoveries,
   industrial designs,
   trade marks, service marks, and commercial names and designations,
   protection against unfair competition,
and all other rights resulting from intellectual activity in the industrial, scientific, literary or artistic fields.

It is probably fair to say that, for the purposes of Article 36 EEC, the concept of industrial and commercial property is no more static than the principles of private law to which those conventions refer. The European Court has so far had occasion to concentrate on patents, trade marks, copyright, and rights akin to it.[176]

Although industrial and commercial property is intangible, and is subject to many specialized national and international rules, it is nevertheless a form of property. As such it falls within Article 222 EEC, which provides that the Treaty shall in no way prejudice the rules in member states governing the system of property ownership.

There is also Article 1 of the First Additional Protocol[177] to The European Convention for the Protection of Human Rights, which reads:

Every natural or legal person is entitled to the peaceful enjoyment of his possessions. No one shall be deprived of his possessions except in the public interest and

[173] TS No. 61 (1970).
[174] The draft of 25 June 1979, sent by the Intergovernmental Preparatory Committee for the consideration of the Diplomatic Conference in Geneva, 4 February–4 March 1980, added a reference to 'inventors certificates'.   [175] TS No. 52 (1970).
[176] The Court also considered registered designs in Case 144/81, *Keurkoop* v. *Nancy Kean Gifts* [1982] *ECR* 2853. With regard to the performing rights in cinematographic films, see Case 62/79, *Coditel* v. *Cine Vog* [1980] *ECR* 881, and Case 262/81, *Coditel* v. *Cine Vog* (No. 2) [1983] 1 *CMLR* 49. See also Case 177/83, *Kohl* v. *Ringelhan*, judgment of 6/11/84.   [177] TS No. 46 (1954).

subject to the conditions provided for by law and by the general principles of international law.

The preceding provisions shall not, however, in any way impair the right of a State to enforce such laws as it deems necessary to control the use of property in accordance with the general interest or to secure the payment of taxes or other contributions or penalties.

This Article was cited by the European Court in *Hauer* v. *Land Rheinland—Pfalz*,[178] which concluded:

The right to property is guaranteed in the Community legal order in accordance with the ideas common to the constitutions of the Member States, which are also reflected in the first Protocol to the European Convention for the Protection of Human Rights.[179]

Applying those rules to the facts, the Court concluded that a Council regulation prohibiting for a period the planting of new vines[180] did not deprive the owner of his property, because the latter could be disposed of or put to other uses. The regulation restricted the owner's use of the property, but that was permitted if necessary for the protection of the general interest. In the Court's view, the regulation did not entail any undue limitation on the exercise of the owner's rights in respect of the property.

The maintenance of this distinction between unlawful deprivation of property and lawful restriction of its use has enabled the Court to maintain a somewhat uneasy truce between those who would defend the attributes of ownership of industrial property and those who would defend the competition rules of the Treaty (Articles 85 and 86 in particular) and the maintenance of freedom from quantitative restrictions and measures of equivalent effect. The distinction was drawn in *Parke, Davis* v. *Centrafarm*.[181] In that case the Court was asked:

whether the concept of practices prohibited under Articles 85(1) and 86, possibly considered with Articles 36 and 222 of the Treaty, includes the action of the holder of a patent issued in a Member State when, by virtue of that patent, he requests the national courts to prevent all commercial dealing in the territory of that State in a product coming from another Member State which does not grant an exclusive right to manufacture and sell that product.

---

[178] Case 44/79 [1979] *ECR* 3727.

[179] Ibid., p. 3745. For the place of fundamental rights in the Community legal order, see also Case 11/70, *Internationale Handelsgesellschaft* [1970] *ECR* 1125, and Case 4/73, *Nold* v. *Commission* [1974] *ECR* 491.

[180] Reg. 1162/76, *OJ* 1976, L135/32, as amended by Reg. 2776/78, *OJ* 1978, L333/1.

[181] Case 24/67 [1968] *ECR* 55. See also Joined Cases 56 and 58/64, *Consten and Grundig* v. *Commission* [1966] *ECR* 299.

After a brief reference to Article 36, the Court turned to Article 85. It held that:

the existence of the rights granted by a Member State to the holder of a patent is not affected by the prohibitions contained in Articles 85(1) and 86 of the Treaty.[182]

However, in its reasoning the Court concluded that Article 85 might apply to the use, in concert between undertakings, of one or more patents.

Another example of the distinction between ownership and use of industrial property for the purposes of Articles 36, 85, and 86 is *Sirena* v. *Eda*.[183] This case concerned an American undertaking which owned a trade mark on a cosmetic cream. It sold the Italian rights in the mark to an Italian company, and the German rights to a German company. The Italian company sought to prevent the circulation of the German cream, so marked, in Italy. This attempt to partition the common market induced the Court to adopt a cautious attitude. It took the view that Article 85 applies to the extent to which trade mark rights are invoked to prevent imports of products originating in different member states, which carry the same trade mark on account of the fact that the owners have acquired it, or the right to use it. This is so whether they invoke agreements between themselves or agreements with third parties. The exercise of trade mark rights would not infringe Article 86 merely because the proprietor prevented third parties from putting into circulation, on the territory of a member state, products bearing the same mark. The proprietor would however have a dominant position within the meaning of that Article if he could impede effective competition over a considerable part of the relevant market. The Court mentioned Article 36 only briefly, drawing attention to the second sentence. It appears to have taken the view that the same principle applies to the free movement provisions of the Treaty as to the competition rules, i.e. that, although the existence of industrial property rights is not affected, their exercise may be prohibited. It would seem that if Articles 85 or 86 are infringed this will almost inevitably mean that there is 'arbitrary discrimination or a disguised restriction on trade between Member States' so as to attract the second sentence of Article 36.

One of the problems with the notion that, although ownership must not be taken away, the exercise of rights appertaining to it may be limited is that it is not always easy to determine the point at which restrictions become so extensive that they are tantamount to expropriation. A *reductio ad absurdum* would be to say that you may own a motor car but you must not allow its wheels to revolve. The problem in such a case is to identify the hard core of essential rights of ownership which must be protected, and without which the property becomes of little or no value to the owner. In

---

[182] Ibid., p. 71.
[183] Case 40/70 [1971] *ECR* 69.

other words, what in the present context is the specific subject-matter of industrial property which is to be preserved. The relevance of the specific subject-matter was referred to in *Deutsche Grammophon* v. *Metro*.[184] In that case a German company sought to use its exclusive right to distribute sound recordings in order to prevent the marketing in Germany of records which it had originally supplied to its French subsidiary. Although asked about Articles 85 and 86, the Court also considered Article 36. After referring in familiar terms to the distinction between owning and exercising industrial property rights, the Court said:

Although it permits prohibitions or restrictions on the free movement of products, which are justified for the purpose of protecting industrial and commercial property, Article 36 only admits derogations from that freedom to the extent to which they are justified for the purpose of safeguarding rights which constitute the specific subject-matter of such property.[185]

The Court did not attempt to define what was the specific subject-matter of the industrial property rights in question, which were akin to copyright. It simply held:

It is in conflict with the provisions prescribing the free movement of products within the common market for a manufacturer of sound recordings to exercise the exclusive right to distribute the protected articles, conferred upon him by the legislation of a Member State, in such a way as to prohibit the sale in that State of products placed on the market by him or with his consent in another Member State solely because such distribution did not occur within the territory of the first Member State.[186]

The Court did however take the opportunity in *Centrafarm* v. *Sterling Drug*[187] to define the specific subject-matter of a patent. It did so in the following terms:

In relation to patents, the specific subject matter of the industrial property is the guarantee that the patentee, to reward the creative effort of the inventor, has the exclusive right to use an invention with a view to manufacturing industrial products and putting them into circulation for the first time, either directly or by the grant of licences to third parties, as well as the right to oppose infringements.[188]

The key phrase here is 'putting them into circulation for the first time'. In a common market this must mean circulation for the first time by the patentee or with his consent in any one of the member states. It follows that in Community terms a patentee's right thereby becomes exhausted.[189] The Court accordingly held:

1. The exercise, by the patentee, of the right which he enjoys under the legislation

---

[184] Case 78/70 [1971] *ECR* 487.   [185] Ibid., p. 500.   [186] Ibid., p. 502.
[187] Case 15/74 [1974] *ECR* 1147.   [188] Ibid., p. 1162.
[189] Confirmed by Article 32 of the Community Patent Convention, *OJ* 1976, L17/1.

of a Member State to prohibit the sale, in that State, of a product protected by the patent which has been marketed in another Member State by the patentee or with his consent is incompatible with the rules of the EEC Treaty concerning the free movement of goods within the Common Market.

2. In this connection, it is of no significance to know whether the patentee and the undertakings to which the latter has granted licences do or do not belong to the same concern.

3. It is also a matter of no significance that there exist, as between the exporting and importing Member States, price differences resulting from governmental measures adopted in the exporting State with a view to controlling the price of the product.[190]

In *Centrafarm* v. *Winthrop*[191] the Court defined the specific subject-matter of a trade mark in the following terms:

In relation to trade marks, the specific subject matter of the industrial property is the guarantee that the owner of the trade mark has the exclusive right to use that trade mark, for the purpose of putting products protected by the trade mark into circulation for the first time, and is therefore intended to protect him against competitors wishing to take advantage of the status and reputation of the trade mark by selling products illegally bearing that trade mark.[192]

In *Centrafarm* v. *American Home Products Corporation*[193] the Court added:

In order to establish in exceptional circumstances the precise scope of the exclusive right granted to the proprietor of the mark regard must be had to the essential function of the trade mark, which is to guarantee the identity of the origin of the trade marked product to the consumer or ultimate user.[194]

Once again, in Community law, the owner's right becomes exhausted when he, or someone acting with his consent, puts the goods into circulation in any member state. He cannot thereafter use any national trade mark rights to prevent free circulation of those goods in the Community.

It is possible to discern a change of emphasis on the part of the Court in *Van Zuylen* v. *Hag*,[195] which concerned rival users of a trade mark on coffee, the essential part of which was the word 'Hag'. Previously the emphasis had been on the competition Articles (85 and 86). In this case, however, the Court found Article 85 to be inapplicable, and examined the matter exclusively on the basis of free movement of goods. After describing on familiar lines the effect of Article 36, the Court expressed its antipathy towards trade marks by saying:

The exercise of a trade mark right tends to contribute to the partitioning off of the

[190] Ibid., p. 1168. See also Case 187/80, *Merck* v. *Stephar and Petrus* [1981] *ECR* 2063.
[191] Case 16/74 [1974] *ECR* 1183.
[192] Ibid., p. 1194.
[193] Case 3/78 [1978] *ECR* 1823.
[194] Ibid., p. 1841.
[195] Case 192/73 [1974] *ECR* 731.

markets and thus to affect the free movement of goods between Member States, all the more so since—unlike other rights of industrial and commercial property—it is not subject to limitations in point of time.

Accordingly, one cannot allow the holder of a trade mark to rely upon the exclusiveness of a trade mark right—which may be the consequence of the territorial limitation of national legislation—with a view to prohibiting the marketing in a Member State of goods legally produced in another Member State under an identical trade mark having the same origin.[196]

It accordingly ruled:

To prohibit the marketing in one Member State of a product legally bearing a trade mark in another Member State for the sole reason that an identical trade mark, having the same origin, exists in the first State, is incompatible with the provisions for the free movement of goods within the Common Market.[197]

An important concept included in this judgment was that of the common origin. Thus, if identical marks have been acquired by different persons in different member states, but the root of title can be traced back to a common owner, it is not open to either of them to exert his national rights, so as to block the marketing in his own member state of the other's goods produced in the other member state. This is so whether he tries to block the other holder of the mark from marketing the goods, or a third party who has duly acquired the product in the other member state.[198]

The Community principle of common origin, in so far as it requires free movement of goods bearing the trade mark in question, in circumstances such as those in the *Van Zuylen* v. *Hag* case,[199] does not however apply where the common origin is outside the Community, and one of the holders of the mark has exclusive rights to its use throughout the Community. This is true even if the two immediate protagonists are both undertakings established within the Community, and even if all the goods in question are also produced within the Community. A common origin outside the Community may, however, be relevant if there are two or more holders who each have the exclusive right to use the mark in different parts of the Community, if that situation presents opportunities for partitioning the common market.

All this was illustrated by three cases, all decided on 15 June 1976, concerning the sale of gramophone records bearing the mark 'Columbia'. The first was *EMI Records* v. *CBS United Kingdom*.[200] The case concerned records made in the UK by the plaintiffs and sold under the Columbia label, and records made outside the Community and bearing the same

[196] Ibid., p. 744.
[197] Ibid., p. 745.
[198] Ibid., p. 745.
[199] Case 192/73 [1974] *ECR* 731.
[200] Case 51/75 [1976] *ECR* 811.

mark but imported and sold within the UK by the defendants, a company incorporated in the UK which was a subsidiary of the American manufacturer. The plaintiffs sought an injunction prohibiting not only the import and sale but also the production of records bearing the mark. The European Court therefore dealt with the question whether the plaintiffs could use their trade mark rights to prevent the importation or marketing of marked records, whether they were manufactured inside or outside the Community. The facts reveal a complicated web of companies. The bare bones of the story, however, were that the mark had originally been owned by a common American ancestor. The plaintiffs had acquired the exclusive right to use it in all member states, and the defendants the exclusive right to use it in certain countries outside the Community. The Court, after noting that Article 30 was concerned only with trade between member states, took the view that the exercise of trade mark rights against the marketing of goods coming from third countries was not prohibited by the Article.[201] If the same proprietor held the rights in all member states (as in this case) there were no opportunities for partitioning the common market, and the principle of common origin was therefore irrelevant.[202] Moreover, the Court considered that the owner of the mark in the Community could use his rights to prevent the owner of the mark outside from manufacturing within the Community, because otherwise Article 36 would be rendered meaningless.[203] It accordingly held:

The principles of Community law and the provisions on the free movement of goods and on competition do not prohibit the proprietor of the same mark in all the Member States of the Community from exercising his trade mark rights, recognized by the national laws of each Member State, in order to prevent the sale or manufacture in the Community by a third party of products bearing the same mark, which is owned in a third country, provided that the exercise of the said rights does not manifest itself as the result of an agreement or of concerted practices which have as their object or effect the isolation or partitioning of the common market.[204]

The Court's ruling in *EMI Records* v. *CBS Grammophon*[205] and *EMI Records* v. *CBS Schallplatten*[206] were in identical terms.

The doctrine of common origin, as expounded by the Court in *Van Zuylen* v. *Hag*,[207] is open to criticism. When, as in that case, the original common owner no longer has any sort of control over at least one of the two current owners of similar trade marks, and when there is no agreement or concerted practice which would infringe Article 85, it is difficult to see why

---

[201] Ibid., p. 845.
[202] Ibid., p. 846.
[203] Ibid., p. 847.
[204] Ibid., p. 850.
[205] Case 86/75 [1976] *ECR* 871.
[206] Case 96/75 [1976] *ECR* 913.
[207] Case 192/73 [1974] *ECR* 731.

there is any more scope for partitioning or manipulating the common market than could exist whenever any trade mark owner protects his rights under Article 36. One point in support of the doctrine was made by the Court in *Terrapin* v. *Terranova*,[208] where the Court said that when the right relied upon was the result of a voluntary or enforced subdivision of a trade mark right originally owned by one proprietor 'the basic function of the trade mark to guarantee to consumers that the product has the same origin is already undermined by the sub-division of the original right'.[209] This view of the basic function of a trade mark right does not appear to reflect the Court's original definition of the specific subject-matter of a trade mark in *Centrafarm* v. *Winthrop*,[210] which made no mention of the protection of the consumer. However, the Court expanded that definition in *Centrafarm* v. *American Home Products Corporation* to include a reference to the consumer.[211]

In view of these criticisms it is not surprising that in *Terrapin* v. *Terranova*,[212] seven member states,[213] perhaps fearing a further diminution of the rights of the trade mark owner, participated and argued in favour of protecting his rights in the circumstances of that case. The facts can be distinguished from those in *Van Zuylen* v. *Hag*[214] in that there was no common origin. In *Terrapin* v. *Terranova*[215] the Court was asked:

Is it compatible with the provisions relating to the free movement of goods (Articles 30 and 36 of the EEC Treaty) that an undertaking established in Member State A, by using its commercial name and trade mark rights existing there, should prevent the import of similar goods of an undertaking established in Member State B if these goods have been lawfully given a distinguishing name which may be confused with the commercial name and trade mark which are protected in State A for the undertaking established there, if there are no relations between the two undertakings, if their national trade mark rights arose autonomously and independently of one another (no common origin) and at the present time there exist no economic or legal relations of any kind other than those appertaining to trade marks between the undertakings?[216]

It held:

It is compatible with the provisions of the EEC Treaty relating to the free movement of goods for an undertaking established in a Member State, by virtue of a right to a trade mark and a right to a commercial name which are protected by the

[208] Case 119/75 [1976] *ECR* 1039.
[209] Ibid., p. 1061.
[210] Case 16/74 [1974] *ECR* 1183, p. 1194, quoted above.
[211] Case 3/78 [1978] *ECR* 1823, p. 1840, quoted above.
[212] Case 119/75 [1976] *ECR* 1039.
[213] Belgium, Denmark, Germany, France, Ireland, the Netherlands, and the United Kingdom.
[214] Case 192/73 [1974] *ECR* 731.
[215] Case 119/75 [1976] *ECR* 1039.
[216] Ibid., p. 1059.

legislation of that State, to prevent the importation of products of an undertaking established in another Member State and bearing by virtue of the legislation of that State a name giving rise to confusion with the trade mark and commercial name of the first undertaking, provided that there are no agreements restricting competition and no legal or economic ties between the undertakings and that their respective rights have arisen independently of one another.[217]

In *Keurkoop* v. *Nancy Kean Gifts*,[218] which concerned registered designs, the Court added a further proviso, namely that the products in question have not been put into circulation in the other member states by, or with the consent of, the proprietor of the right or a person legally or economically dependent on him.

If the Court had wished to extend its principle of common origin it might have taken the opportunity presented by *Hoffmann—La Roche* v. *Centrafarm*,[219] but it did not do so. In that case, British and German subsidiaries of a multinational group of pharmaceutical companies were involved. The Swiss parent company owned the trade mark 'Valium', and the two subsidiaries manufactured and marketed the product under licence in their respective territories. In the United Kingdom the retail price was lower than in Germany. The defendants bought English pills, repackaged them to suit German practices, and resold them in Germany. The object of the litigation was to stop them from doing so. There was a common origin. Moreover, it could not be said to be irrelevant for the same reason as was given in *EMI Records* v. *CBS United Kingdom*,[220] i.e. that the same proprietor held the rights in all member states and that there were therefore no opportunities for partitioning the common market.[221] Also, a common origin outside the Community may be just as capable of affording opportunities to partition the common market as one within it.[222] In the event the parties seem to have made only brief references to *Van Zuylen* v. *Hag*[223] and the Court made no mention of it. It ruled:

1.(*a*) The proprietor of a trade mark right which is protected in two Member States at the same time is justified pursuant to the first sentence of Article 36 of the EEC Treaty in preventing a product to which the trade mark has lawfully been applied in one of those States from being marketed in the other Member State after it has been repacked in new packaging to which the trade mark has been affixed by a third party.

(*b*) However, such prevention of marketing constitutes a disguised restriction on trade between Member States within the meaning of the second sentence of Article 36 where:

— It is established that the use of the trade mark right by the proprietor,

[217] Ibid., p. 1062.
[218] Case 144/81 [1982] *ECR* 2853.
[219] Case 102/77 [1978] *ECR* 1139.
[220] Case 51/75 [1976] *ECR* 811.
[221] Ibid., p. 846.
[222] See Case 40/70, *Sirena* v. *Eda* [1971] *ECR* 69.
[223] Case 192/73 [1974] *ECR* 731.

having regard to the marketing system which he has adopted, will contribute to the artificial partitioning of the markets between Member States;
— It is shown that the repackaging cannot adversely affect the original condition of the product;
— The proprietor of the mark receives prior notice of the marketing of the repackaged product; and
— It is stated on the new packaging by whom the product has been repackaged.[224]

The repackaging of pharmaceutical products has given rise to further litigation. In *Centrafarm* v. *American Home Products*[225] the proprietor was held to be justified under Article 36 in preventing others from putting one of his marks without his authority on goods which had originally been sold in another member state under another of his marks, even though the two products were therapeutically identical. It was for the national court, however, to decide whether such a proprietor was using different marks for the same product for the purpose of partitioning the markets. In *Pfizer* v. *Eurim—Pharm.*[226] the Court considered that there was no impairment of the guarantee of origin of a pharmaceutical product when a parallel importer repackaged it, leaving visible through a window of the package the internal package bearing the manufacturer's trade mark. The owner of the trade mark was not therefore entitled under Article 36 to prevent such parallel imports.

In pursuance of its own external relations, the Community has concluded agreements with third countries. One example was the Agreement between the EEC and Portugal, signed on 22 July 1972.[227] Articles 14(2) and 23 of that Agreement bore a striking resemblance to Articles 30 and 36 EEC, and in *Polydor* v. *Harlequin*[228] the question arose as to whether the case law of the European Court concerning the protection of industrial property applied in respect of trade between Portugal and a member state (the United Kingdom). The plaintiff manufactured and sold gramophone records in the UK under its exclusive licence from the owner of the copyright. Other licensees lawfully manufactured and sold the same products in Portugal. The two defendants bought them in Portugal and imported them into the UK. The plaintiff sought an injunction to stop them. If Portugal had been a member state, and if Articles 30 and 36 EEC had applied, the defendants would have been able to rely on *Terrapin* v. *Terranova*[229] to defeat the claim. The European Court held, however, that the similarity of terms between the relevant provisions of the Agreement and the EEC

---

[224] Case 102/77 [1978] *ECR* 1139, p. 1167.
[225] Case 3/78 [1978] *ECR* 1823.
[226] Case 1/81 [1982] *ECR* 2913.
[227] Adopted on behalf of the Community by Reg. 2844/72, *OJ* 1972, L301/166.
[228] Case 270/80 [1982] *ECR* 329.
[229] Case 119/75 [1976] *ECR* 1039.

Treaty was not a sufficient reason for transposing to the Agreement the case law on the EEC Treaty. The object of the latter (unlike that of the Agreement) was to unite national markets into a single market having the characteristics of a domestic market. The Community had machinery to achieve uniform application of Community law within the Community, but no equivalent existed in the context of relations between the Community and Portugal. The plaintiff was therefore entitled to protect its industrial property in the UK in accordance with Article 23 of the Agreement.

Some measure of European integration should be achieved in the field of industrial property as a result of two conventions, both of which relate to patents.

The first is the convention on the Grant of European Patents (European Patent Convention) signed on 5 October 1973[230] by member states of the EEC and certain other European states. It established the European Patent Organization (with its seat in Munich) and set up the European Patent Office (also in Munich, and with a branch at the Hague). Although setting up a common system of law for the grant of a 'European patent', the effect of such a patent in each of the states for which it is granted is, generally speaking, the same as a national patent granted by that state (Articles 1 and 2).

The second is the convention for the European patent for the common market (Community Patent Convention), signed on 15 December 1975[231] by the member states of the EEC only. It will establish a common system of law concerning patents for all member states (Article 1) which will provide for the granting of Community patents (Article 2). It will be a special agreement within the meaning of Article 142 of the first convention, and envisages the administration of Community patents by special divisions of the European Patent Office, as provided for in Article 143 of the first convention. Although the national courts will have jurisdiction under Articles 69 to 72, provision is made in Article 73 (closely modelled on Article 177 EEC) for preliminary rulings to be given by the European Court of Justice.

The Commission has also proposed a Community trade mark.[232]

DIRECT EFFECT

Article 30 has direct effect as law in the member states, and thus creates rights which the national courts must protect, and which prevail over any national law or constitutional provision to the contrary.

In *Iannelli* v. *Meroni*[233] the Court held that because the prohibition in

---

[230] Entered into force 7 Oct. 1977, TS No. 16 (1982) Cmnd. 8510.
[231] Not yet in force, *OJ* 1976, L17/1.
[232] *OJ* 1980, C351.   [233] Case 74/76 [1977] *ECR* 557, pp. 575, 579.

Article 30 was mandatory and explicit, and its implementation did not require any subsequent action by the member states or the Community institutions, it therefore had direct effect at the end of the transitional period at the latest for all persons subject to Community law. In *Joseph Danis*,[234] the Advocate General was of the opinion that, in relation to national rules which, without distinction between imported and domestic products, required a producer or importer to delay price increases until they had been notified to the competent national authorities, Article 30 did not confer on manufacturers any right which might be protected by national courts.[235] His reason was that courts were not equipped to adjudicate upon questions of macro-economics concerning the functioning of the common market. However, the Court said nothing on this aspect, and it can only be assumed that it declined to modify its earlier view that Article 30 has direct effect.

The normal situation in which the principle of direct effect is invoked is where persons seek to challenge the legality of some act of a national government, whether legislative or administrative, which infringes a Community rule. In *Openbaar* v. *Van Tiggele*,[236] however, Advocate General Capotorti expressed the opinion that Article 30 precluded not only the state but also public agencies with powers delegated from the state from fixing uniform minimum retail prices if such a high level was fixed that it made the marketing of imported products more difficult than that of domestic products.[237] The context was a prosecution by the state for infringement of a rule imposed by a public agency (the Production Board for Spirits). Any direct effect of Article 30 was presumably therefore being invoked against the prosecuting authority of the state rather than the production board. Nevertheless it seems that the Advocate General was treating the state and the board as being on an equal footing so far as concerned the applicability of Article 30. The Court, however, did not say anything about the direct effect of Article 30, and indeed the national court did not ask it to do so. In *Pigs Marketing Board* v. *Redmond*[238] the national court did ask about this aspect, and the European Court ruled that Articles 30 and 34 were 'directly applicable' and conferred on individuals rights which the courts of the member states must protect.

Since Article 30 was accorded direct effect, it seems inevitable that Article 36 should have similar effect. In *Denkavit*[239] the Court reviewed the rules for the interpretation and application of Article 36, and concluded:

It is in each case for the national courts to apply these criteria in the light of all the circumstances relating to the actions brought before them taking into account the

[234] Cases 16–20/79 [1979] *ECR* 3327.
[235] Ibid., p. 3348.
[236] Case 82/77 [1978] *ECR* 25.
[237] Ibid., p. 53.
[238] Case 83/78 [1978] *ECR* 2347.
[239] Case 251/78 [1979] *ECR* 3369.

fact that it must always be the duty of a national authority relying on Article 36 to prove that the measures which it enforces satisfy these criteria.[240]

The implication of this statement is that Article 36 has direct effect, which is why national courts must apply the criteria. There also seems to be a similar implication in *Deutsche Grammophon* v. *Metro*[241] that the second sentence of Article 36 has direct effect just as much as the first sentence, because the Court, having referred to that Article, held that it would conflict with the Treaty if, under various national laws, nationals of member states were able to partition the market and bring about arbitrary discrimination or disguised restrictions on trade.[242] In other words, when applying national laws on copyright (the type of industrial property in issue in that case), the national courts must also apply the brake in the second sentence of Article 36.

TRADE WITH THIRD COUNTRIES

Article 113 envisages a common commercial policy based on agreements between the Community and third countries. The Community has concluded agreements with each member of the European Free Trade Association (EFTA). They follow a common pattern. An example is the agreement with Norway of 14 May 1973.[243] Articles 13(2) and 20 of that agreement are very similar to Articles 30 and 36 EEC. The Community has also concluded agreements with other countries, and the one with Portugal[244] has already been noted earlier in this chapter in connection with *Polydor* v. *Harlequin*.[245] As has been seen, that case shows that the Court's decisions on the interpretation and application of Articles 30 and 36 EEC do not necessarily apply to identical, or almost identical, provisions in agreements with third countries. It is also questionable whether such provisions should be regarded as having direct effect. In principle there seems no reason why they should. There is no guarantee that the third countries would enforce the agreements in their own courts in that way. The reciprocity which is achieved within the Community in relation to intra-Community trade would thus be lacking. On the other hand, the Community has often concluded agreements by means of Community regulations, thus possibly having paved the way for a ruling by the Court that parts of the agreements, like the regulations, have direct effect. In the *Polydor* case[246] the United Kingdom Court of Appeal asked the European

---

[240] Ibid., p. 3392.
[241] Case 78/70 [1971] *ECR* 487.
[242] Ibid., p. 500, paragraphs 12 and 13.
[243] European Communities No. 3 (1974), Cmnd. 5556.
[244] Signed on 22 July 1972. See Reg. 2844/72, *OJ* 1972, L301/166.
[245] Case 270/80 [1982] *ECR* 329.
[246] Ibid.

Court whether Article 14(2) of the Portuguese agreement was directly enforceable by individuals within the EEC, but the latter found it unnecessary to answer the question in view of the answers it gave to the other questions. The Court's ruling in the more recent case of *Kupferberg*[247] has been examined in Chapter 1.

Trade with third countries is also sometimes regulated by internal Community rules. An example is Reg. 120/67 on the common organization of the market in cereals.[248] Article 18(2) of that regulation dealt with third countries, and as a general rule prohibited quantitative restrictions and measures having equivalent effect. In *Orlandi, Carapelli, Saquella, and Franceschi*,[249] the Court had to consider that provision. It held that Article 30 EEC and Article 18(2) of the regulation were to be interpreted in the same sense, in so far as they referred to measures having equivalent effect. It seems, therefore, that judgments interpreting Articles 30 and 36 EEC can be taken as authority for the interpretation of regulations of this kind governing trade with third countries. Moreover, the provisions, which are contained in regulations and are therefore governed by Article 189 EEC, also have the direct effect accorded by that Article.

Not all trade with third countries is as yet covered by agreements or internal Community rules. In such cases national policies may differ, and some member states may be more liberal than others. In order to avoid undue deflection of trade, which would occur if goods were imported from a third country into a liberal member state and then, after getting into free circulation, were re-exported to a less liberal one, Article 115 EEC enables the Commission to authorize member states to take protective measures. Since, however, such protective measures would normally only be effective if they erected barriers to intra-Community trade, the Commission does not often resort to Article 115. Nor has it received much encouragement from the Court to do so. In *Kaufhof* v. *Commission*[250] the Court annulled a Commission decision which allowed Germany to take protective measures against the import of Chinese beans. It did so on the ground that the Commission had failed to review the reasons advanced by the member state for requesting the measures. In *Donckerwolcke*[251] the Court said that, since they were exceptions to Articles 9 and 30, which were fundamental to the operation of the common market, and since they were also an obstacle to the implementation of the common commercial policy under Article 113,

---

[247] Case 104/81 [1982] *ECR* 3641.
[248] *OJ*, English Special Edition, 1967, p. 33. See also, e.g., Regs. 1765/82 and 1766/82, *OJ* 1982, L195.
[249] Joined Cases 206, 207, 209, and 210/80 [1982] *ECR* 2147. The Court had already decided in Case 34/73, *Variola* [1973] *ECR* 981 that 'charge having equivalent effect' in Article 18 of Reg. 120/67 had the same meaning as in Article 9 EEC.
[250] Case 29/75 [1976] *ECR* 431.
[251] Case 41/76 [1976] *ECR* 1921.

the derogations permitted under Article 115 must be strictly interpreted and applied.[252] The member state concerned (France) could require an importer to do no more than give an indication of the origin of the goods in so far as he knew it or might reasonably be expected to have known it, and the state could only impose proportional penalties for his failure to do so.[253] Thus, although Article 115 still applies after the end of the transitional period, its use has been severely curtailed. This Article and other Articles containing general exceptions are considered further in Chapter 10.

FURTHER READING

F. Capelli, 'Les Malentendus Provoqués par l'Arrêt sur le "Cassis de Dijon"', (1981) *Revue du Marché Commun* 421.

B. I. Cawthra, *Industrial Property Rights in the EEC* (1973).

A. Dashwood, 'Quantitative Restrictions and Measures Having Equivalent Effect', (1981) 6 *EL Rev.* 287.

T. L. Early, 'National Price Control and Community Law: Some Observations', (1982) 11 *AMLR* 117.

R. K. Gardiner, 'Industrial and Intellectual Property Rights: Their Nature and the Law of the European Communities', (1972) *LQR* 507.

B. Harris, 'The Application of Article 36 to Intellectual Property', (1976) 1 *EL Rev.* 515.

K. Lewis, 'Café Hag: A Critical Comment', (1976) 1 *EL Rev.* 71.

A. W. H. Meij and J. A. Winter, 'Measures Having an Effect Equivalent to Quantitative Restrictions', (1976) 13 *CML Rev.* 79.

A. C. Page, 'The Concept of Measures Having an Effect Equivalent to Quantitative Restrictions', (1977) 2 *EL Rev.* 105.

D. L. Perrott, 'Pricing Policy and Community Rules on Competition and Free Movement of Goods', (1981) 1 *YEL* 207.

J. Usher, 'National Non-tariff Restrictions at the External Borders of the Community: Towards Community Control?', (1977) 2 *EL Rev.* 304.

D. Wyatt, 'Quantitative Restrictions and Measures Having Equivalent Effect', (1981) 6 *EL Rev.* 185.

---

[252] Ibid., p. 1937.
[253] Ibid., pp. 1938–9.

III

State Monopolies

STATE monopolies existed in all the original six member states of the European Communities in the fields of postal, telephonic, telegraphic, and railway services, and there were other nationalized industries.[1] In a common market based, inter alia, on free movement of goods and services, freely competing with one another, these monopolies could pose problems. For example, such a monopoly might have the exclusive right to import and market a particular product. It would be little comfort to the manufacturer of that product in another member state to know that all customs duties and quantitative restrictions had been removed by the government in question, if he nevertheless found that the same government, acting through the monopoly, simply chose not to purchase the product and instead gave instructions that the home-produced equivalent should always be purchased, or alternatively required the cheapest to be bought and then subsidized the domestic manufacturer.

The Treaty tackles this sort of problem in Articles 37 and 90. Each will be considered in turn.

ARTICLE 37

This Article reads:

1. Member States shall progressively adjust any State monopolies of a commercial character so as to ensure that when the transitional period has ended no discrimination regarding the conditions under which goods are procured and marketed exists between nationals of Member States.

The provisions of this Article shall apply to any body through which a Member State, in law or in fact, either directly or indirectly supervises, determines or appreciably influences imports or exports between Member States. These provisions shall likewise apply to monopolies delegated by the State to others.

2. Member States shall refrain from introducing any new measure which is contrary to the principles laid down in paragraph 1 or which restricts the scope of the Articles dealing with the abolition of customs duties and quantitative restrictions between Member States.

---

[1] For examples see G. van Hecke, 'Government Enterprises and National Monopolies under the EEC Treaty', (1965–6) 3 *CML Rev.*, p. 450.

3. The timetable for the measures referred to in paragraph 1 shall be harmonised with the abolition of quantitative restrictions on the same products provided for in Articles 30 to 34.

If a product is subject to a State monopoly of a commercial character in only one or some Member States, the Commission may authorise the other Member States to apply protective measures until the adjustment provided for in paragraph 1 has been effected; the Commission shall determine the conditions and details of such measures.

4. If a State monopoly of a commercial character has rules which are designed to make it easier to dispose of agricultural products or obtain for them the best return, steps should be taken in applying the rules contained in this Article to ensure equivalent safeguards for the employment and standard of living of the producers concerned, account being taken of the adjustments that will be possible and the specialisation that will be needed with the passage of time.

5. The obligations on Member States shall be binding only in so far as they are compatible with existing international agreements.

6. With effect from the first stage the Commission shall make recommendations as to the manner in which and the timetable according to which the adjustment provided for in this Article shall be carried out.

ARTICLE 37(1) AND (2)

The provisions of Article 37(1) and (2) are not a model of clarity, and, as will be seen, the European Court has picked its way rather cautiously through them.

Article 37(1) requires a particular result to be achieved by the end of the transitional period. The position during that period is of little practical interest, except in the case of Greece. Article 40 of the Greek Act of Accession deals with state monopolies and requires Greece to achieve the same result by 31 December 1985. Paragraphs 3 and 6 of Article 37 EEC also contain provisions which had application only during the transitional period. Article 37(2) prohibits new measures which would be contrary to the principles in Article 37(1).

Questions of interpretation

The first difficulty of interpretation arises because Article 37(1) only relates to 'State monopolies of a commercial character'. Given that in most, if not all, cases there is a commercial aspect to state monopolies, and that they are usually capable of being exploited for profit, it is not easy to see what is excluded by the qualification implied by the words 'of a commercial character'. Is that phrase intended to exclude monopolies which are created primarily, but not necessarily exclusively, to fulfil some purpose which is not commercial in nature, e.g. to meet a social need? If that were the test, a monopoly to run a national health service might be said to be of a non-commercial character, even though that service was in theory capable of being run at a profit. The Advocate General drew the distinction between main and secondary purposes in the *Manghera* case.[2] More significant guidance was given by the Court in *Costa* v. *ENEL*.[3] After referring to the fact that Article 37(1) applies only to state monopolies 'of a commercial character', the Court said:

To fall under this prohibition the State monopolies and bodies in question must, first, have as their object transactions regarding a commercial product capable of being the subject of competition and trade between Member States, and secondly must play an effective part in such trade.[4]

Applying that test to the hypothetical example of a national health service, the conclusion can be reached that since its object would be to heal the sick, and since the making of a profit, if any, would be only incidental, the service would not fall within the provisions of Article 37, even though it was run as a monopoly.

Even the meaning of the word 'monopoly' is not entirely free from ambiguity. Its primary meaning is the exclusive possession of the trade in some commodity, but it is sometimes used to refer to a company which has that exclusive right.[5] However, as used in the first and third sentences of Article 37(1), it seems reasonably clear that the word is being used in its primary sense.

Another difficulty, which the Court has now largely resolved, was to know whether in the first sentence of Article 37(1) a wide or narrow interpretation was to be given to 'the conditions under which' goods are procured and marketed. For example, it was arguable that national rules whereby goods might or might not be advertised represented part of the general conditions under which goods might be marketed. Moreover, if a monopoly existed over some particular kind of advertising, it was possible to visualize how the use of that monopoly could manipulate the market in favour of certain producers, to the disadvantage of others. To take a stark example, if a national monopoly on advertising were operated in such a way that only home-produced goods could be advertised this could have had a seriously adverse effect on the free movement of goods from other member states.

The question how far, if at all, Article 37 would be relevant to such a situation can now be answered as a result of the Court's judgment in *Sacchi*.[6] The case concerned the Italian monopoly over televised commercial advertising. As part of the monopoly system Italian law prohibited anybody else from receiving any television signals from home or abroad for the

---

[2] Case 59/75 [1976] *ECR* 91, p. 106.
[3] Case 6/64 [1964] *ECR* 585.
[4] Ibid., p. 598.
[5] See *The Shorter Oxford Dictionary*.
[6] Case 155/73 [1974] *ECR* 409.

purpose of retransmission. Mr Sacchi operated an unauthorized cable television relay system, and was prosecuted. The national court asked various
questions, some of which were to enable it to determine the validity of the
Italian law in the light of Article 37. The Court first reasoned as follows:

Article 37 concerns the adjustment of State monopolies of a commercial character.
It follows both from the place of this provision in the Chapter on the elimination of
quantitative restrictions and from the use of the words 'imports' and 'exports' in
the second indent of Article 37(1) and of the word 'products' in Article 37(3) and (4)
that it refers to trade in goods and cannot relate to a monopoly in the provision of
services. Thus televised commercial advertising, by reason of its character as a
service, does not come under these provisions.[7]

However, the Court made it clear that the transmission of television
(including advertisements) was governed by the rules of the Treaty
concerning services (Articles 59–66).[8] Moreover, it intimated that trade in
films, recordings, and similar television material was caught by the rules on
free movement of goods, with the result that, although the existence of the
monopoly on advertising did not contravene the principle of free movement of goods, the monopoly would contravene that principle if it discriminated in favour of national material.[9]

Another difficulty is to determine whether the second sentence of Article
37(1) exhaustively defines the bodies to which the provisions of the Article
as a whole apply (the 'exhaustive' theory), or whether it is to be read
cumulatively with the first sentence, so that it may be regarded as adding to
the list of bodies which are caught by the Article (the 'cumulative' theory).
The importance of the question lies in the fact that, while in one respect the
second sentence goes wider than the first, in that it applies to any body
through which a member state, in law or in fact, either directly or indirectly
operates, in another way it narrows the field down by referring only to
bodies through which the member state supervises, determines, or
appreciably influences imports or exports between member states. Should
therefore the rule in the first sentence be confined to those bodies through
which the member state supervises, determines, or appreciably influences
imports or exports? Alternatively, does it also apply to monopolies which
discriminate regarding the conditions under which goods are procured
and marketed between nationals of member states, even though the state
does not supervise or determine imports or exports between member states
and does not influence such imports or exports at all, or at least not
appreciably?

[7] Ibid., p. 428. See also Case 271/81, *Société Coopérative etc.* v. *Mialocq* [1983] *ECR* 2057; Case 161/
82, *Commission* v. *France* [1984] 2 *CMLR* 296.
[8] Ibid., p. 431. See Case 52/79, *Procureur du Roi* v. *Debauve* [1980] *ECR* 833 for the interpretation
of Articles 59 and 60 in relation to advertisements transmitted by cable television, and Case 62/79,
Coditel v. *Ciné Vog Films* [1980] *ECR* 881 as to freedom to provide services and the enforcement of
performing rights. [9] Ibid., p. 427.

The first of these alternative interpretations (based on the exhaustive theory) would seem sufficient to satisfy the general need to ensure free movement of goods between member states, and Article 37 is indeed the last Article in the chapter entitled 'Free movement of goods'. However, from the point of view of freedom of establishment, the second interpretation (based on the cumulative theory) might be preferable. For example, if a national of one member state established a subsidiary in another member state to manufacture goods for the latter's home market using local raw materials, then any discrimination against it by or through a state monopoly would presumably have no influence on imports or exports of goods between member states. Nor would it be easy to maintain that the export of capital[10] was being influenced, even indirectly, because what was being influenced was the subsidiary's ability to acquire capital in the shape of accumulated profits, rather than its freedom to export it. Yet discrimination by the monopoly against the subsidiary in the way its goods were marketed on the domestic market could have a seriously adverse effect on its operations and deprive it substantially of the fruits of its establishment.

Moreover, the exhaustive theory could have an unduly restrictive effect on the interpretation of the first sentence of Article 37(1), if full weight is given to the fact that the second sentence only applies when there is a 'body' *through which* the member state operates. This clearly applies to a legal entity which is separate from the state itself, but it is less clear that it would apply to a department of the central government, or to a single minister who has power to make regulations. Yet it would be anomalous to hold that a state's activities are restricted by the first sentence of Article 37(1) if conducted through the agency of a separate legal body, but unrestricted if conducted directly by the central government. Under the cumulative theory, therefore, it would be easier to attack a member state which, for example, by ministerial order or other subordinate legislation ordered that a certain commodity could not, if produced within that member state, be purchased or marketed within that state without a licence, and then made it a condition of granting such a licence that the commodity must be purchased from, and sold by, its own nationals.

If for these reasons the cumulative theory is to be preferred, the basic structure of Article 37(1) would appear to be as follows. The first sentence requires member states to adjust monopolies which they possess, in order to achieve a given result. The third sentence, assuming 'these provisions' means 'the provisions of this Article', requires member states to achieve the same result in respect of monopolies which they do not themselves possess, but which they have delegated to others. The second sentence requires the same result again to be achieved (the removal of the discrimination referred to in the first sentence) in the case of any monopoly which is

[10] See Title III, chapter 4 of the Treaty.

possessed neither by the state, nor by its agent, but by a body through which the state supervises, determines, or appreciably influences imports or exports. This analysis seems to be broadly in line with the views of the Advocate General, as expressed in *Albatros* v. *Sopéco*:[11]

Article 37 relates to widely varying situations: not only State monopolies but also monopolies delegated by the State to others and finally any body through which a State directly or indirectly supervises, determines or appreciably influences imports or exports between the Member States; in other words, not only cases in which the State reserves to itself the exclusive right to manage a product, but also those in which it transfers that exclusive right to a representative which it appoints, a concessionaire for example, and finally—a situation at once vaguer and more comprehensive—cases in which it exercises a control, some guidance, an appreciable influence on imports or exports between Member States.[12]

Exclusive rights to import, export, or market

One earlier doubt about the interpretation of Article 37(1) has now been removed by the decision in *Pubblico Ministero* v. *Manghera*.[13] It had been argued by some, and was so argued by the Italian government in that case, that since the obligation was to 'adjust' the monopoly this could not mean 'abolish' it, and that therefore a member state need not adjust its monopoly in the way described if to do so would so emasculate the monopoly that it would effectively be destroyed. The case arose out of the monopoly which Italy had conferred on the Amministrazione Autonoma dei Monopoli di Stato to manufacture, prepare, import, and sell tobacco in Italy. The main question was whether a member state was obliged by Article 37(1) to abolish a monopoly's exclusive right to import. The Court held that it was, because it was a discrimination of the kind prohibited by the Article and it infringed the fundamental rule of free movement of goods throughout the common market. In that particular case the monopoly had other exclusive rights as well, but the Advocate General was of the opinion that even if its only exclusive right had been to import, the obligation under Article 37(1) would have been to adjust it out of existence during the transitional period.[14] Thus, while the obligation to adjust the monopoly does not necessarily require its abolition, this may in practice be the case if every part of the monopoly involves discrimination of the prohibited kind. The Advocate General also thought[15] that by analogy with Article 30, as interpreted in *Dassonville*[16] Article 37(1) precluded potential as well as actual restrictions on trade, but the Court did not expressly confirm this in its judgment. What it said was:

The exclusive right to import manufactured products of the monopoly in question

---

[11] Case 20/65 [1965] *ECR* 29.   [12] Ibid., p. 44.

[13] Case 59/75 [1976] *ECR* 91. See also Case 91/78, *Hansen* v. *Hza Flensburg* [1979] *ECR* 935.

[14] Ibid., p. 107.   [15] Ibid., p. 108.   [16] Case 8/74 [1974] *ECR* 852.

thus constitutes, in respect of Community exporters, discrimination prohibited by Article 37(1).[17]

Since a monopoly's exclusive right to import must, therefore be eliminated, it seems right in principle that its exclusive right to export must similarly be abolished. An exclusive right in a member state to export can discriminate against foreign importers established in other member states (or for that matter against foreign exporters established in the first member state) just as much as an exclusive right to import can discriminate against Community exporters. Indeed, there is a good deal of force in the argument, advanced by the Commission in *Hansen* v. *Hauptzollamt Flensburg*,[18] that state monopolies should not be allowed to retain exclusive rights to import, export, or market. An exclusive right to market can be used to discriminate against nationals of other member states wishing to buy or sell goods from those other member states in the member state in question. In that case the Court preferred to deal with the matter on the basis of Article 95. However, the point also arose in an oblique way in *Pubblico Ministero* v. *Manghera*,[19] where the Court was asked whether the Council Resolution of 21 April 1970[20] could vary the effect of the provisions of Article 37(1). The Court not surprisingly answered this question in the negative. The interesting point, however, is that this resolution, which recorded an undertaking by the French and Italian governments to abolish discrimination arising out of national monopolies of a commercial character, added:

The abolition of exclusive rights relating to importation and wholesale marketing must be achieved by 1 January 1976 at the latest.

The Court described that resolution as the expression of the political will of the Council and the two governments concerned 'to put an end to a state of affairs contravening Article 37(1) . . .'.[21] However, the Court did not go on to say whether that political will, in so far as it referred to marketing, corresponded exactly with the obligations of Article 37(1) or whether it went further. Instead the Court took the entirely correct course of simply answering the question put by the national court.

Discrimination regarding the conditions under which goods are procured and marketed may relate not only to the final product but also the procurement of the raw materials from which it is made. This is illustrated in *Peureux* v. *Services Fiscaux*,[22] concerning oranges steeped in alcohol which were imported into France from Italy. Under the rules relating to the

---

[17] Case 59/75 [1976] *ECR* 91, p. 101.
[18] Case 148/77 [1978] *ECR* 1787, p. 1797.
[19] Case 59/75 [1976] *ECR* 91.
[20] *OJ* C50, 28 Apr. 1970.
[21] Case 59/75 [1976] *ECR* 91, p. 102.
[22] Case 119/78 [1979] *ECR* 975—not to be confused with Case 86/78 between the same parties and decided on the same day: n. 55 below.

French ethyl alcohol monopoly, these materials could not be used by French distillers but their domestic equivalent could. The national court asked whether this infringed Article 37. As usual, the European Court declined specifically to answer that question, because although Article 177 gives it power to rule on questions of interpretation it confers no power to determine the compatibility of a national provision with Community law. The Court ruled in general terms to the effect that when a national provision prohibits distillation of products reserved to a national commercial monopoly from raw materials coming from other member states, but this prohibition does not apply to identical raw materials produced within the national territory, this constitutes discrimination under which goods are procured and marketed, within the meaning of Article 37(1).[23]

Discriminatory charges

If a member state imposes charges on the import of goods from other member states, or charges which discriminate against such goods after they have been imported, it will fall foul of Articles 9 or 12 (customs duties) or Article 95 (internal taxation). If such charges are linked to the existence of a state monopoly of a commercial character, they may also amount to discrimination of the kind prohibited by Article 37. In *Cinzano* v. *Hauptzollamt Saarbrücken*[24] the Court had occasion to consider in the light of Article 37 the German laws concerning alcohol—a subject to which it was to return on more than one occasion. The case concerned a state monopoly over the marketing of domestically produced ethyl alcohol, and a new charge on imports of that product which was intended to offset the fiscal charge imposed on the domestic equivalent. The case might have turned on Article 12, or possibly Article 95, but the national court chose, without prejudice to the compatibility of the charge with those Articles, to ask the European Court to interpret Article 37.[25] The latter considered that an import duty on a product, a constituent part of which was subject to a monopoly, could amount to a new measure within the meaning of Article 37(2), and would be prohibited if it produced or aggravated discrimination of the kind referred to in Article 37(1), or if, as stated in Article 37(2), it restricted the scope of the Articles dealing with the abolition of customs duties or quantitative restrictions between member states. The first question, therefore, was whether the new duty had the effect of imposing higher charges on the imported product than on the domestic equivalent. There would be no infringement of Article 37 if the imported product were subjected to the same conditions as the domestic product which was

[23] Ibid., p. 988.
[24] Case 13/70 [1970] *ECR* 1089.
[25] The national court did not ask whether, in relation to Articles 12 and 95, Article 37 was to be regarded as a *lex specialis*. But see n. 46 below.

subject to the monopoly.[26] The Court, having also concluded for similar reasons that there was no customs duty or quantitative restriction or equivalent measure, accordingly ruled:

A duty levied on imports of products from other Member States linked to the existence of a State monopoly and applied for the first time after the entry into force of the Treaty does not amount to an infringement of Article 37(2) as long as such new charge is imposed on the imported product only to the same extent as on domestic products affected by the monopoly.[27]

The judgment in *Cinzano* v. *Hauptzollamt Saarbrücken*[28] was delivered on 16 December 1970. On 23 December 1970 a new German law was enacted, concerning the imposition of a special equalization charge on alcohol imports. This charge did not correspond in amount to the charges levied in respect of domestically produced alcohol, so as to equalize the tax burden imposed on imports and home products and thus enable them to compete on equal terms. Its object was to deal with a different problem, which had arisen because the price paid by the monopoly for certain types of alcohol produced in the Federal Republic exceeded the price of similar alcohol produced in other member states. The former was therefore at a commercial disadvantage. In essence, the equalization charge was levied in such a way that the price of the foreign product, after paying that charge, was always brought up to the price paid by the monopoly to domestic producers. This in effect destroyed the competitive advantage of the imported alcohol. The legality of this equalization charge was questioned in *Hauptzollamt Göttingen* v. *Miritz*.[29] The Court considered that the matter fell within the scope of Article 37 and took the following view:

Article 37(1) is not concerned exclusively with quantitative restrictions but prohibits any discrimination, when the transitional period has ended, regarding the conditions under which goods are procured and marketed between nationals of Member States. It follows that its application is not limited to imports or exports which are directly subject to the monopoly but covers all measures which are connected with its existence and affect trade between Member States in certain products, whether or not subject to the monopoly, and thus covers charges which result in discrimination against imported products as compared with national products coming under the monopoly. It follows from these provisions and their structure that the obligation laid down in paragraph (1) aims at ensuring compliance with the fundamental rule of the free movement of goods throughout the common market, in particular by the abolition, in trade between Member States, of customs duties and charges having equivalent effect. A charge of the type at issue introduced after the entry into force of the EEC Treaty is, accordingly, contrary to Article 37(2).[30]

---

[26] Case 13/70, *Cinzano* v. *HZA Saarbrücken* [1970] *ECR* 1089.
[27] Ibid., p. 1097.
[28] Case 13/70 [1970] *ECR* 1089.
[29] Case 91/75 [1976] *ECR* 217.
[30] Ibid., p. 229.

On the same day the Court gave its judgment in *Rewe v. Hauptzollamt Landau*.[31] The Court was required to consider in somewhat greater detail some aspects of the German alcohol taxation system. That system was complex, owing partly to the existence of exceptions and qualifications to the basic rules. But its essential elements, so far as can be deduced from the report of the case, appear to have been as follows. There were three taxation régimes, covering (i) domestic alcohol subject to the monopoly, (ii) domestic alcohol free from the monopoly, and (iii) imported alcohol (also free from the monopoly). For present purposes, and at the risk of some over-simplification, it may be assumed that type (ii) alcohol was the domestic equivalent of type (iii). Type (i) can therefore be ignored, and type (ii) may for the sake of simplicity be called just 'domestic alcohol'.

Domestic alcohol was subject to a spirits surcharge ('Branntweinaufschlag') which in effect consisted of:

(*a*) a tax equivalent to that imposed on monopoly alcohol (Branntweinsteuer), plus
(*b*) the spirits surcharge margin (Branntweinaufschlagspitze), which was a contribution to the costs of the monopoly, minus
(*c*) a sum roughly corresponding to the costs saved by the monopoly by not having to handle the alcohol.

Imported alcohol was subject to a monopoly equalization duty ('Monopolausgleichsteuer') which in effect was made up by:

(i) the equivalent of the tax at (*a*) above, plus
(ii) a surcharge which was the equivalent of (*b*) above, but called the 'Monopolausgleichspitze', which, unlike (*b*), went into the national coffers.

By a mysterious arithmetical process the total tax for domestic alcohol was made to equal the total tax for imported alcohol in the case of certain large distilleries (notwithstanding the allowances at (*c*) above), but this does not appear to have been so in the case of small producers.[32]

The Court dealt first with the position under Article 95, and concluded that whenever such a system resulted in more tax[33] on imported alcohol than its domestic equivalent it infringed that Article, but not otherwise. Turning to Article 37(1), the Court held that even if a national measure complies with Article 95 this does not imply that it is valid in relation to Article 37. To extract a contribution to the monopoly costs from importers alone, even in the form of a duty, was in principle incompatible with Article 37(1).[34] This conclusion was relatively easy for the Court to reach because

---

[31] Case 45/75 [1976] *ECR* 181.
[32] Ibid., p. 193, quoting the observations of the German Government.
[33] Or less refund of tax: Case 17/81, *Pabst and Richarz* [1983] 3 *CMLR* 11.
[34] Ibid., p. 199.

in such a case there would be clear discrimination as between the marketing conditions for imports and those for home products. The Court went on to say that there would be no infringement, however, if the same tax were applied to imports and domestic products, even if part of the tax on the domestic product went to finance the monopoly, whereas all the tax on imports went into the state's general budget.[35] In its 'dispositif' the Court ruled:

Article 37(1) must be interpreted as meaning that the discrimination regarding the conditions under which goods are procured and marketed which is referred to therein includes the extraction of a contribution to the monopoly costs from an imported product, even in the form of a duty, but that the provision does not prohibit the imposition of identical taxation on an imported product and a similar domestic product, even if the charge imposed on the latter is, in part, allocated for the purposes of financing the monopoly, whilst the charge levied on the imported product is imposed for the benefit of the general budget of the State.[36]

In short, however complicated the national system, one must look at its practical effect in each individual case. Whenever, in connection with a monopoly, there is a higher levy on an import than on its domestic equivalent there will be an infringement of Articles 95 and 37, if the levy takes the form of taxation, and of Article 37 if it takes some other form. However, if a discriminatory taxation system is not intrinsically connected with the specific business of the monopoly it will not infringe Article 37, although it may contravene Article 95: *Pabst and Richarz* v. *HZA Oldenburg*[37] (concerning German taxation of spirits).

Following the *Miritz*[38] and *Rewe*[39] cases, the cold wind of competition blew on the German alcohol monopoly. Alcohol imports increased and the market price of spirits fell. The monopoly continued to buy German alcohol at a higher price, but had to reduce its selling price substantially. To prevent the monopoly sustaining losses, the consumption tax on spirits was increased in 1976. With regard to imported spirits, this was levied through the 'monopolausgleichsteuer', noted above. It was against this background that the second case of *Hansen* v. *Hauptzollamt Flensburg*[40] arose. The plaintiffs imported certain spirits into Germany. Under the revised tax system they became liable to pay a fixed tax on each hectolitre of wine-spirits. The same amount was charged on domestic and imported spirits, although the terminology differed.[41] The plaintiffs argued that nevertheless this alignment of the taxes was more apparent than real,

[35] Ibid.
[36] Ibid., p. 201.
[37] Case 17/81 [1983] 3 *CMLR* 11.
[38] Case 91/75 [1976] *ECR* 217.
[39] Case 45/75 [1976] *ECR* 181.
[40] Case 91/78 [1979] *ECR* 935.
[41] Ibid., p. 949.

because it only applied in the case of spirits distilled by small distilleries, of which Germany alone had a substantial number. There was no alignment, the plaintiffs complained, in the case of taxes on spirits produced by large distilleries at home and abroad. The increased tax was moreover designed to discourage imports and to finance the monopoly's operations.[42] Finally the plaintiffs attacked the tax on the ground that it amounted to a state aid which had not been reported in advance to the Commission under Article 93(3).[43]

The national court focused first of all on this latter point and asked if Article 37 was a *lex specialis* in relation to Articles 92 and 93. The European Court considered that Articles 37, 92, and 93 pursued the same objective, i.e.:

to ensure that the two categories of intervention on the part of a Member State, namely action by a State monopoly and the granting of aids, do not distort the conditions of competition within the common market or create discrimination against the products or trade of other Member States.[44]

However, the two sets of provisions had different legal consequences, notably in that the Commission had a much more important role to play in the implementation of Articles 92 and 93. The Court concluded:

A measure effected through the intermediary of a public monopoly which may also be considered as an aid within the meaning of Article 93 is consequently governed both by the provisions of Article 37 and by those applicable to State aids.[45]

The Court accordingly ruled:

Article 37 of the EEC Treaty constitutes in relation to Articles 92 and 93 of that Treaty a *lex specialis* in the sense that State measures, inherent in the exercise by a State monopoly of a commercial character of its exclusive right must, even where they are linked to the grant of an aid to producers subject to the monopoly, be considered in the light of the requirements of Article 37.[46]

The next questions concerned the monopoly's pricing policy, which generally speaking seems to have been to purchase from German producers at inflated prices, and to resell at deflated prices. The Court held this sort of policy to infringe Article 37(1) on the grounds that the equal opportunities which the Article was designed to secure for products imported from other member states would be jeopardized. The Court ruled:

Any practice by a State monopoly which consists in marketing a product such as spirits with the aid of public funds at an abnormally low resale price compared to

[42] Ibid., p. 940.
[43] Ibid., p. 939.
[44] Ibid., p. 953.
[45] Ibid.
[46] Ibid., p. 958.

the price, before tax, of spirits of comparable quality imported from another Member State is incompatible with Article 37(1) of the EEC Treaty.[47]

Discrimination unconnected with the monopoly

In the *Cassis de Dijon* case,[48] the plaintiff relied on the fact that the German rule, which prohibited the marketing of alcoholic drinks below a certain strength, was contained in the federal law on the monopoly in spirits which also created a monopoly. The plaintiff argued that the prohibition in effect discriminated as between importers of alcoholic drinks and the monopoly, and accordingly infringed Article 37.[49] However, as the Advocate General pointed out,[50] the rule about minimal alcoholic content, while contained in the law relating to the monopoly, did not logically pertain to the monopoly. It was a rule of quite general application and did not relate to the operation of the monopoly at all. He considered that Article 37 did not therefore apply. The Court agreed, and said:

> That provision is therefore irrelevant with regard to national provisions which do not concern the exercise by a public monopoly of its specific function—namely, its exclusive right—but apply in a general manner to the production and marketing of alcoholic beverages, whether or not the latter are covered by the monopoly in question.[51]

The Court has since repeated the same point, for example in *Peureux* v. *Services Fiscaux*.[52]

Reverse discrimination

One general question concerning Article 7, and the other Articles of the EEC Treaty which refer to discrimination on grounds of nationality, is whether those provisions prohibit discrimination which puts a member state's own nationals in a worse position than the nationals of other member states, i.e. 'reverse discrimination'. Article 37 is in slightly different terms from, for example, Articles 7, 48(2), and 67(1) because the latter refer to discrimination 'based on nationality' whereas the former speaks of discrimination 'between nationals of Member States'. Nevertheless the way in which the Court has dealt with the notion of reverse discrimination for the purpose of Article 37 is not without relevance to the wider question. The Court dealt with this aspect twice on the same date, in one case obliquely and in the other more directly. In *Hansen* v. *Hauptzollamt Flensburg*,[53] the Court indicated that the object of Article 37 was to avoid

---

[47] Ibid.
[48] Case 120/78, *Rewe* v. *Bundesmonopolverwaltung für Branntwein* [1979] *ECR* 649—see also Chapter 2.
[49] Ibid., p. 654.   [50] Ibid., p. 667.   [51] Ibid., p. 662.
[52] Case 119/78 [1979] *ECR* 975, p. 986.   [53] Case 91/78 [1979] *ECR* 935.

discrimination against the products or trade of other member states.[54] This implies that its object is not to prevent discrimination by a member state against its own nationals as a result of the way in which the monopoly is conducted.

The point was raised more directly in *Peureux* v. *Services Fiscaux*.[55] France's monopoly for the production and marketing of most forms of ethyl alcohol bore some similarity to the German system, described earlier in this chapter. Producers in metropolitan France had to restrict production and sell to the monopoly at prices fixed by the Minister of Finance. The monopoly sold at fixed official prices. There were three kinds of alcohol—'free alcohol' (not subject to the monopoly), 'reserved alcohol' (bought by the monopoly), and 'freed alcohol' (in principle subject to the monopoly, but in fact left in the hands of the producers, on payment of the cash adjustment which was the subject of the action). Prior to 1977, and as a result of Article 37, France allowed ethyl alcohol in consumable form to be imported from other member states and to be marketed free from the monopoly. It was subject in some cases to a compensatory surcharge which resembled the cash adjustment. But it attracted, instead of the compensatory surcharge, a compensatory charge when the minimum sale price in its country of origin was less than that in France. The plaintiff complained in respect of this period that the compensatory charge was incompatible with the Treaty, and not payable, whereas domestic producers had in similar situations to pay the cash adjustment. The plaintiff (a French undertaking) complained that in that way it was the victim of discrimination.

In 1977, and as a result of *Rewe*[56] and *Miritz*,[57] France had abolished the compensatory charge for imported alcohol. If such alcohol was identical to domestic 'reserved alcohol' (but not otherwise) it attracted the same cash adjustment as domestic 'freed alcohol'. In respect of the period after 1977, the plaintiff complained that importers of similar (but not identical) alcohol did not have to pay the cash adjustment, but the plaintiff did, and again this was a form of reverse discrimination.

The Court dealt with both claims by ruling as follows:

Whether or not a domestic product—in particular certain potable spirits—is subject to a commercial monopoly, neither Article 37 nor Article 95 of the EEC Treaty prohibits a Member State from imposing on that domestic product internal taxation in excess of that imposed on similar products imported from other Member States.[58]

[54] Ibid., p. 953, quoted above.
[55] Case 86/78 [1979] *ECR* 897, not to be confused with Case 119/78 between the same parties and referred to in n. 22 above.
[56] Case 45/75 [1976] *ECR* 181.
[57] Case 91/75 [1976] *ECR* 217.
[58] Case 86/78 [1979] *ECR* 897, p. 915.

At first sight it might be thought that the Court's judgment rules out the possibility of any kind of reverse discrimination falling within the scope of Article 37. A closer study of the Court's reasoning, however, seems to show that this is not necessarily so. The Court's logic[59] seems to have been that the relationship between internal taxation on national products and on imported products is governed by Article 95, which by its very terms is directed against taxing products imported from other member states more severely than domestic products, and not against the reverse situation. During the transitional period Article 37(1) might have allowed exceptions to that rule, because the kind of discrimination with which Article 37 deals only had to be abolished by the end of that period. But Article 37 no longer allows derogations from Article 95, and the latter alone now governs the matter. Having reached that point in its reasoning, the Court then said:

Even if it had to be accepted that Article 37 prohibits not only discrimination against imported products as compared with national products subject to the monopoly but also discrimination against the latter in relation to imported products, this would not mean that the Member States are prevented from imposing internal taxation on national products, whether or not coming under the monopoly, in excess of that on similar imported products.[60]

Thus, although reverse discrimination is not prohibited in the matter of taxation, the first half of the sentence quoted above seems to leave open the question whether Article 37 rules out reverse discrimination when it takes a form other than taxation.[61]

Direct effect

The first two paragraphs of Article 37 now have direct effect as law in the member states, and confer rights on individuals which the national courts must protect. Article 37(1) has had this effect only since the end of the transitional period.[62] Article 37(2) has had direct effect since the entry into force of the Treaty.

In *Pubblico Ministero* v. *Manghera and Others*[63] the accused relied on Article 37(1) to defend themselves against the charge of importing tobacco into Italy without passing through the state monopoly. The national court asked the European Court whether Article 37(1) was directly applicable, and whether it created individual rights which the national judicial bodies must protect. The European Court applied its usual criteria[64] and

[59] Ibid., pp. 912–13.
[60] Ibid., p. 913.
[61] For a discussion of reverse discrimination and a review of earlier cases, see the Advocate General's opinion at ibid., pp. 920–1.
[62] 31 Dec. 1969.
[63] Case 59/75 [1976] *ECR* 91.
[64] Described e.g. by Advocate General Mayras in Case 41/74, *Van Duyn* v. *Home Office* [1974] *ECR* 1337, p. 1354.

concluded that Article 37(1) established a very precise objective which was to be achieved, subject to a clause postponing its operation (until the end of the transitional period). After that date the obligation on member states to achieve the stated objective was unconditional. It was not contingent upon the introduction of any Community or national measure. The Court accordingly ruled that Article 37(1) was capable of being relied on by nationals of member states before national courts. Shortly afterwards the Court repeated this principle in *Rewe* v. *Hauptzollamt Landau*.[65]

The operation of Article 37(2) was not suspended, and before the end of the transitional period its direct effect was in issue in *Costa* v. *ENEL*.[66] The plaintiff, having refused to pay his bill to the national electricity board in which the assets of all private electricity companies had been vested, maintained that this nationalization created a monopoly and that in proceedings in Italy he was entitled to rely on Article 37(2), which the monopoly infringed. The Court held that Article 37(2) was 'in all its provisions a rule of Community law capable of creating individual rights which national courts must protect'.[67]

Goods from third countries

The first sentence of Article 37(1) suggests that it is discrimination between nationals of member states which is to be eliminated, irrespective of the origin of the goods which they are seeking to procure or market. Taken literally this could mean that it makes no difference whether those goods come from other member states or from third countries. However, the second sentence of the same paragraph focuses on imports or exports between member states. Moreover, Article 37 is part of a chapter in which the previous Articles are all concerned with intra-Community trade.

In *Hansen* v. *Hauptzollamt Flensburg*[68] the national court asked whether the sphere of application of Article 37 extended to measures which affect the importation of goods from third countries. The European Court held that it did not. Its reasons were that, from the wording of the Article and its place in Chapter 2 of Title I, it was clear that the Article was intended (i) to promote free movement within the Community of goods which were the subject of a state monopoly, and (ii) to maintain normal conditions of competition 'between the economies of Member States'.[69]

In another judgment delivered on the same date the Court added a qualification to its ruling in the *Hansen* case. The plaintiff in *Peureux* v. *Services Fiscaux*[70] had imported from Italy into France oranges steeped in

[65] Case 45/75 [1976] *ECR* 181.
[66] Case 6/64 [1964] *ECR* 585.
[67] Ibid., p. 599.
[68] Case 91/78 [1979] *ECR* 935.
[69] Ibid., p. 956.
[70] Case 119/78 [1979] *ECR* 975.

alcohol of which some originated in Italy and some came from outside the Community. The latter had however got into free circulation in Italy, having satisfied the requirements of Article 10. The Court, having concluded that certain kinds of national restrictions would infringe both Article 30 and Article 37(1), ruled in that context:

There are no grounds for drawing a distinction between products duly put into free circulation in another Member State after having been imported from a third country and products originating in that Member State.[71]

Thus an importer who is impeded in a member state by a state monopoly in the procurement and marketing of goods coming directly from a third country has no remedy under Article 37. However, he may have one if he can show that he is the victim of discrimination, and if he takes the precaution of first importing the goods into another member state in order to get them into free circulation.

ARTICLE 37(4) AND (5)

Paragraphs (3) and (6) of Article 37 contain transitional provisions. Their operation expired on 31 December 1969. Paragraphs (4) and (5), although sandwiched between them, do not appear to be confined to the transitional period. Paragraph (4) speaks of steps taken in applying the rules contained in 'this Article', which presumably means the whole of it. Indeed, in the *Miritz* case,[72] which concerned events occurring after the end of the transitional period, the German Government submitted that this paragraph continued to apply.[73] The defendant disagreed.[74] The Court did not deal expressly with the point, but it is implicit in its judgment that Article 37(4) was not spent. The Court concentrated on the argument of the German Government that its equalization charge was justified under that paragraph, and that Article 37(1) did not affect that fact. The Court concluded that Article 37(4) did not derogate from Article 37(1), and said:

Article 37(1) lays down a specific and unconditional obligation to achieve results by the end of the transitional period. Far from providing for an exception in the case of certain rules of a monopoly, Article 37(4) is intended to have effect 'in applying the rules' contained in the article. Its purpose is to enable the national authorities, if necessary in cooperation with the Community institutions, to promulgate various measures designed to compensate for the effects which the abolition of the discrimination which a monopoly specifically implies may have on the employment and standard of living of the producers concerned. Nevertheless these equivalent safeguards must themselves be compatible with the provisions of Article 37(1) and (2).[75]

---

[71] Ibid., p. 988.   [72] Case 91/75 [1976] *ECR* 217.
[73] Ibid., p. 221.   [74] Ibid., p. 224.   [75] Ibid., p. 230.

The ruling of the Court is consistent with the language of Article 37(4), which uses terminology more appropriate for a recommendation than for an obligation—'steps should be taken'.

It is interesting to compare Article 37(5) with Article 234. The latter preserves the rights and obligations arising from agreements concluded before the entry into force of the EEC Treaty between one or more member states on the one hand, and one or more third countries on the other.[76] However, it also provides that, to the extent that such agreements are not compatible with the EEC Treaty, member states shall take all appropriate steps to eliminate the incompatibility. Article 37(5) may, in relation to that Article, be regarded as a *lex specialis*. It differs in two respects. First, it contains no obligation to take any steps to remove any incompatible obligations. As a result, Germany, for example, was able to rely on an agreement dated 26 October 1926 to avoid any obligation to adjust its monopoly on matches.[77] Secondly, instead of referring to agreements concluded before the entry into force of the EEC Treaty, it refers to 'existing' agreements. It is often tempting when a draftsman uses different language to think that he means something different. The temptation probably ought to be resisted in this instance, if only because it is difficult to attribute to the words 'existing international agreements' any meaning other than 'international agreements in force at the date of entry into force of this Treaty', i.e. 1 January 1958. Yet this interpretation produces its own anomalies. Although Article 5 of the Act of Accession makes Article 234 EEC apply, for the new member states, to agreements concluded before accession,[78] the Act makes no corresponding adaptation to Article 37(5) EEC. Article 44 of the Act of Accession[79] gives a new transitional period for the new member states for the purposes of Article 37(1), ending on 31 December 1977, but it does not mention Article 37(5). It seems therefore that the new member states can only rely on Article 37(5) in respect of agreements in force on 1 January 1958.

ARTICLE 90

This Article reads:

1. In the case of public undertakings and undertakings to which Member States grant special or exclusive rights, Member States shall neither enact nor maintain in force any measure contrary to the rules contained in this Treaty, in particular to those rules provided for in Article 7 and Articles 85 to 94.

[76] See Case 10/61, *Commission* v. *Italy* [1962] *ECR* 1.
[77] According to Y. van der Mensbrugghe in W. J. Ganshof van der Meersch, M. Waelbroeck *et al.*, *Droit des Communautés européennes* (1969), p. 672.
[78] See also Article 5 of the Greek Act of Accession.
[79] Article 40 of the Greek Act of Accession.

2. Undertakings entrusted with the operation of services of general economic interest or having the character of a revenue-producing monopoly shall be subject to the rules contained in this Treaty, in particular to the rules on competition, in so far as the application of such rules does not obstruct the performance, in law or in fact, of the particular tasks assigned to them. The development of trade must not be affected to such an extent as would be contrary to the interests of the Community.

3. The Commission shall ensure the application of the provisions of this Article and shall, where necessary, address appropriate directives or decisions to Member States.

ARTICLE 90(1) AND (2)

Interpretation

Articles 37 and 90 reveal a common concern that monopolies should not be operated in such a way as to undermine basic principles of the Treaty. Another common feature is the lack of precision in the drafting. Whereas Article 37 is concerned with free movement of goods, Article 90, by its position in Part Three, Title I, Chapter 1 (Rules on Competition) and by its wording, shows a primary interest in preserving the effectiveness of the rules of competition. However its terms show that it is not exclusively confined to competition.

Three points can be made about Article 90(1). First, although it applies to cases where a monopoly exists, i.e. where an undertaking has been granted 'exclusive rights', it also applies in relation to the activities of all 'public undertakings', whether or not they enjoy a monopoly, and to the activities of non-public undertakings to which member states have granted special, but not necessarily exclusive, rights. Secondly, it does not regulate the voluntary activities of the undertakings themselves, to which Articles 85 and 86 apply in any event in matters of competition, but is directed towards member states, who are forbidden to enact or maintain in force any measure contrary to the Treaty. Thirdly, although special mention is made of the Treaty provisions concerning discrimination on grounds of nationality (Article 7), competition (Articles 85 and 86), dumping (Article 91), and state aids (Articles 92–4), the prohibition extends to measures which are contrary to any provision anywhere in the Treaty. It can therefore be regarded as a detailed application of the second sentence of Article 5, which in general terms obliges member states to abstain from any measure which can jeopardize the attainment of the objectives of the Treaty.

Article 90(2) does regulate the activities of the undertakings to which it applies. These are not defined in the same terms as in Article 90(1), although some undertakings will no doubt fall within the scope of both sets of provisions. The main effect of Article 90(2) is to grant undertakings 'entrusted with the operation of services of general economic interest or having the character of a revenue producing monopoly' a limited exemption from the rules contained in the Treaty. Since this permits a derogation from the basic, as well as the peripheral, provisions of the Treaty, it is not surprising that the Court held in *BRT* v. *SABAM and NV Fonior*[80] that 'there must be strict definition of those undertakings which can take advantage of it'.[81] That case concerned an undertaking which enjoyed a *de facto* monopoly for the management of copyrights. The Court considered that Article 90(2) did not apply to an undertaking to which the state had not assigned any tasks, and which managed private interests.[82] In so holding, the Court appears incidentally to have removed one of the ambiguities of the text by indicating that it must be a state which does the entrusting, and the assignment of tasks. Further clarification can be gleaned from some, but not all, of the other cases in which the Court has had occasion to consider Article 90.

In *Ministère Public Luxembourg* v. *Muller*[83] the first undertaking in question had been entrusted by law with the operation of a port on the river Moselle. It enjoyed tax exemptions and the state of Luxembourg paid its maintenance charges. Under the same law, other port undertakings could only operate with permission. One such undertaking broke a condition upon which permission had been granted and it was prosecuted. Its defence was to challenge the privileged position of the first undertaking as contrary to Articles 86 and 90. In the course of its judgment the Court threw a little light on the scope of Article 90(2). It did not attempt to define exhaustively what kind of undertakings fell within that paragraph, or even reach a firm view on whether the first undertaking did so. It said:

An undertaking which enjoys certain privileges for the accomplishment of the task entrusted to it by law, maintaining for this purpose close links with the public authorities, and which is responsible for ensuring the navigability of the State's most important waterways, may fall within this provision.[84]

The facts in *Sacchi*[85] have already been referred to earlier in this chapter in connection with Article 37. The national court also asked, however, about the interpretation of Article 90 in relation to the Italian monopoly over television broadcasting and advertising. Although both broadcasting and television advertising were held to come within the rules of the Treaty relating to services (and therefore Article 37 did not apply) the Court appears to have accepted that these services fell, or could fall, within the

[80] Case 127/73 [1974] *ECR* 313.
[81] Ibid., p. 318.
[82] Ibid.
[83] Case 10/71 [1971] *ECR* 723.
[84] Ibid., p. 730.
[85] Case 155/73 [1974] *ECR* 409.

scope of Article 90(1) and (2). Rather curiously, the Court appears to have left it to each member state to decide whether or not to treat undertakings entrusted with the operation of television and television advertising as undertakings entrusted with the operation of services of general economic interest, and therefore falling within Article 90(2).[86]

The starting-point in the Court's analysis was that the Treaty did not prevent member states, for non-economic reasons, from removing all forms of broadcasting from the field of competition by conferring monopolies on one or more undertakings. Thus the existence or extension of such a monopoly did not as such infringe Articles 7 or 86. The Court's handling of the question of discrimination is interesting. It held in its 'dispositif':

The grant of the exclusive right to transmit television signals does not as such constitute a breach of Article 7 of the Treaty. Discrimination by undertakings enjoying such exclusive rights against nationals of Member States by reason of their nationality is however incompatible with this provision.[87]

By referring to undertakings enjoying 'exclusive rights' the Court was taking up the language of Article 90(1), and there could have been no doubt that the actions of member states in respect of undertakings falling within that paragraph were caught by Article 7 (no discrimination on grounds of nationality). However, the remainder of the sentence in the judgment seems to relate to Article 90(2) because it refers to the conduct of the undertakings themselves. It indicates that the rule in Article 7 applies to the undertakings as well as to the Member States which have assigned their tasks to them. The judgment gives no guidance as to the circumstances in which such an undertaking could escape from the rule in Article 7. In principle it could do so if it could show that it would obstruct the performance of its tasks to obey that Article (or indeed any other Treaty rule) and that to break it would not affect the development of trade contrary to the interests of the Community. In spite of its very general terms, the Court's 'dispositif' did not rule out this possibility. Nor could it have done so in view of the express terms of Article 90(2). However, in view of the fundamental nature of the rule in Article 7, any undertaking seeking to establish that it could escape from that Article via Article 90(2) would have a heavy onus when seeking to show that it was obstructed by the rule and that the second sentence of Article 90(2) did not apply.

The judgment has however a wider significance. Some Articles, e.g. Article 90(1), are addressed to the conduct of member states. Others, e.g. Article 85, relate to the activities of undertakings. A third category, of which Article 7 is only one example, establish a general principle which is not

---

[86] Ibid., p. 430, para. 15.
[87] Ibid., p. 432.

specifically addressed to the conduct of member states or undertakings, although they are usually taken to apply only to the former. Article 30 falls into this category. The Court's judgment therefore raises the question whether an undertaking falling within Article 90(2) is prohibited by Article 30 from maintaining a measure equivalent to a quantitative restriction, e.g. by adopting an internal rule or practice not to purchase any foreign goods. It could be argued that a quantitative restriction is by its very nature a governmental measure and that undertakings in general are not capable of taking any equivalent measures, at least if they act independently of the government and not merely as its agent. The argument would however be somewhat weaker in the case of those undertakings falling within Article 90(2). In respect of the latter, it could be argued that a member state which cannot hinder imports from other member states because of Article 30 should not allow undertakings to which it entrusts services of general economic interest to do so either. To impose on member states a duty to prevent undertakings from maintaining measures contrary to Article 30 would go beyond the strict terms of Article 90(1), which refers only to measures enacted or maintained by the member states themselves. However, in the light of the *Sacchi* case[88] these questions cannot be regarded as settled.

The Court's judgment in *Van Ameyde* v. *UCI*[89] was concerned more with the intepretation of Articles 85 and 86 (competition) than Article 90, but because of the terms of the questions put by the national court it had to consider the latter Article as well. Its ruling accordingly interprets Article 90 only 'in conjunction with' Articles 85 and 86. Moreover, its references to Article 90 are confined to the first paragraph of that Article. The case does at least, however, provide another example of an undertaking within the meaning of that paragraph. The undertaking in question was the Italian motor insurance bureau (UCI) to which had been entrusted the task of acting as the 'handling bureau' in Italy for dealing with and settling motor accident claims on behalf of the 'paying bureaux' in other countries. The latter were the foreign bureaux who had undertaken to insure the motorists in question under the 'green card' system while visiting Italy. For the purpose of Article 90, the significant fact was that the Italian bureau had been entrusted with a special and exclusive task by Italian law. It was only incidental that this was in pursuance of internationally agreed procedures, and in accordance with Community secondary legislation designed to assist the free movement of persons.[90] The latter did not enable the Italian bureau to escape from the provisions of Article 90.

---

[88] Case 155/73 [1974] *ECR* 409.
[89] Case 90/76 [1977] *ECR* 1091.
[90] Dir. 166/72, *OJ* 1972, L103/1, Commission Rec. 185/73 of 15 May 1973, and Commission Dec. 167/74, *OJ* 1974, L87/14.

In other cases the Court has either displayed a lack of interest in the question whether a particular undertaking falls within Article 90, or expressed doubts about whether it does so without reaching any conclusion on the matter, or decided that Article 90 does not apply. In *Pigs Marketing Board* v. *Redmond*[91] the Court seems to have taken the view that it did not matter whether the Northern Ireland Pigs Marketing Board, to or through which all bacon pigs had to be sold, was caught by Article 90. It simply pointed out that its classification as such an undertaking would not exempt its activities from the provisions of Community law.[92] In *INNO* v. *ATAB*[93] the Belgian tobacco tax system was scrutinized. Broadly speaking, this required cigarette manufacturers to pay tax by purchasing tax labels. These had to state the retail price (on which the tax was calculated) and the labels had to be inserted under the cellophane wrappers of the cigarette packets. When this had been done, Belgian law then required retailers to sell at the stated price. This gave cigarette manufacturers, unlike makers of other goods, the power in effect to fix retail prices. It was argued that the cigarette manufacturers were therefore undertakings to which the Belgian Government had granted (albeit indirectly) special or exclusive rights. The Advocate General found no difficulty in accepting this argument.[94] The Court however took a different view. It said:

It should be pointed out that the fiscal system in question leaves the manufacturer or importer free to fix for his products a retail selling price lower than the selling price of competing products of the same kind and quality and which have the same characteristics. Since that possibility is open to all those, including retailers, who become producers or importers of manufactured tobacco, and consequently to an indefinite class of undertakings, it is questionable whether those undertakings can properly be described as having been granted 'special', and at all events 'exclusive', rights.

However, since it has already been indicated in the reasons given for the answer to the first question that in any case Article 90 is only a particular application of certain general principles which bind the Member States, it does not appear necessary to give an answer to the second question.[95]

In *Züchner* v. *Bayerische Vereinsbank*[96] the Court found that banks were not undertakings which could take advantage of Article 90(2). The Court's reasoning was:

Although one transfer of customers' funds from one Member State to another normally performed by banks is an operation which falls within the special task of banks, particularly in connection with international movements of capital, that is

[91] Case 83/78 [1978] *ECR* 2347.
[92] Ibid., p. 2369.
[93] Case 13/77 [1977] *ECR* 2115.
[94] Ibid., p. 2169.
[95] Ibid., p. 2146.
[96] Case 172/80 [1981] *ECR* 2021.

not sufficient to make them undertakings within the meaning of Article 90(2) of the Treaty unless it can be established that in performing such transfers the banks are operating a service of general economic interest with which they have been entrusted by a measure adopted by the public authorities.[97]

Direct effect

The three conditions which have to be fulfilled in order to give a provision of the EEC Treaty direct effect are well known.[98] In short, it must be (i) clear and precise, (ii) unconditional, and (iii) not subject to the adoption by the Community or the member states, with some discretion, of subsequent rules. Judged by those criteria it would be difficult to find a less likely candidate for direct effect than either of the first two paragraphs of Article 90. They are classic examples of the sort of 'framework' provisions which are in general and unclear terms, which need to be spelled out in greater detail later, after due assessment for example of what, in various individual situations, is to be regarded as 'special or exclusive rights', 'services of general economic interest' and 'the interests of the Community', and which might therefore be thought to be conditional upon further legislative steps being taken. Indeed, the third paragraph of the Article envisages further action by the Commission in the shape of directives.

In *Ministère Public Luxembourg* v. *Muller*[99] the Court invited the parties to address oral observations on the 'direct applicability' of Article 90(1) and (2).[100] When delivering judgment the Court did not say whether Article 90(1) had direct effect. It held in its 'dispositif' that Article 90(2) could not 'at the present stage' create individual rights which the national courts must protect (i.e. it did not then have direct effect). It gave as its reasons:

Article 90(2) does not lay down an unconditional rule. Its application involves an appraisal of the requirements, on the one hand, of the particular task entrusted to the undertaking concerned and, on the other hand, the protection of the interests of the Community.

This appraisal depends on the objectives of general economic policy pursued by the States under the supervision of the Commission.[101]

The statement that there was no direct effect at the present stage suggests that Article 90(2) could have direct effect at some later stage, and it is interesting to consider by what process that could be achieved. Short of being amended in accordance with Article 236, it is difficult to see how the terms of Article 90(2) could ever be regarded as satisfying the conditions for

[97] Ibid., p. 323.
[98] See e.g. the Advocate General in Case 2/74, *Reyners* v. *Belgium* [1974] ECR 631, pp. 659–61, and again in Case 41/74, *Van Duyn* v. *Home Office* [1974] ECR 1337, p. 1354.
[99] Case 10/71 [1971] ECR 723.
[100] Ibid., p. 727.
[101] Ibid., p. 730.

direct effect. It is possible the Court was thinking that some provisions in the Commission's directives made under Article 90(3) might, read in conjunction with Article 90(2), have direct effect in respect of individual member states which themselves neglected to give effect to the directives. Or it may have envisaged the adoption of Council regulations under Article 235 which again could be said to have direct effect taken together with Article 90(2). In the case of a regulation it would be easy to conclude that it had direct effect. Even a directive could, in the light of the Court's jurisprudence,[102] be found to have direct effect. But in each case it would seem more logical to regard the regulation or the directive as having that effect rather than the Treaty provision to which it referred. Nevertheless a clue to the Court's thinking may be found in *Sacchi*,[103] where the Court held Article 86 to have direct effect 'within the framework of Article 90'. It may be that the Court will at some future stage hold a directive made under Article 90(3) to have direct effect within the same framework.

ARTICLE 90(3)

The third paragraph of Article 90 requires the Commission to ensure the application of the provisions of the Article. This is merely repetitive of the general duty imposed on the Commission by Article 55, first indent. Article 90(3) goes on to say that the Commission 'shall where necessary, address appropriate directives or decisions to Member States'. It may be noted that this text says 'to Member States', and not 'to the Member States'. At first sight, therefore, it may have been thought that the paragraph was referring to directives or decisions which were limited in their application to individual member states, and to cases where the latter had shown by their conduct that this was necessary. However this fine linguistic point was not reflected in the French text, which says 'aux états membres'. A more substantial reason for having thought that the Commission had no power under Article 90(3) to address a directive or decision to all member states, and thereby to enact secondary legislation of general application, was that the contrary interpretation would have given the Commission a virtually unlimited legislative competence in relation to public undertakings. This would have made a curious comparison with the limited powers accorded to the Commission and the Council respectively, for example, in Article 94 (state aids) in the same chapter.

All this became a live issue when the Commission, acting under this paragraph, addressed to all member states directive 723/80 of 25 June 1980.[104] Its legality was challenged by France, Italy, and the UK in actions

---

[102] See e.g. Case 41/74, n. 98 above.
[103] Case 155/73 [1974] *ECR* 409.
[104] *OJ* 1980, L195/35.

against the Commission. Germany and the Netherlands supported the Commission. The Court dismissed the applications.[105] It considered that the powers of the Commission were not to be inferred from some general principle concerning the respective legislative powers of the Council and Commission, but from the particular wording of each relevant provision.[106] For the same reason, the Commission's powers under Article 90(3) to gather information, inter alia, were not limited by the fact that it had a general power of fact-finding under Article 213 (which was subject to overall control by the Council).[107] Nor did the Council's power under Article 94 to make general regulations in respect of state aids affect the Commission's power under Article 90(3) to watch over state aids, as granted to the particular classes of undertakings to which that Article related.[108] The Commission needed the information required by the directive, the provisions of which were proportional to that need.[109] The Directive did not discriminate against public undertakings because they were not comparable with private undertakings.[110] The Directive did not amplify Articles 90, 92, and 93 because it did not define 'aid' for the purpose of those Articles.[111] Nor did it define the concept of public undertaking for the purpose of Article 90. Its definition of a public undertaking was only for the purpose of the Directive.[112] However, the latter could not, and did not, apply to undertakings operating on the market in coal and steel because the ECSC Treaty had its own rules about aids, and Article 232 EEC preserved them.[113]

Commission Directive 80/723/EEC[114] is designed to make the financial relations between member states and public undertakings transparent. This is a first step towards ensuring that they do not receive aids which are incompatible with the common market. As the preamble acknowledges, some public undertakings may be required to pursue non-commercial ends, e.g. by giving an unprofitable social service, and they may be compensated by the state for the resulting financial burdens. In principle financial assistance to them should also be made transparent, although Article 4 of the Directive exempts from its scope those financial relations between public authorities and public undertakings as regards the supply of services which is not likely appreciably to affect trade between member states. Public undertakings are also exempted by that Article if they concern the supply of water, energy, transport, or posts and telecommunications. So too are public credit institutions and public undertakings

---

[105] In Joined Cases 188–90/80, *France, Italy, UK* v. *Commission* [1982] *ECR* 2545.
[106] Ibid., para. 6.
[107] Ibid., para. 10.
[108] Ibid., paras. 12–13.
[109] Ibid., paras. 18–19.
[110] Ibid., paras. 20–1.
[111] Ibid., paras. 22–3.
[112] Ibid., para. 24.
[113] Ibid., para. 31.
[114] *OJ* 1980, L195/35.

whose turnover excluding taxes has not reached 40 million EUA during the two financial years preceding their receipt of public financial assistance. The assistance which is covered by the Directive includes setting off operating losses, provision of capital, soft loans, and the foregoing of a normal return on public funds.[115] Information on all such assistance must be kept for five years and supplied to the Commission on request.[116] Article 2 defines 'public authorities' as state and regional or local authorities. 'Public undertakings', a concept with no precise connotation in the UK, is defined for the purpose of the directive as:

> any undertaking over which the public authorities may exercise directly or indirectly a dominant influence by virtue of their ownership of it, their financial participation therein, or the rules which govern it.

The concept, continental in origin, of 'professional secrecy' is not defined. It is no excuse for refusing to supply information to the Commission, but the latter enjoins itself under Article 6 not to disclose information covered by such secrecy.

FURTHER READING

A. C. Evans, 'Public Enterprise and EEC Law: The Case of the British National Oil Corporation', (1982) *ECLR* 86.

G. van Hecke, 'Government Enterprises and National Monopolies Under the EEC Treaty', (1965–6) 3 *CML Rev.* 450.

S. D. Kon, 'Aspects of Reverse Discrimination in Community Law', (1981) 6 *EL Rev.* 75.

P. Oliver, 'Recent Case Law on Article 37 EEC', (1980) 17 *CML Rev.* 251.

---

[115] Article 3.
[116] Article 5.

PART II

PERSONS

IV
Workers

ONE of the fundamental principles of the common market is that workers should be able to move freely from one member state to another without any unnecessary governmental interference. If that goal were to be fully achieved, a worker would in principle be able to move across international frontiers as easily as he can within his own national boundaries. It is taken for granted, for example, that a worker from Devon who wishes to take a job in Somerset will be able to drive his car over the county boundary without first having to take out special insurance. He will not at any stage need to produce a passport (with or without an exit or entry visa), and indeed he will not be hindered by any customs or immigration formalities. He will be able to take with him whatever relatives or friends he wishes. Whatever social insurance benefits he or they were entitled to enjoy in Devon will still be available in Somerset. He will not be required on arrival to re-register his car or to buy new number plates for it. Nor will he be told that, although it may comply with the vehicle safety and construction regulations in Devon, it does not satisfy those in Somerset, for example, because the warning lights on the instrument panel are the wrong colour, or because his exterior lights are one centimetre too high or too low. He would be astounded if he even had to present it for fresh technical inspection simply because he had moved to Somerset. He will not have to seek either a residence or a work permit from his new local authorities. Whatever forms of education are available to other inhabitants of Somerset will be available to him and his family, without discrimination. If he seeks fresh employment in Somerset no law will discriminate against him because he comes from Devon.

All this can be achieved because in Devon and Somerset the same national laws apply. So long, however, as member states retain their national identities, in the shape of national laws, the migrant worker is almost bound to be subjected to some restrictions and inconveniences which he would not suffer if he remained within his own national boundaries. An obvious example is that he could reasonably be expected to dip the headlights of his car the other way if he moves from a country where they drive on the left to one where they drive on the right. A less obvious example is that, whereas an English-speaking worker who moves to Glamorgan will not be obliged to fill in complicated forms in the Welsh language in order to register with the Welsh local authority, a French-speaking Belgian who moves within Belgium to a Flemish-speaking commune may not be so lucky, and an Englishman who goes to work in the same commune will fare no better. The Englishman may reasonably expect (at least if he has read Article 7 EEC) to be treated in the same way as the Belgian, but he can also expect more administrative inconvenience than if he had moved to Glamorgan.

The extent to which the European worker has achieved unfettered mobility and the right to live and work anywhere in the Community on equal terms with any other European worker will be examined in the course of this chapter.

The first step towards creating free movement of persons was taken in Article 69 ECSC. That Article requires member states to remove any restrictions based on nationality on the employment of workers in the coal and steel industries, subject to three restrictions: (i) the workers must be nationals of a member state; (ii) they must have qualifications in a coal-mining or steel-making occupation which are 'recognized'; and (iii) their rights are subject to limitations imposed by the 'basic' requirements of health and public policy. The text of the Article gives rise to one or two uncertainties. It is unclear whether the qualifications must have some form of Community recognition, e.g. through the guidance of the High Authority (now the Commission[1]) under Article 69(5), or whether they must be recognized by the state of which the worker is a national, or by the receiving state, or by a combination of one or more of those bodies. Nor is the effect of including the word 'basic' clear. Does this simply signify that all requirements of health and public policy are regarded as basic (in which case the word is redundant), or does it purport to limit the cases in which free movement can be refused on those grounds? If it means the latter, the scope for limiting free movement of these workers may be less than it is as a result of Articles 48(3) and 56 EEC. Lastly, does the omission of any reference to public security mean that it cannot be relied upon as a ground for refusing free movement to a qualified coal or steel worker? These are unresolved questions, but whatever Article 69 ECSC means, it prevails by virtue of Article 232(1) EEC over the EEC Treaty.

Article 96 EURATOM also provides for the abolition of restrictions based on nationality affecting the right of nationals of a member state to take 'skilled' employment in the field of nuclear energy. The need for recognition of qualifications has thus in this context disappeared, and has been replaced by the need to be 'skilled'. The permissible limitations on the right of free movement are stated to be those resulting from the basic requirements of public policy, public security, or public health. The Article allows the Council to issue directives for its application. On 5

---

[1] Article 9 of the Merger Treaty.

March 1962 such a directive was issued.[2] Articles 2 and 3 and the Annex contain a fairly elaborate definition of what is 'skilled'. Perhaps as an indication that the Council's attention was likely to be turned in future to the more general provisions of the EEC Treaty, Article 5 of the Directive declared that, with regard to any matter which it did not cover, member states should apply the measures taken under that Treaty relating to freedom of movement for workers. However, in so far as Article 96 EURATOM and the Directive contain special rules for this class of worker they prevail over the EEC Treaty by virtue of Article 232(2) of the latter.

Without prejudice to these special rules for coal, steel, and atomic energy workers, the free movement of all kinds of worker is now governed by the EEC Treaty, and in particular Articles 48–51. The remainder of this chapter will be devoted to these provisions and the secondary legislation adopted pursuant to them.

DEFINITIONS

Workers

Although Title III of Part Two of the EEC Treaty is entitled 'Free movement of persons, services and capital', Chapter 1 of that Title is headed 'Workers', and it is the free movement of workers which Article 48(1) requires to be secured within the Community by the end of the transitional period at the latest.[3] The use of the wider expression 'persons' in the heading to the whole of Title III can be explained by the fact that, although Chapter 1 is confined to a limited class, the application of Chapter 2 (establishment) and of Chapter 3 (services) involves the movement of natural and legal persons, even though they are not workers within the meaning of Chapter 1. In fact, although not explicitly stated, it seems reasonably clear from its language as a whole that as a general rule Chapter 1 is concerned with individuals who are employees, whereas Chapters 2 and 3 deal with self-employed individuals and companies. Thus, for example, Article 48 speaks of accepting offers of employment, and Article 49 refers to applications for employment. Even more clearly, Article 1(1) of Regulation 1612/68[4] speaks of the right 'to take up an activity as an employed person'.[5] Also, the Community residence permit refers to 'the right to take up and pursue an activity as an employed person'.[6]

---

[2] *OJ*, Special Edition, 1959–62, p. 245.

[3] For the original member states and for Denmark, Ireland, and the UK the transitional periods have how expired. Articles 44–8 of the Greek Act of Accession established various transitional periods, the last of which expires on 1 January 1988. Article 45(1) of the Greek Act of Accession was interpreted by the Court in Case 77/82, *Peskeloglou* v. *Bundesanstalt für Arbeit* [1983] *ECR* 1085.

[4] *OJ*, Special Edition, 1968, p. 475.

[5] But see Article 11 of the same regulation and Case 17/76, *Brack* [1976] *ECR* 1429.

[6] Annex to Dir. 360/68, *OJ* 1968, L257/13.

In *Hoekstra (née Unger)* v. *Bedrijfsvereniging Detailhandel*[7] the Court was asked to interpret the words 'wage-earner or assimilated worker' in Article 19 of Regulation 3.[8] The Court approached the question by pointing out that freedom of movement for workers was part of the 'foundations'[9] of the Community, that attainment of this freedom was the principal objective of Article 51 and that this therefore conditioned the regulations (of which Regulation No. 3 was one) adopted under that Article.[10] The expressions 'workers' and 'migrant workers' each had to be given a Community definition, because if left to national interpretation this would leave member states free to modify the meaning.[11] The Court declined to supply a Community definition, but it did indicate that the words 'wage-earner or assimilated worker' had a meaning only within the limits of the concept of 'workers' as used in the Treaty.[12] With regard to the former, the Court said:

The concept of 'wage-earner or assimilated worker' has thus a Community meaning, referring to all those who, as such and under whatever description, are covered by the different national systems of social security.[13]

It may safely be said therefore that the term 'worker' is at least as wide as the definition quoted above, although the Court did not preclude the possibility of its being wider.

Regulation 3 was also considered in *Caisse Primaire d'Assurance Maladie Sélestat* v. *Football Club d'Andlau*.[14] Some German musicians went to France in 1970 to play at three football club dances. The question was whether they were subject to German or French social security legislation, because if the latter applied the club was obliged to pay contributions. The Court interpreted the regulation in the light of these facts. In doing so, it implicitly accepted that casual workers of this kind were 'wage-earners and assimilated workers' within the meaning of the regulation. When called upon to interpret the same regulation in *Hessische Knappschaft* v. *Singer*[15] the Court treated two German workers as still remaining 'workers' for social security purposes even when they were on holiday in France. After referring to the objective of Article 51 EEC as being to establish as complete freedom of movement for workers as possible, the Court said:

It would not be in conformity with that spirit to limit the concept of 'worker' solely to migrant workers *stricto sensu* or solely to workers required to move for the

[7] Case 75/63 [1964] *ECR* 177.
[8] *OJ*, 16 Dec. 1958, p. 561. See also Article 2 of Dir. 79/7, *OJ* 1979, L6/24, which refers to self-employed persons and workers as two distinct categories.
[9] A reference to the heading to Part Two of the Treaty.
[10] Case 75/63 [1964] *ECR* 177, p. 184.
[11] Ibid.
[12] Ibid.
[13] Ibid., p. 185.
[14] Case 8/75 [1975] *ECR* 739.
[15] Case 44/65 [1965] *ECR* 965.

purpose of their employment. Nothing in Article 51 imposes such distinctions, which would in any case tend to make the application of the rules in question impracticable.[16]

Regulation 3 was followed by Regulation 1408/71 on the application of social security schemes to employed persons and their families moving within the Community.[17] Instead of using the expression 'wage-earner or assimilated worker', the new regulation[18] used the word 'worker', and defined it for the purpose of the regulation in Article 1. The test remained whether the person was insured under a social security scheme and was, or had been, so insured as an employed person. In *Brack* v. *Insurance Officer*[19] the European Court had to consider that definition, to assist the English court to decide whether the plaintiff fell within it. The problem was that the plaintiff had at some times been employed, and at others self-employed, in the UK. He was self-employed at the time when he visited France to convalesce from an illness, and the question was whether at that time he qualified as a 'worker' and was thus entitled under Regulation 1408/71[20] to sickness benefits in respects of the period he spent in France. The Court first noted that the heading to the Regulation referred to 'employed persons', but the Court then went on to illustrate how in some cases, e.g. under Article 2(1), the Regulation applied to persons who, when the contingency arose, did not have the status of employed persons. It also applied, e.g. under Article 34, to persons who were not actual workers, but who in certain circumstances were to be deemed to be workers. This enabled the Court to conclude that the Regulation could apply to persons who had lost their status as employed persons, and that it did apply to persons who, under the UK legislation, were obliged to pay contributions as if they were employed persons, even though they did not at the time in question have that status.[21] Such persons were to be regarded as workers for the purpose of Article 1(a) of the Regulation.

Thus it appears that, in circumstances such as arose in the *Brack* case,[22] a person may for social security purposes be treated as a 'worker' even though at the time in question he was not actually working, and even though when he did last work he was not an 'employed person'. The first part of this proposition is in line with the Court's earlier decision, already mentioned, in *Hessische Knappschaft* v. *Singer*.[23] Indeed, when a person

[16] Ibid., p. 971.
[17] *OJ*, Special Edition, 1971, 416; amended by Act of Accession, Article 29 and Annex I, Treaty Series No. 1 (1973)—Part I, Cmnd. 517-I, p. 143 et seq.
[18] As originally adopted. But see the amendments made by Reg. 1380/81, *OJ* 1981, L143/1, and Reg. 2000/83, *OJ* 1983, L230/1.
[19] Case 17/76 [1976] *ECR* 1429.
[20] *OJ*, Special Edition, 1971, p. 416.
[21] See also Case 32/75, *Cristini* v. *SNCF* [1975] *ECR* 1085, p. 1094.
[22] Case 17/76 [1976] *ECR* 1429.
[23] Case 44/65 [1965] *ECR* 965.

needs social security one would normally expect the need to have arisen because that person is not able to continue working, e.g. on account of sickness or old age. The objective of Article 51 EEC is expressed to be 'to provide for freedom of movement for workers', but although this may imply that the beneficiaries are to be persons who at some stage must be regarded as workers it does not imply that they must be in work at the time the benefit is sought. It is not without significance in this context that sub-paragraph (*b*) of Article 51, which requires certain social benefits to be paid, speaks of 'persons' rather than workers. On the other hand, the decision to treat as a worker a person who, when last in work, was self-employed, could probably be explained in the light of the particular facts of the *Brack* case,[24] the wording of Article 51, and the terms of the regulation.[25] The proposition that Articles 48–50 EEC apply as a general rule only to employees remains unaffected.

In *Walrave* v. *Union Cycliste Internationale*[26] the Court had to consider the position of sportsmen (motorcycle pacemakers and cyclists), and to what extent they were entitled, as workers, to the benefits of Articles 7, 48, and 59 of the Treaty. The Court first found that the practice of sport was subject to Community law only to the extent that it constituted an economic activity within the meaning of Article 2. On this ground it concluded that Article 7 (non-discrimination on grounds of nationality) did not apply to the composition of sports teams, in particular national teams, because in the Court's view their formation was a question of purely sporting interest which (so the Court asserted) had nothing to do with economic activity.[27] Nevertheless, it is implicit in the remainder of the judgment[28] that professional sportsmen generally speaking are to be regarded as workers, and that they accordingly gain the benefit of Articles 48–51 and 59–66. The judgment also provides an answer to the question whether a person is a worker, for the purposes of the Treaty, only in relation to his activities within the boundaries of the Community. The Court said:

> By reason of the fact that it is imperative, the rule on non-discrimination applies in judging all legal relationships in so far as these relationships, by reason either of the place where they are entered into or of the place where they take effect, can be located within the territory of the Community.[29]

From this it can be seen that if a person's contract of employment is concluded within the Community it matters not that he will work outside

---

[24] Case 17/76 [1976] *ECR* 1429.

[25] Reg. 1380/81, *OJ* 1981, L143/1, extended the rules on social security to self-employed persons because, as the preamble states, free movement for persons extends to self-employed persons in the framework of the freedom of establishment and the freedom to supply services.

[26] Case 36/74 [1974] *ECR* 1405.

[27] See also Case 13/76, *Donà* v. *Mantero* [1976] *ECR* 1333, p. 1340.

[28] And in Case 13/76, as above.

[29] Ibid., p. 1420.

the Community, either partly or exclusively. He may in either case still be a worker for Community purposes. In *Commission* v. *France*[30] the Court treated seamen working, or seeking work, on French ships as workers for the purposes of Article 48(2) and Regulation 1612/68.[31] The judgment made no mention of where the contract of employment was made, and it can therefore be taken to have been immaterial in the case of employment on ships registered in a member state.

From the cases reviewed so far it can be seen that the European Court has attributed a fairly wide meaning to the word 'worker'. There is however a limit to the concept, and the person concerned must presumably at least establish some genuine link between himself and work. In *R.* v. *Secchi*[32] the Metropolitan Magistrate sitting at Marylebone felt no need to consult the European Court before deciding that a national of a member state who, during his four months' stay in the UK committed various crimes, and who in the past two years had generally wandered across Europe living the life of an itinerant vagrant, was not a worker within the meaning of Article 48.[33] In the case of *D. M. Levin*[34] the European Court confirmed that the term 'worker' must be explained in the light of principles obtaining within the Community legal order, and not with reference to the laws of the member states.[35] The term included permanent, seasonal, and frontier workers, and persons who were employed, or intended to take up employment, only on a part-time basis. But in the case of part-time workers the occupation must be really genuine, and thus did not include activities which were minimal[36] although it did include genuine employment yielding an income lower than that which the member state considered necessary as the minimum required for subsistence.[37] Another qualification of the definition of worker might have been made by the Court in *R.* v. *Saunders*[38] when it was asked whether Miss Saunders's rights as a worker under Article 48 had been infringed. The Court might have said that she was not a worker for the purposes of that Article. It did not, however, say whether she was or was not. Instead it said that Article 48 did not apply to situations which were wholly internal to a member state (Miss Saunders, a British national, having been sent back to Northern Ireland and ordered not to return to England or Wales within three years). In *Monson and Jhanjan* v.

---

[30] Case 167/73 [1974] *ECR* 359.
[31] *OJ*, Special Edition, 1968, p. 475.
[32] [1975] 1 *CMLR* 383. But a person who is looking for work has the right to take up residence in another member state for that purpose: Case 48/75, *Royer* [1976] *ECR* 497, p. 512.
[33] Ibid., p. 392.
[34] Case 53/81 [1982] *ECR* 1035.
[35] Ibid., p. 1049.
[36] Ibid., p. 1050.
[37] The Advocate General considered an 'au pair' girl to be a worker: Case 118/75, *Watson and Belmann* [1976] *ECR* 1185, p. 1202.
[38] Case 175/78 [1979] *ECR* 1129.

Netherlands[39] there was again an opportunity to consider what was a Community 'worker', but the Court did not take it. The plaintiffs, who were nationals of Surinam, wished to join their son and daughter in the Netherlands. The latter had never worked in another member state. The plaintiffs relied on Article 10(1) of Regulation 1612/68[40] concerning the right of a worker to be joined by his family. The Court seems to have accepted that the son and daughter were workers, but held that the provisions in question could only be relied on in a situation to which some principle of Community law, such as the right of free movement of workers, applied. They therefore had no application in the case of workers who had exercised no right of free movement within the Community, i.e. from one member state to another.

Workers of the member states

Article 48(1) EEC speaks simply of 'workers'. As if struck by conscience that they might have gone too far, the draftsmen confined the operation of Article 48(2) to 'workers of the Member States'—still a somewhat naïve expression. Does it cover only a worker who is a national of a member state, or does it include a worker who is a national of a non-member state, but who permanently resides in, or ordinarily resides in, or works in, or even is just on holiday in a member state? Subsequent provisions in the chapter speak of 'nationals of a Member State'. Regulation 1612/68[41] has no inhibitions. It opts firmly for 'national of a Member State' as the beneficiary of the rights under Article 48 of free movement for workers. It may with reasonable confidence be assumed, therefore, that nationality of a member state is the criterion.

It is primarily for each member state to define who are its own nationals. Of the original member states, only Germany presented any problem, and that was on account of the division between the Federal Republic of Germany and the (then unrecognized) German Democratic Republic. Since only the former was a member of the Community it was thought necessary to clarify what was meant by 'German national' for the purposes of the Treaty. The Federal Republic of Germany accordingly declared:

All Germans as defined in the Basic Law for the Federal Republic of Germany shall be considered nationals of the Federal Republic of Germany.[42]

Although this was a unilateral declaration, it was accepted by the other member states and may be taken to represent an agreed definition for the purposes of the Treaty.

---

[39] Joined Cases 35 and 36/82 [1983] 2 *CMLR* 221.
[40] *OJ*, Special Edition, 1968, p. 475.
[41] Ibid.
[42] Cmnd. 7460, p. 171.

The United Kingdom presented more difficult problems owing to its complex nationality law and the agreed limitations on the territorial application of the Treaty.[43] Following the German precedent, the UK made a similar declaration on accession to the Community treaties.[44] As a consequence of the British Nationality Act of 1981 this statement was replaced by another. The agreed definition of a UK national now reads:

As to the United Kingdom of Great Britain and Northern Ireland, the terms 'nationals', 'nationals of Member States' or 'nationals of Member States and overseas countries and territories' wherever used in the Treaty establishing the European Economic Community, the Treaty establishing the European Atomic Energy Community or the Treaty establishing the European Coal and Steel Community or in any of the Community acts deriving from those Treaties, are to be understood to refer to:
(*a*) British citizens;
(*b*) persons who are British subjects by virtue of Part IV of the British Nationality Act 1981 and who have the right of abode in the United Kingdom and are therefore exempt from United Kingdom immigration control;
(*c*) British Dependent Territories citizens who acquire their citizenship from a connection with Gibraltar.
The reference in Article 6 of the third Protocol to the Act of Accession of 22 January 1972, on the Channel Islands and the Isle of Man, to 'any citizen of the United Kingdom and Colonies' is to be understood as referring to 'any British citizen'.[45]

NON-DISCRIMINATION

Article 48

The first paragraph of Article 48 (EEC) states the general principle that freedom of movement for workers shall be secured within the Community by the end of the transitional period[46] at the latest. The next two paragraphs of the Article each say what this principle shall entail. The first point to note is the use of the word 'entail'. Although the word is not followed in either paragraph by words such as 'inter alia', it is clear from the very existence of the two paragraphs, each stating different things, that in neither case can the word 'entail' be intended to indicate that what follows is an exhaustive catalogue. It is reasonable to suppose, therefore,

[43] Article 227.
[44] Cmnd. 5179–I, p. 282.
[45] *OJ* 1983, C23/1. Part IV of the British Nationality Act 1981 (c. 61) provides for the continuance as British subjects of certain classes of person, i.e. British subjects without citizenship, alien women married to British subjects of certain descriptions, and some persons having dual British and Irish nationality.
[46] Generally expired, but see Articles 44–7 of the Greek Act of Accession.

that the legislative power conferred by Article 49 for the purposes of bringing about freedom of movement for workers, as required by Article 48(1), is
not confined to matters falling within the scope of Article 48(2) and (3).

Article 48(2) establishes the first subrule of the principle of free movement by providing for non-discrimination on grounds of nationality. It
does so in these terms:

Such freedom of movement shall entail the abolition of any discrimination based
on nationality between workers of the Member States as regards employment,
remuneration and other conditions of work and employment.

Article 48(3) lists a number of ⸦enefits which the right of free movement
entails, subject to limitations justified on grounds of public policy, public
security, or public health. The paragraph refers to the right to accept offers
of employment actually made, to move freely within the Community for
that purpose, and, subject to certain conditions, to stay in the member
states concerned both during and after employment. It is sometimes
suggested that this paragraph only lists particular examples of the application of the principle of non-discrimination on grounds of nationality. If that
view were correct it could affect the application of the Article as a whole.
Let us suppose, for example, that a French worker were to be offered a job
with a private British shipbuilder, and that before he could take up that
employment the government introduced a new law forbidding the
recruitment of new workers (of any nationality) by such undertakings, the
objective of the law being to allow the expansion of state-owned ship-
builders but not others. If Article 48(3) were only an application of the rule
in Article 48(2) there could be no objection to the new law. But if the provisions of Article 48(3) were to be regarded as standing independently of
Article 48(2) the government would be in some difficulty. Leaving aside the
question of any conceivable implications for public security, the government's only possible escape would be via the defence of public policy, and
it would have to establish a convincing case on that ground, if it could.
However it is questionable whether Article 48(3) could properly be
regarded as no more than an amplification of the principle of non-
discrimination. There is no support for that view in the text of the Article.
Moreover, there is some evidence that the Council does not share it either.
Thus, in the preamble to Regulation 1612/68[47] it is said that the attainment
of the objective of free movement entails:

the abolition of any discrimination based on nationality . . . as well as the right of
such workers to move freely within the Community . . .

This suggests that the requirement of non-discrimination and the right to
move freely (Article 48(3)(*b*)) are two separate things.

[47] *OJ*, Special Edition 1968, p. 475.

The secondary legislation

Whatever the answer to the question posed above, it is however clear that the principle of non-discrimination pervades the relevant secondary legislation. Regulation 1612/68[48] on freedom of movement for workers within the Community seems to be almost exclusively inspired by the principle. The European worker is accorded the right to take up available employment in another member state 'with the same priority as nationals of that State' (Article 1(2)). Employers and employees may conclude and perform contracts of employment 'without any discrimination resulting therefrom' (Article 2). Member states must not by their laws or practices limit a worker's employment prospects or subject his employment 'to conditions not applicable in respect of their own nationals' (Article 3(1)). There must be no 'special recruitment procedure for foreign nationals' (Article 3(2)). Discrimination in the form of action by member states to restrict the number or percentage of foreign nationals employed in an undertaking must not apply to nationals of other member states (Article 4). Employment offices must give the European worker 'the same assistance . . . as their own nationals seeking employment' (Article 5). As a general rule, his recruitment must not depend on vocational or other criteria 'which are discriminatory on grounds of nationality' (Article 6). He may not, so far as concerns conditions of employment and work, 'be treated differently from national workers' and he enjoys the same social, tax, and vocational training and re-training advantages as national workers (Article 7). 'Equality of treatment' as regards membership of trade unions is his for the asking (Article 8). He enjoys all the housing advantages 'accorded to national workers' (Article 9). When he exercises his right to install his family with him,[49] he must have available suitable housing but this however 'must not give rise to discrimination between national workers and workers from other Member States' (Article 10).

Article 11 is the first Article which appears to be unconcerned about discrimination (a worker's spouse and children, even if not nationals of any member state, are to have the right to take up employment). Article 12 immediately reverts however to the normal pattern by requiring general educational, apprenticeship, and vocational training courses to be open to a worker's children. Thus in the whole of Part I of the Regulation, which contains all the substantive rules, only one Article omits to mention non-discrimination on grounds of nationality.

Council Directive 360/68[50] on the abolition of restrictions on movement and residence within the Community for workers of member states and their families recites in the preamble that 'the rules applicable to residents

---

[48] Ibid.
[49] See Case 267/83, *Aissatou Diatta* v. *Land Berlin*, judgment of 13 February 1985.
[50] *OJ* 1968, L257/13.

should, as far as possible, bring the position of workers from other Member States and members of their families into line with that of nationals'. Regulation 1408/71[51] on the application of social security schemes to employed persons and their families moving within the Community similarly recites that 'equality of treatment for all nationals of Member States under the various national legislations' is the desired aim in the field of social security.

The case law

In *Südmilch* v. *Ugliola*,[52] an Italian worker had interrupted his employment in Germany to perform his military service in Italy. He wanted to lose no seniority on rejoining his employers, and therefore claimed the same rights as a German worker under the German law on security of employment during military service. The Court held that he was entitled to count his Italian military service in calculating his seniority in the same way as a German national could count German military service. In that sort of situation there would be no direct, overt discrimination if a national law simply stated that service with the national armed services conferred a particular benefit. But, since foreigners are not usually eligible to serve with the forces, there would be an indirect discrimination if service with their own foreign armed services was not allowed to count. The Court summarized the position:

Apart from the cases expressly referred to in paragraph (3), Article 48 of the Treaty does not allow Member States to make any exceptions to the equality of treatment and protection required by the Treaty for all workers within the Community by indirectly introducing discrimination in favour of their own nationals alone based upon obligations for military service. Consequently, [as] a rule of national law protecting workers from the unfavourable consequences, as regards conditions of work and employment in an undertaking, arising out of absence through obligations for military service must also be applied to the nationals of other Member States employed in the territory of the State in question who are subject to military service in their country of origin.[53]

It may be noted that the Court described the rule against discrimination on grounds of nationality as 'the equality of treatment and protection' required by the Treaty. This language recognizes the fact that discrimination could take the form not only of some positive act against a foreigner, but also the withholding of some benefit which is granted to the state's own nationals.

Even if a member state actually treats nationals of other member states in the same way as its own, it will be guilty of a breach of Article 48 if its laws

---

[51] *OJ*, Special Edition, 1971, p. 416.
[52] Case 15/69 [1969] *ECR* 363.
[53] Ibid., p. 369.

(which are waived in practice) appear to require discriminatory treatment. This is so even when the Treaty provisions in question have direct effect and, by virtue of their character as Community law, take precedence over national law. The maxim that everybody is presumed to know the law does not apparently apply in this situation. The man in the street is not presumed to know that, when Community law has direct effect, all contrary provisions of national law are rendered inoperable. The Court's view appears to be that a worker who is confronted with the express provisions of a national law may be misled by them and may in fact not know of his overriding Community rights. This was illustrated in *Commission* v. *France.*[54] In that case French laws required key jobs on French merchant ships to be given to French nationals, and the majority of all the crew had to be French. The French Government pointed out that oral instructions had been given to naval authorities to treat Community nationals as French nationals. The Court nevertheless held France to be in breach of Article 48 EEC and Article 4 of Regulation 1612/68.[55] It said:

It thus follows from the general character of the prohibition on discrimination in Article 48 and the objective pursued by the abolition of discrimination that discrimination is prohibited even if it constitutes only an obstacle of secondary importance as regards the equality of access to employment and other conditions of work and employment.

The uncertainty created by the maintenance unamended of the wording of Article 3 of the Code du Travail Maritime constitutes such an obstacle.[56]

Discrimination is not always expressed in a way which refers specifically to the nationality of the worker. In *Sotgiu* v. *Deutsche Bundespost*[57] an increased separation allowance for postal workers whose employment took them away from their families was only paid to persons whose place of residence was in Germany. The question was whether this discriminated against an Italian worker whose home and family remained in Italy, and was therefore contrary to Article 7(1) and (4) of Regulation 1612/68[58] which prohibited such a worker from being treated differently from national workers by reason of his nationality. The Court answered this question as follows:

The reply to the question put should be that the taking into consideration, as a criterion for the grant of a separate allowance, of the fact that a worker has his residence in the territory of another Member State may, according to the circumstances, constitute discrimination forbidden by Article 7(1) and (4) of Regulation No 1612/68.

[54] Case 167/73 [1974] *ECR* 359.
[55] *OJ*, Special Edition, 1968, p. 475.
[56] Case 167/73 [1974] *ECR* 359, p. 373.
[57] Case 152/73 [1974] *ECR* 153.
[58] *OJ*, Special Edition, 1968, 475.

This is not the case however if the scheme relating to such an allowance takes account of objective differences in the situation of workers according to whether their residence at the time when they take up their employment is within the territory of the State concerned or abroad.[59]

In reaching this conclusion the Court took the view that covert as well as overt discrimination was prohibited, and that the application of a criterion such as origin or place of residence could be covert discrimination on grounds of nationality. However, the fact that different allowances were paid to national and foreign workers could be objectively justified when the larger allowance for nationals was temporary and conditional on changing residence to the place of employment, whereas the allowance to foreigners was permanent and subject to no such condition.[60]

There can be no doubt that, subject to the limitations and exceptions referred to later in this chapter, Article 48(2) prohibits the retention of national laws or local bye-laws, and the exercise of governmental powers (centrally or locally), which involve discrimination on grounds of nationality, and which adversely affect workers who are nationals of other member states.[61] But does the prohibition against discrimination go further, and apply to the conduct of persons or bodies who have no connection with central or local government? Does it apply, for example, to employers generally, so that a firm which decides only to employ British or Irish workers (because it believes that only such persons are likely to be fluent in the English language) is guilty of contravening Article 48(2)? Some guidance can be found in *Walrave* v. *Union Cycliste Internationale*,[62] to which reference has already been made. The cyclists and pacemakers in that case were in conflict with the union, which was an international association of national bodies concerned with the sport of cycling, and which had decreed that a cyclist and his pacemaker must be of the same nationality. There does not appear, however, to have been any connection between the union and its constituent national bodies on the one hand and the government of any member state on the other. Yet the Court held the union's activities to be governed by Article 48. The Court ruled:

Prohibition on such discrimination does not only apply to the action of public authorities but extends likewise to rules of any other nature aimed at collectively regulating gainful employment and services.[63]

That case was followed by *Donà* v. *Mantero*.[64] The defendant was the chairman of an Italian football club, and he rejected his talent scout's efforts to

---

[59] Case 152/73 [1974] *ECR* 153, p. 165.   [60] Ibid.
[61] Or which deny a social advantage to a worker's family, after his death: Case 32/75, *Cristini* v. *SNCF* [1975] *ECR* 1085; or deny social benefits to a handicapped adult who has never worked but who qualified for equality of treatment as a child of a worker: Case 7/75, *Mr and Mrs F.* v. *Belgium* [1975] *ECR* 679.   [62] Case 36/74 [1974] *ECR* 1405.
[63] Ibid., p. 1421.   [64] Case 13/76 [1976] *ECR* 1333.

recruit non-Italian players for the club. In doing so he relied on the rules of the Italian Football Federation, which again does not appear to have been in any sense an arm of central or local government. The Court held that Article 48 must be taken into account (as well as Articles 7 and 59) by the national court when judging the validity of the effects of a provision in the rules of a sporting organization. In its 'dispositif' the Court referred to 'rules or a national practice, even adopted by a sporting organization' as being subject to Article 48. This phrase, and the corresponding inclusion of the word 'collectively' in the ruling in the *Walrave* case quoted above, seems to suggest that the Court was in each case referring only to some form of collective action taken by bodies which, although not governmental, nevertheless in practice controlled the activities of the individual employers. These two cases did not therefore go so far as to say that individual employers were caught by the rule in Article 48(2).

Limits of the notion of discrimination

Complete equality of treatment as between national workers and workers from other member states is not assured by Article 48(2). This can be seen in the case of *Watson and Belmann*.[65] Miss Watson, a British national, was charged in Italy with failing to report to the police, and Mr Belmann, with whom she stayed, with failure to report her presence. If one thing is clear, it is that Italian legislation required foreign nationals to report to the police but did not require Italian nationals to do so. In this respect there was therefore no equality of treatment, and it could be argued that in strict logic this must have meant that there was discrimination against foreign nationals, since a burden was imposed on them which was not shared by Italians. Furthermore it was a hindrance, albeit slight, to free movement of workers. It appears that Miss Watson was a worker because while in Italy she became an 'au pair'.[66] In addition, even as between foreign workers from other member states there was discrimination, in that some of them were exempted from the requirement to register. The question therefore arose as to whether Italian legislation contravened Article 48. After referring to the fundamental nature of the principle of free movement of persons the Court concluded, however, that it did not exclude the power of member states to collect information on population movements affecting their territory. National measures to that end did not infringe Articles 48–66 of the Treaty. The Court then added in its best Delphic style:

However, such an infringement might result from the legal formalities in question if the control procedures to which they refer were such as to restrict the freedom of movement required by the Treaty or to limit the right conferred by the Treaty on nationals of the Member States to enter and reside in the territory of any other Member State for the purposes intended by Community law.[67]

[65] Case 118/75 [1976] *ECR* 1185.　　　[66] Ibid., p. 1202.　　　[67] Ibid., p. 1198.

Since the whole point of the reference was to ascertain whether the Italian laws were compatible with 'the freedom of movement required by the Treaty', the national court may not have found this statement particularly illuminating. However, the following two sentences in the judgment were more helpful:

In particular as regards the period within which the arrival of foreign nationals must be reported, the provisions of the Treaty are only infringed if the period fixed is unreasonable.

   Among the penalties attaching to a failure to comply with the prescribed declaration and registration formalities, deportation, in relation to persons protected by Community law, is certainly incompatible with the provisions of the Treaty since, as the Court has already confirmed in other cases,[68] such a measure negates the very right conferred and guaranteed by the Treaty.[69]

The Court added that penalties, other than deportations, such as fines or detention were compatible with the Treaty if not disproportionate.

   Although this case thus limits the notion of discrimination, it is interesting to speculate whether the Court would have reached the same conclusions if its attention had not been drawn to Article 8(2) of Directive 360/68[70] and Article 4(2) of Directive 148/73.[71] Those provisions permitted the competent authorities of member states to require the nationals of other member states to report their presence, and the Court concluded on this account that an obligation to report could not in itself be regarded as an infringement of the rules of free movement. Indeed, the Court could hardly have held otherwise without impugning the validity of those parts of the Directives. This case is therefore an illustration of the fact that, even when establishing fundamental principles, the Treaty often provides little more than a framework within which the Council, as the principal legislative body, can operate in order to spell out the details. In the process it can introduce a degree of pragmatism and caution which enable practical realities to be taken into account.

   In *Sagulo, Brenca and Bakhouche*[72] the Court was asked about German penalties imposed on nationals of other member states for failure to acquire identity documents. The permissible penalties were more severe than in the case of German nationals who committed similar offences. In principle this looked like discrimination against foreign nationals. The Court however followed *Watson and Belmann*.[73] Its reasoning was that, since the requirement to obtain an identity document was expressly contained in Directive 360/68,[74] the power of member states to punish a breach of this

---

[68] See Case 48/75, *Royer* [1976] *ECR* 497.
[69] Case 118/75 [1976] *ECR* 1185, p. 1199.
[70] *OJ* 1968, L257/13.
[71] *OJ* 1973, L172/14.
[72] Case 8/77 [1977] *ECR* 1495.
[73] Case 118/75 [1976] *ECR* 1185.
[74] *OJ* 1968, L257/13.

requirement could not be contested. Some member states impose no corresponding obligation or penalties on their own nationals. There could not therefore be equality of treatment in those countries, and it would be equally wrong to require equality in others which had decided to punish their own nationals and foreigners, but the latter more severely. The Court did add a word of caution. The penalties must not be disproportionate, or 'so severe as to cause an obstacle to the freedom of entry and residence provided for in the Treaty'.[75] It is at present left to the national court to decide where to draw the line between proportionate and disproportionate, and between so severe as to cause an obstacle and not so severe.

Reverse discrimination

In connection with Article 48, as well as other provisions of the Treaty prohibiting discrimination on grounds of nationality, the question arises whether a member state infringes the Article if it treats its own nationals worse than those of other member states. The possibility that reverse discrimination might be prohibited by a number of Treaty provisions, including Articles 7 and 48, was considered by the Advocate General in *Peureux* v. *Services Fiscaux*,[76] where he reviewed the opinions of other Advocates General as well as his own previously stated views.[77] He also cited the following passage from the judgment of the Court in *Kenny* v. *Insurance Officer*:

By prohibiting every Member State from applying its law differently on the ground of nationality, within the field of application of the Treaty, Articles 7 and 48 are not concerned with any disparities in treatment which may result, between Member States, from divergences existing between the laws of the various Member States, so long as the latter affect all persons subject to them in accordance with objective criteria and without regard to their nationality.[78]

To take a concrete example, does Article 48(3)(*b*), while obliging the member state to permit free movement within its territory of workers who are nationals of other member states, nevertheless allow it to hinder the movement of its own nationals within those boundaries, for whatever reason it chooses? The language of Article 48, read on its own or with Article 7, and viewed in the light of the Advocate General's encouraging remarks, might have been interpreted as prohibiting even reverse discrimination of that kind. However, the Court decided otherwise in *R.* v. *Saunders*.[79] Vera Ann Saunders, a British national, was convicted of theft

---

[75] Case 8/77 [1977] *ECR* 1495, p. 1506.
[76] Case 86/78 [1979] *ECR* 897.
[77] Ibid., pp. 920–1.
[78] Case 1/78 [1978] *ECR* 1489, p. 1498.
[79] Case 175/78 [1979] *ECR* 1129.

and bound over, on condition that she went to Northern Ireland and did not return to England or Wales within three years. The European Court held that the Treaty had no application to a wholly domestic situation which fell outside the scope of the rules of free movement of workers.

At first sight this seems to rule out the possibility that any form of reverse discrimination is prohibited. But this does not necessarily flow from the 'dispositif'. It is true tht a wholly domestic situation will not fall within the ambit of Articles 7 and 48, whereas if the worker is a national of another member state it will. But some different kind of foreign factor may be present. If restrictions imposed by a member state inhibit its own nationals from working for a foreign employer, either at home or abroad,[80] or from working for another of its own nationals in a foreign country, what then is the position? The answer is not clear from the 'dispositif'. Is it possible that in some of these cases this form of discrimination against a state's own nationals is prohibited—not necessarily in order to protect the national workers themselves but to protect those persons from other member states who have an interest in the mobility of their labour? If that were the case it would not be clear what kind or degree of foreign element must be present. There would presumably in any event be a point beyond which the foreign factor was too remote to be protected. For example, it would surely be too remote if the prospective employer was a locally incorporated subsidiary of a foreign holding company.

However, although it is interesting to speculate about these possibilities, the Court's reasoning in the *Saunders* case[81] seems to indicate that the relevant foreign factor for the purposes of Article 48 is the nationality of the worker himself. The Court summarized the position in this way:

Under Article 7, any discrimination on grounds of nationality is prohibited within the scope of application of the Treaty and without prejudice to any special provisions contained therein. In application of that general principle, Article 48 aims to abolish in the legislation of the Member States provisions as regards employment, remuneration and other conditions of work and employment—including the rights and freedoms which that freedom of movement involves pursuant to Article 48(3)— according to which a worker who is a national of another Member State is subject to more severe treatment or is placed in an unfavourable situation in law or in fact as compared with the situation of a national in the same circumstances . . .

The provisions of the Treaty on freedom of movement for workers cannot therefore be applied to situations which are wholly internal to a Member State, in other words, where there is no factor connecting them to any of the situations envisaged by Community law.[82]

---

[80] But see Article 2(1) of Dir. 360/68, *OJ* 1968, L257/13.
[81] Case 175/78 [1979] *ECR* 1129.
[82] Case 175/78 [1979] *ECR* 1129, p. 1134.

MOVEMENT AND RESIDENCE

By virtue of Article 48(3)(*b*) EEC a worker is entitled, subject to limitations justified on grounds of public policy, public security, or public health, to move freely within the territory of member states in order to accept offers of employment actually made. Flesh is put onto these bones by Directive 360/ 68 on the abolition of restrictions on movement and residence within the Community for workers of member states and their families.[83] While this directive does not put the worker into quite the same position as the worker who wishes to move from Devon to Somerset, it does go some way towards ensuring that he can cross frontiers and settle where he chooses within the Community without being thwarted by undue formalities, paperwork, or other more serious obstacles.

The beneficiaries

Article 1 of the Directive defines the beneficiaries of this right of free movement as nationals of the member states and members of their families to whom Regulation 1612/68[84] applies. Since that Regulation was made under the powers conferred by Article 49 EEC, the nationals concerned must also be 'workers'. A person whose employers in one member state send him to work at one of their establishments in another falls squarely within Article 48(1). Somebody who goes to another member state to accept an offer of employment already made to him would equally clearly fall within Article 48(3)(a). But if he has lost his employment and wishes to go to another member state to seek a job, is he still a worker? If he has just left school, has never worked, and wishes to look for employment, is he entitled to take up residence in another member state for that purpose? It requires a fairly generous interpretation of the word 'worker' to answer these questions in the positive, particularly in the case of the schoolboy. Yet both these categories would seem to fall within the terms of the Court's *dictum* in *Royer*[85] which said:

(*a*) It follows from the foregoing that the right of nationals of a Member State to enter the territory of another Member State and reside there for the purposes intended by the Treaty—in particular to look for or pursue an occupation or activities as employed or self-employed persons, or to rejoin their spouse or family—is a right conferred directly by the Treaty, or, as the case may be, by the provisions adopted for its implementation.[86]

Moreover, once it is established that a person genuinely wishes to pursue an activity as an employed person, his motive for travelling to a particular member state for that purpose is irrelevant, as the Court made clear in *Levin* v. *Staatssecretaris van Justitie*.[87]

---

[83] *OJ* 1968, L257/13.
[84] *OJ*, Special Edition, 1968, p. 475.
[85] Case 48/75 [1976] *ECR* 497.
[86] Ibid., p. 512.
[87] Case 53/81 [1982] *ECR* 1035, p. 1053.

Article 10(1) of Regulation 1612/68[88] does not define a worker's family, but provides that the following persons have the right to install themselves with him when employed in the territory of another member state:

(*a*) his spouse and their descendants who are under the age of 21 years or are dependants;
(*b*) dependent relatives in the ascending line of the worker and his spouse.

Paragraph 2 of the Article goes on to extend the concept of 'family' for a limited purpose. It provides that member states are to 'facilitate' the admission of any other member of the family 'if dependent on the worker referred to above or living under his roof in the country whence he comes'. In each of these categories it is safe to assume that references to the masculine are deemed to include the feminine and accordingly women workers may take their husbands, whether dependent on their spouses or not. Whether a nephew who lives in a separate flat in the same building as the worker lives 'under his roof' is not entirely clear, although a teleological approach to the interpretation of the text would probably exclude him.

Preparing to travel and frontier formalities

Whatever else he may need to do to prepare for travel, a worker need not apply for an exit visa or any other kind of permission to leave the member state of which he is a national (Article 2(1) and (4) of Directive 68/360[89]). Acceptance of these provisions involved no change in its practice when the UK joined the Community, since exit visas and the like were not previously required. The worker will need to have, and the member state concerned must provide him with, an identity card or passport, showing in particular his nationality (Article 2(2) of the Directive). It is possible that the Crown's prerogative powers to grant or withhold passports in its absolute discretion may to some extent have been circumscribed by these provisions. A further constraint may be added by Section 2(1) of the European Communities Act 1972[90] if, as may well be the case, Article 2(2) of the Directive is regarded as having direct effect. It is not however entirely clear that the royal prerogative has been diminished in this way. The Directive allows either a passport or an identity card to be issued. Even if the UK would contravene the directive if it failed to provide either, it does not follow that this constraint removes the absolute power of the Crown to withhold a passport, because any breach of the directive could be remedied by the grant of an identity card. If an alleged breach of the Directive came to be tested in the courts of the UK, some interesting constitutional issues could arise. However, it should be remembered that Article 10 of the Directive

[88] *OJ*, Special Edition, 1968, p. 475.
[89] *OJ*, 1968, L257/13.
[90] 1972, c. 68.

allows derogations on grounds of public policy, public security, and public health, and that in practice the Crown only denies passports in certain very limited cases in which the public interest so demands.[91] A further development is the idea of introducing a 'European' passport. However, the Resolution of 23 June 1981[92] involves only the adoption of a more or less common format for documents which will remain national passports. Agreement on format will not affect the right of member states to continue to grant or withhold passports in accordance with their own national rules.

If the worker intends to travel by car to take up his new post in another member state he may avail himself of the benefits of Directive 166/72 on the approximation of the laws of member states relating to insurance against civil liability in respect of the use of motor vehicles, and to the enforcement of the obligation to insure against such liability.[93] The philosophy of the directive is explained in its preamble. Frontier checks on 'green cards' for vehicles normally based[94] in a member state could be abolished. National law should provide for the compulsory insurance of vehicles against civil liability, the insurance to be valid throughout Community territory. The directive proceeds to achieve that objective and to make special provision for certain exceptional cases.[95] After checking therefore that his car is insured in his home state, and if he is content to be covered only against 'third party' risks while travelling to his new job, the worker need take out no new car insurance until he has arrived, settled down, and sorted out what his insurance requirements will be in future.

On arrival at the frontier, by whatever mode of travel, the worker and his family should be faced with the minimum of formalities. According to Article 3 of Directive 360/68[96] they must be allowed to enter the member state's territory simply on production (at most) of a valid identity card or passport. Entry visas or the equivalent may not be demanded, except in the case of members of the worker's family who are not nationals of any member state (Article 3(2)). These provisions were interpreted by the Court in *R.* v. *Pieck*.[97] The accused was Dutch and was charged with having remained in the United Kingdom after the time allowed him. On arrival in the UK his passport had been endorsed with the words 'given leave to enter the United Kingdom for six months'. In the context of this endorsement, the Pontypridd Magistrates' Court asked the European

---

[91] For a list of these cases, see Hansard, House of Lords Debates, 22 Jan. 1981, col. 558.

[92] *OJ* 1981, C241/1.

[93] *OJ* 1972, L103/1, as amended by Dir. 72/430/EEC, *OJ* 1972, L291/162.

[94] See Case 64/83, *Bureau Central Français* v. *Fonds de Garantie Automobile* [1984] 2 *CMLR* 16.

[95] Supplemented by Commission Dec. 166/74, *OJ* 1974, L087/13; Commission Dec. 167/74, *OJ* 1974, L087/14; Commission Dec. 23/75, *OJ* 1975, L006/33. For an interpretation of Article 2(2) of the Directive in the case of stolen vehicles, see Case 116/83, *Bureau Belge* v. *Fantozzi* [1984] 3 *CMLR* 720.

[96] *OJ* 1968, L257/13.

[97] Case 157/79 [1980] *ECR* 2171.

Court first what was meant by 'entry visa or equivalent document' in Article 3(2) of Directive 68/360.[98] The European Court dismissed the argument of the UK Government to the effect that an entry visa or equivalent is something which is issued to a traveller before he arrives at the frontier. The Court held that the time of issue was immaterial. It defined 'entry visa or equivalent requirement' as:

any formality for the purpose of granting leave to enter the territory of a Member State which is coupled with a passport or identity card check at the frontier, whatever may be the place or time at which that leave is granted and in whatever form it may be granted.[99]

Residence permits and control of foreigners

The penultimate preambular paragraph of Directive 68/360[100] refers to bringing the position of workers from other member states into line, as far as possible, with that of nationals. Read in the light of this, Article 4 requires member states to issue to each worker or member of his family who is a national of another member state, and who is present in its territory, a 'residence permit' in the form prescribed in the Annex to the Directive. It is the only kind of residence permit which a member state can require the worker to have, and it replaces any general national permits issued to aliens: *R.* v. *Pieck*.[101] This special Community residence permit is to be given as proof of the right of residence, so that the worker can use the document to convince employers and others of his right to remain in the territory. But his right to reside stems from Community law, and not from the act of the host state in granting the residence permit. Put another way, his right to remain does not depend upon the issue of a residence permit or upon whether the member state in question is willing to comply with its obligation to give him this evidence of his rights.

In *Royer*[102] the Court referred to Article 48(3), Articles 1 and 10 of Regulation 1612/68,[103] Article 4 of Directive 360/68[104] and the preamble to Directive 148/73[105] (which requires a residence permit to be issued to self-employed persons from other member states who exercise their rights of establishment) before concluding that the right of residence was conferred by the Treaty and by the provisions adopted for its implementation, and not by the residence permit. It said:

It must therefore be concluded that this right is acquired independently of the issue of a residence permit by the competent authority of a Member State.

[98] *OJ* 1968, L257/13.
[99] Case 157/79 [1980] *ECR* 2171, p. 2188.
[100] *OJ* 1968, L257/13.
[101] Case 157/79 [1980] *ECR* 2171.
[102] Case 48/75 [1976] *ECR* 497.
[103] *OJ*, Special Edition, 1968, p. 475.
[104] *OJ* 1968, L257/13.
[105] *OJ* 1973, L172/14.

The grant of this permit is therefore to be regarded not as a measure giving rise to rights but as a measure by a Member State serving to prove the individual position of a national of another Member State with regard to provisions of Community law.[106]

That the residence permit is only to facilitate the free movement of workers, and that the procedure for its issue is not therefore to be used to hinder them, is further illustrated by Article 5 of Directive 360/68,[107] which provides that the formalities for its issue shall not hinder the commencement of employment.

A question which needs to be asked is whether the presence or absence of a residence permit, while amounting to evidence that a person is or is not a worker with the consequent right of residence, is also conclusive evidence. Neither the Treaty, nor the Directive, nor the decision in *Royer*,[108] gives an answer to that specific question. In principle, however, it would seem wrong to regard this particular form of evidence as conclusive, in the sense of being incapable of being rebutted by other evidence. It would be anomalous, for example, if a member state issued a residence permit in good faith, and then on discovering that the holder had made a fraudulent application for it, based on a forged certificate of employment, was not able to rebut the holder's claim to be a worker. A better view would seem to be that the existence of a residence permit, or its absence, gives rise to prima facie evidence of the status of the person concerned. As such it affects the burden of proof, so that once a permit has been issued, it is for the member state to rebut the presumption that the holder is a worker. Conversely, the burden is on the individual who does not hold a permit, either because he has never applied for one, or is not entitled to one, or has had one which has expired, to prove that notwithstanding those facts he is a worker, with the consequence that he is entitled to reside.

To obtain his residence permit the worker need produce only the document with which he entered the territory, and evidence from his employer that he is employed, or has been engaged as an employed person (Article 4(3) of Directive 68/360,[109] which also specifies the documentary evidence needed by members of the worker's family to prove their relationship, and, where relevant, their dependency). When granted, the permit must be valid throughout the territory of the member state which issued it (Article 6 of the Directive). If therefore Miss Saunders[110] had been a national of another member state it would have been necessary objectively to justify her confinement to Northern Ireland under one of the exceptions which are

[106] Case 48/75 [1976] *ECR* 497, p. 512. See also Case 118/75, *Watson* v. *Belmann* [1976] *ECR* 1185, p. 1197.
[107] *OJ* 1968, L257/13.
[108] Case 48/75 [1976] *ECR* 497.
[109] *OJ* 1968, L257/13.
[110] Case 175/78, *R.* v. *Saunders* [1979] *ECR* 1129.

considered later in this chapter. Special rules are contained in Article 8 of the Directive exempting short-term workers (where the work is not expected to last for more than three months), and frontier workers who commute across the border, from the need to have residence permits. The same rules, however, allow member states to require workers in this category to report their presence. The latter requirement has, as has already been seen, been accepted by the Court as a permissible discrimination against foreigners in *Watson and Belmann*.[111] The issue of residence permits and this requirement to report are the main means by which each member state is able to monitor the movement of workers from other member states, but they give no scope for impeding that movement.

In those cases where residence permits are required, their duration must not be for less than five years, after which they are automatically renewable (Article 6(1)(*b*) of Directive 68/360).[112] When renewed for the first time they may be restricted in time, but the period must still be not less than 12 months (Article 7(2) of the Directive). Article 7 of the Directive provides that if a person is temporarily incapable of work because of sickness or accident, or because he is *involuntarily* unemployed, his residence permit may not be withdrawn solely on these grounds. The Directive is silent about the case where a person voluntarily gives up his job, but seeks fresh employment. On the basis of the *dictum* in *Royer*[113] he would seem to be entitled to continue to reside, at least for a reasonable length of time and provided he makes genuine efforts to find employment. The difference between a person who is dismissed and a person who resigns is that the former is entitled to the residence permit which is prima facie evidence of his continued status as a worker, whereas the latter is not. The ultimate test, however, is whether, upon all the evidence available, the person concerned can be regarded as a genuine 'worker', for which purpose temporary periods of unemployment may be ignored.

Right to remain after employment ceases

Mention has already been made of the right of residence continuing in accordance with Article 7(1) of Directive 68/360.[114] These provisions are primarily designed to apply during periods of temporary unemployment which may occur during the course of a working life. More permanent situations are dealt with in Article 48(3) (EEC) and the regulations to which it refers. That paragraph provides that, subject to the usual limitations justified on grounds of public policy, public security, or public health, the right of free movement for workers entails the right to remain in the

---

[111] Case 118/75 [1976] *ECR* 1185.
[112] *OJ* 1968, L257/13.
[113] Case 48/75 [1976] *ECR* 497, p. 512, quoted above.
[114] *OJ* 1968, L257/13.

territory of a member state after having been employed in that state, subject to conditions to be included in implementing regulations drawn up by the Commission. Such regulations are contained in Commission Regulation 1251/70.[115] They deal mainly with retirement, permanent incapacity to work, and the right of the worker's family to remain in residence after his death, all on the basis of equality of treatment with national workers who have come to the end of their working lives. As in the case of Directive 68/360, 'family' is defined in Article 1 by reference to Article 10 of Regulation 1612/68,[116] which is discussed earlier in this chapter. Article 2 of the Directive gives the right of permanent residence in a member state to any worker who:

(*a*) when ceasing to work has already reached the national age for an old-age pension, having been employed there for at least the last year, and having resided there continuously for more than three years; or

(*b*) having resided continuously for more than two years stops work because of permanent incapacity, or, irrespective of his length of residence, suffers his incapacity as a result of his work; or

(*c*) after three years' continuous employment and residence starts to commute across the border of another Member State as a 'frontier worker'.

If a male worker marries a local girl he may escape the above provisions as to length of residence and employment (Article 2(2)). Once the worker has acquired the right of permanent residence, so too does his family, and the latter's right continues after his death (Article 3(1)). In some circumstances the family can continue to reside after his death even if the worker did not himself acquire the right to remain (Article 3(2)). The remainder of the Directive contains provisions dealing with interruptions of qualifying periods of residence, occasioned by short absences or military service (Article 4), periods within which the right to remain must be exercised (Article 5), acquisition of residence permits (Article 6), and the right to discriminate against one's own nationals by giving them less favourable treatment than nationals from other member states (Article 8(1)). Finally, the Directive contains special provisions in Article 9, based on the Protocol on the Grand Duchy of Luxembourg, which is annexed to the EEC Treaty.

EXCEPTIONS TO FREE MOVEMENT

The phrase 'limitations justified on grounds of public policy, public security or public health' appears only in the preambular part of paragraph (3) of Article 48. A straightforward literal interpretation of the Article therefore leads to the conclusion that these exceptions only apply to the application

---

[115] *OJ* 1970, L142/24. For the right to remain after being self-employed, see Dir. 34/75, *OJ* 1975, L14/10.

[116] *OJ* Special Edition, 1968, p. 475.

of the rights referred to in paragraph (3), i.e. broadly speaking, the right to accept offers of employment, to move freely between member states for the purpose, and to settle in any member state and to retire there. If that is so, the exceptions do not apply to the rule against discrimination based on nationality, which is in Article 48(2). This point arose in *Südmilch* v. *Ugliola*.[117] The German Government argued that they were entitled on grounds of public security to maintain their law which gave a certain benefit to workers whose employment was interrupted by service in the German armed forces, but not to workers in Germany who did military service in other member states. A preliminary question was therefore whether the exception of public security applied to matters falling within Article 48(2) but outside the scope of Article 48(3). The Advocate General said:

It is clear that all these situations deal with the search for employment and the right to carry on a trade or profession. On grounds of public policy or public security a foreigner may not be permitted to enter a country and take up employment there, but these considerations have no bearing on conditions of work once employment has been taken up in an authorized manner. In the field of remuneration, for example, no reason based on public policy or public security may cause a foreign worker to be treated differently from a national. This is a sphere in which the 'discrimination' allowed by Article 48(3) cannot operate.[118]

The Court's judgment, however, is not so clear on this point. After referring to the abolition in Article 48 of any discrimination based on nationality the Court said:

This provision is subject to no reservations other than the restriction set out in paragraph (3) concerning public policy, public security and public health.[119]

This could be read as suggesting that the exceptions do apply to Article 48(2). However, the Court proceeded to hold that the principle of equality of treatment (a reference to Article 48(2)) entitled the worker to have his period of military service in another member state taken into account in the same way as national workers. The Court made no specific reference to the arguments of the German Government. The Court has subsequently gone some way towards dispelling the uncertainty left by this judgment in the *Ugliola* case in *R.* v. *Pieck*[120] where in a similar passage it said:

Admittedly the right of entry for the workers in question is not unlimited. Nevertheless the only restriction which Article 48 of the Treaty lays down concerning freedom of movement in the territory of Member States is that of limitations justified on grounds of public policy, public security or public health. This restriction must be regarded not as a condition precedent to the acquisition of the right of

---

[117] Case 15/69 [1969] *ECR* 363.
[118] Ibid., p. 375.
[119] Ibid., p. 369.
[120] Case 157/79 [1980] *ECR* 2171.

entry and residence but as providing the posibility, in individual cases where there is sufficient justification, of imposing restrictions on the exercise of a right derived directly from the Treaty.[121]

This more general formulation is more readily reconciled with the views of the Advocate General in the *Ugliola* case.

These cases could be logically explained by the following interpretation of the interrelationship between paragraphs (2) and (3) of Article 48. Article 48(2) repeats a basic principle of non-discrimination which is stated more generally in Article 7, and which permeates the whole Treaty. The principle must be applied in a general way in the application of all provisions of the Treaty, including Article 48(3). It can only be displaced by clearly stated exceptions. Therefore as a general rule the provisions of sub-paragraphs (a)–(d) of Article 48(3) must be applied in such a way as to avoid discrimination on grounds of nationality. The application of those sub-paragraphs is however subject to exceptions justified on grounds of public policy, public security, or public health. If in any particular case an exception can be so justified, then the exception may be made even though this discriminates against nationals of other member states.[122]

An actual example was in *Van Duyn* v. *Home Office*[123] where public policy justified the exclusion of a Dutch national from entering the United Kingdom to take up an offer of employment, even though UK nationals were allowed to take up employment with the same organization. The Court so concluded because the facts fell within the scope of Article 48(3). It did however give as an added reason that, under international law, 'which the EEC Treaty cannot be assumed to disregard in relations between Member States', a state may not refuse entry and residence to its own nationals.[124] On the other hand, if a particular situation concerns the free movement of workers, but does not fall within the scope of any of sub-paragraphs (a)–(d) of Article 48(3) then Article 48(2) applies, and no exception can be made on grounds of public policy, public security or public health. An extreme example of the latter would be if a member state said that every foreign worker must work for nothing and for seven days every week. Such a policy would in effect negate free movement, contrary to Article 48(1), infringe the rule in Article 48(2), and be incapable of being defended on grounds of public policy, etc.

The importance of the word 'justified' in Article 48(3) is no less significant than it is in the case of Article 36. The member state may in the first

---

[121] Ibid., p. 2185.

[122] Case 41/74, *Van Duyn* v. *Home Office* [1974] *ECR* 1337, p. 1350. But see Case 36/75, *Rutili* v. *Minister for the Interior* [1975] *ECR* 1219, pp. 1236–7, which took account, inter alia, of Article 8 of Reg. 1612/68, *OJ*, Special Edition, 1968, p. 475.

[123] Case 41/74 [1974] *ECR* 1337.

[124] Ibid., p. 1351.

instance fix the bounds of public policy, public security, and public health, but it must be prepared to justify, on the basis of objective criteria the application of which can be tested in the courts, the limitations it chooses to impose. The Court summarized the position in *Van Duyn* v. *Home Office*:[125]

> The application of these limitations is, however, subject to judicial control, so that a Member State's right to invoke the limitations does not prevent the provisions of Article 48, which enshrine the principle of freedom of movement for workers, from conferring on individuals rights which are enforceable by them and which the national courts must protect.[126]

Even allowing for the existence of ultimate judicial control of what is to be interpreted as being justified on grounds of public policy, public security, and public health, it would have been possible for these escape routes to have allowed more departures from the principle of free movement than the Council would have wished. It accordingly adopted, on 25 February 1964, Directive 221/64 on the coordination of special measures concerning the movement and residence of foreign nationals which are justified on these grounds.[127]

This Directive adopts a somewhat restrictive interpretation of the individual exceptions, as will be seen later in this chapter. It also has some general provisions. Article 1 applies the Directive to any national of a member state who resides in or travels to another member state, either to pursue an activity as an employed or self-employed person, or as a recipient of services, as well as to his spouse and other members of his family.[128] Article 2 provides that exceptions based on public policy, public security, or public health shall not be invoked 'to service economic ends'. A decision to grant or refuse a first residence permit must be taken within six months after an application is made (Article 5). The person against whom one of the exceptions is invoked must be told the grounds, unless this is precluded by interests of state security (Article 6). He must be given at least fifteen days to pack up and go, and at least one month if he has a residence permit (Article 7). He must have the same legal remedies as are enjoyed by nationals of the state concerned in respect of acts of administration (Article 8). He must be given some rights of appeal, but these may in certain cases be no more than a right of recourse to a different administrative authority from the one which took the decision against him (Article 9).

---

[125] Case 41/74 [1974] *ECR* 1337.

[126] Ibid., p. 1347. The application of the limitations is also subject to control by the institutions of the Community: ibid., p. 1350.

[127] *OJ* Special Edition, 1963, p. 117. The Directive was extended by Dir. 35/75, *OJ* 1975, L14/14, to persons who exercise the right under Dir. 34/75, *OJ* 1975, L14/10, to remain after having been self-employed.

[128] See Art. 10 of Reg. 1612/68, *OJ* Special Edition, 1968, p. 475, on what constitutes 'family'.

Public policy

Article 3(1) of Directive 64/221[129] requires measures taken on grounds of public policy (or of public security) to be based exclusively on the personal conduct of the individual concerned. Article 3(2) provides that previous criminal convictions shall not in themselves constitute grounds for the taking of such measures.

The scope and effect of the duty to base a measure exclusively on the personal conduct of the individual was considered by the Court in *Van Duyn* v. *Home Office*.[130] In particular, was it a matter of personal conduct if the individual concerned was associated with an organization whose activities were considered by the member state to be contrary to the public good, although its operations were lawful? The Court was disinclined to regard a person's past association with such a body as amounting to personal conduct, but it accepted that present association did.[131] Moreover, a member state necessarily had 'an area of discretion within the limits imposed by the Treaty' in assessing, subject to the control of the Community institutions, the circumstances which justified recourse to the concept of public policy. This led the Court to say:

It follows from the above that where the competent authorities of a Member State have clearly defined their standpoint as regards the activities of a particular organization and where, considering it to be socially harmful, they have taken administrative measures to counteract these activities, the Member State cannot be required, before it can rely on the concept of public policy, to make such activities unlawful, if recourse to such a measure is not thought appropriate in the circumstances.[132]

In *Bonsignore* v. *Stadt Köln*[133] an Italian worker in Germany unlawfully possessed a firearm and accidentally killed his brother with it. He was found guilty of unlawful possession and of causing death by negligence. The Aliens Authority ordered his deportation. If only those facts had been presented by the national court to the European Court, and if Article 3(2) of Directive 64/221[134] had never been adopted, it may be that the European Court would not on the basis of Article 48(3) EEC have rejected a plea that the deportation was justified on grounds of public policy. However, the national court had to take into account Article 3(2) of the Directive, which requires something more than previous criminal convictions in order to justify reliance upon public policy. The added factor was that the deportation was considered desirable in order to deter other immigrants from

---

[129] *OJ*, Special Edition, 1963, p. 117.
[130] Case 41/74 [1974] *ECR* 1337.
[131] Ibid., p. 1349.
[132] Ibid., p. 1350.
[133] Case 67/74 [1975] *ECR* 297.
[134] *OJ*, Special Edition, 1963, p. 117.

illegally possessing firearms, in view of the resurgence of violence in the German cities. In its preliminary ruling on this aspect, however, the European Court held that Article 3(1) and (2) of the Directive prevented the deportation of a national of a member state if it was ordered for the purpose of deterring other aliens. The desire to deter others was extraneous to the individual case and could not be regarded as 'personal conduct' of the worker.

The importance of the restriction in Article 3(2) of Directive 64/221,[135] i.e. that criminal convictions are 'in themselves' not enough to justify expulsion, was underlined in *R.* v. *Bouchereau*.[136] A French worker in the UK was convicted of two drug offences, the second within six months after the first. The magistrate was minded to recommend his deportation, but first sought a preliminary ruling from the European Court on the meaning of the words 'in themselves'. Did they leave the national court free to regard previous convictions as evidence of likely future conduct? The European Court considered that a member state in each case needed to carry out a specific assessment of what was required by public policy— which might or might not coincide with what was required to support a criminal conviction. In short:

> The existence of a previous criminal conviction can, therefore, only be taken into account in so far as the circumstances which gave rise to that conviction are evidence of personal conduct constituting a present threat to the requirements of public policy.[137]

During the course of its judgment the Court also took the bold step of defining 'public policy' for the purposes of Article 48(3). The Court first recalled its earlier decision in *Van Duyn* v. *Home Office*[138] that the concept of public policy must be interpreted strictly, since it derogated from a fundamental principle of free movement, and must be subject to control by Community institutions. The Court also repeated the view that public policy could justifiably be invoked in circumstances which varied from country to country, and from one period to another. The minimum elements required to enable an exception to be made on grounds of public policy were:

> In so far as it may justify certain restrictions on the free movement of persons subject to Community law, recourse by a national authority to the concept of public policy presupposes, in any event, the existence, in addition to the perturbation to the social order which any infringement of the law involves, of a genuine and sufficiently serious threat affecting one of the fundamental interests of society.[139]

---

[135] Ibid.
[136] Case 30/77 [1977] *ECR* 1999.					[137] Ibid., p. 2012.
[138] Case 41/74 [1974] *ECR* 1337, p. 1350.					[139] Case 30/77 [1977] *ECR* 1999, p. 2015.

This formulation shows that, whatever may be the extent or limits of the concept in national law of 'public policy', 'ordre public', etc., nevertheless Community law requires certain irreducible elements to be present. Having thus narrowed the concept of public policy, the Court at the same time attributed a wide meaning to the word 'measures', as used in the expression 'Measures taken on grounds of public policy . . .' in Article 3(1) of Directive 221/64.[140] It included a recommendation by a UK court to the Home Secretary that an alien should be deported. The national court was therefore obliged, before making any such recommendation, to take into account the provisions of the Directive, and to ensure that it was correctly applied.

Public policy may justify not only a refusal to admit a national of another member state (*Van Duyn* v. *Home Office*[141]) or a decision to expel him (*R.* v. *Bouchereau*[142]). It may also, subject to stringent conditions, afford grounds for refusing to allow him to move freely within the territory of a member state, even though he has been offered employment in a place from which he is excluded, and not withstanding Article 48(3)(*b*). An obvious case would be where a worker who is convicted of a criminal offence is either imprisoned, or required to report regularly to a probation officer in a particular district. A more difficult situation was considered in *Rutili* v. *Minister for the Interior*.[143] In that case an Italian national, born and bred in France, engaged in trade union activities in one French department. The French Minister for the Interior prohibited him from residing in that department or in adjacent departments. He then applied for, and was given, a residence permit as a national of a member state, but the permit contained the same residence restrictions. He sought an annulment of these territorial restrictions. On a reference under Article 177, the national court first asked whether the expression 'subject to limitations justified on grounds of public policy', in Article 48, concerned merely legislative decisions or whether it also concerned individual decisions in the application of legislation. The European Court replied that it also concerned individual decisions. The second question asked about the meaning of 'justified' in the same phrase. The Court answered that question at length. First, the limitation must 'fulfil the requirements of the law, including those contained in Community law'.[144] From this it appears that there must first of all be some provision of national law, the application of which requires the limitation to be imposed. Secondly, there must be a 'genuine and sufficiently serious threat to public policy'[145] (a phrase to be echoed later in *R.*

[140] *OJ*, Special Edition, 1963, p. 117.
[141] Case 41/74 [1974] *ECR* 1337.
[142] Case 30/77 [1977] *ECR* 1999.
[143] Case 36/75 [1975] *ECR* 1219.
[144] Ibid., p. 1230.
[145] Ibid., p. 1231.

v. *Bouchereau*[146]), and the decision must not be invoked to service economic ends, must be based on the individual circumstances of the person concerned (Articles 2 and 3 of Directive 64/221[147]), and must not infringe Article 8 of Regulation 1612/68[148] which requires equality of treatment with nationals of the state concerned as regards trade union activities. The Court finally ruled:

An appraisal as to whether measures designed to safeguard public policy are justified must have regard to all rules of Community law the object of which is, on the one hand, to limit the discretionary power of Member States in this respect and, on the other, to ensure that the rights of persons subject thereunder to restrictive measures are protected . . .

In particular, measures restricting the right of residence which are limited to part only of the national territory may not be imposed by a Member State on nationals of other Member States who are subject to the provisions of the Treaty except in the cases and circumstances in which such measures may be applied to nationals of the State concerned.[149]

The last sentence in the ruling is not easy to reconcile with the *Van Duyn* case,[150] where on grounds of public policy the exclusion from an activity of a foreign national was justified, although a national of the state concerned could lawfully have engaged in the same activity. One difference was that in the *Rutili* case[151] there was a rule of secondary legislation (Article 8 of Regulation 1612/68[152]) which specifically ousted any discrimination on grounds of nationality in matters concerning the activities of trade unions. This difference is however more apparent than real, because in view of Articles 7 and 48(2) EEC Article 8 of Regulation 1612/68 ought to be regarded as having been included only *ex abundanti cautela*. One clue to the way in which the two cases could be reconciled lies in the reference in the *Van Duyn* case[153] to the 'principle of international law, which the EEC Treaty cannot be assumed to disregard in the relations between Member States, that a state is precluded from refusing its own nationals the right of entry or residence'.[154] No such consideration applied to restrictions on movement within a member state. Thus in *Rutili*[155] there was no compelling reason to allow discrimination on grounds of nationality, whereas in *Van Duyn* there was. In the latter case, therefore, it was justifiable on

---

[146] Case 30/77 [1977] *ECR* 1999.
[147] *OJ*, Special Edition, 1963, p. 117.
[148] *OJ*, Special Edition, 1968, p. 475.
[149] Case 36/75 [1975] *ECR* 1219, pp. 1236–7.
[150] Case 41/74 [1974] *ECR* 1337.
[151] Case 36/75 [1975] *ECR* 1219.
[152] *OJ*, Special Edition, 1968, p. 475.
[153] Case 41/74 [1974] *ECR* 1337.
[154] Ibid., p. 1351.
[155] Case 36/75 [1975] *ECR* 1219.

grounds of public policy to refuse entry to an alien, because although this involved some discrimination on grounds of nationality there was no unnecessary degree of discrimination.

The extent to which discrimination against aliens is allowed in this sort of case was explained further in *Adoui and Cornouaille* v. *Belgian State*.[156] Each of the plaintiffs worked in a bar in which waitresses displayed themselves in the window and which was suspected from the point of view of morals. Prostitution as such was not prohibited by Belgian law, although certain ancillary activities were. The national court asked various questions, the essence of which was to determine whether a member state could refuse admission to, or expel, a national of another member state on grounds of public policy, by reason of activities which did not give rise to repressive measures against the former state's own nationals. The European Court (without actually referring to the *Van Duyn* case[157]) said first:

The reservations contained in Articles 48 and 56 of the EEC Treaty permit Member States to adopt, with respect to the nationals of other Member States and on the grounds specified in those provisions, in particular grounds justified by the requirements of public policy, measures which they cannot apply to their own nationals, inasmuch as they have no authority to expel the latter from the national territory or to deny them access thereto.[158]

The Court went on to indicate that although this sort of difference of treatment was permissible, the member state must not allow the application of an arbitrary distinction to the detriment of nationals of other member states. It ruled:

A Member State may not, by virtue of the reservation relating to public policy contained in Articles 48 and 56 of the Treaty, expel a national of another Member State from its territory or refuse him access to its territory by reason of conduct which, when attributable to the former State's own nationals, does not give rise to repressive measures or other genuine and effective measures intended to combat such conduct.[159]

This ruling appears to place an important restriction on the principle established in the Court's decision in *Van Duyn*.[160] It seems to demonstrate that if the facts of the latter case were to be repeated, the member state refusing entry would only be able to defend itself successfully if it could satisfy the Court that, although it placed no restriction on its own nationals who wished to take up the employment in question, it did nevertheless take some steps to repress the activities which it found socially harmful and on which it based its decision to exclude the alien.

[156] Joined Cases 115 and 116/81 [1982] 3 *CMLR* 631.
[157] Case 41/74 [1974] *ECR* 1337.
[158] Joined Cases 115 and 116/81 [1982] 3 *CMLR* 631, p. 661.
[159] Ibid., p. 665.   [160] Case 41/74 [1974] *ECR* 1337.

Public health

Article 4 of Directive 221/64[161] provided that the only diseases or disabilities justifying refusal of entry or refusal of a residence permit were to be those listed in the annex to the Directive. The annex is in two parts. The first lists various infectious or contagious diseases which might endanger public health. The second lists diseases and disabilities (e.g. drug addiction or profound mental disturbance) which, while not being a danger to public health in the sense of being infectious or contagious, might threaten public policy or public security. Article 6 of the Directive requires the person concerned to be informed of the public health grounds (or grounds of public policy or public security) on which he is refused entry or a residence permit 'unless this is contrary to the interests of the security of the state involved'. The circumstances in which the latter proviso could be applied in a public health case is not clear.

Public security

The main restriction on the use of this exception is contained in Article 3 of Directive 221/64,[162] which requires measures taken on grounds of public security (as well as public policy) to be based exclusively on the personal conduct of the individual concerned. It has already been considered in relation to public policy.

The Court seems to have laid the foundations of another restriction in its judgment in *Rutili* v. *Minister of the Interior*.[163] In that case the Court once more drew inspiration from European treaties in the field of human rights.[164] The case was concerned with public policy rather than security, but the Court held that the limitation on grounds of public policy on the powers of member states to control aliens was a specific manifestation of a more general principle enshrined in Articles 8, 9, 10, and 11 of the Convention for the Protection of Human Rights and Fundamental Freedoms, signed in Rome on 4 November 1950, and in Article 2 of Protocol No. 4 to the same convention, signed in Strasbourg on 16 September 1963. The Court also went on to point out that, according to these provisions, no restrictions in the interests of national security (or public safety) could be placed on the rights secured by those Articles other than such as are necessary for the protection of those interests 'in a democratic society'.[165] It may be that the Court regards this as part of the law the observance of which it is obliged by Article 164 EEC to ensure. If that proves to be so, it will in future only be possible to rely on public security if to do so would be necessary in a democratic society.

---

[161] *OJ*, Special Edition, 1963–4, p. 117.   [162] Ibid.
[163] Case 36/75 [1975] *ECR* 1219.
[164] See also Case 4/73, *Nold* v. *Commission* [1974] *ECR* 491, p. 507.
[165] Case 36/75 [1975] *ECR* 1219, p. 1232.

Public service

Article 48(4) EEC states that the provisions of Article 48 shall not apply to employment in the public service. Its counterpart in the chapter on Right of Establishment (Articles 52–8) is Article 55, first sentence. The two Articles are however drafted in quite different terms. The former refers to 'employment in the public service' whereas the latter refers to activities 'connected, even occasionally, with the exercise of official authority'. The strict constructionalist would argue that the two Articles are therefore intended to have a different scope, and that there is no reason to import the wording of the latter into the former. The argument would continue that the concept of 'public service' need not be confined to those forms of public service which, in the words of Article 55, involve the exercise of public authority. On the other hand, those who would wish to restrict the scope of any exception to the rules of free movement would argue that the objective of the two Articles was similar, and that Article 48(4) should by analogy with Article 55 indeed be interpreted as relating only to those employees in the public service who exercise public authority. It would be more difficult to argue conversely that Article 55 should by analogy with Article 48(4) be regarded as extending only to those persons exercising official authority who are employed in the public service, since the establishment chapter relates to the self-employed.

The Court considered the scope of Article 48(4) in *Sotgiu* v. *Deutsche Bundespost*.[166] It did not define 'the public service' but it did define the extent of the exception, and did so restrictively. The Court concluded that the purpose of Article 48(4) would be served by allowing member states to restrict the 'admission of foreign nationals to certain activities in the public service'.[167] It went on, however, to say:

On the other hand this provision cannot justify discriminatory measures with regard to remuneration or other conditions of employment against workers once they have been admitted to the public service. The very fact that they have been admitted shows indeed that those interests which justify the exceptions to the principle of non-discrimination permitted by Article 48(4) are not at issue.[168]

It therefore seems that in the case of the public service Article 48(4) provides an escape route from the obligation to allow nationals of other member states to take up employment. It may also allow such a national to be dismissed if changes take place in the nature of his employment, so that, having originally been outside the public service, the employment subsequently comes within it. Such a change might conceivably occur in the event of an activity being brought within the public domain.[169]

---

[166] Case 152/73 [1974] *ECR* 153.   [167] Ibid., p. 162.   [168] Ibid.

[169] Conversely, the application of Article 48(4) may become no longer appropriate if an activity passes into the private domain.

But apart from such theoretical possibilities Article 48(4) seems to provide little, if any, further scope for evading the principle of free movement enshrined in Article 48. The real difficulty left by the *Sotgiu* case was to know what is meant by 'the public service'. There is no ground for saying that this means service by persons who under some, but not all, of the laws of the member states have a special status such as 'fonctionnaires'. So much the Court made clear in its judgment when it said:

it is of no interest whether a worker is engaged as a workman ['ouvrier'], a clerk ['employé'] or an official ['fonctionnaire'] or even whether the terms on which he is employed come under public or private law.[170]

The Court did not however give positive guidance as to what the expression 'the public service' meant, in spite of submissions by the Commission and the Advocate General. The Court had been invited by the Commission to say that Article 48(4) applied as a general rule (although not exclusively) to persons usually entrusted with powers involving the exercise of public authority.[171] The Advocate General had advised more categorically that Article 48(4) was intended to enable member states to reserve to their own nationals 'such of the public appointments as put those who held them in a position to participate directly in the exercise of public authority'.[172]

An opportunity to consider the matter again arose in *Commission* v. *Belgium*.[173] Belgian nationality was required for a wide variety of posts with Belgian local authorities and public undertakings, ranging from unskilled railway workers to garden hands and children's nurses. The Commission argued that Article 48(4) covered the holders of posts which 'put the holders thereof in the position of directly participating in the exercise of official authority or of making use of prerogatives in the nature of powers conferred by public law in regard to members of the public'.[174] They therefore once more resorted to the language of Article 55. Again the Court shied away from it, and said of Article 48(4):

That provision removes from the ambit of Article 48(1) to (3) a series of posts which involve direct or indirect participation in the exercise of powers conferred by public law and duties designed to safeguard the general interests of the State or of other public authorities. Such posts in fact presume on the part of those occupying them the existence of a special relationship of allegiance to the State and reciprocity of rights and duties which form the foundation of the bond of nationality.[175]

The Court's formulation does however coincide with the Commission's views to the extent that it requires an appraisal of the post in question,

[170] Case 152/73 [1974] *ECR* 153, p. 163.
[171] Ibid., p. 160.
[172] Ibid., p. 170.
[173] Case 149/79 [1980] *ECR* 3881.
[174] Ibid., p. 3886.
[175] Ibid., p. 3900.

rather than an assessment of the institution as a whole and its functions. On the other hand this approach, which means that some posts within an organization may be in the public service and some may not, leaves open the possibility of blocking an alien's promotion, or transfer to other duties within the organization in question, when this would adversely affect the general interests of the state. Following the Court's judgment, difficult questions may arise when seeking to determine whether the incumbent of a particular post participates 'indirectly' in the powers to which the Court refer. The Court itself recognized that there could be difficulties in applying its interpretation of Article 48(4).[176] Nor did it have sufficient information to decide which of the posts in issue were covered by the exception and which were not. It accordingly ordered the Commission and Belgium to re-examine the issue in the light of the Court's interim judgment and to report back to the Court. This procedure resulted in a second and final judgment by the Court.[177] Since the two parties had by that stage agreed (rightly in the Court's view)[178] that the posts of head technical office supervisor, principal supervisor, works supervisor, stock controller, and nightwatchman with the municipality of Brussels, and the post of architect with the municipalities of Brussels and Auderghem, might fall within the exception of Article 48(4), those posts were no longer in issue. The Court held Belgium to have failed to fulfil its obligations under the Treaty in respect of all the other posts. Unfortunately the separate reports given to the Court by Belgium and the Commission are not reproduced in the report of the judgment, and it is therefore difficult to see what factors led the authorities and the Court to put the posts into one category or the other. Further litigation in this sphere may therefore in practice prove to be necessary, before the position is fully clarified.

DIRECT EFFECT

Like many other provisions of the Treaty, Article 48 provides a framework of principles within which more detailed rules can be developed through secondary legislation. During this process the Court was inevitably asked about the extent to which the Article and the secondary legislation had direct effect. It soon became apparent from the Court's decisions that the principle of freedom of movement, which Article 48(1) required to be secured by the end of the transitional period at the latest, was to be protected as effectively as possible by the national courts.

In *Rutili* v. *Minister for the Interior*[179] the Court had the opportunity to consider paragraphs (1) to (3) of Article 48, Regulation 1612/68,[180] Directive

---

[176] Ibid.
[177] Case 149/79, *Commission* v. *Belgium* [1982] *ECR* 1845.
[178] Ibid., p. 1851.
[179] Case 36/75 [1975] *ECR* 1219.   [180] *OJ*, Special Edition, 1968, p. 475.

221/64,[181] and Directive 360/68.[182] The Court dispelled any possible argument that whereas the rules of free movement might have direct effect, the exceptions in Article 48(3) based on public policy, public security, and public health were for the member states themselves to determine without judicial interference. The Court, in answer to a question about whether the exceptions covered individual as well as legislative decisions, went out of its way to point out that all the provisions in question, including those in Directive 64/221 concerning these exceptions, came within the protection of the national courts, i.e. had direct effect. It said:

Inasmuch as the object of the provisions of the Treaty and of secondary legislation is to regulate the situation of individuals and to ensure their protection, it is also for the national courts to examine whether individual decisions are compatible with the relevant provision of Community law.

This applies not only to the rules prohibiting discrimination and those concerning freedom of movement enshrined in Articles 7 and 48 of the Treaty and in Regulation No 1612/68, but also to the provisions of Directive No 64/221, which are intended both to define the scope of the reservation concerning public policy and to ensure certain minimal procedural safeguards for persons who are the subject of measures restricting their freedom of movement or their right of residence.[183]

The Court thus stopped short of holding that all the provisions of Directive 64/221 had direct effect. In addition to those provisions described by the Court, the Directive also contains some provisions which would not normally fall within the Court's criteria for deciding whether a rule of Community law has direct effect.[184] An example is Article 5(2), which says that a member state may ask another for information concerning any previous police record. In the *Van Duyn* case the Court confined itself to holding that Article 3(1) of the Directive had direct effect.[185] In later decisions the Court seemed to regard the secondary legislation not so much as having direct effect itself but rather as spelling out the meaning and effect of Article 48, and the Court emphasized the direct effect of the latter. Thus in *Royer*[186] the Court described Article 48(1), (2), and (3) as having:

the effect of conferring rights directly on all persons falling within the ambit of the above-mentioned articles, as later given closer articulation by regulations or directives implementing the Treaty.[187]

The concept of Article 48 being given 'closer articulation' by the secondary legislation was repeated in *Watson and Belmann*.[188] However, in *Sagulo*[189] the

---

[181] *OJ*, Special Edition, 1963–4, p. 117.
[182] *OJ*, Special Edition, 1968 (II), p. 485.   [183] Case 36/75 [1975] *ECR* 1219, p. 1229.
[184] For a statement of these criteria see the Advocate General's opinion in Case 41/74, *Van Duyn* v. *Home Office* [1974] *ECR* 1337, p. 1354.   [185] Ibid., p. 1349.
[186] Case 48/75 [1976] *ECR* 497.   [187] Ibid., p. 511.
[188] Case 118/75 [1976] *ECR* 1185, p. 1197. See also Case 1/78, *Kenny* v. *Insurance Officer* [1978] *ECR* 1489, p. 1499.   [189] Case 8/77 [1977] *ECR* 1495.

Court reverted to the notion that both the Treaty and the relevant secondary legislation (in that case Articles 2 and 4 of Directive 68/360) have direct effect, when stating that the rights of nationals of a member state followed 'directly from the Treaty, or, as the case may be, from the provisions adopted for its implementation'.[190]

Article 48(4) seems to have been considered by the Advocate General in *Sotgiu* v. *Deutsche Bundespost*,[191] to have direct effect, so that individuals could ask the national courts to determine whether there was or was not a public service exception which limited their right of free movement, and the national courts could in turn seek rulings from the European Court. He said:

Article 48(4) seems to me to require an interpretation which is both strict and uniform in each of these States, thus excluding the possibility of referring for this purpose to national criteria.[192]

In other words, the national court making the reference under Article 177 should not look to national laws to determine whether a post was in the public service, but should determine the applicant's rights by reference to Article 48(4) as interpreted by the European Court.

When a Community law has direct effect, it would be misleading to the general public for a member state to maintain on its statute book an inconsistent law, even though the former took precedence over the latter. The Court condemned this practice in *Commission* v. *France*.[193] It follows that if a national law is found to conflict with Article 48 or with those provisions of Community law which have given it closer articulation, the only safe course is to repeal the national law, rather than give administrative instructions to disregard it, or leave it to the national courts to ensure that Community law prevails.

SOCIAL SECURITY

In an ideal common market, where workers enjoyed completely free and uninhibited movement, it is possible to envisage a comprehensive Community system of social security, under which all workers throughout the Community would pay subscriptions on a uniform scale to the Community, and they and their families would receive from the Community the same social benefits upon satisfying the same conditions. Wherever he went, and for however long he stayed, the worker's contributions to the Community, and the scale of benefits received, would remain the same. Movement from one member state to another would therefore involve no changes in his

[190] Ibid., p. 1503.
[191] Case 152/73 [1974] *ECR* 153.
[192] Ibid., p. 169.
[193] Case 167/73 [1974] *ECR* 359, pp. 372–3.

position with regard to social security. It has been accepted so far, however, that such a system is impractical. Owing to the wide diversity of the details of the various social security schemes in operation in the various member states, both before and after the enlargement of the Community, a Community scheme which adopted the most favourable national scheme as its model would have involved considerable financial burdens for the other member states, whereas anything less would have meant a diminution of the standard of living of some workers, in direct contravention of one of the basic aims of the Community as expressed in Article 2.

The general scheme

The solution adopted in Article 51 was more practical, more modest in its goal, and at the same time considerably more complex in its application, than an exclusively Community system would have been. The simple underlying principle is that national systems of social security are retained, but they are co-ordinated so that, generally speaking, the migrant worker continues to be credited with past subscriptions, wherever within the Community they were made, and he continues to be entitled to appropriate benefits. Article 51 expresses the principle in the following terms:

The Council shall, acting unanimously on a proposal from the Commission, adopt such measures in the field of social security as are necessary to provide freedom of movement for workers; to this end, it shall make arrangements to secure for migrant workers and their dependants:

(*a*) aggregation, for the purpose of acquiring and retaining the right to benefit and of calculating the amount of benefit, of all periods taken into account under the laws of the several countries;

(*b*) payment of benefits to persons resident in the territories of Member States.

The basic secondary legislation is Regulation 1408/71 on the Application of Social Security Schemes to Employed Persons and their Families Moving within the Community, as subsequently amended.[194] The need for this regulation to contain 100 Articles and seven annexes in itself illustrates the complexity of the Council's task in seeking to give effect to Article 51 EEC. It is not surprising that the Regulation, its predecessor (Regulation No. 3)[195] and the implementing Regulation 574/72,[196] have in turn given rise to a considerable volume of litigation in the European Court, much of it on points of fine detail. Only some of the more important of these cases will be considered in this chapter.

---

[194] A consolidated text of the Regulation, incorporating all previous amendments, is set out in Annex I to Reg. 2001/83, *OJ* 1983, L230/6. References in this chapter to Reg. 1408/71 are to the Regulation as amended.

[195] Ibid., Annex II.

[196] *OJ* 1972, L74/1, as amended (see Reg. 3795/81, *OJ* 1981, L378/1). References to Reg. 574/72 are to the amended Regulation.

The Court set out its ground rules for the handling of these cases in *Kals-beek* v. *Sociale Verzekeringsbank*[197] as follows:

By the said Article 177 the Court, when giving a preliminary ruling, is entitled only to pronounce on the interpretation of the Treaty and of acts of the institutions of the Community, but can neither apply them to a particular case nor give judgment by means of this Article on the propriety of a measure of a domestic character. It is only subject to this provision that the Court can accept the questions submitted to it in this case.[198]

Adherence to this principle is particularly important when most of the substantive rules are to be found in national legislation, and the Community role, as codified in Regulation 1408/71, is one of co-ordination.

The Community system of co-ordination was described by the Court in *De Moor* v. *Caisse De Pension*[199] in the following terms:

Regulation No 3 did not provide for a common system of social security giving the beneficiary a single entitlement based on a simple apportionment of such benefits between national institutions, but allowed separate systems to continue, creating separate claims against separate institutions against which the beneficiary has direct rights either under national law alone or national law supplemented, if necessary by the system of the aggregation of insurance periods provided for by Article 51 of the Treaty.[200]

It can thus be seen that one of the main aims is to leave each national social insurance scheme intact,[201] but to ensure that when that scheme makes benefits proportional to a particular period of time, for example, for which the applicant has resided in a particular territory or has contributed to a certain scheme, that time must be deemed to include all periods completed under the legislation of any other member state. If a worker therefore pays contributions in one member state for a year and then moves to another, pays a year's contributions in the latter member state and then makes a sickness claim against its fund, he must be allowed to claim on the basis of having made two years' contributions, notwithstanding any rule of national law to the contrary.

Although in this way a worker who moves within the Community is able to keep his accrued rights to social security benefits, the other side of the coin is that he ought not to receive overlapping benefits from different member states. For the latter reason such benefits should in general be limited to the greatest amount to which a worker would have been entitled from one of the member states if he had spent his working life there.[202] At

[197] Case 100/63 [1964] *ECR* 565.
[198] Ibid., p. 572.
[199] Case 2/67 [1967] *ECR* 197.
[200] Ibid., p. 207.
[201] See Case 275/81, *Koks* v. *Raad van Arbeid* [1982] *ECR* 3013, p. 3024.
[202] Preamble to Reg. 1408/71, *OJ*, Special Edition, 1971, p. 416.

the same time, if the application of national rules against overlapping produces results which are more favourable to the worker than the application of Community rules on apportionment and aggregation, it is the national rules which are to apply: *Romano* v. *Institut National*.²⁰³ Unemployment produces its own special problems. The unemployed worker who is drawing unemployment benefit may wish to go to another member state to seek employment, and for a limited period he should be able to draw the same unemployment benefit.²⁰⁴ His family too should not suffer on account of his travels, whether they accompany him or stay behind.

The persons and matters covered

Article 2 of Regulation 1408/71²⁰⁵ defines the persons covered in the following terms:

1. This Regulation shall apply to employed or self-employed persons who are or have been subject to the legislation²⁰⁶ of one or more Member States and who are nationals of one of the Member States or who are stateless persons or refugees residing within the territory of one of the Member States, as also to the members of their families²⁰⁷ and their survivors.

2. In addition, this Regulation shall apply to the survivors of employed or self-employed persons who have been subject to the legislation of one or more Member States, irrespective of the nationality of such employed or self-employed persons, where their survivors are nationals of one of the Member States, or stateless persons or refugees residing within the territory of one of the Member States.

3. This Regulation shall apply to civil servants and to persons who, in accordance with the legislation applicable, are treated as such, where they are or have been subject to the legislation of a Member State to which this Regulation applies.

Employed persons, self-employed persons, stateless persons, refugees, and members of the family are, inter alia, defined in Article 1. By virtue of Article 69 an 'employed' or 'self-employed' person may upon certain conditions be deemed to include an unemployed person who goes to one or more member states to seek employment.

A literal reading of paragraphs (1) and (2) of Article 2 of the Regulation might suggest that it applies to a worker and his survivors who have never been subject to the legislation of more than one member state, because they have spent all their lives in that state. However, for the Regulation to apply to the facts of any particular situation those facts must include a foreign element. This is for two reasons: first, because the detailed provisions of

---

²⁰³ Case 98/80 [1983] 2 *CMLR* 698, p. 717.
²⁰⁴ Preamble to Reg. 1408/71.
²⁰⁵ See n. 194 above.
²⁰⁶ See Case 143/79, *Margaret Walsh* v. *Insurance Officer* [1980] *ECR* 1639.
²⁰⁷ This includes a handicapped adult who is dependent upon a worker: Case 63/76, *Inzirillo* v. *Caisse Allocations Familiales Lyon* [1976] *ECR* 2057.

the regulation as a general rule refer to situations containing a foreign element, and secondly, because, even more generally, the Treaty does not apply to matters which are of concern only to one member state—as has been seen earlier in this chapter in relation to *R.* v. *Saunders*.[208] But the foreign element does not have to relate to the worker in question or to his movements. He could indeed have spent all his life in one member state, but his survivors would still fall within the provisions of Article 2(2) if their circumstances introduced the necessary foreign element. In *Laumann* v. *Landesversicherungsanstalt Rheinprovinz*[209] the Court, after referring to the fact that under Article 2 of the regulation both workers and their survivors are covered, said:

> The general terms in which those provisions are couched show that the application of the regulation is not limited to workers or their suvivors who have had employment in several Member States or who are, or have been, employed in one State whilst residing or having resided in another.

> Thus the regulation also applies when the residence in another Member State was not that of the worker himself but of a survivor of his.[210]

In that particular case the foreign element was introduced by the survivors changing their residence from Germany to Belgium.

To fall within the provisions of Article 2(1) of the Regulation the worker must not only be, or have been, subject to the legislation of one or more member states. He must also be a national of a member state, or a stateless person or a refugee as defined in Article 1. The reference to nationality presents no particular problem of interpretation since there are, as has already been seen, agreed definitions of nationality in the two difficult cases of the Federal Republic of Germany[211] and the UK.[212] A temporal doubt arose from the fact that the text of Article 2(1) speaks of persons who 'are or have been' subject to the legislation of a member state whereas it refers to persons who 'are' nationals of one of the member states. This doubt was dispelled by the Court in *Belbouab* v. *Bundesknappschaft*.[213] In that case an applicant who was French, because he had been born in Algeria, worked in France and Germany. He applied in Germany for a pension, but was rejected because by the time he applied Algeria had become independent and he had in consequence lost his French nationality. The Court however held that the material time at which such an applicant must satisfy the nationality test was the time when he completed the periods which qualified him for his pension under Article 94(2) of the Regulation and not the date when he applied for his pension.[214]

---

[208] Case 175/78 [1979] *ECR* 1129.
[209] Case 115/77 [1978] *ECR* 805.
[210] Ibid., p. 814.
[211] Cmnd. 7460, p. 171.
[212] *OJ* 1983, C231/1.
[213] Case 10/78 [1978] *ECR* 1915.
[214] Ibid., p. 1925.

The matters covered by the Regulation are set out in Article 4, which reads:

1. This Regulation shall apply to all legislation concerning the following branches of social security:
(*a*) sickness and maternity benefits;[215]
(*b*) invalidity benefits, including those intended for the maintenance or improvement of earning capacity;
(*c*) old-age benefits;[216]
(*d*) survivors' benefits;
(*e*) benefits in respect of accidents at work and occupational diseases;
(*f*) death grants;[217]
(*g*) unemployment benefits;[218]
(*h*) family benefits.[219]
2. This Regulation shall apply to all general and special social security schemes, whether contributory or non-contributory, and to schemes concerning the liability of an employer or ship owner in respect of the benefits referred to in paragraph 1.
3. The provisions of Title III of this Regulation shall not, however, affect the legislative provisions of any Member State concerning a ship owner's liability.
4. This Regulation shall not apply to social and medical assistance, to benefit schemes for victims of war or its consequences,[220] or to special schemes for civil servants and persons treated as such.[221]

One underlying difficulty in interpreting and applying Article 4 of the Regulation stems from the fact that it covers the specified items of social *security* (paragraph 1), but social *assistance* is excluded (paragraph 4), and yet to complicate matters further a migrant worker must enjoy the same social *advantages* as national workers (Article 7(2) of Regulation 1612/68).[222] The classification of 'security', 'assistance', and 'advantage' is not always easy, as the Court discovered in *Frilli* v. *Belgium*.[223] However, a good deal of the uncertainty as to what national schemes were covered by Article 4(1) and (2) has been removed by the declarations of the member states, made

---

[215] See Art. 1 (*t*) and the Court's interpretation of the term in Cases 14/72, *Helmut Heinze* v. *Landesversicherungsanstalt Rheinprovinz* [1972] *ECR* 1105, 15/72, *Land Niedersachsen* v. *Landesversicherungsanstalt* [1972] *ECR* 1127, and 16/72, *Allgemeine Ortskrankenkasse Hamburg* v. *Landesversicherungsanstalt Schleswig—Holstein* [1972] *ECR* 1141.
[216] See Case 1/72, *Frilli* v. *Belgium* [1972] *ECR* 457.
[217] See Art. 1 (*v*).
[218] See Case 39/76, *Mouthaan* [1976] *ECR* 1901.
[219] See Art. 1 (*u*).
[220] See Case 93/75, *Alderblum* [1975] *ECR* 2147; Case 9/78, *Directeur régional de la sécurité sociale de Nancy* v. *Gillard, etc.* [1978] *ECR* 1661; Case 139/82, *Paulo Piscitello* v. *Istituto Nazionale della Previdenza Sociale* [1983] *ECR* 1427.
[221] See Case 129/78, *Bestuur van de Sociale Verzekeringsbank* v. *Lohmann* [1979] *ECR* 853.
[222] *OJ*, English Special Edition, 1968, p. 475. See also Case 32/75, *Cristini* v. *SNCF* [1975] *ECR* 1085.
[223] Case 1/72 [1972] *ECR* 457, p. 465. The essential characteristic of social assistance is that it prescribes consideration of each individual case. See also Case 139/82, *Piscitello* v. *Istituto Nazionale della Previdenza Sociale* [1983] *ECR* 1427.

under Article 5 of the Regulation.[224] Those declarations are not always conclusive as to whether a national law falls within the scope of the Regulation (because the law deals with social security), or outside (because the law regulates social assistance). The Court, as a result of its judgment in *Beerens* v. *Rijksdienst voor Arbeidsvoorziening*,[225] has made it as easy as possible for the worker to establish that the Regulation applies. The Court said in that case:

The fact that a national law or regulation has not been specified in the declarations referred to in Article 5 of the regulation is not of itself proof that law or regulation does not fall within the field of application of the said regulation; on the other hand, the fact that a Member State has specified a law in its declaration must be accepted as proof that the benefits granted on the basis of that law are social security benefits within the meaning of Regulation No 1408/71.[226]

Equality of treatment

Article 3(1) of the Regulation reads:

Subject to the special provisions of this Regulation, persons resident in the territory of one of the Member States to whom this Regulation applies shall be subject to the same obligations and enjoy the same benefits under the legislation of any Member State as the nationals of that state.

In this Article, and others, one of the tests to be applied is that of 'residence', a notoriously difficult concept to interpret. The term is defined in Article 1(*h*) of the Regulation as 'habitual residence'. This definition at least excludes the casual visitor who on one occasion stays for a short period in a hotel. But what amounts to habitual residence is not much easier to determine than residence. The Court faced the task in *Angenieux* v. *Hakenberg*.[227] In that case a French national, whose permanent residence was in France, used to spend nine months of the year on business tours in Germany, where he had no fixed abode. The Court had to consider where was his 'permanent residence' for the purposes of Article 13 of Regulation No. 3,[228] as amended. Permanent residence was defined in Article 1(h) of that Regulation as 'the place where a person has his habitual residence'. The Court found it inappropriate for this purpose to take into account itinerant business-canvassing activities of an unstable nature.[229] The Court defined permanent residence in that context as 'the place in which the worker has established the permanent centre of his interests and to which he returns in the intervals between his tours' (i.e. France).[230]

---

[224] See *OJ* 1980, C139/1.
[225] Case 35/77 [1977] *ECR* 2249.
[226] Ibid., p. 2254. See also Case 237/78, *Palermo (née Toia)* [1979] *ECR* 2645, p. 2653.
[227] Case 13/73 [1973] *ECR* 935.   [228] *OJ* 1958, p. 561.
[229] Ibid., p. 951.   [230] Ibid., p. 952.

As has already been seen, the fundamental rule against discrimination on grounds of nationality, which is enshrined in Article 7 EEC, is given detailed expression in other parts of the Treaty and secondary legislation. Article 3(1) of Regulation 1408/71[231] is one such example. As might be expected from other contexts, the Court has been assiduous in condemning such discrimination in all its forms. In *CRAM* v. *Palermo (née Toia)*[232] the Court had to consider a French law which denied to an Italian mother resident in France a certain allowance. To qualify under the law for the allowance the woman had to be over 65, French, and of insufficient means, having brought up at least five dependent children, all of whom had to be French. After indicating that the matter was covered by the Regulation (which applies to old-age benefits under national security schemes) and that the mother was covered by Article 2(1) of the Regulation (which applies to members of a worker's family or the survivors) the Court then interpreted the rule of equal treatment as preventing not only direct discrimination against the mother on account of her nationality but also indirect discrimination against her on account of the nationality of her children. Provided the mother and children were nationals of a member state, the rule in Article 3(1) of the Regulation applied. The Court's reasoning was as follows:

In this regard, it must be observed that the rules on equality of treatment, laid down by Article 3(1) of the regulation, prohibit not only patent discrimination, based on the nationality of the beneficiaries of social security schemes, but also all disguised forms of discrimination which, by the application of other distinguishing criteria, lead in fact to the same result.

A condition concerning the nationality of the children, such as that imposed by the applicable French legislation, is capable of leading in fact to the result that a mother of foreign nationality may benefit from the allowance only in exceptional cases. In particular she will be at a disadvantage in relation to mothers who are nationals of the State of residence when the nationality of the children depends in principle on that of the parents under the legislation of the country of origin and of the country of residence, as is the case with the Italian and French legislation in this regard.

Therefore the condition concerning the nationality of the children must be regarded as indirect discrimination, unless it was justified by objective differences.[233]

An example of the wide scope of the rule of equal treatment can be found in *Inzirillo* v. *Caisse Allocations Familiales Lyon*,[234] which concerned a French benefit for handicapped adults, applicable only to French nationals. An Italian worker's son was an adult who was handicapped, had never worked,

---

[231] See n. 194 above.
[232] Case 237/78 [1978] *ECR* 2645.
[233] Ibid., p. 2653.
[234] Case 63/76 [1976] *ECR* 2057.

and had always in fact been dependent upon his father. It appears that under French law a person over the age of 20 could not be regarded as a dependent child for social security purposes, and the allowance, when payable, went to the handicapped adult himself and not to the worker upon whom he was dependent.[235] The Court gave a liberal interpretation of Article 3 of Regulation 1408/71 by holding that, when a handicapped child qualified for benefits as a member of the worker's family, the rule of equality of treatment did not terminate when he ceased to be a minor, if the handicap prevented him from himself acquiring the status of a worker.[236] Otherwise, so the Court reasoned, the worker parent would be induced to leave the member state where he had established himself, and this would run counter to the principle of freedom of movement for workers.[237]

The result of this overriding rule of equal treatment is that whenever Regulation 1408/71[238] refers to the legislation of member states (as for example in Article 4) it means that legislation after this rule, and indeed also the other rules of Community law, have been incorporated in it: *Sociale Verzekeringsbank* v. *Smieja*.[239]

Once a worker who is resident in a member state has benefited from his right of equal treatment, and has earned an invalidity or old-age benefit for himself or cash benefits for his survivors, these will not be affected if he then takes up residence in another member state,[240] because Article 10(1) of the Regulation provides:

Save as otherwise provided in this Regulation, invalidity, old age or survivors' cash benefits, pensions for accidents at work or occupational diseases and death grants acquired under the legislation of one or more Member States shall not be subject to any reduction, modification, suspension, withdrawal or confiscation by reason of the fact that the recipient resides in the territory of a Member State other than that in which the institution responsible for payment is situated.

The preceding sub-paragraph shall also apply to lump-sum benefits granted in cases of remarriage of a surviving spouse who was entitled to a survivor's pension.[241]

As in the case of other provisions of Community law which prevent discrimination against the nationals of other member states, the question arises as to whether the rule in Article 3(1) of the Regulation prevents reverse discrimination, i.e. discrimination against a member state's own nationals in favour of nationals of other member states. If the words of

[235] Ibid., p. 2071, per the Advocate General.
[236] Ibid., p. 2067.
[237] Ibid., p. 2068.
[238] See n. 194 above.
[239] Case 51/73 [1973] *ECR* 1213.
[240] See Case 110/73, *Fiege* v. *Caisse Régionale* [1973] *ECR* 999.
[241] For an example of the application of the corresponding provision in the former Reg. 3, see Case 24/74 *Caisse Régionale* v. *Biason* [1974] *ECR* 999.

Article 3(1) of the Regulation mean what they say, any national of another member state must be subject to the same obligations and enjoy the same benefits under the member state's legislation as its own nationals, and this would seem to preclude the foreign national from being subjected to less onerous obligations or entitled to more favourable benefits. If that is so, it follows that a national of the member state concerned must not be discriminated against by having more onerous obligations or less favourable benefits. If, prior to the entry into force of the Community rule, there was a difference of treatment, that difference must be removed. There could be some procedural difficulty in enlisting the support of the European Court if in any particular litigation in a national court there was no foreign element, for example, if a national claimant who never set foot outside the member state in question claims greater benefits because he is receiving less than a national from another member state would receive in similar circumstances from the authorities of the claimant's state.[242] However, there was no such difficulty in *Kenny* v. *Insurance Officer*,[243] because the claimant in the UK Court was an Irish national, and the point at issue was whether a certain period which he had spent in Ireland should count towards entitlement to a UK benefit. Under UK legislation a claimant could not count periods spent in prison, and this could include imprisonment outside the United Kingdom. The question was whether there was any rule of Community law to prevent the application of this UK disqualification to the claimant, who had spent part of the relevant period in prison in Ireland. The Court held:

Articles 7 and 48 of the Treaty and Article 3(1) of Regulation No 1408/71 do not prohibit—though they do not require—the treatment by the institutions of Member States of corresponding facts occurring in another Member State as equivalent to facts which, if they occur on the national territory, constitute a ground for the loss or suspension of the right to cash benefits; the decision on this matter is for the national authorities, provided that it applies without regard to nationality and that those facts are not described in such a way that they lead in fact to discrimination against nationals of the other Member States.[244]

This case does not appear to answer the question whether Article 3(1) of the Regulation prohibits reverse discrimination.[245] It might have done so if the facts had been slightly different. If UK law had required periods of imprisonment (wherever served) to be taken into account in the case of claimants who were UK nationals, in order to reduce their claims, it could have been argued that it would have been unlawful discrimination against

---

[242] See Case 175/78, *R.* v. *Saunders* [1978] *ECR* 1129.

[243] Case 1/78 [1978] *ECR* 1489.

[244] Ibid., p. 1499.

[245] For a contrary view, see *Encyclopedia of European Community Law*, Vol. C IV, General Note on Article 3 of the Regulation, Release 28.

UK nationals not to take into account similar periods in the case of nationals of other member states. But those were not the facts. The UK law drew no distinction based on the nationality of the claimant. An Irishman who had spent time in an English prison would have been treated in the same way as a British claimant. The point of doubt would have been the same whether the claimant had been an Irishman or a British national. It was whether it was in accordance with Community law for the UK author-ities, applying UK law, to treat periods of imprisonment in Ireland as equivalent to periods spent in UK prisons. As to that, the Court said in effect that the UK authorities could please themselves, subject to two provisos. The first was that their decision must (as it did) apply 'without regard to nationality'. The use of that phrase sounded like support for the 'no reverse discrimination' thesis. However, the Court's second proviso referred to the need to avoid 'discrimination against nationals of other Member States', and that may have been its real preoccupation. The position therefore appears to be that the Court was not asked to rule on the question of reverse discrimination, did not purport to do so, and uttered no clear *obiter dictum* one way or the other.

International agreements

Article 6 of Regulation 1408/71[246] states the principle that, with certain exceptions, the Regulation replaces the provisions of any social security convention[247] binding either '(*a*) two or more Member States exclusively, or (*b*) at least two Member States and one or more other States, where settlement of the cases concerned does not involve any institution of one of the latter States'. The provisions referred to in (*b*) above thus leave unaffected those multilateral conventions which include non-member states as well as member states when the proviso is not satisfied, i.e. when in any particular case the administrative authorities of a non-member state are involved. This exception is itself qualified by Article 46(4) of the Regu-lation as regards invalidity, old age, and survivors' pensions. In those cases, if the total of the benefits due from two or more member states under the relevant multilateral convention would be less than those which would be due from those member states under Article 46(1) and (3), then Articles 44–51 apply instead of the convention. In this way the rights of those parties to the convention which are not member states of the Community are not affected, but within the Community the worker and his survivors are to get from the member states the more favourable treatment for which the Regulation provides.

---

[246] See n. 194 above.

[247] Even if they would have given more benefits to the worker: Case 82/72, *Walder* v. *Bestuur der Sociale Verzekeringsband* [1973] *ECR* 599. See also the Advocate General's Opinion in Case 99/80 *Galinsky* v. *Insurance Officer* [1981] *ECR* 941, pp. 962–4.

Article 7 of the Regulation and Annex III list by way of exception to the general rule in Article 6 certain conventions which are nevertheless to continue to apply. These include the European Interim Agreements on Social Security of 11 December 1953. Those agreements however do not derogate from, inter alia, international agreements that are more favourable to those entitled. This produces the somewhat ambiguous situation that the Regulation expresses itself as not affecting the agreements, and the agreements say in effect that they do not derogate from the EEC Treaty (which must include the Regulation made under it). Faced with this mutual *renvoi*, the Court interpreted the Regulation as meaning that it could, and should, be applied instead of the agreements when to do so was more favourable to the applicant: *Callemeyn* v. *Belgium*.[248] This case illustrates the Court's tendency to favour the recipient of social security, when the legislative texts allow it to do so.[249] The Court's rationale was expressed in general terms in *Caisse de pension des employés privés* v. *Massonet*,[250] where it said:

In order to define the meaning and scope of Regulation No 3, it must be interpreted in the light of Articles 48 to 51 of the Treaty which constitute the basis, the framework and the bounds of the social security regulations. Since those articles are intended to ensure freedom of movement for workers by conferring on them certain rights, to reduce the rights of workers without conferring upon them the compensating benefits prescribed in the regulations would be to depart from the purpose and framework of the said provisions.[251]

Choice of national law

Having determined the extent to which the Regulation or any relevant national agreement is applicable, the next question, in the case of a migrant worker who has had connections with more than one member state, is which member state's law should be applied to his situation at any particular time. The general rules[252] are set out in Article 13 of the Regulation:

1. Subject to Article 14(*c*), persons to whom this Regulation applies shall be subject to the legislation of a single Member State only. That legislation shall be determined in accordance with the provisions of this Title.

2. Subject to Articles 14 to 17:

    (*a*)   a person employed in the territory of one Member State shall be subject to the legislation of that State[253] even if he resides in the territory of

---

[248] Case 187/73 [1974] *ECR* 553.

[249] For another example see Case 98/80, *Romano* v. *Institut National* [1983] 2 *CMLR* 698.

[250] Case 50/75 [1975] *ECR* 1473.

[251] Ibid., p. 1481.

[252] The rules concern the choice of national law. The content of that law is subject to the provisions of Community law: Case 276/81, *Sociale Verzekeringsbank* v. *Kuijpers* [1982] *ECR* 3027, p. 3044.

[253] And only that state: Case 150/82, *Coppola* v. *Insurance Officer* [1983] *ECR* 43.

another Member State or if the registered office or place of business of the undertaking or individual employing him is situated in the territory of another Member State;

(*b*)   a person who is self-employed in the territory of one Member State shall be subject to the legislation of that State even if he resides in the territory of another Member State;

(*c*)   a worker employed on board a vessel flying the flag of a Member State shall be subject to the legislation of that State;

(*d*)   civil servants and persons treated as such shall be subject to the legislation of the Member State to which the administration employing them is subject;

(*e*)   a person called up or recalled for service in the armed forces, or for civilian service, of a Member State shall be subject to the legislation of that State. If entitlement under that legislation is subject to the completion of periods of insurance before entry into or after release from such military or civilian service, periods of insurance completed under the legislation of any other Member State shall be taken into account, to the extent necessary, as if they were periods of insurance completed under the legislation of the first State. The employed or self-employed person called up or recalled for service in the armed forces or for civilian service shall retain the status of employed or self-employed person.

From this text it will be seen that, subject to one set of exceptions, the worker is at any given time subject only to one national law in matters of social security, and that law is generally the law of the member state in which he is currently working. One result of the application of the general rule is that if a worker is employed in one member state, and resides in another, the latter cannot demand payment of social security contributions in respect of that employment: *Perenboom* v. *Inspecteur der directe belastingen of Nijmegen*.[254] The exceptional cases are specified in Article 14(*c*) and Annex VII, and they relate to persons who are self-employed in one member state while being employed in another. Further special rules on choice of law are contained in Articles 14–17. Article 14 relates to persons, other than mariners, engaged in paid employment (so that, for example, employees posted by their employers for short periods to another member state continue to be subject to the social security laws of the first member state). Article 14(*a*) concerns the self-employed (other than mariners), Article 14(*b*) relates to mariners, and Article 16 deals with persons employed by diplomatic missions and consular posts, and auxiliary staff of the European Communities.

Overlapping of benefits

The general purpose of the Regulation is not to put migrant workers and their families into a privileged class, but rather to protect them from

---

[254] Case 102/76 [1977] *ECR* 815. See also Case 19/67, *Bestuur der Sociale Verzekeringsbank* v. *van der Vecht* [1967] *ECR* 345.

suffering a loss of social security as a result of their exercising their rights of free movement under Article 48 EEC. It follows that, in the example cited earlier in this chapter, the worker who pays a year's contributions in one member state, pays a second year's contributions in another where he works and resides, and then claims and gets sickness benefits on the basis of two years' contributions, cannot in addition expect to make a further claim under Community law from any other member state. He gets his whole benefit from the paying authority, and it is then up to the latter to claim whatever contribution or reimbursement it may be entitled to receive from any other member state.[255] The exclusion of overlapping benefits is referred to somewhat tersely in Article 12(1) of the Regulation, which reads: 'This Regulation can neither confer nor maintain the right to several benefits of the same kind for one and the same period of compulsory insurance . . .'.[256] It is thus up to the national laws to ensure that, while the claimant gets all his benefits in accordance with the Regulation, he cannot claim any Community rights to get paid twice.[257]

Sickness and maternity

By virtue of Article 18 of Regulation 1408/71[258] the usual rule of aggregation of qualifying periods of insurance, employment, and residence must be applied by the competent institution[259] in the competent state.[260] Article 19 contains the general rules to be applied when an employed or self-employed person resides in the territory of a member state other than the competent state, e.g. if he works and is insured in one member state but resides in another. In essence he (and his family) can get benefits in kind (e.g. medical treatment)[261] wherever he happens to be, and if on any occasion this is where he resides, the local authorities act in this matter on behalf of, and are reimbursed by (in the absence of any Treaty to the contrary), the competent institution in the member state where he works.[262] He

---

[255] E.g. under Art. 19 of the Regulation. See also Reg. 574/72, *OJ* 1972, L74/1, above, Arts. 93–107. For the rules determining the appropriate exchange rate to be used when one member state reimburses another, see Case 98/80, *Giuseppe Romano* v. *Institut National d'Assurance Maladie-Invaliditié* [1983] 2 *CMLR* 698.

[256] This is supplemented in respect of particular benefits e.g. by Arts. 19(2), 25(1)(*b*), and 34.

[257] See also Case 238/81, *Raad van Arbeit* v. *Bunt—Craig* [1983] *ECR* 1385. For a review of the earlier cases see Knorpel, 'Social Security Cases in the Court of Justice of the European Communities', 1978–1980, Part II', (1982) 19 *CML Rev*. 105, pp. 130–48.

[258] *OJ*, Special Edition, 1971, p. 416. See also Arts. 15–16 of Reg. 574/72, *OJ*, 1972, L74/1.

[259] Defined in Art. 1(*o*).

[260] Defined in Art. 1(*q*).

[261] As to the limits of 'benefits in kind', see Case 61/65, *Vaassen* v. *Beamtenfonds, etc.* [1966] *ECR* 261; Case 33/65, *Dekker* v. *Bundesversicherungsanstalt* [1965] *ECR* 901.

[262] For a detailed interpretation of the relevant provisions, see Case 117/77, *Bestuur van het Algemeen Ziekenfonds Drenthe—Platteland* v. *Pierik* [1978] *ECR* 825; Case 182/78, *Bestuur van het Algemeen Ziekenfonds Drenthe—Platteland* v. *Pierik* [1979] *ECR* 1977; Case 69/79, *Jordens—Vosters* v. *Bestuur van de Bedrijfsvereniging voor de Leder-en Lederwerkende Industrie* [1980] *ECR* 75.

or she gets cash benefits, i.e. payments to compensate for loss of earnings on account of sickness or maternity, from the competent institution. The rules are further refined in Articles 21 and 22, to cater, e.g. for short trips abroad on holiday, or to receive medical treatment. Frontier workers and their families get certain special treatment under Article 20.

Invalidity

Article 38 of Regulation 1408/71[263] repeats the general principle that, where relevant, insurance periods must be aggregated. Article 39(1) and (2) determines the basic principles in the following terms:

> 1. The institution of the Member State, whose legislation was applicable at the time when incapacity for work followed by invalidity occurred, shall determine, in accordance with that legislation, whether the person concerned satisfies the conditions for entitlement to benefits, taking account, where appropriate, of the provisions of Article 38.
> 2. A person who satisfies the conditions referred to in paragraph 1 shall obtain the benefits exclusively from the said institution, in accordance with the provisions of the legislation which it administers.

Other provisions in this chapter of the Regulation (Chapter 2) cater for situations where in all member states concerned invalidity benefits are independent of the duration of insurance periods (Article 37); where not all member states concerned are of that type (Article 40);[264] where a person is granted benefits, and then later (and perhaps after he has travelled about within the Community) his invalidity becomes aggravated (Article 41); where benefits for some reason become suspended for a time and it later becomes necessary to determine which institution should resume them (Article 42); where invalidity benefits need, with the passage of time, to be converted into old-age benefits (Article 43).

Old age and death (pensions)

In accordance with the underlying principle of Regulation 1408/71,[265] Articles 44–51 seek to ensure that in the matter of pensions payable on account of old age or death the worker, his family, and his survivors will in no way suffer from the fact that he has chosen to exercise his Community right of free movement rather than to spend his working life in only one member state. The system set out in the Regulation was forged out of the earlier provisions of Regulation No. 3[266] concerning aggregation and apportionment, and its interpretation by the Court in *Neimann* v. *Bundes-*

---

[263] *OJ*, Special Edition, 1971, p. 416.
[264] For an interpretation of Article 40(4), see Case 232/82, *Baccini* v. *ONEM* [1983] *ECR* 583.
[265] *OJ* Special Edition, 1971, p. 416.
[266] Reg. 3/58, *OJ* 1958, p. 561.

versicherungsanstalt.[267] In that case it was discovered that by aggregating all the relevant periods, calculating the total pension due on that basis, and apportioning it between the relevant member states, the worker would get less than if the Regulation were ignored and he claimed his pension solely on the basis of German legislation. Yet Article 28(3) of Regulation No. 3 appeared to preclude this. The Court held:

> 1. Article 28(3) of Regulation No. 3, to the extent to which it implies an aggregation of periods and a consecutive apportionment, resulting in the grant of several benefits paid by different Member States, the total amount of which is however less than that of the benefit to which the worker is already entitled by virtue solely of the laws of one Member State, is incompatible with Article 51 and accordingly to that extent void . . .[268]

The complex system adopted in Chapter 3 (Articles 44–51) of Regulation 1408/71 overcomes this problem. Reduced to its essentials, it is as follows. An applicant can apply to each of the member states in which he has worked. The competent institution of each has to make a number of calculations. First, if the applicant qualified for a pension under the laws of that member state without aggregation of periods in other member states, it must calculate the pension in accordance with national law. It must then calculate what would have been its share of a pension based on aggregation. It must then accept the higher of the two figures (Article 46(1)). On the other hand, if the applicant does not qualify for a pension on the basis of national law alone, and he therefore has to rely on aggregation, the competent institution must make various calculations. First it must calculate the theoretical amount[269] he could claim if all the aggregated periods had been completed in that member state. Then it must calculate its own appropriate share of that theoretical amount, based on the proportion of the periods completed[270] under its own legislation to the total of the aggregated periods (Article 46(2)). Finally, the person concerned is entitled, as a normal rule, to the total of the benefits calculated by all the competent institutions, within the limit of the highest theoretical amount of benefits (Article 46(3)). Articles 47, and 49–51, contain further detailed provisions concerning the calculations to be made. Article 48 deals with the situation where the total length of a worker's periods of insurance or residence in a member state does not amount to a year.[271] That member state is not obliged to grant benefits in respect of those periods (Article

---

[267] Case 191/73 [1974] *ECR* 571.

[268] Ibid., p. 581.

[269] See Case 49/75, *Borella* v. *Landesversicherungsanstalt Schwaben* [1975] *ECR* 1461.

[270] Actually, not notionally, completed: Case 793/79, *Menzies* v. *Bundesversicherungsanstalt für Angestellte* [1980] *ECR* 2085.

[271] See Case 76/82, *Malfitano* v. *INAMI* [1982] *ECR* 4309; Case 150/82, *Coppola* v. *Insurance Officer* [1983] *ECR* 43.

48(1)), but the other member states must take the periods into account (Article 46(2)).[272]

Accidents at work and occupational diseases

An employed or self-employed person who is injured at work or contracts an occupational disease and who is resident in a member state other than the one in which he is insured is entitled to receive benefits in kind or in cash in the state where he resides (Article 52). Article 53 gives a frontier worker the right also to obtain benefits in the member state where he is insured. Articles 54 and 55 deal with temporary stays, changes in residence, and cases where the employed or self-employed person is authorized by the competent institution[273] to go to another member state for treatment. Accidents while travelling are deemed to have occurred in the member state in which the competent institution is situated (Article 56). Article 57 caters for the special needs of those who contract occupational diseases after being exposed to risks in several member states. Further complications are dealt with in the remaining articles of this chapter,[274] the underlying principle throughout being that a person who moves about within the Community can get the practical and financial help he needs on the spot from the local institutions, which are ultimately reimbursed by the competent institution in accordance with Article 63.

Death grants

The usual aggregation of periods of insurance or residence has to be made for the purpose of calculating death grants (Article 64) and the competent institution[275] usually bears the cost (Articles 65 and 66).

Unemployment

Once more the Regulation requires aggregation of the relevant periods,[276] although for the purpose of unemployment benefits the relevant periods are those of insurance or employment[277] (Article 67).

One special problem in this field, which may arise also in connection with education (as will be seen later in this chapter), concerns itinerant

---

[272] See Case 274/81, *Besem* v. *Nieuwe Algemene Bedrijfsvereniging* [1982] *ECR* 2995. For further consideration of Article 46, see also Case 171/82, *Biagio Valentini* [1983] *ECR* 2157, in which it was held that guaranteed payments upon cessation of employment provided for by French law were not benefits falling within Article 46 of the Regulation, and that national rules against overlapping with old-age benefits could be applied.

[273] Defined in Article 1(*o*).

[274] For an interpretation of Article 61(5) of the Regulation, see Joined Cases 173 and 174/78, *Villano* v. *Nordwestliche Eisen- und Stahl-Berufsgenossenschaft* [1979] *ECR* 1851; *Barion* v. *Tiefbau-Berufsgenossenschaft* [1979] *ECR* 1851.

[275] See Case 126/77, *Frangiamore* v. *Office National de l'Emploi* [1978] *ECR* 725.

[276] Article 1(*o*).

[277] But see Case 227/81, *Aubin* v. *Union Nationale* [1982] *ECR* 1991 for an interpretation of Art. 71(1)(*b*) of the Regulation.

students who, after completing their studies, seek to avail themselves of public benefits and grants before commencing work. In *Petrus Kuyken* v. *Rijksdienst voor Arbeidsvoorziening*[278] a Belgian, who was educated first in Belgium and then in the Netherlands, returned to Belgium at the end of his studies and claimed unemployment benefit. For the first year after completing studies in Belgium such benefit would have been available to him. But the Belgian authorities said that he was out of time to base his claim on his earlier Belgian education, and that his period of study in the Netherlands could not be counted. The Court rejected his complaint that the Belgian Government was in breach of Articles 69–71 of the Regulation and said:

It is clear from the wording of those provisions that they have no application in the case of an unemployed person who has never been in employment and has never been treated as an employed person under national legislation applicable to employed persons, particularly that relating to unemployment.[279]

It is not clear, however, whether this judgment should be interpreted narrowly, and as relating only to the interpretation of these particular provisions, or whether it has a wider significance, indicating that a person who has never been employed, but is seeking employment, does not become a 'worker' until he succeeds in getting his first job. Once he gets a job somewhere within the Community, there is no doubt that when thereafter he becomes unemployed, and seeks work within a member state, he is entitled to draw unemployment benefit in accordance with Articles 69[280] and 71 of the Regulation. The paying authority can, as usual, obtain reimbursement from the competent authority, which in this case is the authority in the member state to whose legislation he was subject at the time of his last employment (Article 70).

Family benefits and family allowances

After the usual provision for aggregation of relevant periods of insurance and employment (Article 72) Articles 73 and 74 take the unusual (but not unique)[281] step of providing one set of rules for one member state (France) and another for the other member states. Article 75 provides for reimbursement as between the authorities in each of the member states.[282]

---

[278] Case 66/77 [1977] *ECR* 2311.

[279] Ibid., p. 2318.

[280] For an interpretation of Art. 69(2), see Case 139/78, *Coccioli* v. *Bundesanstalt für Arbeit* [1979] *ECR* 99; Joined Cases 41, 121, and 796/79, *Testa, Miggio and Carmine* v. *Bundesanstalt für Arbeit* [1980] *ECR* 1979; Case 27/75, *Bonafini* v. *Istituto Nazionale della Previdenza Sociale* [1975] *ECR* 971.

[281] See e.g. Reg. 1422/78, *OJ* 1978, L171/14.

[282] For an interpretation of Arts. 73 and 76, see Case 149/82, *Robards* v. *Insurance Officer* (No. 1) [1983] 2 *CMLR* 537.

Benefits for dependent children of pensioners and for orphans

When a pensioner draws a pension under the laws of one or more member states, he can receive additional benefits in respect of his dependent children from the relevant authority, under the relevant rules. Perhaps in an attempt to simplify the scheme, Article 77 requires the place of residence of the pensioner and the children to be ignored for the purpose of choosing the rules to be applied, and requires benefits to be granted in accordance with the legislation of the member state responsible for the pension, where there is only one such state, and in accordance with the legislation of the state in which he resides, where there is more than one such state. However, in *CCAF* v. *Laterza*[283] the Court interpreted Article 77(2)(*b*)(i) as meaning that entitlement to benefits from the state of residence does not take away the right to higher benefits awarded previously by another member state.[284] This is another example of the Court straining to ensure that the recipient gets as favourable treatment as possible.

Orphans get treatment under Article 78 similar to dependent children under Article 77, mutatis mutandis.

EDUCATION

The preamble to Regulation 1612/68[285] recites that:

close links exist between freedom of movement for workers, employment and vocational training, particularly where the latter aims at putting workers in a position to take up offers of employment from other regions of the Community . . .

The first three paragraphs of Article 7 of the Regulation read:

1. A worker who is a national of a Member State may not, in the territory of another Member State, be treated differently from national workers by reason of his nationality in respect of any conditions of employment and work, in particular as regards remuneration, dismissal, and should he become unemployed, reinstatement or re-employment;

2. He shall enjoy the same social and tax advantages as national workers.

3. He shall also, by virtue of the same right and under the same conditions as national workers, have access to training in vocational schools and retraining centres.

Article 12 reads:

The children of a national of a Member State who is or has been employed in the territory of another Member State shall be admitted to that State's general

---

[283] Case 733/79 [1980] *ECR* 1915.

[284] See also Case 242/83, *Caisse de Compensation pour Allocations Familiales du Bâtiment, de l'Industrie et du Commerce du Hainault* v. *Salvatore Patteri*, in which the interpretation and validity of this provision was questioned (judgment of 12/7/84).   [285] *OJ*, Special Edition, 1968, p. 475.

educational, apprenticeship and vocational training courses under the same conditions as the nationals of that State, if such children are residing in its territory.
Member States shall encourage all efforts to enable such children to attend these
courses under the best possible conditions.[286]

Before the adoption of the Regulation it might have been argued that the
rules of free movement for workers in Article 48(1) EEC, and of freedom
from discrimination on grounds of nationality in Article 48(2) EEC, should
be strictly interpreted, and that when so interpreted they have nothing to
do with the education of the worker, his children, or anybody else. However, a more liberal approach is apparent in the secondary legislation
quoted above. In relation to Article 12 it may be argued that, while the
denial of educational facilities to the children of a foreign migrant worker
would not constitute any legal bar to his taking up employment in the
member state in question, it could be a powerful disincentive. Whatever
the reasons for adopting this Article the simple rule of equality of treatment
which it contains must be accepted as a valid Community rule unless and
until it should be declared to be invalid by the Court,[287] and it is not the
Court's normal practice to interpret narrowly any of the fundamental
freedoms.

The reasoning behind Article 7(3) of the Regulation is not, however, so
easy to discern. Why, it may be asked, should the right to take up employment in any member state on a footing of equality with workers who are
nationals of that state be regarded as conferring on the migrant worker a
right to obtain education for himself? The preamble to the Regulation gives
little guidance. In the Article itself the reference to 'retraining centres'
suggests that the legislator may have been concerned with the case where a
worker loses his job, for example, because of a general recession in the
particular industry in which he is employed, and is forced to take a break in
his working life while he retrains for another job. But to justify this part of
the Article it may have been necessary to assume that, unless he is sure in
advance that he will in this respect be treated on an equal footing with
national workers, he will be, or may be, deterred from going to the other
member state to take up the initial employment. A similar assumption may
need to be made to justify the inclusion of a right of equal treatment in
respect of access to vocational schools. A clue to the legislator's line of
thought may however be found from the inclusion in Article 7(3) of the
words 'by virtue of the same right'. This could indicate that access to vocational schools and retraining schemes was regarded as a 'social advantage'

---

[286] For an interpretation of this Article, see Case 68/74, *Alaimo* v. *Préfet du Rhône* [1975] *ECR* 109.

[287] See, in another context, Case 101/78, *Granaria* v. *Hoofdproduktschap voor Akkerbouwprodukten*
[1979] *ECR* 623, pp. 636 and 639, for the rule that every regulation which is brought into force in
accordance with the Treaty must be presumed to be valid so long as a competent court has not
made a finding that it is invalid.

of the kind referred to in Article 7(2). A similar thought process can be detected in a *dictum* of the Court in *Casagrande* v. *Landeshauptstadt München*,[288] which suggests that Article 12 of the Regulation (and presumably Article 7(2) also) may have some foundation in the Community's social policy. The Court said:

Although educational and training policy is not as such included in the spheres which the Treaty has entrusted to the Community institutions, it does not follow that the exercise of powers transferred to the Community is in some way limited if it is of such a nature as to affect the measures taken in the execution of a policy such as that of education and training. Chapters 1 and 2 of Title III of Part Two of the Treaty [Social policy] in particular contain several provisions the application of which could affect this policy.[289]

Articles 118 and 128 EEC, both of which appear in Title III (Social Policy), do in fact specifically refer to vocational training.

Questions of interpretation

Some questions arise as to the interpretation of Article 7(3) of the Regulation.[290] 'He' no doubt refers to 'a worker who is a national of a Member State' (Article 7(1)). The question who is included as a national of a member state presents no particular problems in this context, and it has been answered earlier in this chapter. The use of the term 'worker', although considered at length at the beginning of this chapter, does however give rise to some additional questions. Does it for example include a person who works in one particular state and then decides to go for some vocational training in another member state (where it is perhaps provided free of charge), with the intention of returning immediately thereafter to the first member state to continue his employment? Does it include a person who has never worked, but who wishes to go to have training in one member state before commencing work in that or another member state?

These and similar questions are not easy to answer. It would on the one hand be difficult to regard anyone as a worker unless he had some genuine connection with work. On the other hand there is nothing in the Regulation to suggest what that connection must be, or whether the minimum requirement is an intention one day to work somewhere in the Community, or an intention to work in the member state from which the applicant comes, or in which training is sought, or such an intention coupled with actual work in another member state prior to the training, or actual work in the member state in which training is sought and prior to such training, or a combination of two or more of these requirements.

[288] Case 9/74 [1974] *ECR* 773.
[289] Ibid., p. 779.
[290] Reg. 1612/68, *OJ*, Special Edition, 1968, p. 475.

Another example of fertile soil in which litigation may flourish is the expression 'vocational schools'. Does this mean a school devoted entirely to giving students the training which is necessary, or desirable, for the exercise of a particular trade or profession, for example a school for actors or a school for restaurateurs? Or does it mean a school which offers vocational courses, as well as teaching purely academic subjects to some students, for example the average technical school or polytechnic college? Does it go wider still, and include universities, to the extent that they provide courses which are orientated to a particular vocation, e.g. degree courses in law, medicine, engineering, and the like? Should it be construed even more widely still, on the principle that teaching somebody ancient Sanskrit will at least equip him to take up the vocation of teaching ancient Sanskrit to others? In the absence of detailed guidance from the Court, it is only possible to suggest that the narrowest of these views is probably too narrow, and that the widest is too wide. Articles 118 and 128 EEC do not give any assistance in interpreting what is meant by 'vocational schools'. Nor can much be gleaned in this respect from Council Decision 266/63 of 2 April 1963,[291] although the 'Second principle' set out in the Decision includes as a fundamental objective of the common vocational training policy 'to broaden vocational training on the basis of a general education, to an extent sufficient to encourage the harmonious development of the personality and to meet requirements arising from technical progress, new methods of production and social and economic developments'.[292] A slightly more tangible objective, which also appears in the Second principle is 'to organize in due course suitable training facilities to supply the labour forces required in the different sectors of economic activity'.[293] In the case of an Irish car worker in the United Kingdom who decided to retrain as a school teacher, the Chancery Division of the High Court held that training in an approved teacher-training college was training in a vocational school, for the purposes of Article 7(3).[294]

In *Michel S.* v. *Fonds national de reclassement social des handicapés*,[295] which concerned an Italian who had never worked and whose chances of obtaining employment were reduced because of his low mental capacity, the European Court interpreted Article 7 as extending to national measures for the rehabilitation of the handicapped, in so far as such measures concerned workers themselves, and to national measures which allowed the handicapped to realize or improve their aptitude for work, in so far as such measures concerned the children of workers. That case also shows how the difficulties of interpreting Article 7 of the Regulation are compounded by

[291] *OJ*, Special Edition, 1963, p. 25.
[292] Ibid., sub-paragraph (*c*).
[293] Ibid., sub-paragraph (*b*).
[294] *MacMahon* v. *Department of Education and Science* [1982] 3 *WLR* 1129.
[295] Case 76/72 [1973] *ECR* 457, p. 465.

the fact that the quotations set out in the report of the judgment[296] differ from the text of the Regulation as established in the Special Edition of the Official Journal.[297]

Access to education

The equality of treatment with nationals of the host state, which is to be enjoyed by a migrant worker, extends to all the conditions upon which he may have access to training in vocational schools and retraining centres for himself, and to general educational, apprenticeship, and vocational training courses for his children. Such conditions may relate to the payment of fees,[298] so that if the children of a national of the host state are admitted to a school on payment of less than the full fees (because e.g. they are in whole or in part paid by the state or by a local authority), it is an infringement of Article 12 of Regulation 1612/68[299] for the migrant worker to be charged higher fees. The question arose in *Casagrande* v. *Landeshauptstadt München*,[300] where the plaintiff was denied an educational grant of DM 70 per month to which German nationals were entitled under Bavarian law. The Court held:

In providing that the children of a national of a Member State who is or has been employed in the territory of another Member State shall be admitted to educational courses 'under the same conditions as the nationals' of the host State, Article 12 refers not only to rules relating to admission, but also to general measures intended to facilitate educational attendance.[301]

The same principle presumably also applies to cases falling within Article 7(3) of the Regulation. Whether it in addition applies to educational grants which are discretionary, and not required by law, is unclear. However, it should be noted that in a different context (interest-free loans given at childbirth), the Court has held 'social advantage' to include a discretionary advantage: *Reina* v. *Landeskreditbank Baden Wurtemberg*.[302] This may have some relevance if it is correct to regard Articles 7 and 12 of the Regulation as having some foundation in the Community's social policy, as the Court has hinted in the *Casagrande* case.[303] Moreover in that case there appears to have been an element of discretion in that although the grant was obligatory under Bavarian law, it was only payable when the child did not have 'sufficient means',[304] in the assessment of which some discretion presumably had to be exercised.

[296] Ibid., p. 463.
[297] *OJ*, Special Edition, 1968, p. 477.
[298] Including registration fees: see Case 152/82, *Forcheri* [1983] *ECR* 2323.
[299] Supra.
[300] Case 9/74 [1974] *ECR* 773.
[301] Ibid., p. 780.
[302] Case 65/81 [1982] *ECR* 33.
[303] Case 9/74 [1974] *ECR* 773.
[304] Ibid., p. 775.

In *Forcheri* v. *Belgium*[305] the Court took a broad view of the right in Community law of access to education. It analysed the situation in this way. Article 7 of the Treaty prohibited within the scope of application of the Treaty, and without prejudice to any special provisions contained therein, any discrimination on grounds of nationality. The question therefore was whether access to educational courses came within the scope of application of the Treaty. Article 128 required the Council to lay down principles for implementing a common vocational training policy. The Council indeed adopted Decision No. 266/63[306] for that purpose. The Court's conclusion therefore was:

It follows that, although it is true that educational and vocational training policy is not as such part of the areas which the Treaty has allotted to the competence of the Community institutions, the opportunity for such kinds of instruction falls within the scope of the Treaty.[307]

The type of instruction in question was in fact a three-year training course catering primarily for the profession of social worker, and given at the 'Institut supérieur de sciences humaines appliquées' in Brussels.

The judgment poses almost as many questions as it answers, and it may well breed further litigation. Article 7(3) of Regulation 1612/68[308] speaks of a worker's right, under the same conditions as national workers, to train in vocational schools. This provision does not therefore extend to training in any particular establishment unless it is a 'vocational school'. A school for waiters would easily fall into that category, but the English department of a university would hardly do so. The 'dispositif' in the judgment speaks however of courses rather than establishments. It reads:

If a Member State organizes educational courses relating in particular to vocational training, to require of a national of another Member State lawfully established in the first Member State an enrolment fee which is not required of its own nationals in order to take part in such courses constitutes discrimination by reason of nationality, which is prohibited by Art. 7 of the Treaty.[309]

If the criterion is the nature of the course, rather than the type of establishment in which it is given, this could have far-reaching consequences, as well as giving rise to a number of possible interpretations. At one end of the scale it could include only courses the successful completion of which results in the acquisition of a professional qualification, which in itself entitles the holder to practise a particular profession. At the other end it might include almost any educational course on any subject at any type of

[305] Case 152/82 [1983] *ECR* 2323.
[306] *OJ*, Special Edition, 1963–4, p. 25.
[307] Case 152/82 [1983] *ECR* 2323, p. 2336. See also Case 293/83, *Gravier* v. *City of Liège* [1985] 3 CMLR 1.
[308] *OJ*, Special Edition, 1968, p. 475.
[309] Case 152/82 [1983] *ECR* 2323, pp. 2337–8.

institution, on the basis that virtually any form of education can help a person to obtain better employment than he could without it. Thus, for example, to acquire a degree in the classics may well result in a job in the public or private sector which would not be open to a person having no degree at all. Further, a degree in law can exempt the holder from certain parts of his professional examinations. Yet if such a broad interpretation were to be adopted this would seem to be straying far beyond the notion in Article 128 that the Council should adopt a 'common vocational training policy'. Further guidance will be needed from the European Court before this difficult area can be clarified.

FURTHER READING

A. Barav, 'Court Recommendation to Deport and the Free Movement of Workers in EEC Law', (1981) 6 *EL Rev.* 139.

G. Druesne, 'Liberté de Circulation des Personnes. Les Prolongements de la Libre Circulation des Salariés: Droit de Séjour et Progrès Social', (1982) 3 *RTDE* 556.

H. ter Heide, 'The Free Movement of Workers in the Final Phase', (1968–9) 6 *CML Rev.* 466.

H. Knorpel, 'Social Security Cases in the Court of Justice of the European Communities', (1981) 18 *CML Rev.* 579, (1982) 19 *CML Rev.* 105, (1984) 21 *CML Rev.* 241.

D. O'Keeffe, 'The Scope and Content of Social Security Regulation in European Community Law', in *Essays in European Law and Integration* (1982).

J.-C. Séché, 'Free Movement of Workers under Community Law', (1977) 14 *CML Rev.* 385.

D. W. Williams, 'British Passports and the Right to Travel', (1974) 23 *ICLQ* 642.

F. Wooldridge, 'Free Movement of EEC Nationals: The Limitation Based on Public Policy and Public Security', (1977) 2 *EL Rev.* 190.

D. Wyatt, 'The Social Security Rights of Migrant Workers and their Families', (1977) 14 *CML Rev.* 411.

——, 'Residence Permits for Nationals of the Member States', (1977) 2 *EL Rev.* 445.

V

Establishment

In Chapter 4 consideration was given to the worker from Devon who wished to go to Somerset to take up employment. The same person might however have wished to open a new business in Somerset, or to purchase an existing one, and then either to run it from his home in Devon or to take up residence in Somerset for that purpose. He might have decided to run the business solely in his own name, or in partnership with others, or he might have wished to run it through the medium of a company. Whichever of those plans he had chosen to pursue he would have expected no impediments to have been put in his way by any national or local authority on account solely of the fact that he came from Devon, and he would in fact have been entitled to compete on an equal footing with the people of Somerset. It can readily be seen, therefore, that in our ideal common market he will, when moving from one member state to another, need to enjoy rights which in many respects are similar, or complementary, to those of the migrant worker. Indeed, under the EEC Treaty the dividing line between a worker and a person who seeks to exercise the right of establishment[1] is sometimes blurred, and sometimes non-existent. So, for example, he will, as a self-employed person who runs the business on his own account, fall within the scope of Regulation 1408/71[2] with regard to social security, since by virtue of Article 2 the Regulation applies to employed and self-employed persons. Moreover, if he chooses to float a new company in which he owns virtually all the shares, and to get himself employed by the company, he is in every sense a worker exercising his right of free movement, as well as a person who is enjoying the right of establishment.

The basic Treaty provisions are as follows:

Article 52

Within the framework of the provisions set out below, restrictions on the freedom of establishment of nationals of a Member State in the territory of another Member State shall be abolished by progressive stages in the course of the transitional period. Such progressive abolition shall also apply to restrictions on the setting up of agencies, branches or subsidiaries by nationals of any Member State established in the territory of any Member State.

[1] Or the right to provide services under Art. 59. For the link between Arts. 48, 52, and 59, see Case 48/75, *Procureur du Roi* v. *Royer* [1976] *ECR* 497, p. 509.   [2] See Chapter 4.

Freedom of establishment shall include the right to take up and pursue activities as self-employed persons and to set up and manage undertakings, in particular companies or firms within the meaning of the second paragraph of Article 58, under the conditions laid down for its own nationals by the law of the country where such establishment is effected, subject to the provisions of the Chapter relating to capital.

Article 53

Member States shall not introduce any new restrictions on the right of establishment in their territories of nationals of other Member States, save as otherwise provided in this Treaty.

Article 58

Companies or firms formed in accordance with the law of a Member State, and having their registered office, central administration or principal place of business within the Community shall, for the purposes of this Chapter, be treated in the same way as natural persons who are nationals of Member States.

'Companies or firms' means companies or firms constituted under civil or commercial law, including cooperative societies, and other legal persons governed by public or private law, save for those which are non-profit making.

DEFINITIONS

Nationals of a member state

In Chapter 4 the meaning of 'national of a Member State' was considered in relation to workers. So far as individuals are concerned, the phrase has the same meaning in the context of establishment, and indeed wherever it occurs in the Treaty. A special problem arises, however, in the case of companies, which for establishment purposes must, generally speaking, be treated in the same way as natural persons (Article 58, first paragraph). The idea that legal persons are to be equated with natural persons, and treated as nationals of a state, has long prevailed in international affairs. A state has traditionally been regarded as entitled in international law to afford diplomatic protection to its own companies, but differences of opinion have persisted over what, for the purposes of international law, should be the test of a company's nationality. There have even been lingering doubts as to whether a reference in a treaty to 'nationals' includes companies, so that, for example, it was felt necessary in Article 5 of the Vienna Convention on Consular Relations[3] to add after each reference to a state's nationals the words 'both individuals and bodies corporate'. The EEC Treaty deals with these questions, first by reserving the use of the phrase 'nationals of a Member State' for natural persons, and secondly by requiring 'companies or firms' formed in accordance with the law of a member state and having

[3] 24 April 1963, TS No. 14 (1973), Cmnd. 5219.

their registered office, central administration, or principal place of business within the Community to be treated in the same way as individuals who are nationals of member states (Article 58, first paragraph).

From this one may deduce that to be treated in the same way as a national of a member state a company must satisfy two conditions. The first is to be incorporated in accordance with the law of a member state. The second is to have either its registered office, or its central administration, or its principal place of business within the Community. If a company satisfies both conditions then it must for establishment purposes be treated in the same way as a natural person who is a national of a member state. It is tempting to go on to conclude that it is then not necessary to go further and ask what nationality should be attributed to the company. On that view one should simply regard the company as falling within the meaning of the phrase 'nationals of a Member State', in Article 52, first sentence. The difficulty with that approach, however, is what meaning then to attribute to the words 'in the territory of another Member State', because 'another Member State' in the context of Article 52 prima facie means a state other than the one of which the person concerned is a national. It is possible to deal with that question in three different ways. First one could say that 'another Member State' means a member state other than the one under whose laws the company is formed, and other than the one where it has its registered office, central administration, or principal place of business within the Community. Alternatively, one could say it means a member state other than the one of which it is to be regarded as a national, taking account of the criteria specified in Article 58, first paragraph, and the rules of international law for determining a company's nationality. The difficulty with this latter approach is that there is no uniform view within the Community of what factors determine a company's nationality. The United Kingdom's traditional view is that the place of incorporation determines the company's nationality, but some member states adhere to the view that the place of central management is the determining factor. Whichever approach is adopted, difficult questions could arise when the relevant factors (registered office, etc.) are connected with different member states or with a mixture of member and non-member states. A third possibility would be to regard the phrase 'in the territory of another Member State' as referring, not to a territory other than the one of which the applicant is a national, but to a territory other than the one in which it has hitherto been established. This would be consistent with the approach of the Court in the case of individuals in *Knoors* v. *Secretary of State for Economic Affairs*.[4]

At the present stage of Community jurisprudence it is not possible to forecast with certainty which of the various conflicting views will eventually

---

[4] Case 115/78 [1979] *ECR* 399.

prevail. However, it would seem to be consistent with the Court's general approach to the interpretation of the fundamental freedoms not to take too narrow a view. A broad 'communautaire' approach would suggest that for the purpose of applying Article 52 to companies, Article 58 either replaces all considerations as to nationality or spells out the sole test of nationality which is to be applied for the purpose of both Articles. Thus, provided a company is formed in accordance with the law of one member state, and provided it has its registered office, or its central administration, or its principal place of business somewhere within the Community, it should, if nationality is relevant at all, be counted as a Community national and enjoy rights of establishment, throughout the Community, even though addition-ally it may have connections with non-member states. There need be only two qualifications to this. First, in any particular case there must be factors connecting the situation with more than one member state, because of the principle in *R.* v. *Saunders*,[5] according to which the Community is not concerned with purely domestic situations. Secondly, under Title I of the General Programme[6] a company must also show a real and continuous link with the economy of a member state or of an overseas country,[7] which link must not be one of nationality, if it wishes to claim the benefits of Article 52, second sentence, by establishing only an agency, branch, or subsidiary within the territory of a particular member state.

Companies or firms

Article 58, second paragraph, contains the following definition:

'Companies or firms' means companies or firms constituted under civil or commercial law, including cooperative societies, and other legal persons governed by public or private law, save for those which are non-profit making.

Before applying therefore the tests in Article 58, first paragraph, to deter-mine whether a company or firm qualifies to be treated in the same way as a national of a member state, one must first ask whether the body in question is 'constituted under civil or commercial law'. Behind those words there hides a deep division of opinion (as yet unresolved) as to what conditions must be satisfied before a body must be regarded as constituted under the law of a particular member state. If a body takes all the necessary steps to become incorporated in the United Kingdom, to comply with its legal requirements, and to be registered on the companies' register accordingly, it will be regarded as constituted under the law of the United Kingdom, and it will retain that status until it is dissolved in accordance with the relevant laws related to dissolution. It matters not that its main functions

---

[5] Case 175/78 [1979] *ECR* 1129.
[6] *OJ*, Special Edition, 1974, part ix, p. 7.
[7] See Part IV of the EEC Treaty.

may be exercised outside the United Kingdom or that it may have other foreign connections. The same situation obtains in the Netherlands, for example. In some other member states, however, a company must satisfy an additional condition. In those countries it must have and maintain a functional connection with the state of incorporation, before that incorporation can be regarded as valid. It must in short have its real seat ('siège réel', or 'siège social') in that state. The theoretical possibility exists, therefore, that a body which is recognized as a company in one member state might be refused rights of establishment in another on the grounds (albeit dubious) that the latter did not recognize it as a company or firm which was legally constituted in the former.

This potential difficulty was foreseen in the Treaty. Article 220 requires member states to enter into negotiations with each other with a view to securing for their nationals (inter alia):

the mutual recognition of companies or firms within the meaning of the second paragraph of Article 58, the retention of legal personality in the event of transfer of their seat from one country to another, and the possibility of mergers between companies or firms governed by the laws of different countries.[8]

A convention on the mutual recognition of companies and bodies corporate was duly negotiated and signed on 29 February 1968,[9] by the original six member states, but it never entered into force because it was not ratified by all signatories. It is still not in force, and there is no indication that the underlying difficulties over ratification are likely to be overcome in the near future.

One question which arises in connection with the second paragraph of Article 58 is whether a partnership under English law should for the purpose of establishment be regarded as amongst the 'legal persons governed by public or private law'. Traditionally an English partnership is not regarded as having legal personality in the full sense of having an identity in law which is entirely separate from that of its members.[10] Nor can complete reliance be placed on the facts that the Treaty uses the term 'firms' as well as companies, and that Section 4 of the Partnership Act 1890 provides that partners are called collectively a firm, because terms used in one text of a multilingual treaty do not necessarily have the meaning ascribed to them by the law of one party to the treaty. Nevertheless, it is the case that actions may be brought in the English courts by and against partners in the name of the firm,[11] and, if judgment is given against such a

[8] See also Art. 3(2) of the Act of Accession and Art. 3(2) of the Greek Act of Accession.
[9] See *Bulletin of the European Communities*, Supplement 2 (1969). The text of the convention is in *Encyclopedia of Community Law* vol. B II, together with an extensive commentary.
[10] See Farwell LJ in *Sadler* v. *Whiteman*, [1910] 1 KB 868, p. 889. But see S. 4(2) of the Partnership Act 1890, which states that in Scotland a firm is a legal person distinct from the partners of whom it is composed.   [11] Order 81, Rule 1, RSC.

firm, execution may be levied against any property of the firm within the jurisdiction,[12] although in certain limited cases the leave of the court is required.[13] In these circumstances it would not require a very generous interpretation of the word 'firms', as used in the Treaty, to regard it as covering partnerships. Moreover, it is not customary for the European Court to adopt restrictive interpretations of the basic freedoms.

Establishment

The Treaty does not define what is meant by 'establishment'. The second paragraph of Article 52 says that freedom of establishment includes the right to take up and pursue activities as self-employed persons and to set up and manage undertakings. The reference to self-employment, and the fact that the Treaty established an economic community, imply that the activity must be pursued for economic ends. But there is no other limitation on the type of lawful activity which is covered. Nor, by virtue of the use of the word 'includes', can this paragraph be regarded as an exclusive definition which confines the activities to those of the self-employed. However, it seems to be implicit in the scheme of Title III that, generally speaking, free movement of workers concerns employed persons, whereas the right of establishment relates to the self-employed.

The difficulty of defining 'establishment' is not new. During a period extending many years before accession, the United Kingdom had negotiated a series of bilateral treaties designed, inter alia, to secure rights of establishment, although they did not expressly attempt to define the term. To give only one example, the Treaty of Commerce, Establishment, and Navigation between the United Kingdom and Iran, signed on 11 March 1959,[14] secured rights of establishment in the territory of the other party on an equal footing with nationals of any other foreign country. In describing those rights in Article 3(4) it referred to engaging 'in every lawful employment, profession, business or occupation'. That description goes wider than the EEC Treaty, in that it covers the provision of services, whereas the latter draws a distinction between establishment (Chapter 2) and services (Chapter 3). Precedents of that kind are thus of little help in interpreting the EEC Treaty, except possibly as some indication that the very word 'establishment' has for a long time been used by at least one member state in a very wide sense. Although they do not use the word 'establishment', other examples of treaties conferring wide reciprocal rights to enter, travel, and reside, and to engage in commerce, industry, a profession, or any other occupation, are to be found in bilateral agreements between the United Kingdom and France, signed on 12 May 1882,[15] Germany, signed on 2

[12] Order 81, Rule 5, RSC.
[13] Order 81, Rule 6, RSC.　　　　　　　　　　　[14] Cmnd. 698.
[15] Foreign Office Handbook of Commercial Treaties, 4th edn., p. 225.

December 1924,[16] Greece, signed on 16 July 1926,[17] and Italy, signed on 15 June 1883.[18]

Linguistically the word 'establishment' seems to imply (i) some degree of permanence and (ii) some fixed base or bases from which the economic activity is conducted.

The first of these implications has received some support.[19] However, it is an unreliable guide either as to the meaning of establishment, or as a method of differentiating from services. Article 52 gives no indication as to how permanent an arrangement should be to qualify as establishment. Nor does it seem right in principle to regard only what is permanent as a form of establishment, and only what is ephemeral as a form of services. For example, it would seem more logical to regard the acquisition and operation of a factory, even though it performs for only a short time before becoming unprofitable and being closed down, as a form of establishment, and the selling of postal tuition from abroad, even if this activity is conducted over a very long period, as a form of service.

Some indication that permanency is not the test of establishment is given by Article A(*h*) of Title III of the General Programme,[20] although unfortunately it is ambiguous. That paragraph provides that all measures must be eliminated which prohibit foreign nationals from becoming members of companies or firms, or which restrict their rights as members, in particular as regards the functions which they may perform within the company or firm. If this is regarded as referring only to companies or firms which have themselves been set up in exercise of the right of establishment it might be regarded as being merely ancillary to that right, because it would hinder a foreigner from establishing a company or firm if he could not make key personnel from his own member state members of it. But it is possible to interpret the Article in a wider sense, as demonstrating that acquisition of membership of a company or firm whose nationality is that of the receiving state may itself be a form of establishment. For example, a national of one member state may wish to establish himself in another member state, not entirely on his own account but in partnership with a national of the latter state. On that view, it may also be possible to regard establishment as including even the acquisition and holding of shares in a local company, because although the shareholder is only engaging in the economic affairs of the company in an indirect way, he has some say in those affairs, even as a shareholder. If that is the case it is difficult to regard establishment as implying some permanent kind of arrangement, since in the nature of things shares are easily and freely disposed of by the average investor.

---

[16] Ibid., p. 299.

[17] Ibid., p. 325.

[18] Ibid., p. 369.

[19] See the Advocate General in Case 33/74, *Van Binsbergen* [1974] *ECR* 1299, p. 1316.

[20] *OJ*, Special Edition, 1974, part IX, p. 7.

The second implication (that establishment involves some fixed base or bases from which the economic activity is conducted) is probably correct, and indeed it may well represent the best way of distinguishing establishment from services. Yet even this concept may cause difficulty in some cases. The acquisition of business premises would be clear enough evidence of establishment, but what about the case of an ice-cream vendor who resides in one member state and who drives his van every day to the same selling pitch in another member state? Is the latter a sufficiently fixed point to constitute an example of establishment, or is the vendor providing a service? No confident answer can be given in this and other borderline situations.

Further difficulty may arise if one considers the role, if any, of residence in assessing where a person is established. If the place of residence and the place of business coincide no problem arises. But if a person owns and occupies premises in one member state exclusively as his residence, and owns and occupies premises in another member state exclusively for business, it would seem logical to regard him as established in the latter and not in the former. Moreover, if the 'person' concerned happens to be a company, a residence test would seem to be even more inappropriate. Of course to deny an individual the right of residence in a member state may in practice be tantamount to denying him the practical opportunity to conduct his economic activity there, and thus infringe his right of establishment. Conversely, to insist that he should reside in the state where he wishes to conduct his business may deny him appropriate opportunities and equally infringe his right of establishment, as can be seen from Article A(*d*) of Title III of the General Programme,[21] which provides that the receiving state must not make prior residence a condition for taking up or pursuing an activity as a self-employed person. But none of this alters the principle that when trying to identify what constitutes establishment, and where it should be regarded as being situated, the acid test should be to consider the nature of the activity and where it is conducted, and not where the person concerned resides. However, it must be admitted that on occasion it has been suggested that residence is an ingredient of establishment.[22] This aspect will be considered further in Chapter 6 ('Services'), in connection with the requirement in Article 59 that the provider of services must be established in another member state.

In spite of these difficulties it is possible to attempt a definition of 'establishment'. Like most such attempts it may not be appropriate to cover all cases, but it probably covers most, and it is as follows. Establishment in a state means the conduct of an economic activity from a fixed base or bases

[21] *OJ*, Special Edition, 1974, part IX, p. 7.
[22] See e.g. the Advocate General in Case 33/74, *Van Binsbergen* v. *Bedrijfsvereniging Metaalnijverheid* [1974] *ECR* 1299, p. 1315.

in that state, which will usually involve the occupation of premises there, to be used wholly or partly for that purpose, and which may also, in the case of individuals, be accompanied by residence.

Article 54(1) EEC required the Council to draw up a general programme for the abolition of existing restrictions on freedom of establishment within the Community. This the Council did on 18 December 1961.[23] Although the procedure specified in Article 54 for adopting the General Programme was similar to the procedure for the adoption of secondary legislation, the Programme does not belong to one of the categories of legislation referred to in Article 189. It would however appear to amount to an act of the Council within the meaning of Article 173 because it satisfies the test established in the *AETR* case,[24] being one of the 'measures adopted by the institutions which are intended to have legal force'.[25] It is true that Title VII (Aids) appears to be a statement of intention, rather than of legal obligation. However the main bulk of the document is expressed in binding terms. Title II says that certain steps 'are to be taken'. Title III records that certain restrictions 'are to be eliminated', while Titles IV and V use the imperative verb 'shall'. Moreover it seems right to regard the General Programme as an agreed interpretation of the matters which fall within the scope of the Treaty provisions on establishment. Thus one might say that the Treaty imposes the general obligations, and that the General Programme spells out in some detail the meaning of those obligations.

In *Reyners* v. *Belgium*[26] the German Government argued that 'the "General Programme" and the directives provided for by Article 54 were of significance only during the transitional period, since the freedom of establishment was fully attained at the end of it'.[27] The Court concentrated on the role of the directives, but it did also refer to the General Programme in the following passage:

It appears from the above that in the system of the Chapter on the right of establishment the 'general programme' and the directives provided for by the Treaty are intended to accomplish two functions, the first being to eliminate obstacles in the way of attaining freedom of establishment during the transitional period, the second being to introduce into the law of Member States a set of provisions intended to facilitate the effective exercise of this freedom for the purpose of assisting economic and social interpenetration within the Community in the sphere of activities as self-employed persons.[28]

[23] *OJ*, Special Edition, 1974, part IX, p. 7, gives the full official English text.
[24] Case 22/70, *Commission* v. *Council* [1971] *ECR* 263.
[25] Ibid., p. 276.   [26] Case 2/74 [1974] *ECR* 631.
[27] Ibid., p. 649.   [28] Ibid., p. 651.

This seems to fall short of endorsing the submission of the German Government, and it is not inconsistent with the view that the General Programme remains an agreed interpretation of the scope of Article 52.[29]

The beneficiaries (Title I)

Title I of the General Programme defines the persons (both natural and legal) entitled to benefit from the abolition of restrictions on freedom of establishment. It naturally covers the individuals and companies referred to in Articles 52 and 58 of the Treaty.

In relation to individuals, the General Programme introduces one new concept, namely 'nationals ... of the overseas countries and territories'. This must be read subject to the agreed definition, in relation to the United Kingdom, of the phrase 'nationals of Member States and overseas countries and territories'.[30]

The Court has given further guidance as to the categories of natural persons who qualify as beneficiaries. In *Knoors* v. *Secretary of State for Economic Affairs*[31] the plaintiff was a Dutch plumber, residing in Belgium. At first he was an employed worker, but later he became head of an independent business and thereafter, and at all material times, he may be regarded as having been established in Belgium. He then applied to the Dutch authorities for permission to carry on the same trade in the Netherlands. He was refused, because he did not have the qualifications required by Dutch law. The conditions for access to the plumbing trade had not been harmonized within the Community, but Directive 427/64[32] provided that member states should, in the trades to which the Directive related, accept as sufficient the fact that the activity had been pursued in another member state. The question which then arose was whether the beneficiaries of the right of establishment included persons who had always been nationals of the host member state, and of no other. The application referred to the meaning of beneficiaries in Directive 64/427, but it could equally have referred to the General Programme which, as the Court said, forms the basis and framework of the directive.[33] The Court held that such persons were included as beneficiaries. In the light of this judgment it would seem that, when Article 52 refers to 'freedom of establishment of nationals of one Member State in the territory of another Member State', it may be interpreted as if it said 'freedom of nationals of a Member State,

---

[29] The Court has described it as the basis and framework for subsequent directives: Case 115/78, *Knoors* v. *Secretary of State for Economic Affairs* [1979] *ECR* 399, p. 407. In Case 71/76, *Thieffry* [1977] *ECR* 765, the Court also said that the Programme provides useful guidance for the implementation of the relevant provisions of the Treaty (p. 777).

[30] *OJ* 1983, C231/1.

[31] Case 115/78 [1979] *ECR* 399.

[32] *OJ* 1964, L59/8.

[33] Case 115/78 [1979] *ECR* 399, p. 407.

who are established in any Member State, to establish themselves in any Member State other than the one in which they are currently established'. The Court analysed the situation as follows:

It may therefore be stated that Directive No 64/427 is based on a broad definition of the 'beneficiaries' of its provisions, in the sense that the nationals of all Member States must be able to avail themselves of the liberalizing measures which it lays down, provided that they come objectively within one of the situations provided for by the directive, and no differentiation of treatment on the basis of their residence or nationality is permitted.

Thus the provisions of the directive may be relied upon by the nationals of all the Member States who are in the situations which the directive defines for its application, even in respect of the State whose nationality they possess.

This interpretation is justified by the requirements flowing from freedom of movement for persons, freedom of establishment and freedom to provide services, which are guaranteed by Articles 3(*c*), 48, 52 and 59 of the Treaty.

In fact, these liberties, which are fundamental in the Community system, could not be fully realized if the Member States were in a position to refuse to grant the benefit of the provisions of Community law to those of their nationals who have taken advantage of the facilities existing in the matter of freedom of movement and establishment and who have acquired, by virtue of such facilities, the trade qualifications referred to by the directive in a Member State other than that whose nationality they possess.[34]

The last paragraph quoted above shows that the Court was considering a case where there was a foreign element, in that the plaintiff had already exercised his right of establishment in another member state (Belgium), and indeed appears still to have been established there at the time of his application to the Dutch authorities. It should not be assumed from this case that a national from a member state who has never left that member state could claim rights of establishment there, because the Community is not concerned with purely domestic situations.[35]

The *Knoors* case[36] has been followed in *Broekmulen*,[37] where a Dutch doctor, qualified in Belgium, was regarded as entitled to practise in the Netherlands, even though there were more requirements for the training of doctors in the Netherlands than in Belgium. One factor in each of these cases was that the applicant was either established, or at least resident, in one member state and wished to establish himself in another. That foreign element was sufficient to create a Community interest in the situation. However, a more important element, upon which these cases seem to have turned, was that in each case there was a Community directive, and the

[34] Ibid., p. 409.
[35] Case 175/78, *R. v. Saunders* [1979] *ECR* 1129; Case 115/78, *Knoors v. Secretary of State* [1979] *ECR* 399, p. 410.
[36] Case 115/78 [1979] *ECR* 399.
[37] Case 246/80 [1981] *ECR* 2311.

Court founded its judgments on the precise provisions of those directives. Thus in *Knoors*[38] the directive required activity in another member state to be accepted as a qualification to practise. In *Broekmulen*[39] the directive required qualifications in another member state to be recognized as qualifications to practise.

In *Ministère* v. *Auer*[40] there was at the times in question no directive upon which the person claiming establishment could rely. The facts were that an Austrian national obtained veterinary qualifications in Italy and then went to live in France in 1958, where he practised veterinary medicine, first as an assistant and then on his own account. Later he became a French national. All was well until 1962, when a French decree required him to have his professional competence tested, because he had 'acquired or reacquired French nationality' and because he did not have a French qualification. He was rejected on a number of occasions by the French authorities, continued to practise, and was prosecuted. The Court ruled:

Article 52 of the Treaty must be interpreted as meaning that for the period prior to the date on which the Member States are required to have taken the measures necessary to comply with Council Directives Nos 78/1026 and 78/1027 of 18 December 1978, the nationals of a Member State cannot rely on that provision with a view to practising the profession of veterinary surgeon in that Member State on any conditions other than those laid down by national legislation.[41]

As in *Knoors*[42] and *Broekmulen*[43] there was a foreign element, in that qualifications acquired in another member state were involved. However, the *Auer* case[44] is distinguishable from those cases in that the defendant had already lawfully established himself (from 1958 to 1962) in the member state in which he subsequently claimed the right to remain established. He was therefore not established or resident in one member state and seeking establishment in another.[45] A more important distinction, however, seems to have been the absence at the material time of any secondary legislation requiring his Italian qualifications to be recognized, and for that reason he could not be regarded as a beneficiary of Article 52 or the General Programme.

In all three cases, *Knoors*,[46] *Broekmulen*,[47] and *Auer*,[48] the person concerned was claiming rights of establishment against the member state

[38] Case 115/78 [1979] *ECR* 399.
[39] Case 246/80 [1981] *ECR* 2311.
[40] Case 136/78 [1979] *ECR* 437.
[41] Ibid., p. 451.
[42] Case 115/78 [1979] *ECR* 399.
[43] Case 246/80 [1981] *ECR* 2311.
[44] Case 136/78 [1979] *ECR* 437.
[45] That this is not a decisive factor is illustrated by the *Thieffry* case; Case 71/76 [1977] *ECR* 765.
[46] Case 115/78 [1979] *ECR* 399.
[47] Case 246/80 [1981] *ECR* 2311.
[48] Case 136/78 [1979] *ECR* 437.

of which he was a national, and as has been seen his success depended upon his ability to demonstrate the existence of a directive within whose terms he could bring himself. If the claimant is a national of one member state, and wishes to establish himself in another, he has no need to discharge this particular burden. In *Thieffry*[49] the plaintiff was a Belgian lawyer who practised at the Brussels Bar and then established himself in legal practice in Paris. In 1974 he obtained from the University of Paris recognition that his Belgian doctorate was equivalent to a French law degree. In 1975 he passed the French professional examination for advocates. In 1976 the Bar Council in Paris rejected his application to register for a period of practical training at the Paris Bar, on the ground that he had no degree in French law. The Court left it to the competent national authorities (whoever they were) to decide, in the light of Community requirements, whether recognition by a university (supplemented as in this case by a professional qualifying certificate obtained according to the law of the country of establishment) can constitute valid evidence of a professional qualification. It then held:

When a national of one Member State desirous of exercising a professional activity such as the profession of advocate in another Member State has obtained a diploma in his country of origin which has been recognised as an equivalent qualification by the competent authority under the legislation of the country of establishment and which has thus enabled him to sit and pass the special qualifying examination for the profession in question, the act of demanding the national diploma prescribed by the legislation of the country of establishment constitutes, even in the absence of the directives provided for in Article 57, a restriction incompatible with the freedom of establishment guaranteed by Article 52 of the Treaty.[50]

The Court repeated in *Patrick* v. *Ministre des Affaires Culturelles*[51] the principle that, where a national of one member state seeks establishment in another, the absence of any directives under Article 57 is no bar to the application of Article 52. The case concerned a British architect whose British qualifications had been accepted by the French authorities as equivalent to the certificate required in France for French architects.

Title I of the General Programme also introduced, in relation to companies and firms, two additional factors, of which one widened the scope of the right of establishment and the other introduced a restriction.

The first of these new elements relates to companies formed under the law of an overseas country or territory, which are declared to be entitled to establish themselves, provided that, as in the case of companies and firms covered by Article 58, they have either the seat prescribed by their statutes, or their centre of administration, or their main establishment, within the

---

[49] Case 71/76 [1977] *ECR* 765.
[50] Ibid., p. 779.
[51] Case 11/77 [1977] *ECR* 1199.

Community. In this formulation 'main establishment' replaced 'principal place of business' as used in Article 58, but no substantial difference seems to be intended. The French texts of Article 58 and Title I of the General Programme in fact use the same expression—'principal établissement'. The phrase 'overseas country or territory' is taken from Article 227(3) EEC and Part IV of the Treaty (Articles 131–6) and it refers to the territories having special relations with certain member states which are to enjoy associated status. That status is now regulated by Council Decision 1186/80 of 16 December 1980.[52] Article 137 of the decision contains provisions relating to establishment (and services) and reads:

As regards the arrangements that may be applied in matters of establishment and provision of services, the competent authorities of the countries and territories shall treat nationals and companies or firms of Member States on a non-discriminatory basis. However, if, for a given activity, a Member State is unable to provide similar treatment to nationals or companies or firms of the French Republic, the Kingdom of the Netherlands or the United Kingdom of Great Britain and Northern Ireland, established in a country or territory, or to companies or firms subject to the laws of the country or territory concerned and established therein, the relevant authorities of that country of territory shall not be bound to accord such treatment.[53]

In this way member states have now reserved the right not to grant rights of establishment to nationals, companies, and firms from the overseas countries and territories, the penalty for doing so being to lose any similar rights in those countries and territories for their own nationals, companies, and firms.[54] In this respect Title I of the General Programme must now be regarded as having been modified. The countries and territories concerned were originally listed in Annex IV to the Treaty, but owing to a number of them having disqualified themselves by becoming independent that list is now obsolete. The current list is in Annex I to Decision 80/1186,[55] except that as a result of the independence of Belize and Antigua those territories no longer qualify.

The second new element, which has already been mentioned, is that where companies and firms which qualify for establishment wish to exercise their rights by setting up only agencies, branches, or subsidiaries in a member state they only gain the benefit of the General Programme if they satisfy the following proviso:

that, where only the seat prescribed by their statutes is situated within the Community or in an overseas country or territory, their activity shows a real and

[52] *OJ* 1980, L361/1, as subsequently amended.
[53] Art. 160 of the Second ACP–EEC Convention, signed at Lomé on 31 October 1979, TS No. 3 (1983), is in similar terms. This Article is identical to Art. 62 of the first Lomé Convention, which the Court interpreted in Case 65/77, *Razanatsimba* [1977] *ECR* 2229.
[54] This may be regarded as a special provision under Art. 136 EEC, rather than as falling within Art. 132(5) EEC.   [55] *OJ* 1980, L361/1.

continuous link with the economy of a Member State or of an overseas country or territory; such link shall not be one of nationality, whether of the members of the company or firm, or of the persons holding managerial or supervisory posts therein, or of the holders of the capital.[56]

Whether failure to satisfy this proviso merely disqualifies such companies and firms from gaining the benefit of the General Programme, or whether it disqualifies them from claiming the benefits of Article 52 remains to be determined by the Court. Since the *fons et origo* of the General Programme is in Articles 52 and 58 EEC, and since neither contains any such proviso, the first interpretation may be preferable.

Entry and residence (Title II)

This part of the Programme required that, subject to the exceptions listed in Article 56, member states should remove any restrictions on the entry and residence of nationals of other member states which would be liable to hinder self-employed persons in the exercise of their rights of establishment.

Directive 148/73[57] achieves this objective for nationals of member states who wish to establish themselves. Article 1(1) also widens the category of beneficiaries of the right of entry and residence to include as of right the spouse, children under 21 years of age, and dependent relatives of such nationals and of the spouse of such nationals in the ascending and descending lines, irrespective of their own nationality. Article 1(2) goes even further, and requires member states to 'favour' the admission of any other dependent relative of the national or of his or her spouse who in the country of origin was living 'under the same roof'. Article 2 assures all such persons of the right to leave a member state on production of a valid identity card or passport. This applies to the member state of which the person concerned is a national, as well as any other member state in which he may establish himself.

As is made clear in Article 8 of the Directive, this right of free movement (and indeed all other provisions of the Directive) is subject to the provisions of Article 56 EEC, so that for example a member state is not obliged by the Directive to release a convicted criminal from prison simply because he expresses a wish to take advantage of Article 2(1) of the Directive.

Article 2 also requires member states to issue to their own nationals either an identity card, or a passport valid for all member states and all countries through which the holder must pass when travelling between member states. In each case the document must state the holder's

[56] Ibid., p. 7.
[57] *OJ* 1973, L172/14. The Directive follows closely Dir. 360/68, *OJ* 1968, L257/13, which applies to employed persons.

nationality. If a passport is required to leave the country, it must be valid for at least five years. No exit visas may be demanded (Article 2(4)). Article 3 requires member states to allow entry merely on production of a valid identity card or passport, and entry visas may only be required in respect of members of the family who are not nationals of any member states.

Article 4 requires the right of permanent residence to be granted (and evidenced by a document entitled 'Residence Permit for a National of a Member State of the European Communities', valid for five years and automatically renewable) to nationals of other member states who establish themselves in order to pursue activities as self-employed persons, 'when the restrictions on these activities have been abolished pursuant to the Treaty'. The latter qualification may have been added because at the time it was thought that the rights of establishment under Article 52 were dependent, even after the expiry of the transitional period, upon the adoption of a relevant directive under Articles 54 or 57. However, in the light of the Court's decision in *Reyners* v. *Belgium*[58] the qualification may be regarded as no longer having any legal effect. Article 5 requires the right of residence to be effective throughout a member state's territory. Article 6 prevents a member state from requiring, as a condition of issuing a residence permit, the production of anything other than an identity card or passport, and proof that the applicant is a beneficiary under the Directive.

Directive 34/75[59] takes the matter further, and at the same time fills a gap which exists under the Treaty, because whereas Articles 48(3)(*d*) of the Treaty expressly confers a right on workers to remain in the territory of a member state after having been employed there, neither Article 52 nor Article 54 does so in the case of self-employed persons. The reasoning behind the Directive, as explained in the preamble, appears to be that it is normal for a person to prolong a period of permanent residence in a member state after he has ceased to exercise his self-employed activity there, and that the absence of a right to do so is an obstacle which may inhibit him from exercising his rights of establishment. Accordingly the Directive requires member states to abolish restrictions on such a person's right to remain (Article 1). The conditions which he must satisfy to gain recognition of his right to remain permanently in a member state are the same, mutatis mutandis, as those contained in Commission Regulation 1251/70,[60] which apply in the case of a worker who ceases to be employed. The applicant must have either reached retirement age or become incapacitated, and have completed a minimum period of residence. The details are described in Chapter 4 ('Workers') in connection with Regulation 1251/70.

[58] Case 2/74 [1974] *ECR* 631.
[59] *OJ* 1975, L14/10.
[60] *OJ* 1970, L142/24.

Removal of restrictions (Title III)

This part of the General Programme is particularly valuable as an indication, in some detail, of the scope and extent of the right of establishment. It is worth quoting in full:

Subject to the exceptions or special provisions laid down in the Treaty and in particular to:
  Article 55 concerning activities which are connected with the exercise of official authority in a Member State; and to
  Article 56 concerning provisions on special treatment for foreign nationals on grounds of public policy, public security or public health,
the following restrictions are to be eliminated in accordance with the timetable laid down under Title IV:

A. Any measure which, pursuant to any provision laid down by law, Regulation or administrative action in a Member State, or as the result of the application of such a provision, or of administrative practices, prohibits or hinders nationals of other Member States in their pursuit of an activity as a self-employed person by treating nationals of other Member States differently from nationals of the country concerned.

Such restrictive provisions and practices are in particular those which, in respect of foreign nationals only:

(*a*) prohibit the taking up or pursuit of an activity as a self-employed person;

(*b*) make the taking up or pursuit of an activity as a self-employed person subject to an authorization or to the issue of a document such as a foreign trader's permit;

(*c*) impose additional conditions in respect of the granting of any authorization required for the taking up or pursuit of an activity as a self-employed person;

(*d*) make the taking up or pursuit of an activity as a self-employed person subject to a period of prior residence or training in the host country;

(*e*) make the taking up or pursuit of an activity as a self-employed person more costly through taxation or other financial burdens, such as a requirement that the person concerned shall lodge a deposit or provide security in the host country;

(*f*) limit or hinder by making it more costly or more difficult access to sources of supply or to distribution outlets;

(*g*) prohibit or hinder access to any vocational training which is necessary or useful for the pursuit of an activity as a self-employed person;

(*h*) prohibit foreign nationals from becoming members of companies or firms, or restrict their rights as members, in particular as regards the functions which they may perform within the company or firm;

(*i*) deny or restrict the right to participate in social security schemes, in particular sickness, accident, invalidity or old age insurance schemes, or the right to receive family allowances;

(*j*) grant less favourable treatment in the event of nationalization, expropriation or requisition.

The like shall apply to provisions and practices which, in respect of foreign nationals only, exclude, limit or impose conditions on the power to exercise rights normally attaching to an activity as a self-employed person, and in particular the power:

(*a*) to enter into contracts, in particular contracts for work, business or agricultural tenancies, and contracts of employment, and to enjoy all rights arising under such contracts;

(*b*) to submit tenders for or to act directly as a party or as a subcontractor in contracts with the State or with any other legal person governed by public law;

(*c*) to obtain licences or authorizations issued by the State or by any other legal person governed by public law;

(*d*) to acquire, use or dispose of movable or immovable property[61] or rights therein;

(*e*) to acquire, use or dispose of intellectual property and all rights deriving therefrom;

(*f*) to borrow, and in particular to have access to the various forms of credit;

(*g*) to receive aids granted by the State, whether direct or indirect;

(*h*) to be a party to legal or administrative proceedings;

(*i*) to join professional or trade organizations;

where the professional or trade activities of the person concerned necessarily involve the exercise of such power.

Furthermore, included among the abovementioned provisions and practices are those which limit or impair the freedom of personnel belonging to the main establishment in one Member State to take up managerial or supervisory posts in agencies, branches or subsidiaries in another Member State.

B. Any requirements imposed, pursuant to any provision laid down by law, Regulation or administrative action or in consequence of any administrative practice, in respect of the taking up or pursuit of an activity as a self-employed person where, although applicable irrespective of nationality, their effect is exclusively or principally, to hinder the taking up or pursuit of such activity by foreign nationals.

Discrimination

As a guide to the meaning of 'establishment' the provisions of Title III of the General Programme have been considered earlier in this chapter. At their root is the general principle, first referred to in Article 7 and then repeated in other Articles of the Treaty (including Article 52, second paragraph), that a member state must not discriminate on grounds of nationality against the nationals of any other member state. This is clear from the opening lines of paragraph A of Title III of the General Programme. The corresponding part of paragraph B, while referring to restrictions which are applicable irrespective of nationality, nevertheless only applies where the effect of those restrictions is exclusively or principally to hinder foreign

---

[61] With regard to land and buildings, see also Art. 54(3)(*e*) EEC.

nationals from taking up a self-employed activity. It thus brings disguised discrimination on grounds of nationality within the ambit of the prohibition. The Court referred in *Thieffry* v. *Conseil, etc.*[62] to Title III B as evidence of the principle that disguised discrimination against foreign nationals in matters of establishment is prohibited just as much as overt discrimination.

It can be argued that discrimination on grounds of nationality is an essential ingredient of any breach of Article 52, and that this Article is indeed no more than a particular application of the principle in Article 7. Thus in *Costa* v. *ENEL*[63] the Court made a general pronouncement which can be taken to indicate that discrimination is an essential ingredient of any breach of the rules on establishment. It said:

Article 53 is therefore satisfied so long as no new measure subjects the establishment of nationals of other Member States to more severe rules than those prescribed for nationals of the country of establishment, whatever the legal system governing the undertaking.[64]

The Court also demonstrated the very close link between Article 52 and Article 7 in *Van Ameyde* v. *UCI*,[65] where it said:

Article 7 of the Treaty prohibits in general terms all discrimination based on nationality.

In the respective spheres of the right of establishment and the freedom to provide services Articles 52 and 59 guarantee the application of the principle laid down by Article 7.

It follows therefore that if rules are compatible with Articles 52 and 59 they are also compatible with Article 7. Articles 52 and 59 prohibit directly any discrimination based on nationality.[66]

It should be noted, however, that the penultimate sentence in this quotation does not say that if rules are compatible with Article 7 they are also compatible with Articles 52 and 59.

This argument as to whether Article 52 is only an application of the equal treatment rule was not resolved in *Reyners* v. *Belgium*,[67] although parts of the judgment are relevant to it. It is not altogether easy to follow the Court's reasoning, because the text of the judgment does not clearly record when the Court is reproducing the arguments of others and when it is stating its own views. Thus paragraph 11 is attributed to the German Government.

[62] Case 71/76 [1977] *ECR* 765, p. 777.
[63] Case 6/64 [1964] *ECR* 585.
[64] Ibid., p. 597.
[65] Case 90/76 [1977] *ECR* 1091.
[66] Ibid., pp. 1126–7. See also Case 182/83, *Robert Fearon & Co. Ltd.* v. *Irish Land Commission*, judgment of 6/11/84, in which the Court referred to 'the fundamental rule of non-discrimination which underlies the chapter of the Treaty relating to the right of establishment'.
[67] Case 2/74 [1974] *ECR* 631.

Paragraphs 12 and 13 are not, although in fact paragraph 13 records a view which had been advanced by the German Government (that the Directives provided for by Article 54 were of significance only during the transitional period) and which is inconsistent with the Court's view as expressed in paragraph 31 of the judgment. Paragraph 14 refers to the Commission's argument that Article 52 has at least partial direct effect to the extent that it prohibits discrimination on grounds of nationality. It is however by no means clear whether the following paragraph 15 records the Court's views or, if that and any subsequent paragraphs merely repeat the Commission's thoughts, at what point the Court begins to voice its own.

It may well be that in paragraph 15 et seq. the Court is speaking for itself, but this is not free from all doubt. Paragraph 18 describes as the guiding principle in Article 52 that freedom of establishment is to *include* the right to take up and pursue activities as self-employed persons 'under the conditions laid down for its own nationals by the law of the country where such establishment is effected'. This rule on equal treatment with nationals is again described by the Court as one of the fundamental legal provisions of the Community.[68] The rule is then said by the Court in paragraph 30 to have direct effect after the expiry of the transitional period.

This approach raises, but does not answer, the question whether, if Article 52 only *includes* (in its second paragraph) the nationality rule and it is only the latter which is to have direct effect, the first paragraph of the Article goes wider, and creates some additional kind of right of establishment. Although the question is not answered directly, some indication that the Court in effect regarded Article 52 as a whole as only a particular application of the nationality rule is to be gained from the fact that the first conclusion in the 'dispositif' is that Article 52 (i.e. as a whole) is directly applicable, whereas all the Court's previous arguments had been directed to explaining why the nationality rule had direct effect.

On the other hand, when referring to the Directives under Articles 54, 56, and 57, the Court said:

After the expiry of the transitional period the directives provided for by the Chapter on the right of establishment have become superfluous with regard to implementing the rule on nationality, since this is henceforth sanctioned by the Treaty itself with direct effect.

These directives have however not lost all interest since they preserve an important scope in the field of measures intended to make easier the effective exercise of the right of freedom of establishment.[69]

Thus, if the directives are superfluous for the purpose of removing discrimination on grounds of nationality, but are in other respects useful to

---

[68] Ibid., p. 651.
[69] Ibid., p. 652.

achieve freedom of establishment, the inference may be that Article 52 goes wider than the nationality rule.

From a practical point of view it seems preferable to regard the Council as having a measure of discretion to adopt directives which will assist the exercise of the right of establishment without always having to demonstrate that what it is doing is applying the nationality rule. A good example of this practical need is the case of a directive which says that a person (of whatever nationality provided he is a national of a member state) is to be regarded as a qualified doctor if he holds one of a number of specified qualifications.[70]

Some support for this view is to be found in *Ministère Public and Auer*.[71] After stating that *in so far* as Article 52 is intended to ensure national treatment it concerns only nationals of other states, the Court went on to say:

> However, it may be seen from the provisions of Articles 54 and 57 of the Treaty that freedom of establishment is not completely ensured by the mere application of the rule of national treatment, as such application retains all obstacles other than those resulting from the non-possession of the nationality of the host State and, in particular, those resulting from the disparity of the conditions laid down by the different national laws for the acquisition of an appropriate professional qualification.
>
> With a view to ensuring complete freedom of establishment, Article 54 of the Treaty provides that the Council shall draw up a general programme for the abolition of existing restrictions on such freedom and Article 57 provides that the Council shall issue directives for the mutual recognition of diplomas, certificates and other evidence of qualifications.[72]

The first paragraph in this quotation does not refer to Article 52, but it does nevertheless suggest that the right of establishment goes wider than a rule of non-discrimination on grounds of nationality. The second paragraph refers to the need for action by the Council in order to achieve complete freedom of establishment. Taken in isolation, that paragraph might have been read as an indication that such action was the only means of securing that freedom, and that in its absence non-discrimination was the only rule. That a successful claim to the right of freedom of establishment may depend upon the existence of relevant secondary legislation has also been demonstrated in *Knoors*[73] and *Broekmulen*.[74]

However, in *Paris Bar Council* v. *Klopp*[75] the Court took a different view. In that case there were no relevant Community directives, and national

---

[70] Arts. 2 and 3 of Dir. 362/75, *OJ* 1975, L167/1.

[71] Case 136/78 [1979] *ECR* 437. See also Case 271/82, *Auer* v. *Ministère Public and Others* [1985] 1 *CMLR* 123.

[72] Ibid., p. 449.

[73] Case 115/78 [1979] *ECR* 399.

[74] Case 246/80 [1982] 1 *CMLR* 91.

[75] Case 107/83 [1985] 1 *CMLR* 99. The quotations below are taken from this report, not the Court's own translation.

rules, applicable irrespective of nationality, required that any person engaging in practice at the French Bar must have only one business or professional address. The application of this rule meant that any barrister established in premises in another member state was required to give up those premises in order to establish himself in France. The Court held this to be contrary to Article 52 (the first paragraph of which refers to the right to retain an establishment in one member state and at the same time to become established in another by opening up there an agency, branch, or subsidiary). Thus the national rule infringed Article 52, although it did not discriminate on grounds of nationality. Although the applicant sought to argue that there was in fact disguised discrimination, the Court left such a question of fact to the national court, and itself dealt with the matter without reference to such a possibility.

The Court's ruling was:

Even in the absence of any directive co-ordinating national provisions governing access to, and the exercise of, the legal profession, Articles 52 et seq. of the EEC Treaty prevent the competent authorities of a Member State from denying, in accordance with their national legislation and the rules of professional conduct which are in force in that State, to a national of another Member State the right to enter and to exercise the legal profession solely on the ground that he simultaneously maintains chambers in another Member State.[76]

The Court explained its reasons in the following passage:

It should be emphasised that, pursuant to Article 52(2) the freedom of establishment includes the right to take up and pursue activities as self-employed persons 'under the conditions laid down for its own nationals by the law of the country where such establishment is effected.' It follows from this provision and its context that, in the absence of specific Community rules on the subject, each Member State is free to regulate the practice of the profession of advocate in its territory.

However, this rule does not imply that the legislation of a Member State may require an advocate to have no more than one establishment in the whole of Community territory. Such a restrictive interpretation would in practice have the consequence that an advocate, once established in a particular Member State, could no longer invoke the benefit of the freedoms given by the Treaty in order to establish himself in another Member State except at the price of giving up his existing establishment.

The view that the freedom of establishment is not confined to the right to open a single establishment within the Community is confirmed by the very terms of Article 52 of the Treaty, which provide that the gradual abolition of restrictions on the freedom of establishment also applies to restrictions on the setting up of agencies, branches or subsidiaries by nationals of any Member State established in the territory of another Member State. This rule must be regarded as a specific

---

[76] Ibid., p. 115.

expression of a general principle applying equally to the liberal professions, whereby the right of establishment includes the right to set up and maintain, in compliance with professional rules, more than one centre of activity in Community territory.[77]

This judgment lends further support to the view that Article 52 is not simply an application of the rule of non-discrimination which is established in Article 7.

Mutual recognition of diplomas and other evidence of formal qualifications (Title V) and the co-ordination of national provisions

Title V of the General Programme indicated that the mutual recognition of diplomas, certificates, and other evidence of formal qualifications could be made at any time, whether before or after the lifting of any particular restrictions on establishment. It also envisaged the possibility in appropriate cases of a transitional system, whereby a certificate of actual and lawful practice in the country of origin should be accepted as evidence of qualification to practise. An example of such a system is in Directive 427/64,[78] which was the subject of litigation in the *Knoors* case.[79] This Title therefore provides a programme for the implementation of Article 57(1) EEC.

Article 57(1) imposes an obligation on the Council, on a proposal from the Commission and after consulting the European Parliament, to issue directives for the mutual recognition of diplomas, certificates, and other evidence of full qualifications. A simplistic view would be that in a common market a qualification judged sufficient to allow a person to practise a profession or occupation in one member state should be regarded as adequate in all other member states. However, owing to the complex structure of some professions it is not always easy to find exact equivalents in all member states. Nor in practice is there uniformity in the standards of training required. Yet it is clearly an impediment to the free movement of a person, whether he is self-employed or employed, if his qualifications are not recognized outside the member state in which they were acquired, and if he is in consequence only allowed to practise there.

Article 57(2) similarly obliged the Council to adopt directives before the end of the transitional period, for the co-ordination of national provisions concerning the taking up and pursuit of activities as self-employed persons.[80]

It is curious that there is no specific equivalent of Article 57 in Chapter 1 of Title III ('Workers'). However, the Council has adopted the habit of

[77] Ibid., p. 113.

[78] *OJ* 1964, L59/8.

[79] Case 115/78 [1979] *ECR* 399.

[80] Art. 57(3), about the medical and allied and pharmaceutical professions, was regarded by the Advocate General as ceasing to have effect at the end of the transitional period: Case 136/78, *Ministère Public and Auer* [1979] *ECR* 437, p. 457.

reciting Articles 49, 57, 66, and 235 in the preambles to directives which fall within the scope of Article 57, thereby acknowledging the need for recognition of qualifications and co-ordination of national laws in order to facilitate the free movement of workers, freedom of establishment, and freedom to provide services.[81]

In this field some progress has been made in the adoption of directives dealing, for example, with agricultural workers,[82] establishment on abandoned agricultural holdings,[83] established farmers,[84] agricultural leaseholders,[85] self-employed persons providing agricultural and horticultural services,[86] intermediaries in commerce, industry, and small craft industries,[87] mining and quarrying,[88] electricity, gas, water, and sanitary services,[89] forestry and logging,[90] food manufacturing and beverage industries,[91] exploration (prospecting and drilling) for petroleum and natural gas,[92] reinsurance and retrocession,[93] co-ordination of laws of direct insurance other than life insurance,[94] abolishing restrictions on establishment in the business of direct insurance other than life insurance,[95] insurance agents and brokers,[96] Community co-insurance,[97] co-ordination of laws on direct life assurance,[98] self-employed activities of banks and other financial institutions,[99] co-ordination of laws on credit institutions,[100] road-haulage operators in national and international operations,[101] road passenger transport operators in national and international operations,[102] reciprocal recognition of navigability licences for inland waterway vessels,[103] training

---

[81] See e.g. Dir. 362/75 (doctors), *OJ* 1975, L167/1.

[82] Dir. 261/63, *OJ*, Special Edition, 1963, p. 19, as amended by the Act of Accession.

[83] Dir. 262/63, *OJ*, Special Edition, 1963, p. 22, as amended by the Act of Accession.

[84] Dir. 530/67, *OJ*, Special Edition, 1967, p. 228, as amended by the Act of Accession.

[85] Dir. 531/67, *OJ*, Special Edition, 1967, p. 230, as amended by the Act of Accession.

[86] Dir. 18/71, *OJ*, 1971, L8/24, as amended by the Act of Accession.

[87] Dir. 224/64, *OJ*, Special Edition, 1964, p. 126, as amended by the Act of Accession and Greek Act of Accession.

[88] Dir. 428/64, *OJ*, Special Edition, 1964, p. 151, as amended by the Act of Accession.

[89] Dir. 162/66, *OJ*, Special Edition, 1966, p. 93, as amended by the Act of Accession.

[90] Dir. 654/67, *OJ*, Special Edition, 1967, p. 287, as amended by the Act of Accession.

[91] Dir. 365/68, *OJ*, 1968, L260/9, as amended by the Act of Accession.

[92] Dir. 69/82, *OJ* 1982, L68/4, as amended by the Act of Accession.

[93] Dir. 225/64, *OJ*, Special Edition, 1964, p. 131, as amended by the Act of Accession.

[94] Dir. 239/73, *OJ*, 1973, L228/3, as amended by the Act of Accession and Dir. 580/76, *OJ* 1976, L189/13.   [95] Dir. 240/73, *OJ* 1973, L228/20.

[96] Dir. 92/77, *OJ* 1977, L26/14, as amended by the Greek Act of Accession.

[97] Dir. 473/78, *OJ* 1978, L151/25.

[98] Dir. 267/79, *OJ* 1979, L63/1, as amended by the Greek Act of Accession.

[99] Dir. 183/73, *OJ* 1973, L194/1.

[100] Dir. 780/77, *OJ* 1977, L322/30, as amended by the Greek Act of Accession.

[101] Dir. 561/74, *OJ* 1974, L308/18, as amended by the Greek Act of Accession and Dir. 1179/80, *OJ* 1980, L350/41.

[102] Dir. 562/74, *OJ* 1974, L308/23, as amended by the Greek Act of Accession and Dir. 1179/80, *OJ* 1980, L350/42.

[103] Dir. 135/76, *OJ* 1976, L21/10, implemented by Decision 527/77, *OJ* 1977, L209/29, extended in duration and amended by Dir. 1016/78, *OJ* 1978, L349/31.

of some road-transport drivers,[104] recognition of diplomas, etc. for goods haulage operators and road passenger transport operators,[105] persons concerned with real estate,[106] the film industry,[107] film distribution,[108] restaurants, hotels, taverns, etc.,[109] retail traders,[110] wholesalers and intermediaries in the coal trade,[111] trade in and distribution of toxic products,[112] freedom of establishment and services in respect of itinerant activities,[113] recognition of qualifications in medicine,[114] co-ordination of laws on doctors,[115] recognition of qualifications of nurses,[116] co-ordination of laws on nurses,[117] recognition of qualifications in dentistry,[118] co-ordination of laws on dentists,[119] qualifications of vets,[120] co-ordination of laws on vets,[121] recognition of qualifications of midwives,[122] co-ordination of laws on midwives.[123] Oddly enough, the lawyers' Directive[124] is concerned solely with the provision of services and therefore does not apply to establishment.

In the absence of any directive issued under Article 57(1) on the mutual recognition of qualifications, the position appears to be that it is for national authorities to determine in accordance with national law whether in any particular case a foreign qualification is to be recognized, provided however the national rules, including those on recognition, draw no

---

[104] Dir. 914/76, *OJ* 1976, L357/36.

[105] Dir. 796/77, *OJ* 1977, L334/37, amended by Dir. 1180/80, *OJ* 1980, L350/43.

[106] Dir. 43/67, *OJ*, Special Edition, 1967, p. 3, amended by the Act of Accession and the Greek Act of Accession.

[107] Dir. 264/65, *OJ*, Special Edition, 1965, p. 62, and Dir. 451/70, *OJ* 1970, L218/37, both amended by the Act of Accession.

[108] Dir. 369/68, *OJ* 1968, L260/22, amended by the Act of Accession.

[109] Dir. 367/68, *OJ* 1968, L260/16, and Dir. 368/68, *OJ*, 1968, L260/19, both amended by the Act of Accession.

[110] Dir. 363/68, *OJ* 1968, L260/1, and Dir. 364/68, *OJ* 1968, L260/6, both amended by the Act of Accession.

[111] Dir. 522/70, *OJ* 1970, L267/14 and Dir. 523/70, *OJ* 1970, L267/18, both amended by the Act of Accession.

[112] Dir. 556/74, *OJ* 1974, L307/1, Dir. 557/74, *OJ* 1974, L307/5.

[113] Dir. 369/75, *OJ* 1975, L167/29.

[114] Dir. 362/75, *OJ* 1975, L167/1, amended by the Greek Act of Accession and Dir. 1057/81, *OJ* 1981, L385/25.

[115] Dir. 363/75, *OJ* 1975, L167/14.

[116] Dir. 452/77, *OJ* 1977, L176/1, amended by the Greek Act of Accession, and by Dir. 1057/81, *OJ* 1981, L385/25.

[117] Dir. 453/77, *OJ* 1977, L176/8.

[118] Dir. 686/78, *OJ* 1978, L233/1, amended by the Greek Act of Accession and Dir. 1057/81, *OJ* 1981, L385/25. See Case 219/83, *Commission* v. *Netherlands*, Case 223/83, *Commission* v. *Germany*.

[119] Dir. 687/78, *OJ* 1978, L233/10, interpreted by *OJ* 1978, C202/1.

[120] Dir. 1026/78, *OJ* 1978, L362/1, amended by the Greek Act of Accession and by Dir. 1057/81, *OJ* 1981, L385/25. See Case 221/83, *Commission* v. *Italy*.

[121] Dir. 1027/78, *OJ* 1978, L362/7.

[122] Dir. 154/80, *OJ* 1980, L33/1, amended by Dir. 1273/80, *OJ* 1980, L375/74.

[123] Dir. 155/80, *OJ* 1980, L33/8.

[124] Dir. 249/77, *OJ* 1977, L78/17, as amended by the Greek Act of Accession, Art. 21 and Annex I.

distinction based on the nationality of the applicant: see *Ministère Public and Auer*,[125] and *Patrick* v. *Ministre des Affaires Culturelles*,[126] where the Court said:

After the expiry of the transitional period the directives provided for by the chapter on the right of establishment have become superfluous with regard to implementing the rule on nationality, since this is henceforth sanctioned by the Treaty itself with direct effect.[127]

Thus in *Auer* the Court left it to the national authorities of the host country to say whether, at the material time, the applicant's qualifications were equivalent to national ones, but the judgment in *Patrick* made it clear that this is subject to the overriding rule against discrimination on grounds of nationality. Once a competent national authority recognizes such equivalence, it may not demand a national diploma as well: *Thieffry* v. *Conseil* etc.[128] The position of course is quite different when a relevant directive has been adopted, as can be seen in the sequel to the first *Auer* case.[129] In *Auer* v. *Ministère Public and Others*[130] the veterinary surgeon succeeded because by that time there were in existence Directives 1026/78 and 1027/78,[131] and it was no longer open to the national law to determine whether or not he was suitably qualified. Such questions could henceforth only be answered by reference to the Directive.

Co-ordination of safeguards required of companies (Title VI), and the harmonization of company laws

Title VI of the General Programme provided a timetable for action by the Council under Article 54(3)(g) EEC, which requires it to co-ordinate

to the necessary extent the safeguards which, for the protection of the interests of members and others, are required by Member States of companies or firms within the meaning of the second paragraph of Article 58 with a view to making such safeguards equivalent throughout the Community . . .

This provision, together with Article 100, formed the basis of extensive Commission plans for the harmonization and approximation of the nationals laws of the member states, and a number of them have come to fruition. The First Directive of 9 March 1968[132] deals with the compulsory disclosure of information by companies, company obligations, and nullity

---

[125] Case 136/78 [1979] *ECR* 437, p. 451.
[126] Case 11/77 [1977] *ECR* 1199.
[127] Ibid., p. 1205.
[128] Case 71/76 [1977] *ECR* 765, p. 780.
[129] Case 136/78 [1979] *ECR* 437.
[130] Case 271/82 [1985] 1 *CMLR* 123. See also Case 5/83, *Hendrik Gerhard Rienks* [1983] *ECR* 4233.
[131] *OJ* 1978, L362/1 and 7.
[132] Dir. 151/68, *OJ* 1968, L65/8.

of companies. The Second Directive of 13 December 1976[133] concerns the formation of companies, and the maintenance, increase, and reduction of their capital. The Third Directive of 9 October 1978[134] is about mergers. The Fourth Directive, which with a fine sense of Community logic predates the Third Directive, is dated 25 July 1978,[135] and deals with annual accounts. The draft for a Fifth Directive[136] included provisions on the structure of companies and employee participation. Major difficulties emerged, and the draft still remains to be finalized. Directive 79/279 of 5 March 1979[137] co-ordinated the conditions for the admission of securities to official stock exchange listing. Directive 80/390 of 17 March 1980[138] co-ordinated the requirements for the drawing up, scrutiny, and distribution of the listing particulars to be published for the admission of securities to official stock exchange listing. Directive 82/121[139] concerns the interim reports required to be published by companies whose securities are listed on a recognized stock exchange. Directive 891/82 ('the Sixth Directive')[140] is about divisions of public limited liability companies. Directive 349/83 ('the Seventh Directive')[141] concerns group accounts of companies.

Failure to comply with the first two directives was the subject of *Commission* v. *Belgium*.[142]

EXCEPTIONS TO FREEDOM OF ESTABLISHMENT

Article 52(2) (capital)

Article 52(2) EEC ends with the words 'subject to the provisions of the Chapter relating to capital', thereby showing that free movement of capital, though needed to enable rights of establishment to be exercised, was to be ensured by action under Articles 67–73 rather than Articles 52–8. In fact, the movement of capital for this purpose was liberalized by the First Directive for the implementation of Article 67,[143] and for practical purposes Article 52(2) need no longer be regarded as making any exception in this respect.

Article 55 (exercise of official authority)

Article 55 EEC reads:

The provisions of this Chapter shall not apply, so far as any given Member State is concerned, to activities which in that State are connected, even occasionally, with the exercise of official authority.

   The Council may, acting by a qualified majority on a proposal from the

[133] Dir. 91/77, *OJ* 1977, L26/1.
[134] Dir. 855/78, *OJ* 1978, L295/36.   [135] Dir. 660/78, *OJ* 1978, L222/11.
[136] *OJ* 1972, C131/49.   [137] *OJ* 1979, L66/21.
[138] *OJ* 1980, L100/1.   [139] *OJ* 1982, L48/26.
[140] *OJ* 1982, L378/47.   [141] *OJ* 1983, L193/1.
[142] Case 148/81 [1982] *ECR* 3555.   [143] *OJ*, Special Edition, 1959–62, p. 49.

Commission, rule that the provisions of this Chapter shall not apply to certain activities.

The Council has not acted under the second paragraph of this Article.

The first paragraph of the Article has a counterpart in Article 48(4) relating to workers employed in the public service.[144] An idea common to both Articles is that some functions, exercised on behalf of the State, require a standard of loyalty which a member state can expect of its own nationals but not of foreigners. In such cases it should not be obliged to allow foreigners to perform them, either as employees or as independent contractors established in its territory. Although they share this common thought, it should not however be concluded that the scope of the two Articles is necessarily the same, mutatis mutandis. Each needs to be interpreted in accordance with its own express provisions and context. The key words in Article 55(1) are 'connected, even occasionally, with the exercise of official authority'.

The meaning of this phrase was considered by the Court in *Reyners* v. *Belgium*.[145] In that case the national court asked whether, within a profession such as that of 'avocat', only activities connected with the exercise of official authority were excluded by Article 55, or whether the profession itself was excluded on the grounds that its exercise involved activities connected with the exercise of official authority. The plaintiff supported the former interpretation. So did the Belgian, Dutch, Irish, and UK governments, and the Commission. The government of Luxembourg and the Belgian Bar supported the latter interpretation. The German government thought that in the case of a particular profession the activities connected with the exercise of official authority could be so preponderant that the whole profession could come within Article 55. The European Court accepted the first interpretation. Its ruling was:

2. The exception to freedom of establishment provided for by the first paragraph of Article 55 must be restricted to those of the activities referred to in Article 52 which in themselves involve a direct and specific connexion with the exercise of official authority; it is not possible to give this description, in the context of a profession such as that of *avocat*, to activities such as consultation and legal assistance or the representation and defence of parties in court, even if the performance of these activities is compulsory or there is a legal monopoly in respect of it.[146]

In its reasoning the Court, after referring to the necessity to interpret strictly an exception to a fundamental Community rule, said:

An extension of the exception allowed by Article 55 to a whole profession would be possible only in cases where such activities were linked with that profession in

---

[144] Considered in Chapter 4 ('Workers').
[145] Case 2/74 [1974] *ECR* 631.   [146] Ibid., p. 656.

such a way that freedom of establishment would result in imposing on the Member State concerned the obligation to allow the exercise, even occasionally, by non-nationals of functions appertaining to official authority. This extension is on the other hand not possible when, within the framework of an independent profession, the activities connected with the exercise of official authority are separable from the professional activity in question taken as a whole.[147]

Article 56 (public policy, public security, public health)

Article 56(1) reads:

1. The provisions of this Chapter and measures taken in pursuance thereof shall not prejudice the applicability of provisions laid down by law, regulation or administrative action providing for special treatment for foreign nationals on grounds of public policy, public security or public health.

The references to public policy, public security, and public health echo the terms of Articles 36 and 48(3). However, the draftsman approaches these concepts in different ways. In the two earlier Articles the right of free movement of workers may only be restricted if the limitations are 'justified' on one of the grounds stated. It was therefore relatively easy for the Court to conclude that the Article only created an exception if the claim to make it was subject to judicial control,[148] and control by the Community institutions.[149] On the other hand, Article 56 makes no mention of justification, and it indicates instead that the Community rules in this chapter are not to prejudice laws, regulations, or administrative action relating to public policy, etc. It could be argued from all this that the authors of the Treaty intended to draw a distinction between the earlier Articles and Article 56, and that under the latter the primary rules, which are not to be affected, are those of national law, even though that law may provide for administrative or other action which is not subject to judicial control or control by Community institutions.

However, to accept such an argument would run counter to the Court's view that Articles 36 and 48 should be interpreted strictly, since they allow departures from the fundamental freedoms.[150] The absence of the word 'justified' from Article 56(1) would be weak evidence of any underlying intention in the Treaty to depart from such an important and basic principle. In fact the Court appears to have equated Article 56 with Article 48, because *Adoui and Cornouaille* v. *Belgium*[151] concerned the interpretation of both Articles, and in that case the Court drew no distinction between them.

[147] Ibid., p. 654.
[148] Case 41/74, *Van Duyn* v. *Home Office* [1974] *ECR* 1337, p. 1347.
[149] Ibid., p. 1350.
[150] Case 46/76, *Bauhuis* [1977] *ECR* 5, p. 15; Case 13/79, *Eggers* [1978] *ECR* 1935, p. 1956; Case 41/74, *Van Duyn* v. *Home Office* [1974] *ECR* 1337, p. 1350.
[151] Joined Cases 115 and 116/81 [1982] 3 *CMLR* 631, pp. 661–3.

The whole of the relevant portion of the judgment related to both Articles. The Court said that they permitted member states to adopt, with respect to the nationals of other member states and on the grounds specified in them, 'in particular grounds justified by the requirements of public policy',[152] measures which they could not apply to their own nationals. It went on to say that the measures must not have the effect of applying 'an arbitrary distinction' to the detriment of nationals of other member states.

If, therefore, the national measures under Article 56 must be justified, and must not be arbitrary, it is reasonable to assume that they must also be subject to judicial control. Indeed, the Court itself proceeded to exercise a degree of judicial control by holding that under Articles 48 and 56 a member state may not expel a national of another member state, or refuse him access to its territory, by reason of conduct of a kind which is not effectively repressed in the case of its own nationals.[153] In reaching that conclusion the Court referred to its judgment in *Bouchereau*,[154] where it said that the concept of public policy presupposed the existence of 'a genuine and sufficiently serious threat affecting one of the fundamental interests of society'.[155] It is reasonably safe to assume therefore that, when considering the scope of the exceptions relating to public policy, public security, or public health the Court will reach similar conclusions whether it is interpreting Articles 36, 48, or 56. It is permissible therefore, in the context of establishment, to refer to the cases already considered in Chapters 2 and 4.

A further link between Articles 48 and 56 is that in Directive 221/64, on the co-ordination of special measures concerning movement and residence of foreign nationals on grounds of public policy, public security, or public health[156] the Council chose in Article 1(1) to apply the provisions of the Directive to both employed and self-employed persons. In relation to employed persons and the application of the exceptions in Article 48(3) the Directive has already been considered in detail in Chapter 4 ('Workers'). In view of Article 1(1) of the Directive and the reference to Article 56(2) in the preamble, there can be no doubt that it deals with the exceptions referred to in Article 56(1) in relation to individuals who wish to exercise rights of establishment. On the other hand, the Directive does not seem apt to deal with companies or firms even though, by virtue of Article 58(1) EEC, they are to be treated in matters of establishment in the same way as natural persons who are nationals of member states. The expression 'self-employed persons' in Article 1(1) of the Directive does not seem entirely apt to describe a company, any more than do references in other Articles to residence permits, diseases, and disabilities. Article 3(1) refers expressly to

---

[152] Ibid., p. 661.
[153] Ibid., p. 662.
[154] Case 30/77 [1977] *ECR* 1999.
[155] Ibid., p. 2015.
[156] *OJ*, Special Edition, 1963–4, p. 117.

'the personal conduct of the individual concerned'. It would seem, there-fore, that the Directive does not apply to the establishment of companies, although it may apply to individuals who are partners in firms.

DIRECT EFFECT

At an early stage in the Community's development Article 53, which prohibits member states from introducing any new restrictions on the right of establishment in their territories of nationals of other member states, was held to have direct effect, in the sense of conferring rights on indi-viduals which the nationals courts must protect. The point arose in *Costa* v. *ENEL*,[157] where the national court seems to have thought that a decree nationalizing an electricity undertaking might possibly have infringed Article 53.[158] In giving its reasons for holding that Article 53 had direct effect the Court said:

By Article 53 the Member States undertake not to introduce any new restrictions on the right of establishment in their territories of nationals of other Member States, save as otherwise provided in the Treaty. The obligation thus entered into by the States simply amounts legally to a duty not to act, which is neither subject to any conditions, nor, as regards its execution or effect, to the adoption of any measure either by the States or by the Commission. It is therefore legally complete in itself and is consequently capable of producing direct effects on the relations between Member States and individuals. Such an express prohibition which came into force with the Treaty throughout the Community, and thus became an integral part of the legal system of the Member States, forms part of the law of those States and directly concerns their nationals, in whose favour it has created individual rights which national courts must protect.[159]

This formulation illustrates the classic elements for direct effect according to the early jurisprudence of the Court, i.e. a treaty provision (not a direc-tive) which imposes an unconditional negative obligation on member states. The result is to produce direct effects as between member states and individuals, there being no question at that stage and in that sort of case of the possibility of horizontal direct effect, i.e. as between individuals.

The idea that direct effect applied to cases where member states were prohibited from doing certain things (and by implication that it did not apply in other cases) persisted, as can be seen from the judgment in *Royer*.[160] The Court referred to the obligations in Article 52 (and 59), which are in fact in positive terms, i.e. 'restrictions ... shall be abolished', and

---

[157] Case 6/64 [1964] *ECR* 585.
[158] A view which appears to be inconsistent with Art. 222.
[159] Case 6/64 [1964] *ECR* 585, p. 596.
[160] Case 48/75 [1976] *ECR* 497.

then proceeded to describe them as having a negative and a direct effect. It said:

These provisions, which may be construed as prohibiting Member States from setting up restrictions or obstacles to the entry into and residence in their territory of nationals of other Member States, have the effect of conferring rights directly on all persons falling within the ambit of the above-mentioned articles, as later given closer articulation by regulations or directives implementing the Treaty.[161]

The use of language referring to a prohibition on 'setting up' restrictions (rather than maintaining existing ones) might be thought to be more appropriate to describe the effect of Article 53. Be that as it may, there seems little logical justification for clinging to any notion that direct effect can only apply to a negative obligation. When Article 52 says to member states in effect: 'abolish existing restrictions', and Article 53 says: 'and do not create new ones', these are each different sides of the same coin. If one of these obligations has direct effect, so from a pragmatic point of view should the other. However, whatever line of reasoning is the better, the final conclusion is as stated in the 'dispositif':

1. The right of nationals of a Member State to enter the territory of another Member State and reside there is a right conferred directly, on any person falling within the scope of Community law, by the Treaty—especially Articles 48, 52 and 59—or, as the case may be, by the provisions adopted for its implementation, independently of any residence permit issued by the host State.[162]

In fact, in the earlier case of *Reyners* v. *Belgium*[163] the Court had already ruled that since the end of the transitional period Article 52 was a 'directly applicable' provision, by which it appears to have meant one having direct effect in the sense already described.[164] In reaching that conclusion, it had made no attempt to convert the positive provisions of the Article into a negative form, nor given any indication that it mattered whether the obligation was of one kind or the other. This case represented a milestone in the law of establishment because hitherto it had been fairly widely assumed that Article 52 had no direct effect, and that although it imposed obligations on member states to produce a particular result, the means by which this was to be achieved lay in the adoption of appropriate directives, in particular under Article 54.[165] Some directives had been adopted within the

---

[161] Ibid., p. 511.

[162] Ibid., p. 519.

[163] Case 2/74 [1974] *ECR* 631.

[164] A comparison of paras. 30 and 32 of the judgment, p. 652, suggests that when using the words 'direct effect' and 'directly applicable' the Court was not seeking to draw any distinction between the two.

[165] See e.g. the written observations of Belgium, Luxembourg, and Ireland, and the oral observations of the UK, although Germany (said by the Court to have been supported in substance by the Dutch government) and (with some hesitation) the Commission, took the opposite view.

time specified in Article 52, and at the time of the judgment the Council was still considering a number of other draft directives which had been proposed by the Commission. The Court's ruling was:

Since the end of the transitional period Article 52 of the Treaty is a directly applicable provision, despite the absence, in a particular sphere, of the directives prescribed by Articles 54(2) and 57(1) of the Treaty.[166]

Thus, whatever the ambit of Article 52, and whether or not it goes wider than to apply the rule of non-discrimination on grounds of nationality (a question discussed earlier in this chapter) it is clear from the terms of this ruling that Article 52 as a whole has direct effect.

Since Article 52 has direct effect, there can be little escape from the conclusion that Article 56 likewise has direct effect. In Chapter 2, Article 36 was found to have direct effect, so that when a national court is required to give direct effect to the rule of free movement of goods in Article 30, it must at the same time exercise its own judgment as to whether any exception pleaded under Article 36 is justified, and it must not simply accept without question any claim by the government of the member state concerned.[167] It has also been seen, in Chapter 4, that the exceptions to free movement of workers in Article 48(3) have direct effect,[168] and so do those in Article 48(4) relating to employment in the public service.[169] There seems no reason to suppose that Article 56 should be regarded any differently.

Provisions in directives adopted under Article 57 may also have direct effect if they satisfy the usual criteria.[170] An example of this in the field of establishment is to be found in *Auer* v. *Ministère Public & Others*,[171] where the Court held:

A national of a Member State entitled to practise the profession of a veterinary surgeon in another Member State which has issued to him one of the diplomas, certificates or other evidence of formal qualification referred to in Article 3 of Directive 78/1026/EEC is entitled, even prior to the implementation of the latter, to carry on that profession in the first-mentioned State as from 20 December 1980, provided always that the competent authorities of the State in which he received his diploma have issued to him an attestation certifying that the diploma is in keeping with the requirements of Article 1 of Directive 78/1027/EEC.

Absence of enrolment with a national body of veterinary surgeons cannot preclude the practice of the profession or justify prosecution for improper practice thereof when such enrolment was refused in contravention of Community law.[172]

---

[166] Case 2/74 [1974] *ECR* 631, p. 656.

[167] Case 251/78, *Denkavit* [1979] *ECR* 3369; Case 78/70, *Deutsche Grammophon* v. *Metro* [1971] *ECR* 487.

[168] Case 36/75, *Rutili* v. *Minister for the Interior* [1975] *ECR* 1219; Case 48/75, *Royer* [1976] *ECR* 497; Case 8/77, *Sagulo* [1977] *ECR* 1495.

[169] Case 152/73, *Sotgiu* v. *Deutsche Bundespost* [1974] *ECR* 153.

[170] The criteria are set out, for example, in Case 41/74, *Van Duyn* v. *Home Office* [1976] *ECR* 1337.

[171] Case 271/82 [1985] 1 *CMLR* 123.   [172] Text as recorded in *OJ* 1983, C289/3.

FURTHER READING

U. Everling, *The Right of Establishment in the Common Market* (1964).

W. van Gerven, 'The Right of Establishment and the Supply of Services within the Common Market', (1965–6) 3 *CML Rev.* 344.

B. Goldman, 'The Convention between the Member States of the European Economic Community on the Mutual Recognition of Companies and Legal Persons', (1969) 6 *CML Rev.* 116.

C. Maestripieri, 'Freedom of Establishment and Freedom to Supply Services', (1973) 10 *CML Rev.* 150.

J. Welch, 'The Fifth Draft Directive—A False Dawn?', (1983) 8 *EL Rev.* 83.

VI

Services

THERE are strong links between the freedom of movement for workers, freedom of establishment, and freedom to provide services.[1] In many cases the same economic purpose will be served whether an individual or undertaking chooses to operate in a member state by becoming established there or through temporary visits for the provision of services, and in either case there may be an incidental need to move workers across frontiers for the purpose of the enterprise. Title III, Chapter 2 of the Treaty ('Establishment') shares common provisions with Title III, Chapter 3 ('Services'), because Article 66 provides that Articles 55–8 (establishment) shall apply to matters covered by the chapter on services. In many cases too it may be difficult to disentangle establishment and services and to decide whether a particular activity falls into one category or the other.[2] In such cases it often may not matter, because the end result will be the same whichever set of Community rules is applied. Nevertheless there are differences of treatment in the two chapters, and it may in some cases be necessary to decide where the dividing line lies. For example, Article 61(1), which provides that freedom to provide services in the field of transport shall be governed by the provisions of the Title relating to transport, has no counterpart in the chapter on establishment. There are also shades of difference in the treatment which the European Court has given to provisions which are similar in each chapter, as will be seen.

The most important Treaty provisions are:

Article 59

Within the framework of the provisions set out below, restrictions on freedom to provide services within the Community shall be progressively abolished during the transitional period in respect of nationals of Member States who are established in a State of the Community other than that of the person for whom the services are intended.

The Council may, acting unanimously on a proposal from the Commission, extend the provisions of this Chapter to nationals of a third country who provide services and who are established within the Community.

[1] See Case 48/75, *Procureur du Roi* v. *Royer* [1976] *ECR* 497, p. 509.
[2] In Case 118/75, *Watson and Belmann* [1976] *ECR* 1185, p. 1197, the European Court decided to leave that task to the national court.

Article 60

Services shall be considered to be 'services' within the meaning of this Treaty where they are normally provided for remuneration, in so far as they are not governed by the provisions relating to freedom of movement for goods, capital and persons.

'Services' shall in particular include:

(*a*) activities of an industrial character;

(*b*) activities of a commercial character;

(*c*) activities of craftsmen;

(*d*) activities of the professions.

Without prejudice to the provisions of the Chapter relating to the right of establishment, the person providing a service may, in order to do so, temporarily pursue his activity in the State where the service is provided, under the same conditions as are imposed by that State on its own nationals.

Article 62

Save as otherwise provided in this Treaty, Member States shall not introduce any new restrictions on the freedom to provide services which has in fact been attained at the date of the entry into force of this Treaty.

These Articles follow the familiar pattern of creating an obligation to remove restrictions during the transitional period (Article 59), so that a particular result is to be achieved by the end of it, coupled with a general 'standstill' provision operating with effect from the entry into force of the Treaty (Article 62). The essential elements of a claim under Article 59, first paragraph, to freedom to provide services are (i) that the claimant should be a national of a member state, and (ii) that he should be established in a state of the Community 'other than that of the person for whom the services are intended'. The latter phrase is particularly loosely drafted. There is not too much difficulty in construing the word 'that' as referring to another member state of the Community. But is the state 'of the person' concerned the member state of which he is a national, the member state where he resides, the member state in which he is present in order to receive in person the services in question, or the member state in which he asks for the service to be performed (whether or not he is himself present in that state)?

In the light of the Court's tendency not to interpret the fundamental freedoms in a restrictive manner it may well be that, if ever put to the test, something like the last interpretation would prevail, even though it is the one which least fits the wording of the Article. On this basis, if a German national pays another German, who is established in Germany, to go and tend the garden of his weekend house in Denmark, the arrangement would fall within the ambit of Article 59. The other interpretations would exclude it. Indeed, any of the other interpretations would be likely to produce all kinds of illogical distinctions. For example, there seems no reason why a Belgian window-cleaner, established in Belgium, who travels on certain days to the Netherlands, should not be entitled to clean windows in buildings in the Netherlands belonging to expatriate Belgians, or to the operators of enterprises in the Netherlands who reside in Belgium, or to Dutch nationals or residents who happen to be on holiday in Belgium. Yet even the notion that the state 'of the person for whom the services are intended' means the state where the service is to be performed may not entirely suit all deserving cases. For example, if a French launderer collects laundry from house to house in Germany, does the laundering in France, and then re-delivers the finished articles, the service is performed partly in Germany and partly in France. This would also be true of a postal advisory service.

With these examples in mind, it is submitted that for the purposes of Article 59 the provider must be a national of a member state, established in a member state (not necessarily the same one), who provides a service wholly or partly in a member state other than the one where he is established. This sort of interpretation would seem to be more in keeping with the concept of a fundamental freedom to provide services than one based on a narrow view of the language of a loosely drafted Article.

This suggested interpretation does not cater for the case where a national of one member state travels to another member state in order to receive services from a person who is established in that other member state. Such a recipient is indeed entitled under Article 1(1)(*b*) of Directive 148/73[3] to travel or even to take up residence there for that purpose. However, it may be preferable to regard this provision as ancillary to the rights of the provider of the service, i.e. on the principle that his clients should be allowed to come to him.[4] Thus, where the provider is established in the member state where the service is rendered, it should be treated as one aspect of his rights of establishment. That the right of establishment includes the right to provide services can be illustrated by the reference in Annex 1 to the General Programme on Establishment[5] to 'business services not elsewhere classified' amongst the activities in respect of which restrictions on freedom of establishment were to be abolished before the end of the second year of the second stage. On the other hand, if the provider of the service is established in a member state other than the one in which the service is provided, it might be regarded as an example of his rights to

---

[3] *OJ* 1973, L172/14.

[4] This appears to be the view taken by the Advocate General in Case 118/75, *Watson and Belmann* [1976] *ECR* 1185, p. 1204. See also Title III of the General Programme, *OJ*, Special Edition, 1974, 36/62, which speaks of restrictions that affect the person providing the services directly, or 'indirectly through the recipient of the service'. See also Joined Cases 286/82 and 26/83, *Graziana Luisi and Carbone* v. *Ministero del Tesoro*, judgment of 31/1/84.

[5] *OJ*, Special Edition, 1974, part IX, p. 3.

provide services. This approach is consistent with the fact that Directive 148/73[6] concerns both establishment and services.

DEFINITIONS

Services

The definition of 'services' in the first paragraph of Article 60 is not comprehensive. After an unpromising start ('Services shall be considered to be "services" ') this paragraph proceeds to impose two qualifications. The first is that to qualify as services they should 'normally' be provided for remuneration. The actual absence or presence of remuneration in any particular case is apparently irrelevant. What seems to matter is whether services of the kind which are to be provided are usually remunerated. The second qualification is that Title III, Chapter 3 ('Services') only applies to the extent that the services are not governed by the provisions of Community law relating to free movement of goods, capital, and persons. Were it not for this provision, the supply of goods or capital across frontiers could in itself be considered as the provision of a service, and its effect therefore is to make clear that such operations as a whole are not to be regarded as the provision of services, and are instead to be governed by the rules on free movement of goods and capital.

Another example of a facility, which would be deemed not to be a service, would be where an employment agency put prospective employers in touch with workers whom the employers eventually engaged under a contract of employment. The freedom of the workers and employers to enter into such relationships would appear to be governed by the provisions of Community law on free movement of workers, rather than Article 60. This latter example is to be distinguished from the situation in the *Webb* case,[7] where the workers remained throughout in the employment of the undertaking which made them available for a fee to the users. In that case the Court held the expression 'services' in Article 60 to include the provision of manpower in that way. It said:

Where an undertaking hires out, for remuneration, staff who remain in the employ of that undertaking, no contract of employment being entered into with the user, its activities constitute an occupation which satisfies the conditions laid down in the first paragraph of Article 60. Accordingly they must be considered a 'service' within the meaning of that provision.[8]

[6] *OJ*, 1973, L172/14.
[7] Case 279/80 [1981] *ECR* 3305.
[8] Ibid., p. 3323.

The question whether television signals were 'goods' or 'services' was answered in *Sacchi*.[9] In explanation of its ruling that they were services, the Court said:

In the absence of express provision to the contrary in the Treaty, a television signal must, by reason of its nature, be regarded as provision of services. Although it is not ruled out that services normally provided for remuneration may come under the provisions relating to free movement of goods, such is however the case, as appears from Article 60, only insofar as they are governed by such provisions.

It follows that the transmission of television signals, including those in the nature of advertisements, comes, as such, within the rules of the Treaty relating to services.

On the other hand, trade in material, sound recordings, films, apparatus and other products used for the diffusion of television signals are subject to the rules relating to freedom of movement for goods.[10]

This ruling was followed by the Court in *Procureur du Roi* v. *Debauve*,[11] and *Coditel* v. *Ciné Vog Films*.[12]

Nationals of member states

The phrase 'nationals of Member States' has the same meaning in respect of individuals as it does in the context of free movement of workers. This class of persons has already been considered in Chapter 4. In Chapter 5 it has been seen that, in the context of establishment, the phrase also needs to be interpreted in relation to companies and firms. The same is true in the field of services because by virtue of Article 66, applying Article 58 to the chapter on services, companies, or firms formed in accordance with the law of a member state and having their registered office, central administration, or principal place of business within the Community are to be treated in the same way as natural persons who are nationals of member states. Companies or firms may thus be the providers or recipients of services in accordance with Article 59. Much of what has been said in Chapter 5 is therefore relevant in this context also. However, it seems rather easier to accept, for the purposes of Article 59, the notion that if a company or firm satisfies the criteria in Article 58, first paragraph, it is not necessary to ask any further questions about its nationality. It is possible, without raising any further such issues, simply to read the phrase 'nationals of Member States' as if it included such companies or firms. The next questions, then, are whether the company or firm is established in one member state, and whether the service is required in another. By stipulating these two conditions, Article 59 itself of course satisfies the rule in *R.* v. *Saunders*,[13]

[9] Case 155/73 [1974] *ECR* 409.
[10] Ibid., p. 427.
[11] Case 52/79 [1980] *ECR* 833.
[12] Case 62/79 [1980] *ECR* 881.
[13] Case 175/78 [1979] *ECR* 1129.

repeated in connection with services in *Procureur du Roi* v. *Debauve*,[14] that the Community is not concerned with purely domestic situations. Finally, if a company or firm has its seat, but not its centre of administration or its main establishment, within the Community, it only falls within Title I of the General Programme for the abolition of freedom to provide services[15] if its activity shows 'a real and continuous link with the economy of a Member State', such link being not one of nationality.

Established

The meaning of the term 'establishment' has already been considered in Chapter 5 ('Establishment') and the word 'established' ought to be inter-preted in the same sense in Article 59 when it requires the provider of the service to be established in one member state and the service to be given in another. In that chapter it has been suggested that the essential ingredient of establishment is a fixed base from which an economic activity is conducted, rather than residence in a member state, although the fixed base and residence may well coincide in the case of individuals.

A good example of the latter situation is to be found in the facts of the *Van Binsbergen* case.[16] In that case the would-be provider of the service in the Netherlands was a lawyer who at the material time resided in Belgium. As previously noted in Chapter 5, the Advocate General in that case thought the word 'established' implied that the self-employed person concerned had 'permanently, or at least for a long time, fixed their habitual or actual residence' in the state in question.[17] The Court did not speci-fically endorse or challenge that proposition. It might be argued that the Court was at least mentally equating residence or habitual residence with establishment, from the fact that, whereas in the recital of facts the Dutch law is said to have provided that only persons 'established' in the Nether-lands could act as legal representatives or advisers, the Court spoke of a national law which imposed a requirement as to 'habitual residence'.[18] Nevertheless, it is submitted that the crucial factor in the case was that the lawyer in question conducted at least part of his professional activities from his residence in Belgium. The Advocate General assumed that the lawyer drew up there the statements of case, which he sent by post to the registries of the courts and tribunals with which he was dealing.[19] He therefore did have a fixed base in Belgium from which he conducted his professional activities, and so, when applying Article 59 to the restrictions imposed upon him by the Dutch law, he satisfied the condition of being established

---

[14] Case 52/79 [1980] *ECR* 833, p. 855.
[15] *OJ*, Special Edition, 1974, part IX, p. 3.
[16] Case 33/74 [1974] *ECR* 1299.
[17] Ibid., p. 1315.
[18] Ibid., p. 1310.
[19] Ibid., p. 1315.

in a state other than the one where the services were to be provided. The fact that the same address in Belgium happened also to be his habitual residence was coincidental. This view is consistent with the Court's summary of the position:

In particular, a requirement that the person providing the service must be habitually resident within the territory of the State where the service is to be provided may, according to the circumstances, have the result of depriving Article 59 of all useful effect, in view of the fact that the precise object of that Article is to abolish restrictions on freedom to provide services imposed on persons who are not established in the State where the service is to be provided.[20]

It might be thought to be correct and significant that, in a passage which was concerned with restrictions based on residence, the Court nevertheless indicated that establishment elsewhere (and not residence elsewhere) was the criterion upon which a claim under Article 59 was to be founded. However in *Coenen* v. *Sociaal-Economische Raad*[21] the Court, in a virtually identical passage, changed the words 'who are not established' to 'who do not reside'.[22] This misleadingly suggests that, for the purposes of interpreting the text of Article 59, 'established' equals 'residing'. For this reason the corresponding passage in *Van Binsbergen*[23] is to be preferred.

In the *Coenen* case[24] the facts were that the plaintiff appears to have been established in the Netherlands, because he, or rather his two private companies of which he was the managing director, had business offices in the Netherlands. He took up residence in Belgium, and there is no suggestion that he conducted any part of his business from his residence. It may therefore be that in fact he was established in the Netherlands and not in Belgium, and that when he became thwarted from doing business in the Netherlands by a Dutch residence qualification his case ought more appropriately to have been dealt with under Article 52 rather than Article 59, because he was being deprived in the Netherlands of the opportunity to exercise his rights of establishment. Indeed, had the point been taken, there would seem to have been good ground for saying that he did not qualify under Article 59, because he was not established in a state other than the one where the service was to be provided. However, as the Advocate General pointed out,[25] the Court, acting under Article 177, must deal with the questions actually put to it, and the question put by the national court (which the European Court answered affirmatively) was whether a residence requirement in the Netherlands was incompatible with Articles

---

[20] Ibid., p. 1309.
[21] Case 39/75 [1975] *ECR* 1547.
[22] Ibid., p. 1555.
[23] Case 33/74 [1974] *ECR* 1299, p. 1309.
[24] Case 39/75 [1975] *ECR* 1547.
[25] Ibid., p. 1559.

59 and 60, and not whether Article 52 was relevant, or whether establishment elsewhere was an essential condition which was to be satisfied
before any claim could be made under Article 59. It is however a pity that
the Court's *obiter dictum* quoted above introduced such an element of
confusion over the meaning of the word 'established' in Article 59.

THE GENERAL PROGRAMME AND ITS IMPLEMENTATION

Article 63(1) EEC (services) is the counterpart of Article 54(1) (establishment), in providing for the drawing up of a general programme for the
abolition of existing restrictions on freedom to provide services within the
Community. The Council drew up both programmes on the same date (18
December 1961). The General Programme on Services,[26] like the one on
establishment, is an act of the Council, as defined in the *AETR* case.[27] It
can also be regarded as a generally agreed interpretation of the scope of the
Treaty provisions on services. The reasons for so concluding are similar to
those advanced in Chapter 5 ('Establishment').

The beneficiaries (Title I)

Title I of the General Programme defines the individuals, companies, and
firms entitled to benefit from the freedom to provide services. Individuals
must be nationals of member states who are established within the
Community. This differs from the definition in the General Programme on
establishment in two respects. First, it requires establishment within the
Community, a qualification which naturally follows from the requirement
in Article 59 that the claimant must be established in a state of the
Community other than that of the person for whom the service is intended.
Secondly, it contains no mention of nationals of the overseas countries and
territories. This curious difference between the two programmes is
however of little significance in view of the very limited rights given to the
overseas countries and territories in Council Decision 1186/80 of 16
December 1980.[28] The effect of Article 137 of that decision, which treats
establishment and services in exactly the same way, has already been
considered in Chapter 5. Article 160 of the second ACP–EEC convention[29]
is in similar terms. For the meaning of nationals of the United Kingdom,
reference should be made to the UK declaration.[30]

The companies and firms which are to be treated as beneficiaries are
defined in similar terms in the two General Programmes. One difference is
that the General Programme on services makes no reference to companies

---

[26] *OJ* Special Edition, 1974, part IX, p. 3, gives the full official English text.
[27] Case 22/70, *Commission* v. *Council* [1971] *ECR* 263.
[28] *OJ* 1980, L361/1, as subsequently amended.
[29] Signed at Lomé on 31 Oct. 1979, TS No. 3 (1983).
[30] *OJ* 1983, C23/1.

and firms formed under the law of an overseas country or territory. Again, this has little practical significance. More importantly, this programme adds that where only the seat of the company or firm is situated within the Community its activity must show a real and continuous link (of a kind other than nationality) with the economy of a member state. It will be remembered that this qualification only applies in the General Programme on Establishment in the case of companies which wish to exercise their rights by setting up only agencies, branches, or subsidiaries in the other member states.

This part of the General Programme on services, after listing the nationals, companies, or firms qualifying as beneficiaries, concludes with the words:

subject to the condition that the service is carried out either personally by the person contracting to provide it or by one of his agencies or branches established in the Community.

In so far as this relates to a natural person, it would seem to exclude the possibility, for example, of his sending any employees into the member state in which the service is to be rendered, because he would not then be personally carrying it out and they would not be the persons who had contracted to carry it out. That this should be so in the case of employees who are not nationals of another member state is perhaps not altogether surprising. But the exclusion seems to apply irrespective of the nationality of the employees, and thus excludes his employees who are nationals of a member state, even if, had they been working on their own account, they would have been entitled to provide the same services. The provision is even more anomalous when one considers that it apparently allows the contractor to set up an agency or branch in any member state other than the one where the service is to be provided, and then to send its employees to carry out the service. Moreover it is inconsistent with Title II of the General Programme, which speaks of persons 'accompanying the person providing the services *or* carrying out the services on his behalf'. It is also difficult to reconcile with the power of the provider of the service, recognized in Title III of the General Programme, to enter into contracts of employment. Prima facie the need for such contracts would seem to be to employ persons in the member state where the service was to be performed, in order to provide that service on behalf of the person who had contracted to provide it.

Be that as it may, since failure by the contractor to carry out a service personally is a factor which is not reflected in the language of the Treaty, and since its introduction as a principle of law would tend to restrict the basic right of freedom to provide services, it may be that the only effect of this provision (at most) is to restrict the application of the General

Programme, and in particular its timetable. In other words, there may have been no programme for the abolition of restrictions on the provision of services by those Community nationals who contracted to provide them, but did not do so personally or through agencies or branches established in the Community. Such persons must on that view rely on the text of the Treaty itself, and such of its provisions as have had direct effect after the end of the transitional period.

Fortunately, by its very terms this particular exclusion seems in any event not to apply to companies or firms which are beneficiaries of the right to provide services. Although a company or firm may be a legal 'person', it is hardly possible to regard it as carrying out a service 'personally'. Nor in its case is it appropriate to speak of 'his' agency or branch.

It has been seen in Chapter 5 that, provided there is a foreign element in the case, and provided the claimant can bring his circumstances within the terms of a relevant directive or other Community legislation, he may qualify as a beneficiary of the right of establishment even in respect of the state of which he is a national: *Knoors* v. *Secretary of State*.[31] Although, on the facts, that case seems to have been primarily concerned with establishment, the Court's judgment indicated that the principle also applied to services.[32] Thus, where a national of a member state goes to another member state and obtains there his professional qualifications (as happened in *Knoors*), he has two options. He can return to his own state and exercise a right of establishment there, or he can establish himself in another member state and exercise his right to provide services in his own state. That a Dutch lawyer, established in Belgium, was entitled to provide services in the Netherlands was demonstrated in the *Binsbergen* case.[33]

The position of a recipient of services has been considered earlier in this chapter, where it has been submitted that it is the provider of services, rather than the recipient, who should be regarded as the beneficiary under Article 59.

Entry, exit, and residence (Title II)
Title II of the General Programme reads —

Before the end of the second year of the second stage of the transitional period provisions laid down by law, Regulation or administrative action which in any Member State govern the entry, exit and residence of nationals of other Member States are to be amended, in particular by the abrogation of provisions having an economic purpose, where such provisions are not justified on grounds of public policy, public security or public health and are liable to hinder the provision of

[31] Case 115/78 [1979] *ECR* 399.
[32] Ibid., p. 409.
[33] Case 33/74 [1974] *ECR* 1299.

services by such nationals, or by staff possessing special skills or holding positions of responsibility accompanying the person providing the services or carrying out the services on his behalf.

The latter part of this text reveals a cautious approach to the question whether the provider of a service should have an unrestricted right to take supporting staff with him for the purpose. It speaks only of staff possessing special skills or holding positions of responsibility. While there might be a good deal of argument about where the dividing line might lie between special and ordinary skills, and between positions which do, and those which do not, involve responsibility, the underlying thought seems to be that if the service involves the use of wholly unskilled labour it should be recruited locally and not imported. Whether this caution is justified is open to question.[34] Moreover, a generous interpretation of what is a special skill could do much to reduce this limitation. For example, one special skill might be to speak the same language as the provider of the service and his foremen, so that instructions can be easily understood.

Effect was given to this part of the Programme, and also to the corresponding part of the General Programme on Establishment, by Directive 148/73.[35] Many of its provisions are common to both establishment and services, and it is only necessary here to concentrate on the latter. Article 1(1) of the Directive requires the abolition of restrictions on movement and residence for persons wishing to provide or receive[36] services. The Directive would only seem to require permission to reside for so long as may be necessary in order to provide the services in question. In many cases this will be for a relatively short period, and if an individual stays for any length of time his activities may shade almost imperceptibly into establishment. But this need not necessarily be so. It is possible to envisage cases where an employer remains established in one member state, provides services in another, and for that purpose requires some of his employees to reside permanently in the latter.[37] One example would be a news agency in the first member state which employed local correspondents to collect news in the second member state and then, after processing the raw material, telexed the finished product to those clients in the second member state who wished to receive that service. Permanent residence could be claimed for the local correspondents and their families (as defined in Article 1).

It might be argued that because Article 4 of the Directive confers rights

[34] Particularly in the light of Joined Cases 62 and 63/81, *Seco* v. *EVI* [1982] *ECR* 223, concerning the employment by a French undertaking in Luxembourg of construction workers who were not nationals of any member state.
[35] *OJ* 1973, L172/14.
[36] See n. 3 above, as regards a recipient of services.
[37] See also Title III of the General Programme, *OJ*, Special Edition, 1974, part IX, p. 3, which lists as one of the rights normally attaching to the provision of services the power to acquire immovable property.

of permanent residence on those wishing to establish themselves, and makes no mention of those engaged in the provision of services, the latter are by implication excluded. However, the better view would appear to be that restrictions on the basic freedoms require either express authority in Community legislation, or at least an inescapable implication. It is not necessary to imply any such exclusion here. Article 4 can be regarded as conferring an additional benefit in the case of establishment, which includes the right to have a particular kind of residence permit, as specified in that Article. This does not affect a claim to permanent residence, in appropriate cases, for persons engaged in the provision of services.

Removal of restrictions (Title III)

This Title is in many respects a repetition, mutatis mutandis, of the corresponding Title in the General Programme on establishment.[38] There are, however, a few significant differences, and since the Title is, like its counterpart on establishment, a valuable indication of the scope of the right to provide services, it is convenient to quote the text in full, before considering those differences. It reads:

Subject to the exceptions or special provisions laid down in the Treaty, and in particular to:
— Article 55 concerning activities which are connected with the exercise of official authority in a Member State;
— Article 56 concerning provisions on special treatment for foreign nationals on grounds of public policy, public security or public health;
— Article 61, which provides that freedom to provide services in the field of transport is to be governed by the provisions of the Title relating to transport; and to
— the provisions concerning the free movement of goods, capital and persons, and those concerning taxation systems;
the following restrictions are to be eliminated in accordance with the timetable laid down under Title V, whether they affect the person providing the services directly, or indirectly through the recipient of the service or through the service itself:

A. Any measures which, pursuant to any provision laid down by law, Regulation or administrative action in a Member State, or as a result of the application of such a provision, or of administrative practices, prohibits or hinders the person providing services in his pursuit of an activity as a self-employed person by treating him differently from nationals of the State concerned.

Such restrictive provisions and practices are in particular those which, in respect of foreign nationals only:
(*a*) prohibit the provision of services;
(*b*) make the provision of services subject to an authorisation or to the issue of a document such as a foreign trader's permit;
(*c*) impose additional conditions in respect of the granting of any authorisation required for the provision of services;

[38] *OJ* 1974, 36/62.

(*d*) make the provision of services subject to a period of prior residence or training in the host country;

(*e*) make the provision of services more costly through taxation or other financial burdens, such as a requirement that the person concerned must lodge a deposit or provide security in the host country;

(*f*) limit or hinder, by making it more costly or more difficult, access to sources of supply or to distribution outlets;

(*g*) deny or restrict the right to participate in social security schemes, in particular, in sickness, accident, invalidity or old age insurance schemes, or the right to receive family allowances;

(*h*) grant less favourable treatment in the event of nationalisation, expropriation or requisition.

The like shall apply to provisions and practices which, in respect of foreign nationals only, exclude, limit or impose conditions on the power to exercise rights normally attaching to the provision of services and in particular the power:

(*a*) to enter into contracts, in particular contracts for work, contracts of hire and contracts of employment, and to enjoy all rights arising under such contracts;

(*b*) to submit tenders for or to act directly as a party or a subcontractor in contracts with the State or with any other legal person governed by public law;

(*c*) to obtain licences or authorisations issued by the State or by any other legal person governed by public law;

(*d*) to acquire, use or dispose of movable or immovable property or rights therein;

(*e*) to acquire, use or dispose of intellectual property and all rights deriving therefrom:

(*f*) to borrow, and in particular to have access to the various forms of credit;

(*g*) to receive aids granted by the State, whether direct or indirect;

(*h*) to be a party to legal or administrative proceedings;

where the professional or trade activities of the person concerned necessarily involve the exercise of such power.

Furthermore, any requirements imposed, pursuant to any provision laid down by law, Regulation or administrative action or in consequence of any administrative practice, in respect of the provision of services are also to be regarded as restrictions where, although applicable irrespective of nationality, their effect is exclusively or principally to hinder the provision of services by foreign nationals.

B. Any prohibition of, or hindrance to, the movement of the item to be supplied in the course of the service or of the materials comprising such item or of the tools, machinery equipment and other means to be employed in the provision of the service.

C. Any prohibition of, or impediment to, the transfer of the funds needed to perform the service.

D. Any prohibition of, or hindrance to, payments for services, where the provision of such services between the Member States is limited only by restrictions in respect of the payments therefor.

However, in respect of the provisions referred to in paragraphs C and D, Member States shall retain the right to verify the nature and genuineness of transfer of funds and of payments and to take all necessary measures in order to prevent contravention of their laws and regulations, in particular as regards the issue of foreign currency to tourists.

The first difference from the General Programme on establishment is the reference to Article 61. This is necessary because, as already noted, that Article provides that freedom to provide services in the field of transport shall be governed by Articles 74–84. The second is the reference to the timetable for the removal of restrictions being subject to the provisions of the Treaty concerning free movement of goods, persons, and capital. This has already been noted when defining 'services'. In connection with the movement of capital it should also be read, however, in conjunction with paragraphs C and D of Title III of the Programme. The latter expressly require free movement of capital in the shape of funds needed to perform services or to pay for them.

The list of restrictive provisions and practices which are to be eliminated, in so far as they apply only to foreign nationals, does not include anything corresponding to the provision in the General Programme on establishment referring to access to vocational training. This omission may reflect an instinctive feeling that establishment is permanent, that services are ephemeral, and that there is no practical need for non-discriminatory vocational training in the state where services are to be provided. This may be so in the majority of cases, but, as has been seen, there may be cases where the provider of a service, or his servants or agents, may need to reside more or less permanently in the receiving state.

Another omission from the same list is the provision in the General Programme on establishment relating to membership of companies or firms. This is understandable, since such membership would almost invariably take the situation into the field of establishment.

One provision, largely common to both Programmes, requires the removal of discriminatory rules and practices limiting the power to enter into contracts, in particular contracts for work, and to enjoy all rights arising under such contracts. The list of examples given in each Programme after the words 'in particular' is, however, different. Whereas the General Programme on establishment refers to 'contracts for work, business or agricultural tenancies, and contracts for employment', the General Programme on services refers to 'contracts for work, contracts of hire and contracts of employment'. There appears to be no significance in this distinction, beyond the thought that tenancies of land (which imply a more permanent presence) are more likely to be of interest to establishment than to services, and that contracts for the hire of movable property (which imply a less permanent presence) are more likely to be appropriate to services than to establishment. The same thought (about the respective degrees of permanence of establishment and services) also seems to underlie the fact that the right to join a professional or trade organization appears in the General Programme on establishment, but not in the one on services. However, as has been seen, the degree of permanence of an activity need not be the ultimate test of the distinction between establishment and services.

Paragraphs B, C, and D of this Title have no counterpart in the General Programme on establishment. Of these, paragraph B (the right to take the materials and tools needed to provide the service) needs no explanation, and paragraphs C (transfer of funds) and D (payments for services) have already been considered.

Discrimination (Title IV)

As a general principle of Community law, and within the scope of application of the treaty, discrimination on grounds of nationality is prohibited (Article 7). In Chapter 5 it was seen that this principle underlay the rules of establishment, although there was room for argument about whether those rules were in all cases confined to an application of the principle. The same is true of the General Programme on the provision of services.[39]

Title IV of the General Programme on services contains, however, provisions which do not figure in the General Programme on establishment. They are transitional in nature because they only apply until the restrictions referred to in the Programme have been abolished. In that interim period member states were enjoined to apply any restrictions temporarily retained without distinction on grounds of nationality *or residence*, and so as to accord (presumably to nationals of other member states) the most favourable treatment under existing practices and treaties. The latter 'most favoured nation' treatment did not extend to other member states the favourable treatment enjoyed by nationals of the Benelux states as a result of their regional union.

Although these provisions are now largely of historical interest, the ghost of the words 'or residence' has continued to haunt the precincts of the European Court. The idea of equating nationality with residence, so that discrimination on the grounds of the latter is also prohibited, persisted in the *van Binsbergen* case.[40] In that case the Court said:

The restrictions to be abolished pursuant to Articles 59 and 60 include all requirements imposed on the person providing the service by reason in particular of his nationality or of the fact that he does not habitually reside in the State where the service is provided, which do not apply to persons established within the national territory or which may prevent or otherwise obstruct the activities of the person providing the service.[41]

---

[39] See Case 118/75, *Watson and Belmann* [1976] *ECR* 1185, p. 1196, para. 9, and Case 33/74, *van Binsbergen* [1974] *ECR* 1299, p. 1313.

[40] Case 33/74 [1974] *ECR* 1299.

[41] Ibid., p. 1309.

It is possible to interpret this passage as an example of how a restriction imposed on persons who are not resident in a member state may be a disguised form of restriction directed against the nationals of other member states. An alternative approach is to regard it as referring to the fact that, if a member state confines the provision of certain kinds of services to persons who are resident in its territory, this is likely in many cases to thwart the freedom of persons who are nationals of, and established in, other member states to provide services. This is so because in practice their places of establishment and residence will often coincide, and will be in their own member states. To prevent foreign residents from providing services is thus an indirect way of preventing nationals of other member states, established in other member states, from doing so. Yet freedom from such restrictions is precisely what Article 59 is designed to ensure. This alternative interpretation also seems to be consistent with the Treaty.

This part of the judgment should not however be read in a wider sense, and as indicating that all restrictions based on residence must necessarily infringe Article 59, in so far as they apply to nationals of other member states. This would not be correct. A Dutchman, established in business in the Netherlands but resident in Belgium, would not be prevented from providing services in Belgium by a Belgian restriction requiring him to reside in Belgium. Nor does the judgment imply that he would. It seems clear that the Court was only condemning restrictions based on residence if one of two alternative conditions was satisfied: i.e. either that they did not apply to persons established within the national territory (and were therefore in that sense discriminatory), or that they in some way prevented or hindered the provider of the service.

Another example of disguised discrimination on grounds of nationality was identified in *Seco* v. *EVI*.[42] In that case a French construction company employed persons who were not nationals of any member state for work on the Luxembourg railway system. The workers remained compulsorily affiliated to French social security. They were exempted from the employee's share of contributions to the Luxembourg social security scheme. However, the company was obliged, as employer, to make certain social security payments in respect of workers who were neither nationals of any member state nor entitled to be treated as such, although this did not confer on the workers any benefits. Employers providing services in Luxembourg escaped from this obligation in respect of workers who were nationals of a member state. After referring to Articles 59 and 60(3), and to earlier jurisprudence on discrimination, the Court said:

Thus they prohibit not only overt discrimination based on the nationality of the person providing a service but also all forms of covert discrimination which,

---

[42] Joined Cases 62 and 63/81 [1982] *ECR* 223.

although based on criteria which appear to be neutral, in practice lead to the same result.[43]

The requirement for employers to make these payments was thus precluded by Community law. The Court added:

Nor would such a requirement be justified if it were intended to offset the economic advantages which the employer might have gained by not complying with the legislation on minimum wages in the State in which the work is performed.[44]

Disguised discrimination on grounds of nationality also featured in the *Webb* case.[45] In that case the English company, established in the United Kingdom, was impeded in the provision of temporary manpower in the Netherlands by a Dutch law which required all persons providing that kind of service, irrespective of their nationality, to have a Dutch licence. On the face of it there was no discrimination against foreign nationals, but in practice there could have been. Whereas its Dutch competitors required only one licence, the English company needed to go to the trouble of getting two—one from the Dutch authorities and one from the British. The Court, after referring to the prohibition in Article 60 of discrimination, went on to say (thus adverting to disguised discrimination):

However it does not mean that all national legislation applicable to nationals of that State and usually applied to the permanent activities of undertakings established therein may be similarly applied in its entirety to the temporary activities of undertakings which are established in other Member States.[46]

Later it stated the position as follows:

It follows in particular that it is permissible for Member States, and amounts for them to a legitimate choice of policy pursued in the public interest, to subject the provision of manpower within their borders to a system of licensing in order to be able to refuse licences where there is reason to fear that such activities may harm good relations on the labour market or that the interests of the workforce affected are not adequately safeguarded. In view of the differences there may be in conditions on the labour market between one Member State and another, on the one hand, and the diversity of the criteria which may be applied with regard to the pursuit of activities of that nature on the other hand, the Member State in which the services are to be supplied has unquestionably the right to require possession of a licence issued on the same conditions as in the case of its own nationals.

Such a measure would be excessive in relation to the aim pursued, however, if the requirements to which the issue of a licence is subject coincided with the proofs and guarantees required in the State of establishment. In order to maintain

[43] Ibid., p. 235.
[44] Ibid., p. 238.
[45] Case 279/80 [1981] *ECR* 3305.
[46] Ibid., p. 3324.

the principle of freedom to provide services the first requirement is that in considering applications for licences and in granting them the Member State in which the service is to be provided may not make any distinction based on the nationality of the provider of the services or the place of his establishment; the second requirement is that it must take into account the evidence and guarantees already furnished by the provider of the services for the pursuit of his activities in the Member State of his establishment.[47]

The concept that member states ought to trust each others' proofs and guarantees, required in the public interest, has already been encountered in connection with the free movement of goods, and the protection of public health.[48]

Mutual recognition of diplomas and other evidence of formal qualifications (Title VI) and the co-ordination of national provisions

Title VI of the General Programme on services is virtually identical to Title V of the General Programme on establishment in providing for the mutual recognition of diplomas, certificates, and other evidence of formal qualifications, which could be achieved either before or after the lifting of any particular restrictions on the provision of services. Likewise, a provisional system is envisaged for the acceptance in appropriate cases of certificates of actual and lawful practice in the country of origin. In effect this Title is concerned with the implementation of Article 57(1), as applied to services by Article 66.

The majority of these Directives are for the purpose of facilitating both establishment and the provision of services. The most important ones are listed in Chapter 5. The lawyers' directive,[49] however, applies only to the provision of services. The aim, as described in the preamble, is not to provide for the mutual recognition of formal qualifications. It is to ensure the recognition as lawyers of those persons practising the profession in each of the member states. The corollary of such recognition, referred to in the preamble and Article 3, is that each beneficiary must adopt the professional title used in the member state in which he is established ('the Member State from which he comes'). There is no indication in the Directive that the draftsman directed his attention to the possibility of a lawyer being established in more than one member state. However, there is no inherent reason why this should not happen, as has been seen in Chapter 5.[50] Presumably in such a case the lawyer may use all or any of his professional titles.

---

[47] Ibid., pp. 3325–6.
[48] See Case 272/80, *Biologische Producten* [1981] *ECR* 3277.
[49] Dir. 249/77, *OJ* 1977, L78/17, as amended by the Greek Act of Accession, Art. 21, and Annex I.
[50] See Case 107/83, *Paris Bar* v. *Klopp* [1985] 1 *CMLR* 99.

Article 1 of the Directive allows member states to reserve to certain kinds of lawyers the preparation of formal documents for obtaining title to administer the estates of deceased persons, and the drafting of formal documents creating or transferring interests in land. UK lawyers are defined as advocates, barristers, and solicitors. Article 4 allows lawyers from other member states to represent clients in legal proceedings or proceedings before public authorities 'under the conditions laid down for lawyers established in that State, with the exception of any conditions requiring residence, or registration with a professional organization, in that State'. This would seem to leave a member state free, for example, to insist that all lawyers practising in litigation in its courts must have passed a professional examination in its law, provided such examination is open to nationals of all member states, and there is no requirement to register with the professional organization which sets the examination, and provided there is no residence requirement. A lawyer taking advantage of his right to represent clients in litigation must observe the rules of professional conduct in the host member state.[51]

The rules of professional conduct applicable when the United Kingdom is the host member state are specified, taking account of the different branches of the profession, and the special position of Irish barristers.[52] The lawyer must also observe the professional rules of the member state in which he is established. In the host member state he must in particular respect its rules on professional secrecy, although this did not prevent the court from holding in the *A. M. & S.* case[53] that his advice to his client is only privileged from production in competition cases if he is in a private practice, and is not an 'in-house' lawyer employed by the undertaking which is being investigated.[54] The host member state may require the lawyer appearing for clients in litigation to work in conjunction with a lawyer 'who practises before the judicial authority in question and who would, where necessary, be answerable to that authority, or with an "avoué" or "procuratore" practising before it'. Article 6 allows member states to prevent 'in-house' lawyers from representing in litigation the undertaking by which they are employed.

EXCEPTIONS TO FREEDOM TO PROVIDE SERVICES

Article 66

Article 66 (EEC) provides that Articles 55–8 shall apply to the matters covered by the chapter on services. The exceptions to free movement

---

[51] Art. 4(2).
[52] Art. 4(3).
[53] Case 155/79, *A. M. & S. Europe Ltd.* v. *Commission* [1982] *ECR* 1575.
[54] Ibid., pp. 1611, 1614.

allowed by Article 55, in relation to activities which are connected, even occasionally, with the exercise of official authority, has already been considered in Chapter 5. The cases cited in that chapter are also relevant when considering the scope of this exception in relation to the provision of services. Article 56, as applied to services by Article 66, allows limitations to be imposed, on grounds of public policy, public security, or public health, on the freedom to provide services. These exceptions too have already been considered in Chapter 5, and again reference may be made to the cases cited there. Directive 221/64,[55] on the co-ordination of special measures concerning movement and residence of foreign nationals on grounds of public policy, public security, or public health has also been reviewed in that chapter and in Chapter 4 ('Workers'). The directive applies equally to self-employed persons who exercise their right of free movement in order to provide services, as is made clear by the preamble, which refers to the General Programme on freedom to provide services.[56]

Application of professional rules

If the last sentence of Article 60 had been interpreted literally, the only constraint upon member states would have been the obligation to apply the same conditions to nationals of other member states as it applied to its own nationals, with regard to the provision of services. Thus, if in national law certain rules of professional conduct had been imposed on all persons exercising a particular calling, no national of another member state would have been entitled under Article 60 to offer that kind of service unless he had submitted to the discipline imposed by those rules. There would therefore have been no need to regard the application of those rules to him as an exception to the rule in Article 60. However, as has already been seen, the Court took a broader view of the right to provide services in the *van Binsbergen* case.[57] Having considered the combined effect of Articles 59 and 60, the Court held that the first paragraph of Article 59 and the third paragraph of Article 60 meant that a member state could not, by imposing a condition as to habitual residence in that state, deny persons established in another member state the right to provide services. In so holding the Court explained:

that the precise object of that Article [59] is to abolish restrictions on freedom to provide services imposed on persons who are not established in the state where the service is to be provided.[58]

[55] *OJ*, Special Edition, 1963–4, p. 117.
[56] *OJ*, Special Edition, 1974, part IX, p. 3.
[57] Case 33/74 [1974] *ECR* 1299.
[58] Ibid., p. 1309.

Having established this broad principle, it became necessary for the Court to consider whether there were any exceptions to it. The Court's conclusions were:

However, taking into account the particular nature of the services to be provided, specific requirements imposed on the persons providing the service cannot be considered incompatible with the Treaty where they have as their purpose the application of professional rules justified by the general good—in particular rules relating to organisation, qualifications, professional ethics, supervision and liability—which are binding upon any person established in the State in which the service is provided, where the person providing the service would escape from the ambit of those rules being established in another Member State.[59]

From this it will be seen that the exception does not authorize the application of all professional rules of conduct, such as those by which the legal, medical, and other professions are bound, but only those which are 'justified by the general good'. This formula no doubt paves the way for the Court itself to consider, in disputed cases, what is and what is not for the general good. The Council could also resolve problems concerning professional rules of conduct, by issuing directives under Article 63, as the Court pointed out later in the *van Binsbergen* case.[60]

In *Ministère Public and ASBL* v. *van Wesemael*[61] the Court widened its exception in one respect, and narrowed it in another. These joined cases concerned fee-charging employment agencies for entertainers. The Court found the application of national professional rules to foreign agencies providing such services to be in accordance with Community law not only if justified by the general good, but also if needed to protect the entertainer. On the other hand the Court applied once more[62] the principle that member states should trust each others' safeguards, so that subjection to national professional rules was not justified if the provider of the service was already subject to similar professional rules in the member state where he was established. It did not say whether subjection to similar rules in any other member state (for example, the state of which the provider of the service is a national, or in which he resides) should be regarded as a sufficient safeguard. The Court said:

Taking into account the particular nature of certain services to be provided, such as the placing of entertainers in employment, specific requirements imposed on persons providing services cannot be considered incompatible with the Treaty where they have as their purpose the application of professional rules, justified by the general good or by the need to ensure the protection of the entertainer, which

---

[59] Ibid. See also Case 39/75, *Coenen* v. *Sociaal-Economische Raad* [1975] *ECR* 1547, p. 1555.

[60] Case 33/74 [1974] *ECR* 1299, p. 1311.

[61] Joined Cases 110 and 111/78 [1979] *ECR* 35.

[62] See Case 272/80, *Biologische Producten* [1981] *ECR* 3277, and Case 279/80, *Webb* [1981] *ECR* 3305, p. 3326.

are binding upon any person established in the said State, in so far as the person providing the service is not subject to similar requirements in the Member State in which he is established.[63]

Services of general economic interest and revenue-producing monopolies (Article 90)

The extent to which member states may, by entrusting the operation of services of general economic interest or having the character of a revenue-producing monopoly, escape the rules on competition has already been considered in Chapter 3 ('State Monopolies'). In that chapter the *Sacchi* case[64] was also considered, and it will be remembered that the provision of television signals was regarded as the provision of a service. The judgment in that case was concerned primarily with the relationship between Article 86 (abuse of a dominant position) and Article 90 (services of general economic interest and revenue-producing monopolies). The Court's views were expressed in the following terms:

Nothing in the Treaty prevents Member States, for considerations of public interest, of a non-economic nature, from removing radio and television transmissions, including cable transmissions, from the field of competition by conferring on one or more establishments an exclusive right to conduct them.[65]

The position with regard to services may be analysed as follows. A particular set of facts may fall within the terms of both Articles 59 and 90. When it does so the latter is the *lex specialis*. The reservation of services to undertakings of the kind referred to in Article 90 may be a justified exception to the rules in Article 59. This is so when, in the language of Article 90(2), it would 'obstruct the performance' of the tasks of those undertakings to hold otherwise, and it would not be 'contrary to the interests of the Community' to allow this exception. The reservation of radio and television signals to undertakings falling within Article 90 is one such exception. The reference by the Court in the above quotation to considerations of a non-economic nature seems therefore to indicate that in the Court's view it would be 'contrary to the interests of the Community', and therefore contrary to Articles 59 and 90, to allow member states for economic reasons to restrict the freedom to provide services.

Control of aliens

An essential part of the freedom to provide services is the freedom of movement for the persons who provide it. National controls over the movement and residence of aliens may not generally, therefore, be used to prevent or hinder such activity. Not every form of national control, however, is

[63] Joined Cases 110 and 111/78 [1979] *ECR* 35, p. 52.
[64] Case 155/73 [1974] *ECR* 409.
[65] Ibid., p. 429.

excluded. One particular example which has survived is to be found in Article 4(2) of Directive 148/73 on the abolition of restrictions on movement and residence within the Community for nationals of member states with regard to establishment and the provision of services.[66] That paragraph deals only with services, and it provides inter alia that for stays of not more than three months the person concerned need not produce any evidence of his right of abode other than the identity card or passport with which he entered the member state in question. It goes on to say that the member state may, however, require him to report his presence in the territory (i.e. to the local authorities). It may be thought that this latter requirement is a very small limitation on his freedom of movement, and that it hardly deserves to be regarded as an exception. Nevertheless, it is an example of the reluctance of the Court to accept any interference with the basic freedoms that, while accepting the validity of this provision, it felt constrained to circumscribe it in *Watson and Belmann*.[67] The Court said:

In particular as regards the period within which the arrival of foreign nationals must be reported, the provisions of the Treaty are only infringed if the period fixed is unreasonable.

Among the penalties attaching to a failure to comply with the prescribed declaration and registration formalities, deportation, in relation to persons protected by Community law, is certainly incompatible with the provisions of the Treaty since, as the Court has already confirmed in other cases, such a measure negates the very right conferred and guaranteed by the Treaty.[68]

Transport

Article 61(1) EEC says:

Freedom to provide services in the field of transport shall be governed by the provisions of the Title relating to transport.

A natural interpretation of this paragraph leads to the conclusion that the provisions of the Title relating to transport (Articles 74–84) are to apply in the case of transport services, to the exclusion of Articles 59–66 (services). This in effect was the argument of the French Government in *Commission v. France*.[69] The Advocate General endorsed it.[70] The Court did not state the position quite so clearly. It said:

Since transport is basically a service, it has been found necessary to provide a special system for it, taking into account the special aspects of this branch of activity.

[66] *OJ* 1973, L172/14.
[67] Case 118/75 [1976] *ECR* 1185.
[68] Ibid., p. 1199.
[69] Case 167/73 [1974] *ECR* 359, pp. 367–8.
[70] Ibid., p. 378.

With this object, a special exemption has been provided by Article 61(1), under which freedom to provide services in the field of transport 'shall be governed by the provisions of the Title relating to transport', thus confirming that the general rules of the Treaty must be applied insofar as they are not excluded.[71]

This passage needs to be considered in its context. The case was principally concerned with Articles 48–51 (workers), and the relationship between those Articles and Articles 74–84 (transport). The Court referred to the object, expressed in Article 2, of establishing a common market, the basis of which was the free movement of goods, persons, services, and capital. The Court concluded:

Conceived as being applicable to the whole complex of economic activities, these basic rules can be rendered inapplicable only as a result of express provision in the Treaty.[72]

As an example of such an express provision the Court cited Article 38(2) (agriculture). Another example is Article 61(1) (transport services), and an indication that the Court thought it was so lies in its use of the word 'exemption' (i.e. from the basic rules) in the first passage quoted above. The second half of that quotation should therefore be taken to mean that the need to create a special exemption in the Treaty for transport services showed an intention to make transport subject to the basic rules in other respects. In other words, the rules on free movement of goods, persons, and capital (but not services) continue to apply in the field of transport, notwithstanding the existence of special rules relating to the common transport policy, because the object of the latter is to 'implement and complement' the basic rules.[73]

This complete exemption of transport services from the basic rules on services was understandable when read with Article 75(2), which required, inter alia, that the Council should lay down during the transitional period the conditions under which non-resident carriers might operate transport services within a member state, and with Article 84(2) which enabled the Council to include sea and air transport within these arrangements. There was thus a reasonable hope that specially adapted rules on all transport services might be adopted, thus avoiding a lacuna in the general scheme for freedom to provide services. To the extent that this has not been achieved there may therefore be a temptation to try to circumvent the blanket exemption in Article 61(1). The language of the Court's judgment in *Commission* v. *France*[74] may just leave the door ajar for this purpose. But the correct interpretation of that decision appears to be that as a result of Article 61(1) the rules on services in Articles 59–66 do not apply to transport services.

---

[71] Ibid., p. 370. [72] Ibid., p. 369. [73] Ibid., p. 370.
[74] Case 167/73 [1974] *ECR* 359. See also Case 13/83, *European Parliament* v. *Council*.

The next question is whether the Council, acting under Article 75, can create rules which run counter to those of free movement. In *Commission* v. *France*[75] the Court was discouraging, but did not rule out the possibility. It said:

> Far from involving a departure from these fundamental rules, therefore, the object of the rules relating to the common transport policy is to implement and complement them by means of common action.
>
>   Consequently the said general rules must be applied insofar as they can achieve these objectives.[76]

There is no doubt that this quotation refers to all the fundamental rules other than those relating to services. But does it also apply to services, so that the Council, when adopting special rules, on transport services must, so far as possible, implement and complement the basic rules on free movement? The point is unsettled, although the Council has in fact exerted some freedom of manoeuvre. An example of a restriction on free movement can be found in Regulation 1463/70 (made under Article 75),[77] which prevented the provision of services by the operators of certain vehicles unless the latter were fitted with a tachograph (Articles 3 and 4 of the Regulation). The validity of this Community rule was not questioned in *Commission* v. *United Kingdom*.[78]

DIRECT EFFECT

Once the Court had decided in *Reyners* v. *Belgium*[79] that since the end of the transitional period Articles 52 (establishment) had direct effect, despite the absence of implementing directives, it was inevitable that it would reach a similar decision in the case of services. The opportunity soon came in the *van Binsbergen* case,[80] in which the Court ruled:

> The first paragraph of Article 59 and the third paragraph of Article 60 have direct effect and may therefore be relied on before national courts, at least in so far as they seek to abolish any discrimination against a person providing a service by reason of his nationality or of the fact that he resides in a Member State other than that in which the service is to be provided.[81]

The Court maintained that directives adopted under Article 63 performed three functions, i.e. (i) to remove restrictions during the transitional period, (ii) to facilitate the exercise of the freedom to provide services, especially by

[75] Case 167/73 [1974] *ECR* 359.
[76] Ibid., p. 370.
[77] *OJ*, 1970, L164/1.
[78] Case 128/78 [1979] *ECR* 419.
[79] Case 2/74 [1974] *ECR* 631.
[80] Case 33/74 [1974] *ECR* 1299.
[81] Ibid., p. 1313.

providing for the mutual recognition of professional qualifications, and (iii) to resolve problems arising because the provider of the service may not be fully subject to the professional rules of conduct in the state where the service is provided. Article 59, read with Article 8(7), expressed an intention to abolish restrictions by the end of the transitional period. The Court went on to say:

The provisions of Article 59, the application of which was to be prepared by directives issued during the transitional period, therefore became unconditional on the expiry of that period.

The provisions of that article abolish all discrimination against the person providing the service by reason of his nationality or the fact that he is established in a Member State other than that in which the service is to be provided.

Therefore, as regards at least the specific requirement of nationality or of residence, Articles 59 and 60 impose a well-defined obligation, the fulfilment of which by the Member States cannot be delayed or jeopardized by the absence of provisions which were to be adopted in pursuance of powers conferred under Articles 63 and 66.[82]

It will be seen that in these quotations the confusion between establishment and residence, and the tendency to equate the two, persists. In considering the meaning of 'establishment' earlier in this chapter, it has been submitted that one of the criteria for the purposes of Articles 59 and 60 is establishment (and not residence) in another member state. Another is discrimination, and it is the case that, in considering whether discrimination exists, one must take into account the fact that a restriction based on residence may amount to a disguised restriction on grounds of nationality. The effect of this judgment may therefore be that Articles 59 and 60 have direct effect, to the extent that they prohibit discrimination against the provider of the service (i) on grounds of nationality (which may be disguised as a residence rule) or (ii) on account of his establishment in another member state. The implication that in some instances Articles 59 and 60 go beyond this, and that when so doing they may not have direct effect, was qualified in *Watson and Belmann*,[83] where the Court, referring to both Articles 52 and 59, said:

These provisions, which may be construed as prohibiting Member States from setting up restrictions or obstacles to the entry into their territory of nationals of other Member States, have the effect of conferring rights directly on all persons falling within the ambit of the above-mentioned articles, as later given closer articulation by certain provisions adopted by the Council in implementation of the Treaty.[84]

[82] Ibid., p. 1311.
[83] Case 118/75 [1976] *ECR* 1185.
[84] Ibid., p. 1197.

In *Ministère Public* v. *van Wesemael*,[85] the Court described the effect of Article 59 in the following equally broad terms (which followed the court's frequent practice of equating 'direct effect' and 'direct applicability'):

In laying down that freedom to provide services shall be attained by the end of the transitional period, that provision, interpreted in the light of Article 8(7) of the Treaty, imposes an obligation to attain a precise result, the fulfilment of which had to be made easier by, but not made dependent on, the implementation of a programme of progressive measures.

It follows that the essential requirements of Article 59 of the Treaty, which was to be implemented progressively during the transitional period by means of the directives referred to in Article 63, became directly and unconditionally applicable on the expiry of that period.[86]

In the *Webb* case[87] the Court was equally general in its conclusions:

It follows that the essential requirements of Article 59 of the Treaty became directly and unconditionally applicable on the expiry of that period.[88]

In *Walrave* v. *Union Cycliste Internationale*[89] the Court was concerned only with discrimination on grounds of nationality, and its ruling on direct effect was therefore confined to that aspect. It held:

The first paragraph of Article 59, in any event in so far as it refers to the abolition of any discrimination based on nationality, creates individual rights which national courts must protect.[90]

The judgment also however settled another question. It was argued in the case that Articles 7, 48, and 59 refer only to restrictions imposed by an authority, and not to those imposed by persons or associations (like the defendants) who did not come under 'public law'. The Court disposed of that argument in the following two passages:

Articles 7, 48, 59 have in common the prohibition, in their respective spheres of application, of any discrimination on grounds of nationality.

Prohibition of such discrimination does not only apply to the action of public authorities but extends likewise to rules of any other nature aimed at regulating in a collective manner gainful employment and the provision of services.[91]

Although the third paragraph of Article 60, and Articles 62 and 64, specifically relate, as regards the provision of services, to the abolition of measures by the State, this fact does not defeat the general nature of the terms of Article 59, which makes no distinction between the source of the restrictions to be abolished.[92]

---

[85] Joined Cases 110 and 111/78 [1979] *ECR* 35.
[86] Ibid., p. 52.
[87] Case 279/80 [1981] *ECR* 3305.
[88] Ibid., p. 3324.
[89] Case 36/74 [1974] *ECR* 1405.
[90] Ibid., p. 1422.
[91] Ibid., p. 1418.
[92] Ibid., p. 1419.

The result so far as concerned direct effect was, in the Court's words:

It follows that the provisions of Articles 7, 48 and 59 of the Treaty may be taken into account by the national court in judging the validity or the effects of a provision inserted in the rules of a sporting organisation.[93]

The use of the word 'may' in this passage can be explained by the fact that earlier in its judgment the Court had indicated that it was for the national court to consider whether the activity in question concerned only the composition of sporting teams (such as national teams) and had nothing to do with economic activity, in which case the Community rules against discrimination on grounds of nationality did not apply. Finally, it should be noted that the relevant provisions in this case which were held to have direct effect were treaty articles. As a result of their direct effect they governed the relationship between individuals and an undertaking which was in no sense part of central or local government. Regulation 1612/68[94] was also mentioned. The Court did not specifically confirm that it had direct effect, perhaps assuming that such confirmation was hardly necessary. No directive was involved. The judgment did not therefore settle the question of whether, to the extent that directives may have direct effect, they may similarly regulate relationships between individuals or undertakings ('horizontal direct effect'), or whether their direct effect is only 'vertical', i.e. so as to impose obligations only upon any member state failing to take action required by it by the Directive, which persons may rely upon in litigation in national courts.[95]

FURTHER READING

C. J. Berr and H. Groutel, 'La Libre Prestation des Services dans le Domaine des Assurances', (1979) 15 *RTDE* 73.

H. Bronkhorst, 'Lawyers' Freedom under the new Directive', (1977) 2 *EL Rev.* 224.

A. Brunois, 'Le Barreau et la Libération des Prestations de Services et des Etablissements dans le CEE', (1977) *RTDE* 397.

P. P. Chappatte, 'Freedom to Provide Insurance Services in the European Community', (1984) 1 *EL Rev.* 3.

A. Th. S. Leenen, 'Recent Case Law of the Court of Justice of the European Communities on the Freedom of Establishment and the Freedom to Provide Services', (1982) 17 *CML Rev.* 259.

G. Morse, 'Provision of Services: the Professional Supervision Exception', (1979) 4 *EL Rev.* 375.

W. Pool, 'Moves Towards a Common Market in Insurance', (1984) 21 *CML Rev.* 133.

---

[93] Ibid.
[94] *OJ*, Special Edition, 1968, p. 475.
[95] Case 148/78, *Pubblico Ministero* v. *Ratti* [1979] *ECR* 1629, pp. 1644–6, is also inconclusive.

E. Steindorf, 'Insurance and Freedom to Provide Services', (1977) 14 *CML Rev.* 133.

D. B. Walters, 'Uncertain Steps Towards a European Legal Profession', (1978) 3 *EL Rev.* 265.

P. S. Wilson, 'EEC: Freedom to Provide Services for EEC Lawyers', (1978) 19 *Harvard International Law Journal* 379.

VII

Sex Discrimination

ALTHOUGH sex discrimination is not dealt with under that part of the Treaty which is specifically devoted to the free movement of persons, services, and capital (Part Two, Title III, Articles 48–73), the subject has a connection with free movement. A woman may with some justification feel that her freedom to work in whatever member state of the Community she chooses is impaired if, although allowed to pursue her career in one or more member states, she is denied the right to do so in others solely on account of her sex. But the quest for sexual equality is also inextricably linked with social factors and *mores*, whether one is considering the case of a male midwife who is allowed to practise in some but not all member states, or of a woman who seeks employment as a coal-miner. In fact, the relevant treaty provisions are compressed into one Article of the Treaty, which appears in Part Three, Title III, Articles 117–28 (social policy). Article 119 reads:

Each Member State shall during the first stage ensure and subsequently maintain the application of the principle that men and women should receive equal pay for equal work.

For the purpose of this Article, 'pay' means the ordinary basic or minimum wage or salary and any other consideration, whether in case or in kind, which the worker receives, directly or indirectly, in respect of his employment from his employer.

Equal pay without discrimination based on sex means:

(a) that pay for the same work at piece rates shall be calculated on the basis of the same unit of measurement;

(b) that pay for work at time rates shall be the same for the same job.

Based wholly as it is on equal pay, it might be thought that one of the underlying objectives of Article 119 was to ensure free competition, so that no member state could gain an unfair advantage by allowing its manufacturers to sell their goods at artificially low prices as a result of using cheap female labour, thus undercutting their foreign competitors in both the home market and in intra-Community trade. Indeed, in *Defrenne* v. *Belgium*[1] the Belgian Government appears to have argued that Article 119 only had an economic objective of that kind.[2] The Court did not find it necessary to consider this contention in that case. It did however reject it in

---

[1] Case 80/70 [1971] *ECR* 445.
[2] Ibid., p. 449.

Defrenne v. *Sabena*,[3] and in doing so drew attention to the fact that Article 119 is among the social provisions of the Treaty. In that case the Court described the dual role of Article 119 in the following terms:

First, in the light of the different stages of the development of social legislation in the various Member States, the aim of Article 119 is to avoid a situation in which undertakings established in States which have actually implemented the principle of equal pay suffer a competitive disadvantage in intra-Community competition as compared with undertakings established in States which have not yet eliminated discrimination against women workers as regards pay.

Secondly, this provision forms part of the social objectives of the Community, which is not merely an economic union, but is at the same time intended, by common action, to ensure social progress and seek the constant improvement of the living and working conditions of their peoples, as is emphasized by the Preamble to the Treaty.[4]

It will also be seen in this chapter that the Community has moved beyond the principle of equal pay by beginning to develop the concept of equal opportunity. Nevertheless, the starting-point of any consideration of the ways in which the Community has dealt with sex discrimination must be the notion of equal pay for equal work,[5] and its development as a concept.

DEFINITION OF PAY

The definition in Article 119 of 'pay' is useful in showing that the term is to be construed in a wide sense. The reference to a worker receiving it 'directly or indirectly' has given rise to some uncertainty, and the need for clarification. In the first of Miss Defrenne's three actions, *Defrenne* v. *Belgium*,[6] the facts were that a Belgian air hostess employed by the Sabena airline company took exception to being compulsorily retired under the terms of her contract at the age of 40, whereas male cabin stewards could continue to work beyond that age. The first question on which the Court was asked for a preliminary ruling was in effect whether the retirement pension, granted under a social security scheme and financed by contributions from workers and employers and by a state subsidy, constituted pay, i.e. a consideration which the worker received indirectly in respect of his employment from his employer. The first point to note is that the social security scheme in question was one which had been established by Belgian law and not by the employer. Miss Defrenne's pension was regu-

---

[3] Case 43/75 [1976] *ECR* 455, p. 472.

[4] Ibid., p. 472.

[5] Or, according to the French text of Article 119, 'l'égalité des rémunérations entre les travailleurs masculins et les travailleurs féminins pour un même travail'.

[6] Case 80/70 [1971] *ECR* 445.

lated by a general Decree on retirement[7] and a special one[8] dealing, inter alia, with air crews. The Court declined in these circumstances to consider the pension as pay, although it hinted that pay could include future benefits to be enjoyed after employment has ceased, provided they come from the employer and are in respect of the former employment. It said:

The provision in the second paragraph of the article extends the concept of pay to any other consideration, whether in cash or in kind, whether immediate or future, provided that the worker receives it, albeit indirectly, in respect of his employment from his employer.

Although consideration in the nature of social security benefits is not therefore in principle alien to the concept of pay, there cannot be brought within this concept, as defined in Article 119, social security schemes or benefits, in particular retirement pensions, directly governed by legislation without any element of agreement within the undertaking or the occupational branch concerned, which are obligatorily applicable to general categories of workers.[9]

The 'dispositif' accordingly reads:

A retirement pension established within the framework of a social security scheme laid down by legislation does not constitute consideration which the worker receives indirectly in respect of his employment from his employer within the meaning of the second paragraph of Article 119 of the EEC Treaty.[10]

This case contrasts with *Worringham and Humphreys* v. *Lloyds Bank Ltd*.[11] In the latter case, the bank had two of its own retirement benefits schemes, one for men and one for women. Men under 25 years of age (but not women) were required to contribute 5 per cent of their salary to the trustees of the scheme, and their gross salary was increased accordingly. The result of paying these contributions was to enhance the amounts of various social benefits and allowances. In certain circumstances the men could, upon leaving their employment, secure the return to them of these particular contributions, with interest. The Court was asked whether (i) the contributions financed by the employer (through the topping up of salary), or (ii) the rights and benefits of the worker under the scheme, were 'pay' within the meaning of Article 119. The Court did not answer the second part of the question, but answered the first in the affirmative by ruling:

A contribution to a retirement benefits scheme which is paid by an employer in the name of employees by means of an addition to the gross salary and which therefore helps to determine the amount of that salary constitutes 'pay' within the meaning of the second paragraph of Article 119 of the EEC Treaty.[12]

---

[7] Royal Decree No. 50 of 24 Oct. 1967.
[8] Royal Decree No. 3 of 3 Nov. 1969.
[9] Case 80/70 [1971] *ECR* 445, p. 451.
[10] Ibid., p. 453.
[11] Case 69/80 [1981] *ECR* 767.
[12] Ibid., p. 795.

Its reasons were:

Sums such as those in question which are included in the calculation of the gross salary payable to the employee and which directly determine the calculation of other advantages linked to the salary, such as redundancy payments, unemployment benefits, family allowances and credit facilities, form part of the worker's pay within the meaning of the second paragraph of Article 119 of the Treaty even if they are immediately deducted by the employer and paid to a pension fund on behalf of the employee. This applies *a fortiori* where those sums are refunded in certain circumstances and subject to certain deductions to the employee as being repayable to him if he ceases to belong to the contractual retirement benefits scheme under which they were deducted.[13]

In *Garland* v. *British Rail*[14] the Court confirmed what it had only hinted in *Defrenne* v. *Belgium*,[15] namely that pay can include benefits in cash or in kind which only accrue after the employment has terminated. But it went further and treated as pay certain non-contractual benefits to which the former employee had no legal right but which he had come to expect. The facts were that British Rail in practice allowed former male employees and their families to continue to enjoy travel benefits after they had retired, but denied the same privileges to former female employees and their families. The Court considered that these benefits were conferred 'directly or indirectly in respect of his employment' (Article 119).[16] In this way the Court may, by omitting the comma after 'indirectly' (and thus departing from the text of Article 119), have regarded that word as qualifying not only the word 'receives' but also the phrase 'in respect of his employment'. Alternatively, it may have equated the phrase 'in respect of his employment' with 'because of his past or present employment'. Whatever may have been the Court's reasons, once it had accepted that this form of consideration was in respect of the employment, it was relatively easy for the Court then to rely on the fact that the Article says 'receives' and not 'is entitled to receive'. The result was that these non-obligatory financial advantages enjoyed during retirement had to be treated as pay. The Court concluded:

It follows from those considerations that rail travel facilities such as those referred to by the House of Lords fulfil the criteria enabling them to be treated as pay within the meaning of Article 119 of the EEC Treaty.[17]

In *Commission* v. *Luxembourg*[18] it was implicitly accepted by the parties and by the Court, without question or argument, that an allowance paid to civil servants having the status of head of a household was 'pay' within the meaning of Article 119.

[13] Ibid., p. 790. See also Case 23/83, *Liefting*, judgment of 18/9/84.
[14] Case 12/81 [1982] *ECR* 359.
[15] Case 80/70 [1971] *ECR* 445.
[16] Case 12/81 [1982] *ECR* 359, p. 369.
[17] Ibid., p. 369.
[18] Case 58/81 [1982] *ECR* 2175.

THE SECONDARY LEGISLATION

Article 119 adopts the deceptively simple test of 'equal pay for equal work'. One of the difficulties is that 'equal work' is capable of being construed restrictively. For example, strictly speaking the person who makes the morning coffee for all the office workers is not doing work which is exactly equal to (in the sense of being the same as) that of the person who makes the afternoon tea, because the two operations are technically different, as well as involving different commodities. Yet such a narrow interpretation would lead to absurd results,[19] and, far from representing the 'social progress' to which the preamble to the Treaty refers, would involve a diminution in the rights of sexual equality previously achieved in a convention drawn up under the auspices of the International Labour Organization, to which all member states of the Community are parties.[20] That convention adopts the standard of equal remuneration for 'work of equal value'.[21] This provision was the source of inspiration for the Community's secondary legislation on equal pay.[22]

Directive 117/75 (equal pay)

The Council recognized in the social action programme set out in its Resolution of 21 January 1974[23] that, as part of the process of harmonizing living and working conditions, priority should be given to action on women's pay. It accordingly adopted Directive 117/75 of 10 February 1975[24] on the approximation of the laws of the member states relating to the application of the principle of equal pay for men and women. The Directive was based on Article 100. That Article requires that any directive made under it must be for the approximation of national provisions which directly affect the establishment and functioning of the common market. This condition was satisfied because, in connection with the establishment of the common market, Article 2 of the Treaty requires a raising of the standard of living, and Article 119 requires equal pay for men and women as part of that process. One consequence of this basic objective of raising standards of living is that it cannot be maintained that Article 119 is satisfied by bringing men's pay down to that of women and thus achieving equality of pay. That this latter action would only be paying lip-service to Article 119 was demonstrated by the Court in *Defrenne* v. *Sabena*[25] when it said:

In particular, since Article 119 appears in the context of the harmonization of working conditions while the improvement is being maintained, the objection that

---

[19] It would also be contrary to Art. 1 of Dir. 117/75, *OJ* 1975, L45/19.
[20] ILO Convention No. 100 concerning equal remuneration for men and women workers for work of equal value, of 29 June 1951, TS No. 88 (1972).   [21] Ibid., Art. 2.
[22] It was also referred to in Case 43/75, *Defrenne* v. *Sabena* [1976] *ECR* 455, p. 473.
[23] *OJ* 1974, C13/1.
[24] *OJ* 1975, L45/19.   [25] Case 43/75 [1976] *ECR* 455.

the terms of this article may be observed in other ways than by raising the lowest salaries may be set aside.[26]

Therefore when Article 3 of the Directive requires member states to abolish all discrimination between men and women arising from laws, regulations, or administrative provisions which is contrary to the principle of equal pay, this should be interpreted in the sense that the pay fixed for the lower-paid worker (usually the woman) must be brought up to the level paid to the worker of the opposite sex. Moreover, it would not be sufficient for some intermediate rate of pay to be fixed for both men and women.

Article 1 of the Directive requires a broad interpretation to be given to the phrase 'equal pay for equal work', as used in Article 119 of the Treaty. Article 1 of the Directive reads:

The principle of equal pay for men and women outlined in Article 119 of the Treaty, hereinafter called 'principle of equal pay' means, for the same work or for work to which equal value is attributed, the elimination of all discrimination on grounds of sex with regard to all aspects and conditions of remuneration.

In particular, where a job classification system is used for determining pay, it must be based on the same criteria for both men and women and so drawn up as to exclude any discrimination on grounds of sex.

The words 'or for work to which equal value is attributed' clearly demonstrate that in the example given earlier in this chapter the tea-maker and the coffee-maker should receive equal pay, even if they are of different sexes.

The extent of the principle of equal pay for work to which equal value is attributed was considered by the Court in *Commission* v. *United Kingdom*.[27] The problem arose out of the way in which the United Kingdom purported to comply with the Treaty through the Equal Pay Act 1970,[28] as amended by the Sex Discrimination Act 1975.[29] Under Section 1 of the 1970 Act, all women's contracts of employment were deemed to include a clause requiring equal pay for men and women. The section drew a distinction between women employed on 'like work', and women engaged on work 'rated as equivalent' with that of a man. 'Like work' was defined as work which was of 'the same' or a 'broadly similar' nature when the differences, if any, between the work done by women and men were not of practical importance with regard to terms and conditions of employment. The difficulty, however, arose in connection with work which was not 'like' work, and which only attracted equal pay under the Act if it could be said to be 'rated as equivalent'. For this purpose Section 1(5) provided that work was only to be rated as equivalent if it had been so rated as a result of a job evaluation

---

[26] Ibid., p. 472.
[27] Case 61/81 [1982] *ECR* 2601.
[28] 1970, Cp. 41.
[29] 1975, Cp. 65.

scheme operated within an undertaking or group of undertakings. To gain the benefit of such a scheme it had to be demonstrated that the woman's job, though not even broadly similar to the man's, was of equal value in terms of effort, skill, decision, etc. But there was no obligation on the employer to institute any job evaluation scheme, and indeed one could not be independently initiated without his consent.[30] If, therefore, an undertaking's female medical adviser claimed that her job should be rated as equivalent to that of the undertaking's male legal adviser, the employer could defeat her claim by saying that there had been no relevant job evaluation scheme.

In the action the Commission claimed that the United Kingdom was in breach of its obligations under Article 1 of Directive 75/117[31] by failing to ensure that all discrimination on grounds of sex must be eliminated in the case of work for which equal value was attributed. The Court pointed out that under Article 1 of the Directive a job classification system was only one of the possible methods for determining pay for work for which equal value was to be attributed, whereas the Equal Pay Act stipulated that it was to be the only method. The Court then rejected the United Kingdom's contention, that the Directive did not confer upon an employee any right to have her pay determined by a job classification scheme, in the following terms:

The United Kingdom's interpretation amounts to a denial of the very existence of a right to equal pay for work of equal value where no classification has been made. Such a position is not consonant with the general scheme and provisions of Directive 75/117. The recitals in the preamble to that directive indicate that its essential purpose is to implement the principle that men and women should receive equal pay contained in Article 119 of the Treaty and that it is primarily the responsibility of the Member States to ensure the application of this principle by means of appropriate laws, regulations and administrative provisions in such a way that all employees in the Community can be protected in these matters.[32]

In cases where an employee sought to rely on the principle of equal pay for 'the same work' or 'work to which equal value is attributed', there must therefore be some machinery for settling disputes.[33] The Court, referring to this obligation, said:

It follows that where there is disagreement as to the application of that concept a worker must be entitled to claim before an appropriate authority that this work has the same value as other work and, if that is found to be the case, to have his rights under the Treaty and the directive acknowledged by a binding decision. Any method which excludes that option prevents the aims of the directive from being achieved.[34]

---

[30] See Case 61/81 [1982] *ECR* 2601, p. 2615.
[31] *OJ* 1975, L45/19.
[33] See Art. 2 of Dir. 117/75, *OJ* 1975, L45/19.

[32] Case 61/81 [1982] *ECR* 2601, p. 2615.
[34] Ibid., p. 2616.

The Court accordingly ruled:

that, by failing to introduce into its national legal system in implementation of the provisions of Council Directive 75/117/EEC of 10 February 1975 such measures as are necessary to enable all employees who consider themselves wronged by failure to apply the principle of equal pay for men and women for work to which equal value is attributed and for which no system of job classification exists to obtain recognition of such equivalence, the United Kingdom has failed to fulfil its obligations under the Treaty.[35]

As a result of this decision, the Equal Pay Act 1970 was amended by the Equal Pay (Amendment) Regulations 1983,[36] made pursuant to Section 2(2) of the European Communities Act 1972.[37]

Although the reference in Article 1 of the Directive to 'work to which equal value is attributed' is useful in recording a broad interpretation of the principle of equal pay, and although its inclusion of the words 'all aspects and conditions of remuneration' confer an equally extended meaning to the word 'pay', the Court, while not casting any doubt on those wide interpretations, prefers to rely in its judgments on Article 119 of the Treaty. In following this tendency the Court seems to have considered that the Directive merely restates in the first sentence the principle in Article 119, and that its second sentence is only an example of the application of that principle. Thus in *Macarthys Ltd*. v. *Wendy Smith*[38] the Court concluded that the dispute which had been brought before the national court could be decided in the framework of an interpretation of Article 119, and that there was therefore no need to answer the national court's questions about the Directive. In that case the woman concerned had succeeded a man in a particular post, but had been paid less. Her employers' argument was that Article 119 required contemporaneous situations to be considered, and did not require a comparison to be made between the pay of a woman employee and that of her predecessor. The Court rejected that contention by saying:

In such a situation the decisive test lies in establishing whether there is a difference in treatment between a man and a woman performing 'equal work' within the meaning of Article 119. The scope of that concept, which is entirely qualitative in character in that it is exclusively concerned with the nature of the services in question, may not be restricted by the introduction of a requirement of contemporaneity.[39]

However, the difference in time between the occupation of a post by a man and woman respectively may result in differences in the work involved, and

---

[35] Ibid., p. 2617. See also Case 143/83, *Commission* v. *Denmark*, judgment of 30/1/85.

[36] SI 1983/1794. See also the Industrial Tribunals (Rules of Procedure) (Equal Value Amendment) Regulations 1983.

[37] 1972, C. 68.

[38] Case 129/79 [1980] *ECR* 1275.

[39] Ibid., p. 1288.

it clearly would not be contrary to Article 119 to pay the successor less if the workload, or its value, had changed, because it would not then be 'equal work' or, in the words of the Directive, 'work to which equal value is attributed'. The Court accordingly said:

It must be acknowledged, however, that, as the Employment Appeal Tribunal properly recognized, it cannot be ruled out that a difference in pay between two workers occupying the same post but at different periods in time may be explained by the operation of factors which are unconnected with any discrimination on grounds of sex. That is a question of fact which it is for the court or tribunal to decide.[40]

In *Jenkins* v. *Kingsgate (Clothing Productions) Ltd.*[41] the Court did answer a question which specifically asked for an interpretation of both Article 119 EEC and Article 1 of the Directive. However, its conclusion was:

It follows, therefore, that Article 1 of Council Directive 75/117/EEC which is principally designed to facilitate the practical application of the principle of equal pay outlined in Article 119 of the Treaty in no way alters the content or scope of that principle as defined in the Treaty.[42]

The Court accordingly based its ruling exclusively on Article 119, and thus once more demonstrated its preference for the Treaty provision. In that case a woman was employed part-time at an hourly rate which was lower than that of her male counterpart, who was employed full-time. Before 1975 the employer paid women lower rates than men, but in the case of each sex there was no difference in the hourly rates paid to part-time and full-time workers. After November 1975 (under a scheme introduced shortly before the entry into force of the Equal Pay Act 1970) the employer paid men and women workers the same hourly rates, but part-time workers of either sex were paid less than full-time workers. After that date, therefore, there was prima facie no discrimination in matters of pay on grounds of sex. The discrimination was as between full-time and part-time workers. But in fact there was only one male worker who had been brought out of retirement to work part-time, and for short periods. The question therefore arose as to whether this scheme in reality involved a disguised discrimination on grounds of sex. The European Court left it to the national court to consider, in the light of the facts and of the employer's intentions, whether this was so. The Court's ruling was:

A difference in pay between full-time workers and part-time workers does not amount to discrimination prohibited by Article 119 of the Treaty unless it is in reality merely an indirect way of reducing the pay of part-time workers on the ground that that group of workers is composed exclusively or predominantly of women.[43]

[40] Ibid., p. 1289.
[42] Ibid., p. 927.
[41] Case 96/80 [1981] *ECR* 911.
[43] Ibid., p. 928.

In *Burton* v. *British Railways Board*[44] the European Court was asked by the national court for an interpretation of Article 1 of Directive 117/75.[45] There a man claimed that he was the victim of discrimination because under a voluntary redundancy scheme men had to reach the age of 60 before they were eligible, whereas women qualified at the age of 55. There is of course no reason why a man should not gain the benefit of Article 119 and Directive 75/117 if he is paid less than a woman worker. However, as the Court pointed out,[46] the real question in the case did not concern the benefits under the redundancy scheme, but whether the conditions of access to it were discriminatory. The Court proceeded therefore to deal with it on the basis of Directive 207/76.[47]

Article 2 of Directive 75/117[48] required the introduction in national legal systems of a judicial process which must be available, after possible recourse to other competent authorities, to all persons who seek redress for failure to apply the principle of equal pay. The Court's reference to this in *Commission* v. *United Kingdom*[49] has already been noted. In that case the Court referred to the worker's right to claim before 'an appropriate authority'. This latter phrase would cover recourse either to the judicial process, or to the other competent authorities, which are mentioned in Article 2 of the Directive. In this context the rules of English law on arbitration are entirely in accordance with the Directive. If an employer and employee agree as part of the contract of employment that their disputes arising out of their relationship are to be referred to arbitration they may, if they draft their contract carefully, succeed in delaying any action in the courts until after the arbitrator has given his award. But they cannot oust the jurisdiction of the courts, and the latter have powers to set aside the award.[50]

Article 3 of Directive 75/117[51] reads:

Member States shall abolish all discrimination between men and women arising from laws, regulations or administrative provisions which is contrary to the principle of equal pay.

It may be thought that this provision added little to what was already stated in the first paragraph of Article 119. To say that equal work must be rewarded with equal pay in effect is the same thing as saying that there must be no discrimination between men and women which contravenes the

---

[44] Case 19/81 [1982] *ECR* 555.
[45] *OJ* 1975, L45/19.
[46] Case 19/81 [1982] *ECR* 555, p. 575.
[47] *OJ* 1976, L39/40.
[48] *OJ* 1975, L45/19.
[49] Case 61/81 [1982] *ECR* 2601.
[50] See vol. 2 of Halsbury's *Laws of England*, 4th edn., London: Butterworth, 1973, paras. 542–5, 555, and 621, and the cases cited therein.
[51] *OJ* 1975, L45/19.

principle of equal pay. Indeed, the third paragraph of Article 119 proceeds to give a definition of the expression 'equal pay without discrimination based on sex', although those words do not appear elsewhere in the Article, and the definition can only be taken to refer to the principle which has already been stated in the first paragraph of the Article. Nevertheless this reformulation is useful because, by focusing on the point that Article 119 is in effect a non-discrimination provision, it draws attention to the fact that the Court's jurisprudence on disguised discrimination is also applicable. The second *Defrenne* case[52] is best known for its ruling on direct effect—an aspect which will be considered later in this chapter. But it also dealt with discrimination. It was agreed between the parties that Miss Defrenne's work as an air hostess was identical to that of a male cabin steward, and that she had suffered discrimination in the matter of pay.[53] The Court took the opportunity, however, of drawing attention to the possibility of disguised discrimination. It said:

For the purposes of the implementation of these provisions a distinction must be drawn within the whole area of application of Article 119 between, first, direct and overt discrimination which may be identified solely with the aid of the criteria based on equal work and equal pay referred to by the article in question and, secondly, indirect and disguised discrimination which can only be identified by reference to more explicit implementing provisions of a Community or national character.

It is impossible not to recognize that the complete implementation of the aim pursued by Article 119, by means of the elimination of all discrimination, direct or indirect, between men and women workers, not only as regards individual undertakings but also entire branches of industry and even of the economic system as a whole, may in certain cases involve the elaboration of criteria whose implementation necessitates the taking of appropriate measures at Community and national level.

This view is all the more essential in the light of the fact that the Community measures on this question, to which reference will be made in answer to the second question, implement Article 119 from the point of view of extending the narrow criterion of 'equal work', in accordance in particular with the provisions of Convention No 100 on equal pay concluded by the International Labour Organization in 1951, Article 2 of which establishes the principle of equal pay for work 'of equal value'.

Among the forms of direct discrimination which may be identified solely by reference to the criteria laid down by Article 119 must be included in particular those which have their origin in legislative provisions or in collective labour agreements and which may be detected on the basis of a purely legal analysis of the situation.[54]

---

[52] Case 43/75, *Defrenne* v. *Sabena* [1976] *ECR* 455.
[53] Ibid., p. 471.
[54] Ibid., p. 473.

Article 4 of Directive 75/117[55] reads:

Member States shall take the necessary measures to ensure that provisions appearing in collective agreements, wage scales, wage agreements or individual contracts of employment which are contrary to the principle of equal pay shall be, or may be declared null and void or may be amended.

This provision is very similar to Article 4(*b*) of Directive 207/76,[56] although the latter deals with the principle of equal access rather than the principle of equal pay. The interpretation of the latter was considered in connection with the Commission's first complaint in *Commission* v. *United Kingdom*.[57] In view of the similarity of the two texts it is reasonable to suppose that the Court would interpret Article 4 of Directive 75/117 in the same way.

The point at issue concerned collective agreements. In the United Kingdom these are not normally binding, and indeed, by Section 18 of the Trade Union and Labour Relations Act 1974,[58] collective agreements made before 1 December 1971 or after the entry into force of the Act were presumed not to be legally enforceable unles they contained a written provision to the contrary. The UK Government informed the Court during the proceedings that it was not aware of there being any legally binding collective agreements then in force in the United Kingdom.[59] Since collective agreements had no legal effect, the United Kingdom argued that the Directive did not require the Government to go further, and take steps to ensure that they were, or might be, declared to be null and void or amended. The Court did not accept the argument, and found that the Directive covered all collective agreements, whether or not they produced legal effects. The Court considered the underlying reason of the Directive to be that, although collective agreements might not be legally binding, they had a *de facto* effect on the employment relationship to which they referred.

It may well be true that in many cases employers and employees alike turn to the bundle of collective agreement texts kept on the premises, rather than to the relevant statutes, in order to decide what should be done in practice. If, therefore, collective agreements contained provisions contravening the principles of equal pay or equal access, they could be not only misleading as to the employees' rights but also likely in practice to cause those principles to be breached. Although the Court did not spell out its reasoning in such detail, this seems to have been the burden of it. Thus far the Court's views are understandable. It is however unfortunate that the Court went on to speak of collective agreements determining the 'rights' of workers, and the conditions which employment relationships 'must'

[55] *OJ* 1975, L45/19.
[56] *OJ* 1976, L39/40.
[57] Case 165/82 [1984] 1 *CMLR* 44.
[58] Cp. 52.
[59] Case 165/82 [1984] 1 *CMLR* 44, p. 59.

satisfy.[60] Such language seems inappropriate to a document which is not legally binding.

Article 5 of Directive 75/117[61] requires member states to protect employees against dismissal as a result of having claimed equal pay. Article 6 requires member states to take the necessary measures to ensure the application of the principle of equal pay, and Article 7 obliges them to see that the relevant revisions on equal pay are brought to the attention of employees 'by all appropriate means'.

Article 8 of the Directive reads:

1. Member States shall put into force the laws, regulations and administrative provisions necessary in order to comply with this directive within one year of its notification and shall immediately inform the Commission thereof.

2. Member States shall communicate to the Commission the texts of the laws, regulations and administrative provisions which they adopt in the field covered by this directive.

On the face of it, this provision allowed member states one year from 19 February 1975 in which to comply with the directive. Since the Directive was designed to give effect to the principle of equal pay contained in Article 119 EEC, it was widely thought that the Council had thereby set the time limit for compliance with Article 119, and that by implication it had authorized member states not to comply fully with that Article until that date. In view of the enormous financial consequences in the member states of introducing equal pay for men and women, this was a reasonable assumption. However, the Court held in *Defrenne* v. *Sabena*[62] that for the original six members of the EEC the application of the principle of equal pay was, by the express terms of Article 119, to be 'fully secured and irreversible' by 1 January 1962 (the end of the first transitional period), and that the same result had to be secured for the new member states with effect from 1 January 1973 (the date of entry into force of the Treaty of Accession).[63] With regard to Article 8 of the Directive, the Court said:

It was not possible for this legal situation to be modified by Directive No 75/117, which was adopted on the basis of Article 100 dealing with the approximation of laws and was intended to encourage the proper implementation of Article 119 by means of a series of measures to be taken on the national level, in order, in particular, to eliminate indirect forms of discrimination, but was unable to reduce the effectiveness of that article or modify its temporal effect.[64]

[60] Ibid., p. 60.
[61] *OJ* 1975, L45/19.
[62] Case 43/75 [1976] *ECR* 455.
[63] Ibid., p. 478.
[64] Ibid., p. 479.

The enormity of this conclusion was, however, reduced by the way in which the Court handled questions of direct effect, and by the way in which it imposed temporal limitations on claims by individuals.[65] This will be considered later in this chapter in connection with direct effect.

Directive 76/207 (equal treatment)

Two legislative problems for the Council have been first, that the Treaty confers on it no legislative powers specifically to give effect to Article 119, and second, that the Article is confined to equal pay and therefore does not extend to equal treatment in other respects. The first difficulty was overcome by resorting to Article 100 (approximation of laws) for the adoption of Directive 75/117,[66] and by asserting in its preamble that implementation of the principle of equal pay was an integral part of the establishment and functioning of the common market. The second difficulty was more troublesome. The Court first recognized the need to ensure equality in working conditions for men and women employed by the institutions of the Community: *Sabbatini (née Bertoni)* v. *European Parliament*,[67] and *Airola* v. *Commission of the European Communities*.[68] It subsequently explained, in *Defrenne* v. *Sabena*,[69] its reasons for taking this view.

The Court started from the position that respect for fundamental personal human rights was one of the general principles of Community law, the observance of which it had a duty to ensure. This was an indirect reference to Article 164 EEC, Article 31 ECSC, and Article 136 EURATOM. It then said: 'There can be no doubt that the elimination of discrimination based on sex forms part of those fundamental rights.'[70] Finally the Court noted that these concepts were recognized by the European Social Charter of 18 November 1961, and by convention No. 111 of the International Labour Organization of 25 June 1958. Having thus justified its position with regard to the two staff cases, the Court then shrank from applying the same principle to other workers. It concluded in *Defrenne* v. *Sabena*[71] that, at the time of the events which were the subject of the litigation in the Belgian courts, the Community had not assumed any responsibility for securing observance of the principle of equality between men and women in working conditions other than pay, although it had in Articles 117 and 118 EEC adopted a social programme.

The Court therefore ruled:

At the time of the events which form the basis of the main action there was, as regards the relationships between employer and employee under national law, no rule of Community law prohibiting discrimination between men and women in the

[65] Ibid., pp. 480–1.
[66] *OJ* 1975, L45/19.
[67] Case 20/71 [1972] *ECR* 345.
[68] Case 21/74 [1975] *ECR* 221.
[69] Case 149/77 [1978] *ECR* 1365.
[70] Ibid.
[71] Ibid., p. 1378.

matter of working conditions other than the requirements as to pay referred to in Article 119 of the Treaty.[72]

The result of this decision appeared to be that, at the time in question in that case, Community law governed the employment of persons working for institutions of the Community, and that for this purpose Community law included the right of equal treatment in all respects. On the other hand, it was left to national law to decide whether other workers in the member states should be accorded that right.

The Council had however by this time taken Community law a step further, by adopting Directive 207/76 on the implementation of the principle of equal treatment for men and women as regards access to employment, functional training and promotion, and working conditions.[73] For this purpose the Council relied on Article 235, rather than any general principle of law. That Article can only, by its terms, be applied when this is necessary in order to attain a Community objective. The preamble to the Directive sought to establish such an objective. It referred to the Council's Resolution of 21 January 1974 concerning a social action programme,[74] which included the achievement of equal treatment in these respects as one of its priorities. The preamble then appeared to maintain that the Directive was necessary to achieve that Community objective, although it is not entirely clear on this point. If this is indeed the Council's reasoning, it might be thought to imply that an objective of the Community can be established by a resolution of the Council, for the purpose of creating legislative competence under Article 235. This in turn raises the question whether a resolution of the European Parliament can do likewise.[75] A better view may be that the institutions can do no more than give greater articulation to the objectives already to be found in Articles 2 and 3 of the Treaty, which are in very broad terms. The reference in these Articles to raising the standard of living and to the abolition of obstacles to the free movement of persons may be a sufficiently broad base on which to have built the edifice of Directive 76/207.[76]

Article 1 of the Directive describes its purpose as being to implement the principle of equal treatment for men and women as regards access to employment, including promotion and vocational training, and as regards working conditions. It also refers to the prospect of future secondary legislation on equal treatment in social security matters.[77]

Article 2 provides that the principle of equal treatment shall exclude any discrimination on grounds of sex 'either directly or indirectly by reference

[72] Ibid., p. 1379.
[73] *OJ* 1976, L39/40.
[74] *OJ* 1974, C13/1.
[75] See, e.g., its Resolution of 11 Feb. 1981, *OJ* 1981, C50.
[76] *OJ* 1976, L39/40.
[77] Subsequently incorporated in Dir. 7/79, *OJ* 1979, L6/24.

in particular to marital or family status'. Article 2(2) states, however, that this is without prejudice to the right of member states to exclude from the field of application of the Directive 'those occupational activities and, where appropriate, the training leading thereto, for which, by reason of their nature or the context in which they are carried out, the sex of the worker constitutes a determining factor'.

The scope of this exception was considered in *Commission* v. *United King-dom*.[78] In the United Kingdom Section 6(3) of the Sex Discrimination Act 1975[79] made an exception to the principle of equal access in the case of employment in a private household, or in undertakings where the number of persons employed did not exceed 5. The Commission complained, and the United Kingdom sought to rely on this exception in Article 2(2) of the Directive. With regard to employment in a private household (which, as the Advocate General pointed out, is not necessarily the same thing as employment as resident domestic staff[80]), the Court found the United Kingdom to be in breach of its obligations on the grounds that, while in some cases of employment in private households the sex of the employee might be a decisive factor, this was not the case for all kinds of such employment.[81] With regard to small undertakings, the Court simply noted that the United Kingdom had advanced no argument to show that in any undertaking of that size the sex of the worker would be a determining factor by reason of the nature of his activities or the context in which they were carried out. The Commission also alleged in this case that the United Kingdom's restrictions on midwifery by men did not fall within the exception. These restrictions were that, under certain temporary provisions in the Midwives Act 1951,[82] men were only allowed to follow midwifery training courses at centres approved by the Minister. The Court concluded that, at least for the present, personal sensitivities might play an important role in relations between midwife and patients, that the United Kingdom was entitled to rely on the exception in such cases, and that it was accordingly not in breach of its Community obligations.[83] The judgment makes no mention of Article 2(3) of the Directive, which says that the directive is without prejudice to provisions concerning the protection of women, particularly as regards pregnancy and maternity. The inference is that it was not thought to be relevant, perhaps because the sort of protection to which it refers does not include protection against offence to a woman's personal sensitivities in such matters.

Article 2(4) of the Directive provides, somewhat unnecessarily, that the

---

[78] Case 165/82 [1984] 1 *CMLR* 44.
[79] 1975, C. 65.
[80] Case 165/82 [1984] 1 *CMLR* 44, p. 55.
[81] Ibid., p. 61.
[82] 1951, C. 53.
[83] Case 165/82 [1984] 1 *CMLR* 44, p. 62.

Directive is without prejudice to measures to promote equal opportunity for men and women. It would, however, have been rather difficult to argue, even without that paragraph, that such a measure (e.g. to remove a male monopoly) infringed the principle in Article 2(1) of no discrimination on grounds of sex.

Article 3 of the Directive enlarges on the principle of equal treatment and no discrimination on grounds of sex with regard to access to jobs. It obliges member states to abolish laws, regulations, and administrative provisions which conflict with the principle. Similarly, they are required to ensure that conflicting provisions in 'collective agreements, individual contracts of employment, internal rules of undertakings or in rules governing the independent occupations and professions shall be, or may be declared, null and void or may be amended'. This is very similar to Article 4 of Directive 117/75 (equal pay),[84] and its interpretation by the Court in *Commission* v. *United Kingdom*[85] has been discussed earlier in this chapter.

Article 4 applies the same principle to access 'to all types and to all levels, of vocational training, advanced vocational training and retraining'. The requirements to abolish conflicting laws, regulations, and administrative provisions, and for the nullification of conflicting provisions in collective agreements, etc. are in identical terms to those in Article 3. Indeed, it was in relation to Article 4(b) of the Directive that the Court gave its ruling in *Commission* v. *United Kingdom*.[86] Article 4(c) adds that member states must ensure that vocational guidance, training and retraining, are available 'on the basis of the same criteria and at the same levels without any discrimination on grounds of sex'. It makes an exception, however, in the case of 'the freedom granted in certain Member States to certain private training establishments'. This latter is a deplorable piece of legislative drafting which gives no indication of how the member states or establishments in question can be identified.

Article 5 applies the principle of equal treatment to working conditions, including conditions for dismissal. It requires, in terms which are identical to those in Articles 3 and 4, the abolition or amendment of conflicting laws, collective agreements, etc. The reference in this Article to 'dismissal' was held in *Burton* v. *British Railways Board*[87] to include termination of employment under a voluntary redundancy scheme.[88] In that case, men could only opt for redundancy at the age of 60 whereas women could do so at the age of 55. However this took account of the national old age pension scheme, under which the qualifying ages were 65 (men) and 60 (women). The effect of the redundancy scheme was therefore that both men and women could

[84] *OJ* 1975, L45/19.
[85] Case 165/82 [1983] *ECR* 3431.
[86] Ibid.
[87] Case 19/81 [1982] *ECR* 555.
[88] Ibid., p. 575.

become voluntarily redundant at any time during the five years imme-diately preceding the qualiyfing age for a national pension. The Court held that in these circumstances there was no discrimination against male rail-way employees with regard to access to the voluntary redundancy scheme.[89]

Article 6 echoes the provisions of Article 2 of Directive 117/75 (equal pay),[90] and requires the maintenance of a national legal system whereby aggrieved persons can 'pursue their claims by judicial process after possible recourse to other competent authorities'. It has been submitted earlier in this chapter that the rules of English law on arbitration accord with this requirement. The Directive is silent on the question of the remedies to be provided as a result of judicial or arbitral process. If an employer denies a worker his or her Community rights, and assuming those rights have direct effect in the member states, one remedy could be damages. But the victim might prefer some kind of specific performance of the Community obligation. In principle it would seem that, since the Com-munity rules have not prescribed the remedies, they should be determined by the laws of the member state in question. The point arose, in relation to the principle of equal access, in two cases in which a female applicant was refused employment because of her sex. In each case the national court sought a preliminary ruling under Article 177 EEC on the question whether national law must provide a remedy whereby the employer is ordered to employ the victim. The two cases are *Colson and Kamann* v. *Minister of Justice*,[91] and *Harz* v. *Firma Deutsche*,[92] and in each case the Court answered the question in the negative.

Article 7 of the Directive is the corollary of Article 6, in that it protects employees from dismissal for having asserted their rights earlier within the undertaking which employes them or in litigation.

The remainder of the Directive requires employees to be informed of measures taken pursuant to it, gives member states periods of grace for compliance, the last of which periods expired in 1980, and requires excep-tions which may be made on the grounds that sex is a determining factor (Article 2(2)) to be kept under review.

Directive 7/79 (social security)

The trilogy of directives on sex discrimination is completed by Directive 7/79 on the progressive implementation of the principle of equal treatment for men and women in matters of social security.[93] This Directive also was

---

[89] Ibid., p. 577.
[90] *OJ* 1975, L45/19.
[91] Case 14/83, [1984] *ECR* 1891.
[92] Case 79/83, [1984] *ECR* 1921.
[93] *OJ* 1979, L6/24.

adopted under Article 235 EEC. Its only indirect reference to a Community objective, the attainment of which must be necessary in order to found any action under Article 235, lies in its mention in the preamble of Directive 76/207.[94] Article 1(2) of the latter Directive had indeed referred to 'the principle of equal treatment in matters of social security'. Although this may now be taken to be a Community objective, it needs to be considered in the light of the wider Community policy with regard to social security generally. It has been seen in Chapter 4 that the pragmatic solution adopted in the latter field has been to retain the various national social security systems, but to co-ordinate them to the extent necessary to give effect to Community principles. This solution is reflected in the preamble to Directive 7/79, which indicates that the principle of equal treatment (and in its context this refers to equal treatment for men and women) should:

be implemented in the first place in the statutory schemes which provide protection against the risks of sickness, invalidity, old age, accidents at work, occupational diseases and unemployment, and in social assistance in so far as it is intended to supplement or replace the abovementioned schemes.

The reference to statutory schemes seems therefore to refer to national schemes, co-ordinated so far as may be required to accord with Community principles.

Article 1 of the Directive declares its purpose to be the progressive implementation of the principle of equal treatment for men and women in matters of social security and 'other elements of social protection' set out in Article 3 of the Directive.

Article 2 makes it clear that the Directive applies to the entire working population, whether they be workers within the meaning of Article 48 EEC or self-employed persons, whether or not their activity has been interrupted by sickness or involuntary unemployment, whether or not they have retired or been invalided, and even if they have never worked but are seeking employment. The scope of application of the Directive is defined in Article 3(1) as extending to:

(*a*) statutory schemes which provide protection against the following risks:
  — sickness,
  — invalidity,
  — old age,
  — accidents at work and occupational diseases,
  — unemployment;
(*b*) social assistance, in so far as it is intended to supplement or replace the schemes referred to in (*a*).

[94] *OJ* 1976, L39/40.

The Article makes an exception, however, in the case of provisions concerning survivors' benefits and family benefits which take the form of increases of benefits due in respect of the risks referred to in Article 3(1).

Article 4 prohibits direct and indirect discrimination on grounds of sex, by reference in particular to marital or family status. It states, but only by way of particular examples, that this principle concerns the scope of the schemes (referred to in Article 3) and conditions of access thereto, the obligation to contribute and the rates of contribution, and the calculation of benefits (including increases due in respect of a spouse and for dependants and the conditions governing the duration and retention of entitlement to benefits).

Article 5, like Article 3 of Directive 117/75[95] and Article 5(2) of Directive 207/76,[96] requires laws, regulations, and administrative provisions contrary to the principle of equal treatment to be abolished. Article 6 corresponds to Article 2 of Directive 75/117 and Article 6 of Directive 76/207, all of which require member states to have machinery whereby aggrieved persons can pursue their claims to equal treatment 'by judicial process, possibly after recourse to other competent authorities'. The way in which the United Kingdom's rules on arbitration comply with this requirement has already been explained in relation to those other Directives.

Article 7(1) contains an important reservation, and is worth quoting in full:

This Directive shall be without prejudice to the right of Member States to exclude from its scope:

(a) the determination of pensionable age for the purposes of granting old-age and retirement pensions and the possible consequences thereof for other benefits;
(b) advantages in respect of old-age pension schemes granted to persons who have brought up children; the acquisition of benefit entitlements following periods of interruption of employment due to the bringing up of children;
(c) the granting of old-age or invalidity benefit entitlements by virtue of the derived entitlements of a wife;
(d) the granting of increases of long-term invalidity, old-age, accidents at work and occupational disease benefits for a dependent wife;
(e) the consequences of the exercise, before the adoption of this Directive, of a right of option not to acquire rights or incur obligations under a statutory scheme.

The UK Government would no doubt rely on this Article if it were alleged in any proceedings in the European Court that the United Kingdom discriminated against men as regards age of entitlement to national old-age pensions.

---

[95] *OJ* 1976, L39/40.
[96] *OJ* 1976, L39/40.

Article 8 gave member states six years in which to comply with the Directive. Since the Directive did not in this respect purport to alter the application of Article 119 EEC, or any other treaty provision, the Court was able to refer to this Article of the directive without comment in *Koks* v. *Raad van Arbeid*.[97]

DIRECT EFFECT

The leading judgment on the direct effect of Article 119 is in the second case of *Defrenne* v. *Sabena*.[98] Miss Defrenne's earlier proceedings in the European Court[99] have already been considered in connection with the meaning of 'pay'. Her third case[100] has been reviewed when considering Directive 76/207 (equal treatment).[101] In this second case the retired Belgian air hostess was claiming arrears of pay. The basis of her claim was that during the period in question she had been paid less than male cabin stewards, although their work was identical to hers. The period of the claim started on 15 February 1963 (because the limitation period in Belgian law precluded earlier claims) and ended on 1 February 1966, the date when Sabena put air hostesses and stewards on the same basic rates of pay. The questions referred under Article 117 to the Court were:

(1) Does Article 119 of the Treaty of Rome introduce directly into the national law of each Member State of the European Community the principle that men and women should receive equal pay for equal work and does it therefore, independently of any national provision, entitle workers to institute proceedings before national courts in order to ensure its observance, and if so as from what date?
(2) Has Article 119 become applicable in the internal law of the Member States by virtue of measures adopted by the authorities of the European Economic Community (if so, which, and as from what date?) or must the national legislature be regarded as alone competent in this matter?[102]

The first question incorporates an unfortunate description of the nature of direct effect, because it assumes that a Community law which has such effect becomes part of the national law of each member state. This is a misleading analysis, which could lead to the false assumption that, having become part of national law, it is subject to national rules of interpretation. Such a conclusion could lead to a wide variety of interpretations of

---

[97] Case 275/81 [1982] *ECR* 3013, p. 3024. See Case 43/75, *Defrenne* v. *Sabena* [1976] *ECR* 455, p. 478, where the Court criticized a similar provision in Dir. 117/75 because it contravened Art. 119 EEC.
[98] Case 43/75 [1976] *ECR* 455.
[99] Case 80/70 [1971] *ECR* 445.
[100] Case 149/77 [1971] *ECR* 1365.
[101] *OJ* 1976, L39/40.
[102] Case 43/75 [1976] *ECR* 455, p. 484.

Community law, whereas one reason for the existence of the European Court and the system of references to it under Article 177 is to achieve as far as possible a uniformity of interpretation throughout the Community, in accordance with the Community's own rules of construction. Thus, for example, the Court's preference for construing Community legislation in accordance with the underlying Community objectives (the teleological approach)[103] is different from the 'strict constructionalist' approach of an English court to the wording of a statute. A better view would therefore seem to be that when a provision of Community law takes direct effect in a Member State it does not become part of the national law, but retains its character as Community law, it being the duty of the national court to construe it and treat it as such, with such guidance from the European Court under Article 177 as may be necessary.

In its judgment the Court in effect rejected the contention of the UK Government that the obligation imposed on member states by Article 119 did not satisfy the Court's criteria of clarity and precision which had to be satisfied before a treaty provision could have direct effect.[104] The Court observed that the Belgian Royal Decree of 24 October 1967, in stating the right of women to commence proceedings for the application of the principle of equal pay set out in Article 119, had simply referred to that Article, thus accepting that it was sufficiently clear and precise for direct interpretation and application by the Belgian courts.

Yet the Court did not treat Article 119 as a whole as having direct effect. It drew a distinction between direct and overt discrimination, capable of being identified solely by applying the test of equal pay for equal work, and indirect and disguised discrimination, identifiable only as a result of more explicitly implementing provisions of Community or national law.[105] This was a novel approach, to the extent that it drew a distinction between 'direct and overt discrimination', in relation to which Article 119 was to have direct effect, and 'indirect and disguised discrimination', in respect of which the Article did not have direct effect, or at least did not have direct effect until given greater articulation by Community or national legislation. In previous cases, such as *Sotgiu* v. *Deutsche Bundespost*,[106] overt and covert discrimination had been treated alike, and no distinction had been drawn between the two for the purpose of determining whether a provision did or did not have direct effect. Nor had the question of directness or indirectness of the discrimination been previously thought to be relevant to the question of direct effect of a Community provision.

This unsettling interpretation of direct effect was criticized along those

---

[103] See, for example, ibid., p. 471, para. 7.
[104] Ibid., p. 459.
[105] Ibid., p. 473.
[106] Case 152/73 [1974] *ECR* 153.

lines by the Advocate General in *Worringham and Humphreys* v. *Lloyds Bank*.[107] He also drew attention to the fact that the actual ruling in *Defrenne* v. *Sabena*[108] did not mention this distinction. Indeed, that ruling was:

The principle that men and women should receive equal pay, which is laid down by Article 119, may be relied on before the national courts. These courts have a duty to ensure the protection of the rights which that provision vests in individuals, in particular in the case of those forms of discrimination which have their origin in legislative provisions or collective labour agreements, as well as where men and women receive unequal pay for equal work which is carried out in the same establishment or service, whether private or public.[109]

In the *Worringham* case[110] the Court appears to have been influenced by the Advocate General's remarks, because it refrained in that case from drawing any such distinction. Instead it maintained the view that Article 119 had direct effect in some respects but not in others. But the criterion for direct effect was stated to be whether or not the discrimination on grounds of sex could be identified solely by reference to the concept of 'equal pay for equal work' (Article 119). The Court said in *Worringham*:

Article 119 of the Treaty applies directly to all forms of discrimination which may be identified solely with the aid of the criteria of equal work and equal pay referred to by the article in question, without national or Community measures being required to define them with greater precision in order to permit of their application.[111]

The Court repeated this formulation verbatim in *Jenkins* v. *Kingsgate (Clothing Productions) Ltd.*,[112] and this may now be regarded as the accepted test. It is for the national courts, therefore, to apply the test of equal pay for equal work whenever they can. For this purpose they will need to decide whether they are able, without the assistance of further Community or national rules, to identify discrimination which infringes the principle. The Court did not give exhaustive guidance on how they should resolve that question, but it did state in *Defrenne* v. *Sabena*,[113] by way of example only, that among the forms of discrimination which could be so identified they must include those originating in legislation or in collective labour agreements.[114]

---

[107] Case 69/80 [1981] *ECR* 767, p. 802.
[108] Case 43/75 [1976] *ECR* 455.
[109] Ibid., p. 481.
[110] Case 69/80 [1981] *ECR* 767.
[111] Ibid., p. 792.
[112] Case 96/80 [1981] *ECR* 911, p. 926. See also Case 12/81, *Garland* v. *British Rail Engineering* [1982] *ECR* 359, p. 370.
[113] Case 43/75 [1976] *ECR* 455.
[114] Ibid., p. 473. In this way Art. 119 may be held to override any inconsistent provision in the Equal Pay Act 1970 and the Sex Discrimination Act 1975. See European Communities Act 1972, section 2(1) and (4).

A more difficult problem arose in *Defrenne* v. *Sabena*,[115] on account of the fact that member states had for a considerable time not always required men and women to be given equal pay for equal work, in the belief that Article 119 stated a general principle, rather than a strict rule of law, that it accordingly did not have direct effect, and that they could await appropriate implementing Community legislation before taking action in any particular field of activity. The Court, as has been seen, took a different view. Its critics might allege that in so doing the Court was exercising a quasi-legislative function. Yet that is not the role given to the Court by the Treaty. Its function, as defined in Article 177, is to give preliminary rulings on the interpretation of the Treaty (and of certain other instruments which are not relevant in this context), and on the validity and interpretation of acts of the institutions. Its only function in relation to Article 119 was therefore to interpret the Article. But the normal consequence when a Court interprets a legislative provision is that such provision must be taken always to have had that meaning. On that basis the result of the Court's ruling could have been to open the floodgates to claims for arrears of pay, dating (subject to any relevant limitation period) to the date when the Treaty entered into force in the member states in question. The economic consequence would have been considerable, as the UK and Irish Governments pointed out to the Court.[116]

The Court therefore took the somewhat surprising step of imposing its own rule of limitation of actions in national courts, thereby again (so its critics would say) indulging in judicial legislation. It referred to the large number of potential claims. It also said[117] that undertakings could not have foreseen them (thereby seemingly admitting that its own judgment was not such as might have been expected), and that some of those undertakings might even as a consequence be driven to bankruptcy. It found that the Commission's failure to commence infringement proceedings against certain member states had been likely to confirm the incorrect impression held by those states as to the effects of Article 119.[118] Moreover, it was impossible to reopen cases when it could no longer be known at what general level pay would have been fixed if Article 119 had been applied.[119] The Court accordingly ruled:

Except as regards those workers who have already brought legal proceedings or made an equivalent claim, the direct effect of Article 119 cannot be relied on in order to support claims concerning pay periods prior to the date of this judgment.[120]

[115] Case 43/75 [1976] *ECR* 455.
[116] Case 43/75 [1976] *ECR* 455, p. 480.
[117] Ibid.
[118] Ibid.
[119] Ibid., p. 481.
[120] Ibid., p. 482.

In the sort of situation uncovered by the *Defrenne* case[121] it was unlikely that the Court, once it had decided to hold that the principle of equal pay for equal work was a rule of Community law having direct effect, would be able to do justice to everybody in all circumstances. But let us suppose that all the female workers in an undertaking had paid subscriptions, for example, through their trade union, to enable one of their members to bring a test case, but had refrained from taking any other action themselves: is it just and equitable that the one should succeed and that all the others should fail? Yet that appears to be the effect of the judgment. It would have avoided discrimination of that kind, as well as establishing a clearer rule, if the Court had simply held that claims could not be presented if they related to pay periods prior to the date of its judgment. That would of course have defeated Miss Defrenne's claim, but in seeking to do justice to her and to similar claimants the Court may not have done justice to others.

The question whether Article 1 of Directive 75/117 (equal pay),[122] as well as Article 119, had direct effect was asked in *Macarthys* v. *Smith*.[123] The Court took the view that this question only arose if the issues in the case could not be resolved by reference to Article 119 alone.[124] Since the Court decided that it was in fact only necessary to refer to Article 119, the Court made no pronouncement on whether Article 1 of the Directive did or did not have direct effect.

In *James Hyndman* v. *Harry S. Spring & Associates*,[125] a case concerning a man who alleged that he had been discriminated against on grounds of sex, the question of the direct effect of Directive 207/76 (equal treatment)[126] was raised, but the case was removed from the Court Register on 9 October 1984.

At present, therefore, the question of direct effect of both Directives remains to be decided. The question whether, if either of them has such effect, it may only be relied upon in the courts in order to determine the rights which an individual or an undertaking can exercise against a member state ('vertical' direct effect), or whether it may also be relied on to determine the rights which individuals or undertakings can exercise against other individuals or undertakings ('horizontal' direct effect), likewise remains unresolved. There is on the other hand no doubt that Article 119 itself has both kinds of direct effect. So far as vertical direct effect is concerned, the fact that individuals can rely on the article in support of claims against a Member State *qua* employer is clear from the reference in *Defrenne* v. *Sabena*[127] to the rights which the article gives to individuals in the same establishment or service, 'whether private or public'.[128] The same

[121] Case 43/75 [1976] *ECR* 455.
[122] *OJ* 1975, L45/19.
[123] Case 129/79 [1980] *ECR* 1275.
[124] Ibid., p. 1288.
[125] Case 132/83.
[126] *OJ* 1976, L39/40.
[127] Case 43/75 [1976] *ECR* 455.
[128] Ibid., pp. 481–2. See also para. 35 of the judgment.

passage, by referring to individuals' rights against the private establishment which employs them, also illustrates the horizontal direct effect of Article 119.

FURTHER READING

J. Forman, 'The Equal Pay Principle under Community Law—A Commentary on Article 119 EEC', (1982) 1 *LIEI* 17.

I. Snaith, 'Equal Pay and Sex Discrimination', (1982) 7 *EL Rev.* 301.

J. Steiner, 'Sex Discrimination under UK and EEC Law: Two plus Four Equals One', (1983) 32 *ICLQ* 399.

Thomson and F. Wooldridge, 'Equal Pay, Sex Discrimination and European Community Law', (1980) 2 *LIEI* 1.

M. Weirich, 'Equality and the Payment of Household Allowances', (1981) 6 *ELR* 489.

D. Wyatt, 'Article 119 EEC: Definition of Pay', (1976) 1 *EL Rev.* 414.

PART III

CAPITAL

VIII

Free Movement of Capital

ARTICLE 3(c) of the EEC Treaty lists as one of the Community's objectives the abolition, as between member states, of obstacles to the freedom of movement for persons, services, and capital. Free movement of capital is thus included amongst the fundamental freedoms of movement.[1] Its close connection with the right of establishment is readily apparent. It is of little avail that a person should have the right to establish an economic activity in another member state if he is at the same time denied the right to transfer sufficient capital to that member state, at a time of his choosing, to enable him to acquire the necessary premises and operational facilities needed for the purposes of his venture. The movement of capital from one state to another is however capable, depending on its amount or its timing, of having a de-stabilizing effect on the economy of one or other of those states. Moreover, Article 2 refers, among the objectives of the Community, to a harmonious development of economic activities, a continuous and *balanced* expansion and an increase in *stability*.[2] In view of the latter objectives, it is not surprising that the principle of free movement of capital is expressed in more qualified terms than in the case of the other freedoms of movement. The main articles of the Treaty in which the free movement of capital is enshrined read:

Article 67

1. During the transitional period and to the extent necessary to ensure the proper functioning of the common market, Member States shall progressively abolish between themselves all restrictions on the movement of capital belonging to persons resident in Member States and any discrimination based on the nationality or on the place of residence of the parties or on the place where such capital is invested.

2. Current payments connected with the movement of capital between Member States shall be freed from all restrictions by the end of the first stage at the latest.

Article 68

1. Member States shall, as regards the matters dealt with in this Chapter, be as liberal as possible in granting such exchange authorisations as are still necessary after the entry into force of this Treaty.

---

[1] See Case 203/80, *Guerrino Casati* [1981] *ECR* 2595, p. 2614.
[2] See also Art. 104, which requires member states to ensure the equilibrium of their overall balance of payments.

2. Where a Member State applies to the movements of capital liberalised in accordance with the provisions of this Chapter the domestic rules governing the capital market and the credit system, it shall do so in a non-discriminatory manner.

3. Loans for the direct or indirect financing of a Member State or its regional or local authorities shall not be issued or placed in other Member States unless the States concerned have reached agreement thereon. This provision shall not preclude the application of Article 22 of the Protocol on the Statute of the European Investment Bank.

Article 71

Member States shall endeavour to avoid introducing within the Community any new exchange restrictions on the movement of capital and current payments connected with such movements, and shall endeavour not to make existing rules more restrictive.

They declare their readiness to go beyond the degree of liberalisation of capital movements provided for in the preceding Articles in so far as their economic situation, in particular the situation of their balance of payments, so permits.

The Commission may, after consulting the Monetary Committee, make recommendations to Member States on this subject.

Article 106

1. Each Member State undertakes to authorise, in the currency of the Member State in which the creditor or the beneficiary resides, any payments connected with the movement of goods, services or capital, and any transfers of capital and earnings, to the extent that the movement of goods, services, capital and persons between Member States has been liberalised pursuant to this Treaty.

The Member States declare their readiness to undertake the liberalisation of payments beyond the extent provided in the preceding sub-paragraph, in so far as their economic situation in general and the state of their balance of payments in particular so permit.

2. In so far as movements of goods, services, and capital are limited only by restrictions on payments connected therewith, these restrictions shall be progressively abolished by applying, *mutatis mutandis*, the provisions of the Chapters relating to the abolition of quantitative restrictions, to the liberalisation of services and to the free movement of capital.

3. Member States undertake not to introduce between themselves any new restrictions on transfers connected with the invisible transactions listed in Annex III to this Treaty.

The progressive abolition of existing restrictions shall be effected in accordance with the provisions of Article 63 to 65, in so far as such abolition is not governed by the provisions contained in paragraphs 1 and 2 or by the Chapter relating to the free movement of capital.

4. If need be, Member States shall consult each other on the measures to be taken to enable the payments and transfers mentioned in this Article to be effected; such measures shall not prejudice the attainment of the objectives set out in this Chapter.

Superficially these articles follow the already familiar pattern of requiring the progressive removal of restrictions on free movement, the abolition of discrimination in the application of national rules, and refraint from introducing new restrictions on free movement (the 'standstill' provisions of Articles 71 and 106). Closer examination reveals qualifications which do not feature in the rules on free movement of goods, persons, and services. The abolition of restrictions is only to be 'to the extent necessary to ensure the proper functioning of the common market' (Article 67); member states are only to be 'as liberal as possible' in granting exchange authorisations (Article 68); they need only 'endeavour to avoid introducing' new exchange restrictions (Article 71); and, although in some respects Article 106 is firmer, it too requires certain action only to be taken by member states 'in so far as the economic situation in general and the state of their balance of payments in particular so permit'. The scope of these provisions, and the limitations to which they are subject, will be considered later in this chapter. So too will the escape routes provided by Articles 104–9 (balance of payments).

Article 221 also deals with capital, in that it provides that, within three years of the entry into force of the EEC Treaty, member states shall accord to nationals of other member states the same treatment as their own nationals as regards participation in the capital of companies or firms within the meaning of Article 58, without prejudice to the application of other provisions in the Treaty. This Article need not necessarily have any effect as regards the movement of capital from one member state to another. It might, depending on the nature of the national rules in question, only have the effect that if a national of one member state has funds in another member state he must be allowed to invest them there in stocks and shares in the same way as nationals of the latter. It is however possible to visualize a situation in which a Member State allowed its own nationals to import funds for the purpose of investing in the capital of companies. If it did, it would be required by Article 221 to permit nationals of other member states also to import funds into its territory for the same purpose. A similar situation could arise if a national rule permitted export of funds for investment purposes. This article is expressed in the form of a rule of non-discrimination on grounds of nationality, whereas national rules on exchange control are usually based on residence. However, a rule relating to residents, as distinct from nationals, may infringe a rule of non-discrimination on grounds of nationality if it is in effect a disguised form of discrimination against nationals of other member states. This has been held to be so in the fields of freedom to provide services and social security,[3] and there seems no reason why it should not apply in cases falling within the provisions of Article 221.

[3] See Case 33/74, *van Binsbergen* [1974] *ECR* 1299, p. 1309, and Cases 62 and 63/81, *Seco* v. *EVI* [1982] *ECR* 223, p. 235. Both cases are discussed in Ch. 6 ('Services').

Capital

Capital

Capital is nowhere defined in the treaty. In *R.* v. *Thompson, Johnson and Woodiwiss*[4] the defendants were charged with certain offences related to the smuggling of gold krugerrands, some silver alloy coins which were still legal tender in the United Kingdom, and other silver alloy coins which were no longer legal tender. Their defence was that the United Kingdom legislation in question contravened the Treaty. In order to deal with that defence it became necessary to consider whether the coins were goods, in which case Articles 30–7 would be relevant, or capital, to which Articles 67–73 applied. The Court of Appeal (Criminal Division) asked the European Court whether the coins were capital, within the meaning of Articles 67–73.[5] The defendants argued that they were goods, because if that were the case the validity of the legislation could only be defended if it could be established that it was covered by Article 36, which they denied. They did not attempt to define 'capital', but focused on the expression 'movement of capital'. They argued that no such movement was involved because the transactions were covered by the treaty provisions concerning the movement of goods.

The UK Government, while not attempting an exhaustive definition of 'capital', maintained that the word was internationally understood as applying to precious metals such as gold and silver and money (including coins).[6] Moreover, so the argument continued, the First Directive for the implementation of Article 67 of the Treaty[7] referred to 'financial assets' and these included gold and means of payment of any kind. The Italian Government thought that 'capital' must include precious metals (gold, platinum, and silver), considered on the basis of their intrinsic value, and thus when not incorporated in goldsmiths' or silversmiths' wares.[8]

The Commission's starting-point was that although Articles 67–73 were headed 'capital' they were not so much concerned with the precise nature of 'capital' itself, but with certain activities concerning capital. By looking at the activities mentioned in those Articles, the Commission thought that some insight would be gained into the meaning of the word 'capital'. The difficulty with that approach is that the Articles give only the barest of clues. Articles 68(2), 68(3), and 73, by referring to 'the capital market', 'credit system', and 'direct or indirect financing', do perhaps give a hint that financial assets of all kinds may amount to capital, particularly if they are used in connection with some economic venture. The Commission,

[4] Case 7/78 [1978] *ECR* 2247.
[5] Ibid., p. 2249.
[6] Ibid., p. 2257.
[7] *OJ*, Special Edition, 1959–62, p. 49.
[8] Case 7/78, *R.* v. *Thompson, Johnson and Woodiwiss* [1978] *ECR* 2247, p. 2261.

adopting in this respect the same approach as the defendants, offered a definition not of 'capital' but of 'movement of capital' in the following terms:

On the basis of all the above considerations, and without seeking to define every circumstance in which a movement of capital can take place, it is considered that in many cases a movement of capital will occur when financial resources situated in one country are used to make an investment in another country, and the investment is not transferred to the country where those resources were originally situated within a reasonable period. In such cases, nothing of equivalent value is received in the country where the resources were originally situated to counterbalance the resources which left it in order to make the investment and, in fact, no matter what form the investments take, no goods cross a national frontier.[9]

From this definition it might appear that the Commission considered capital to consist primarily of financial resources, and not goods. If 'financial resources' are interpreted as including money, and all kinds of credits with banks and other financial institutions, this is a reasonably workable definition. It would exclude, for example, factory plant transferred to a factory in another member state, even though such equipment might sometimes loosely be described as a 'capital' investment in that factory. Whether the Commission intended to exclude all goods from being treated as capital, no matter what were the circumstances of its movement, is not entirely clear. The Commission later referred to the exceptional sort of case in which a movement of capital could be effected by 'the actual physical transfer of assets from one country to another', provided nothing was received in the first country in return.[10] Unless the Commission was thinking of such things as currency, or share certificates, as being assets which could be physically transferred (and it is questionable whether the physical movement of the evidence of title to shares, even in the case of bearer shares, involves movement of the assets themselves), it is possible that it was thinking of the movement of goods. If that was the case, perhaps the Commission's view was that the movement of a piece of factory machinery from one member state to another would be a movement of capital if it was installed by the owner in his own factory in the second member state, but a movement of goods if (i) he sold it to another person for installation in the latter's factory, and (ii) the price was then transferred to the first member state within a reasonable period.[11] In other words, the Commission's analysis may have been that 'capital' includes all financial resources, and can also include goods, but whether the latter are capital depends entirely upon the nature of the transaction in which they are moved from one member state to another. A simpler and, it is submitted, a

9 Ibid., p. 2263.
10 Ibid., p. 2264.
11 Ibid., p. 2264.

more straightforward view would be that financial resources of all kinds are capital, and goods are not. The remaining difficulty then is whether or not to classify coins and bank notes as financial resources or as goods.

The Advocate General thought it was impossible to answer the direct question whether the coins were capital or goods.[12] He noted that some coins at least were treated as goods under UK law.[13] But he thought they were goods of a very special kind which could be assimilated to capital 'by reason of the circumstances and conditions of and methods used in the transactions of which they are the subject matter'.[14] In one respect, therefore, the Advocate General was agreeing with the Commission, i.e. that it is not possible simply to look at coins and say whether they are capital or goods. One must look at all the circumstances surrounding the transaction in question, in order to decide whether they should be treated as one or the other. In the circumstances of the case the Advocate General concluded:

> that capital within the meaning of Community Law must also be taken to mean gold and silver coins which are legal tender or 'means of payment of all kinds'.[15]

The Court shied away from defining 'capital' and from saying what the words 'movement of capital' meant in Article 67. It resorted to its not infrequent practice of taking the questions put by the national court, distilling what it regarded as their essence, and re-formulating the question to be answered. Although the national court had asked whether the coins were 'capital', the European Court considered that the actual purpose behind that question was to find out whether the coins were 'goods' falling within the provisions of Articles 30–7 or constituted a means of payment falling within the scope of other provisions (in particular Article 106).[16] It said:

> An analysis of this system shows that the rules relating to the free movement of goods and, in particular, Articles 30 *et seq.* concerning the elimination of quantitative restrictions and measures having equivalent effect, must be considered not only with reference to the specific rules relating to transfers of capital but with reference to all the provisions of the Treaty relating to monetary transfers, which can be effected for a great variety of purposes, of which capital transfers only comprise one specific category.
>
> Although Articles 67 to 73 of the Treaty, which are concerned with the liberalization of movements of capital, assume special importance as far as one of the aims set out in Article 3 of the Treaty is concerned, namely the abolition of obstacles to freedom of movement for capital, the provisions of Articles 104 to 109,

---

[12] Ibid., p. 2279.

[13] Ibid., pp. 2279–80, referring to the Import, Export and Customs Powers (Defence) Act 1939 and subordinate legislation made thereunder.

[14] Ibid., p. 2282.

[15] Ibid., p. 2289.

[16] Ibid., p. 2273.

which are concerned with the overall balance of payments and which for this reason relate to all monetary movements, must be considered as essential for the purpose of attaining the free movement of goods, services or capital which is of fundamental importance for the attainment of the common market.[17]

Thus analysed it becomes impossible to say whether, considered in isolation, money, financial credits, or anything else is or is not to be treated as 'capital' within the meaning of Article 67. One is forced to look at the transaction in question, in order to decide (i) whether money, etc. is capital, and (ii) whether a question as to its free movement arises. All monetary movements, as the Court indicated, fall within Articles 104–9, concerning overall balance of payments, and the Court seems to have indicated that those provisions must be regarded as paramount, since it said that they were of fundamental importance for attaining free movement of goods, services, and capital. If the Court's judgment is to be interpreted in that sense, it appears that when a question of movement of money arises one should ask first whether Articles 104–9 cover the situation, and if they do, one may ignore Articles 67–73. This may be too wide an interpretation of the Court's judgment, and in any case the Court had no need to establish such a broad principle. It could have taken the view that when, prima facie, two sets of treaty provisions appear to cover a situation, one should first try to apply both sets. If that will produce a conflict, a solution may be found in the rule '*generalia specialibus non derogant*'. The latter principle would have afforded sufficient reason to hold that when coins were used as a means of payment Article 106 contained the *lex specialis* which was to be applied.

However, the way in which the Court went on to deal with the problem was different. It referred to the rule in Article 106, that a member state must authorize payments across the exchanges which are connected with the movement of goods, services, or capital, and any transfer of capital and earnings, to the extent that the movement of goods, services, capital, and persons between member states has been liberalized pursuant to the Treaty. The Court concluded that in view of this freedom to make monetary transfers (and seemingly because Articles 104–9 are paramount in situations to which they apply), it must be inferred that means of payment are not to be regarded as 'goods'.[18] Articles 30–7 were not applicable to silver alloy coins, which were legal tender, or to krugerrands, which on the money markets of those member states which permitted dealings in such coins were treated as equivalent to currency. The Court's argument then leapt to the conclusion that because Articles 30–7 did not apply, it was not necessary to deal with the question under what circumstances the transfer of these two types of coin might possibly be designated either as a movement of capital *or as a current payment*.[19] Since the Court's earlier

[17] Ibid.   [18] Ibid., p. 2274.   [19] Ibid., p. 2275.

reasoning appears to have been that Articles 30–7 did not apply *because* those coins were means of payment and were therefore caught by the more appropriate rule in Article 106, the agility of the jump can be seen. Be that as it may, the fact remains that the Court did not take the opportunity in this part of its judgment to give any substantial guidance as to the meaning of 'capital'. Nor did it do so in the remainder of the judgment. So far as concerns those coins which were no longer legal tender, the Court concluded, quite shortly, that they could not be regarded as means of payment, and therefore could be treated as goods. But the right of a member state to protect its coinage was justified under Article 36.[20]

One principle which emerges is that items of capital cannot be identified in isolation from the transactions of which they form part. Thus money is not capital if it is sent from one member state to another to pay for goods which have been purchased, but it is capital if sent in order to create an undertaking in another member state. What then is the essential feature of a transaction, which enables something which forms part of it to be identi- fied as 'capital'? It is tempting to think that the transaction must at least be one of an economic, trading, or commercial nature, since the Treaty sets up an economic community whose task is first and foremost to establish a common market (Article 1).

However, this is not necessarily so, as can be seen from the First Direc- tive for the implementation of Article 67 of the Treaty,[21] as amended by the Second Council Directive,[22] and in particular the capital movements listed in the Annex.[23] The latter includes in List A a number of personal capital movements which do not readily fit the description suggested above. One example is 'dowries', which can hardly be considered to be concerned with trade or commerce, and are only 'economic' in the very broadest sense of the word. Another example is 'death duties'. Indeed, the disparity in the natures of the transactions in this Annex is such that it is difficult to identify a common thread.

This difficulty is compounded when one makes a comparison between the lists in this Annex with the list of invisible transactions, covered by Article 106(3), which is set out in Annex III to the Treaty. The former includes (in List A) 'transfers of capital belonging to *residents* who emig- rate',[24] while the latter includes 'exchange authorisations granted to *own or foreign nationals* emigrating'. Even allowing for the difference in termino- logy, one and the same transaction may thus be covered both by the 'stand- still' provisions of Article 71, by which member states must only use their

[20] Ibid.

[21] *OJ*, Special Edition, 1959–62, p. 49.

[22] *OJ*, Special Edition, 1963–4, p. 5.

[23] A consolidated text of the Annex to the First Directive, as amended by the Second Directive, is reproduced with its explanatory notes in *OJ*, Special Edition, 1963–4, pp. 9–17. See Appendix.

[24] *OJ*, Special Edition, 1963–4, p. 9.

'best endeavours' not to impose new restrictions, and by those of Article 106(3), by which member states are absolutely prohibited from imposing new restrictions. In that particular instance there is no conflict between the two sets of provisions because Article 1 of the First Directive for the implementation of Article 67 of the Treaty[25] obliges member states to grant all foreign exchange authorizations required for the conclusion or performance of the transactions in List A. Nevertheless, these two items illustrate the difficulty of defining the sort of transaction relating to financial assets which will make those assets 'capital' for the purposes of Article 67 but not for the purposes of Article 106.

In the light of all these difficulties it may be that one can go further than to suggest that a transaction which identifies the financial assets involved as capital for the purposes of Article 67 will be one which is not covered by Articles 30, 106–9, or 221. Such a negative definition is however only of limited value, since it merely provokes the question of the scope of the latter Articles. However, until the Court or the Council provides further guidance as to the meaning of 'capital' as used in Article 67 it is probably not possible to take the matter much further. A pointer to the Court's more recent thinking can be seen in *Graziana Luisi* and *Carbone* v. *Ministero del Tesoro*.[26] In that case the Court said:

In fact we can infer from the general Treaty system, and a comparison of Articles 67 and 106 will bear this out, that current payments are transfers of currency which constitute a counter-payment made in connection with an underlying transaction whereas capital movements are financial operations which essentially involve the placing or investing of the sum in question and not the remuneration of a service. For this reason capital movements can themselves give rise to current payments as Article 67(2) and Article 106(1) imply.[27]

Persons resident

Article 67(1) refers to 'persons resident' in member states. Articles 67–73 do not define the word 'persons', as used in Article 67, and in particular they do not contain anything corresponding to Article 58, which requires companies and firms to be treated in the same way as natural persons for the purposes of the chapter on establishment. However, since the Explanatory Notes[28] attached to the Annexes to the First Directive for the implementation of Article 67 indicate that residents and non-residents are to include 'natural and legal persons according to the definitions laid down in the exchange control regulations in force in each Member State', and the natural or legal persons are 'as defined by the national rules', there can be

---

[25] *OJ*, Special Edition, 1959–62, p. 47.
[26] Joined Cases 286/82 and 26/83, judgment of 31/1/84.
[27] Ibid., para. 21, as it appears in the Court's first typed text.
[28] *OJ*, Special Edition, 1963–4, pp. 16–17.

little doubt that for the purposes of Article 67 'persons' includes both natural and legal persons. The same Explanatory Notes also indicate that whether a person is to be regarded as 'resident' in a member state is to be determined by national law. This is understandable since the Treaty itself establishes no criteria. The term 'resident' may of course not include all persons who are nationals of the member state in question, and it may include persons who are not nationals of any member state. It is unusual for the Treaty to make residence rather than nationality the test, but the practical reason for this is that national exchange control laws are usually based on residence.

THE TREATY PROVISIONS

Article 67

Although providing for the progressive abolition of all restrictions on the free movement of capital, the text of this Article[29] begins with a qualification. This is that the progressive abolition is to be achieved (*a*) during the transitional period, and (*b*) to the extent necessary to ensure the proper functioning of the market. Looking simply at the text of the Article, it might have been possible to construe it in the sense that during the transitional period member states were obliged to take all the necessary steps and that thereafter their obligations were at an end. One consequence of such an interpretation would be that what was necessary for the functioning of the common market would have to be judged with regard to the stage reached by the end of that period in its development. No obligation to continue the process of freeing the movement of capital would thus subsist after the end of the transitional period, even though thereafter the common market might evolve further. However, such a view would be inconsistent with the dynamic nature of the Community. An interpretation more consistent with the Court's jurisprudence would be that the temporal provision, that action was to be taken during the transitional period, did not qualify the extent of the obligation to abolish restrictions, so that even if member states failed to take all the necessary action within that period the obligation would subsist. This accords with the Court's decision in *Reyners* v. *Belgium*,[30] where, in relation to freedom of establishment (Article 52), the Court said:

In laying down that freedom of establishment shall be attained at the end of the transitional period, Article 52 thus imposes an obligation to attain a precise result, the fulfilment of which had to be made easier by, but not made dependent on, the implementation of a programme of progressive measures.

The fact that this progression has not been adhered to leaves the obligation itself intact beyond the end of the period provided for its fulfilment.[31]

[29] Quoted in full at the beginning of this chapter.
[30] Case 2/74 [1974] *ECR* 631.   [31] Ibid., p. 651.

Once that interpretation is accepted in relation to Article 67, it becomes easy to interpret the phrase 'to the extent necessary to ensure the proper functioning of the common market' as referred to the state of the common market as it has been developed at any given time, whether before or after the end of the transitional period. This was indeed the view taken by the Court in *Casati*,[32] where the Court, after referring to the fact that completely free movement of capital might undermine the economic policy of one of the member states, or create an imbalance in its balance of payments, said:

For those reasons, Article 67(1) differs from the provisions on the free movement of goods, persons and services in the sense that there is an obligation to liberalize capital movements only 'to the extent necessary to ensure the proper functioning of the Common Market'. The scope of that restriction, which remained in force after the expiry of the transitional period, varies in time and depends on an assessment of the requirements of the Common Market and on an appraisal of both the advantages and risks which liberalization might entail for the latter, having regard to the stage it has reached and, in particular, to the level of integration attained in matters in respect of which capital movements are particularly significant.[33]

In the light of the *Casati* judgment[34] it is possible, when construing the effect of Article 67(1), to ignore the words 'During the transitional period and'. The remaining qualification in the opening lines is 'to the extent necessary to ensure the proper functioning of the common market', and, subject to that limitation, member states are obliged progressively to abolish between themselves all restrictions on the movement of capital belonging to persons resident in member states and any discrimination based on the nationality or on the place of residence of the parties. The meaning of 'persons' (including companies and other legal persons) and of 'residence' (which is to be determined by national law) has already been noted in the definitions section of this chapter. It should also be noted that the use of the words 'progressively abolish between themselves' indicated a clear need, if only in the interests of legal certainty, for detailed action to be agreed at Community level in order to determine the scope and timetable of the measures of abolition. The way in which that need has been fulfilled will be seen later in this chapter, in the section on secondary legislation.

Article 67(1) also provides for the progressive abolition of discrimination based on the place where capital is invested. It would undermine the freedom of movement of capital if a member state were to discriminate against persons within its jurisdiction on account of the fact that they had chosen to invest capital in another member state. In order to prevent such a situa-

---

[32] Case 203/80 [1981] *ECR* 2595.
[33] Ibid., p. 2614.
[34] Case 203/80 [1981] *ECR* 2395.

tion from arising, the need for this part of Article 67 is readily apparent. On the other hand, there seems to be no such need in the case of a member state which accords benefits to those who invest in certain regions within its national territory, for example in order to encourage economic development in depressed areas, even though this in a sense discriminates against those who prefer to invest in other parts of the territory. However, because in this latter situation there is no question of a person being inhibited from moving his capital from one member state to another, it would seem that Article 67 has no application.

Article 68

The looseness of the obligation in Article 68(1) to be 'as liberal as possible' in granting any necessary exchange authorizations has already been noted. The only means of tightening the rules are to be found in Article 70, and the power which it confers on the Council to issue directives for the progressive co-ordination of the exchange policies of member states in respect of the movement of capital within the Community. In the exercise of that power the Council is exhorted by Article 70(1) to 'endeavour to attain the highest possible degree of liberalisation'.

A rather more concrete provision appears in Article 68(2), prohibiting the discriminatory application of domestic rules governing the capital market and credit system in relation to movements of capital which have been liberalized in accordance with Articles 67–73.

Article 68(3) places a restriction on the free movement of capital. Loans may not be issued or placed by or on behalf of a member state, or its regional or local authorities, in another member state except by agreement between the two states. On the other hand, the European Investment Bank may borrow on the capital market of a member state, either in accordance with the latter's law, or, if it has no legal provisions on the subject, by agreement between that state and the Bank (Article 22 of the Protocol on the Statute of the European Investment Bank).

Article 71

The exhortative character of Article 71 (the 'standstill'), aimed at preventing the introduction of new exchange restrictions on the movement of capital, can be seen from the fact that it uses the word 'endeavour' twice in the first sentence. The following declaration of readiness by the member states 'in so far as their economic situation, in particular the situation of their balance of payments, so permits' to go beyond the degree of liberalization of capital movements provided for in Articles 67–70, is a further example of the tentative nature of the whole of this chapter of the Treaty.

The nearest thing it has to 'teeth' is the provision in the last sentence of Article 71 for the Commission, after consulting the Monetary Committee,[35] to make recommendations to member states.

Article 106

Article 106 has only a limited connection with the free movement of capital. To the extent that capital movements are liberalized pursuant to the Treaty, payments connected with such movements, and transfers of earnings, must be allowed in the currency of the member state in which the creditor or beneficiary resides (Article 106(1)). If, therefore, capital originating in one member state is invested in another pursuant to the provisions of Articles 67–73, the earnings from that investment can be repatriated. In this respect Article 106(1) reinforces Article 67(2). The scope of Article 106 was considered in *Graziana Luisi* and *Carbone* v. *Ministero del Tesoro*.[36] In those cases the legality of Italy's restrictions on transfers of currency for the purpose of tourism was in issue. Amongst the questions on which the Italian court sought a preliminary ruling was one which in essence asked whether, if such a transaction fell within the scope of Article 106(3) and Annex III to the Treaty (which lists 'Tourism' as one of the invisible transactions in connection with which no new restrictions on transfers are to be instituted) it was a movement of capital which, under Articles 67 and 68, need not necessarily be liberalized. The Court drew a distinction between capital movements, which it describes as 'financial operations which essentially involve the placing or investing of the sum in question', and remuneration for a service rendered in another member state to a tourist.[37] It concluded that the physical transfer of bank notes for the latter purpose was not a movement of capital.[38] By virtue of Articles 106(1) and 59, restrictions on payments relating to the provision of services (e.g. to tourists) could no longer be imposed.[39] In *Casati*[40] the Court interpreted the phrase 'in the currency of the Member State in which the creditor or the beneficiary resides'. It concluded that for this purpose the reference to 'currency' did not require a member state to allow the import or export of bank notes. It was not, in the Court's view, in accordance with standard practice to effect transfers by that method.[41]

---

[35] Set up by Art. 105.
[36] Joined Cases 286/82 and 26/83, judgment of 31/1/84.
[37] Ibid., para. 21.
[38] Ibid., paras. 22 and 23.
[39] Ibid., para. 24.
[40] Case 203/80 [1981] *ECR* 2595.
[41] Ibid., p. 2617.

THE SECONDARY LEGISLATION

The First and Second Directives

The Council adopted the First Directive for the implementation of Article 67 of the Treaty on 11 May 1960.[42] The Second Council Directive of 18 December 1962[43] repealed Article 2(3) of the First Directive (which had permitted certain temporary measures restricting the application of Article 2(1)). More importantly, it replaced Annexes I and II to the First Directive with new texts. The text of the First Directive was further amended by the Act of Accession.[44] The texts of the two Directives, as amended and with annotations, are reproduced in the Appendix to this book.

Article 1 of the First Directive obliges member states to permit payments across the exchanges, at exchange rates ruling for payments relating to current transactions, for the benefit of residents of the member states in respect of the capital movements in List A of Annex I to the Directive. Article 2 requires member states to grant 'general permission' for similar foreign exchange payments in respect of capital movements set out in List B of Annex I. So far as concerns exchange rates for List B transactions, Article 2(2) provides that where the rates are not officially restricted, member states must 'endeavour to ensure' a degree of stability, as defined in that Article. Article 3 deals with List C transactions, by requiring the grant of exchange authorizations, subject to the proviso in Article 3(2) that a member state may maintain or re-introduce its original exchange restrictions when free movement of capital might form an obstacle to the achievement of its economic policy objectives. List D of Annex I is dealt with in Article 7, which requires no liberalization for items on this list, and merely requires member states to make known to the Commission any amendments of the provisions governing their movements.

Directive 335/69

On 17 July 1969 the Council adopted Directive 335/69 concerning indirect taxes on the raising of capital.[45] The Directive was designed to deal with discrimination, double taxation, and disparities caused by indirect taxes on the raising of capital, in the shape of duty chargeable on contribution of capital to companies and firms and stamp duties on securities.[46] The Directive provided in Article 1 for a harmonized duty on contributions of capital to 'capital companies', as defined in Article 3(1). Articles 10 and 11 prohibited other forms of taxation on raising of capital, but Article 12 allowed duties to be imposed on the transfer of securities and other

---

[42] *OJ*, Special Edition, 1959–62, p. 49.
[43] *OJ*, Special Edition, 1963–4, p. 5.
[44] Annex I(VII)(3).
[45] *OJ*, Special Edition, 1969, p. 412, supplemented by Dir. 80/73, *OJ* 1973, L103/15.
[46] Ibid., 6th preambular para.

business assets. The Directive was interpreted in *Felicitas* v. *Finanzamt für Verkehrsteuern*.[47] The issue turned on Article 5(2) of the Directive, which in essence required certain harmonized duties to be not less than the actual value of the shares in question or their 'nominal amount' if the latter exceeded their actual value. The question was whether shares in a 'Kommanditgesellschaft' (a sort of limited partnership) had a nominal value. The United Kingdom participated in the proceedings and argued that shares only had a 'nominal' amount if they had a recognized nominal amount under national law.[48] The Court rejected that argument, on the ground that a provision of Community law was to be determined in each member state 'on the basis of objective criteria, having a uniform scope within the Community and free from the influence of national laws'.[49] The Court proceeded to rule:

1. The shares in a company have a nominal amount within the meaning of Article 5(2) of Directive 69/335/EEC when the legal structure of the type of company to which the company concerned belongs includes amounts fixed in cash, intended to quantify the value of the members' contributions to the raising of capital in that company and to characterize in durable fashion the relations between the members and the company.
2. It is for the national court, taking into account the criteria for interpretation laid down by the Court of Justice, to carry out the necessary appraisal both of the relevant national rules and the provisions of the company's documents of constitution in order to establish whether that is the case.[50]

Directive 156/72

On 21 March 1972 the Council adopted Directive 156/72 on regulating international capital flows and neutralizing their undesirable effects on domestic liquidity.[51] The fact that this Directive was needed illustrates that there are some dangers in the notion of completely free movement of capital. It also shows the delicate balance which needs to be struck between upholding that freedom as a general concept and at the same time protecting member states from serious upheaval in their economies. The Directive recited that exceptionally large capital movements had caused serious disturbances in the monetary situation and in economic trends in member states. To prevent recurrence, and in particular (but not exclusively) to discourage exceptionally large capital movements to and from third countries, the Directive requires member states to have available instruments containing certain rules for the effective regulation of international capital

---

[47] Case 270/81 [1982] *ECR* 2771.
[48] Ibid., p. 2777.
[49] Ibid., p. 2784.
[50] Ibid., pp. 2787–8.
[51] *OJ*, Special Edition, 1972, part I, p. 296.

flows.[52] A limited derogation from Article 3(1) of the First Directive[53] is envisaged by Article 1(*a*). However the use of such instruments is not left to the unfettered discretion of individual member states. They are required by Article 2 to take account of the interests of other member states, and the Commission is enjoined to ensure close co-operation to that end between the competent authorities of the member states.

EXCEPTIONS

As has already been seen, Article 67(1) has its own inherent exception to the principle of free movement.[54] In accordance with that Article, the principle does not apply if free movement is not 'necessary to ensure the proper functioning of the common market'. The Council has the power, under Article 69, to assess the extent to which free movement is necessary. This gives the Council a wide measure of discretion. But the Court has not accepted that the Council is to be a sole judge of what degree of liberalization is or is not necessary. The Court would no doubt reserve to itself a residual discretion to determine whether the Council had acted within the limits of its powers. So much is evident from the judgment in *Casati*,[55] where the Court said:

> The conclusion must be drawn that the obligation contained in Article 67(1) to abolish restrictions on movements of capital cannot be defined, in relation to a specific category of such movements, in isolation from the Council's assessment under Article 69 of the need to liberalize that category in order to ensure the proper functioning of the Common Market. The Council has so far taken the view that it is unnecessary to liberalize the exportation of bank notes, the operation with which the accused in the main proceedings is charged, and there is no reason to suppose that, by adopting that position, it has overstepped the limits of its discretionary power.[56]

Article 73

The text of Article 73 reads:

> 1. If movements of capital lead to disturbances in the functioning of the capital market in any Member State, the Commission shall, after consulting the Monetary Committee, authorise that State to take protective measures in the field of capital movements, the conditions and details of which the Commission shall determine.
>
> The Council may, acting by a qualified majority, revoke this authorisation or amend the conditions or details thereof.

---

[52] Ibid., Art. 1.
[53] *OJ*, Special Edition, 1959–62, p. 47.
[54] So too does Art. 68, in the case of loans to member states or their authorities.
[55] Case 203/80 [1981] *ECR* 2595.
[56] Ibid., p. 2615.

2. A Member State which is in difficulties may, however, on grounds of secrecy or urgency, take the measures mentioned above, where this proves necessary, on its own initiative. The Commission and the other Member States shall be informed of such measures by the date of their entry into force at the latest. In this event the Commission may, after consulting the Monetary Committee, decide that the State concerned shall amend or abolish the measures.

As can be seen, this Article enables member states to take urgent action unilaterally, but the last word lies with the Commission, after it has consulted the Monetary Committee. One of the questions put by the national court in the *Casati* case[57] was whether the fact that the Italian Government had not, in relation to an Italian law prohibiting the unauthorized export of currency over a certain value, resorted to the consultative procedure in Article 73 constituted an infringement of the Treaty. However, as the Court pointed out,[58] there is no need to resort to Article 73 (i.e. to seek an exception to the rule in Article 67(1)) in cases where the capital movements in question have not been liberalized. A government wishing to restrict any particular movement of capital should first consider whether it has, prima facie, a duty under Article 67 to liberalise that movement and, if it has such a duty, whether there is any escape from it under Article 73.

Articles 104–6

Articles 104–6 fall within Title II of the Treaty which deals with 'economic policy'. They are concerned more particularly with the need of each individual member state to control its balance of payments. Article 104 is couched in the form of an obligation to do what is needed:

Each Member State shall pursue the economic policy needed to ensure the equilibrium of its overall balance of payments and to maintain confidence in its currency, while taking care to ensure a high level of employment and a stable level of prices.

Article 105 requires the member states, however, to co-ordinate their policies in this respect, and to provide for co-operation between their central banks for this purpose. The Monetary Committee set up by Article 105 keeps each member state's monetary and financial situation under review, and delivers opinions to the Council and Commission. It is against this background that Article 106(1), as has already been seen, requires member states to authorize payments connected with the movement of liberalized capital, and the transfer of such capital and earnings.

Article 106(4) provides, however, a qualification. That paragraph reads:

If need be, Member States shall consult each other on the measures to be taken to enable the payments and transfers mentioned in this Article to be effected; such

---

[57] Case 203/80 [1981] *ECR* 2595.
[58] Ibid., p. 2615.

measures shall not prejudice the attainment of the objectives set out in this Chapter.

This provision seems to be concerned only with measures agreed collectively between member states to facilitate the implementation of the Article. Such measures must not prejudice the objectives of the chapter, which of course includes Article 104. The measures must not therefore prejudice a member state's ability to ensure equilibrium in its overall balance of payments. While, therefore, this paragraph may give the member states, acting collectively, some discretion to restrict the free movement of capital, it does not appear to provide any ground for one member state unilaterally to avoid compliance with its obligations under Article 106(1). The appropriate escape routes for a member state which finds itself in balance of payments difficulties are to be found in Articles 108 and 109. A member state does however have the power to subject transfers of currency to controls aimed at ascertaining whether the capital movements to which they relate have or have not been liberalized: see *Graziana Luisi and Carbone* v. *Ministero del Tesoro*.[59] It may also investigate the genuineness of the transactions in question. In the same case the Court said:

Other than in times of crisis and until freedom of movement for capital has been fully achieved, Member States therefore have the power to check that transfers of currency stated to appertain to liberalized payments are not deflected from their intended purpose and used in connection with unauthorised capital movements. To that end Member States have the right to verify the nature and genuineness of the operations or movements in question.[60]

The opening words of the above quotation show that in this passage the Court was not thinking of Articles 108 and 109, even though it had mentioned those articles in the previous paragraph.

Article 108

Article 108 provides machinery, under the control of Community institutions, for a member state to take action, contrary to the principle of free movement of capital, when it has balance of payments difficulties. Article 108(1) reads:

1. Where a Member State is in difficulties or is seriously threatened with difficulties as regards its balance of payments either as a result of an overall disequilibrium in its balance of payments, or as a result of the type of currency at its disposal, and where such difficulties are liable in particular to jeopardise the functioning of the common market or the progressive implementation of the common commercial policy, the Commission shall immediately investigate the position of

[59] Joined Cases 286/82 and 26/83, judgment of 31/1/84, paras. 31–3.
[60] Ibid., para. 33.

the State in question and the action which, making use of all the means at its disposal, that State has taken or may take in accordance with the provisions of Article 104. The Commission shall state what measures it recommends the State concerned to take.

If the action taken by a Member State and the measures suggested by the Commission do not prove sufficient to overcome the difficulties which have arisen or which threaten, the Commission shall, after consulting the Monetary Committee, recommend to the Council the granting of mutual assistance and appropriate methods therefore.

The Commission shall keep the Council regularly informed of the situation and of how it is developing.

Control over the exercise of these exceptional powers thus remains initially in the hands of the Commission.[61] But if its recommendations do not remedy the difficulties the Commission may further recommend the Council to grant mutual assistance. The Council is empowered by Article 108(2) to grant such mutual assistance and to determine the conditions on which it is to be granted. The assistance may take the form of a concerted approach by member states to other international organizations, or measures to avoid deflection of trade where the member state in difficulties establishes quantitative restrictions against third countries, or the granting of limited credits.

Paragraph 3 of the article contains an unusual provision.[62] As between the Commission and the Council, the Council usually has the last word in deciding what action should be taken. But Article 108(3) provides that, if mutual assistance recommended by the Commission is not granted by the Council, or if it is granted but proves insufficient, the Commission 'shall authorise the state which is in difficulties to take protective measures, the conditions and details of which the Commission shall determine'.

Article 109

In contrast to Article 108, Article 109 allows a member state to take unilateral action in emergency situations, when recourse to the procedure of Article 108 would be too cumbersome and too slow. Paragraph (1) of Article 109 reads:

1. Where a sudden crisis in the balance of payments occurs and a decision within the meaning of Article 108(2) is not immediately taken, the Member State concerned may, as a precaution, take the necessary protective measures. Such measures must cause the least possible disturbance in the functioning of the common market and must not be wider in scope than is strictly necessary to remedy the sudden difficulties which have arisen.

[61] See e.g. Commission Rec. 81/494 of 1 July 1981, *OJ* 1981, L189/60.
[62] Referred to in Joined Cases 6 and 11/69, *Commission* v. *France* [1969] *ECR* 523.

However, paragraphs (2) and (3) of Article 109 make it clear that the Commission and the member states must be informed at once, and that in due course the Council may require the member state concerned to amend, suspend, or abolish the protective measures it has taken.

The Court made some general remarks about Articles 108 and 109 in *Commission* v. *France*,[63] which reveal the reserve with which the Court treats the idea of a member state unilaterally setting aside a Community rule. The Court said:

Articles 108(3) and 109(3) confer powers of authorization or intervention on the Community institutions which would be otiose if the Member States were free, on the pretext that their action related only to monetary policy, unilaterally to derogate from their obligations under the provisions of the Treaty and without being subject to control by the institutions.

The solidarity which is at the basis of these obligations as of the whole of the Community system in accordance with the undertaking provided for in Article 5 of the Treaty, is continued for the benefit of the States in the procedure for mutual assistance provided for in Article 108 where a Member State is seriously threatened with difficulties as regards its balance of payments.

The exercise of reserved powers cannot therefore permit the unilateral adoption of measures prohibited by the Treaty.[64]

The last sentence quoted above seems to be unduly restrictive. However it may be noted that this part of the judgment was given in the context of unilateral measures contravening Articles 92 and 93 (state aids). Given the looseness which has already been noted in the provisions of the Treaty regarding free movement of capital, it would appear that, in the circumstances to which Article 109 relates, this judgment does not rule out temporary interference by a member state with the free movement of capital.

DIRECT EFFECT

Article 67(1) is an unlikely candidate for direct effect. It only requires the abolition of restrictions on the movement of capital 'to the extent necessary to ensure the proper functioning of the common market'. To judge whether free movement is necessary for this purpose requires an assessment of political and economic factors which goes beyond the competence of the courts. As the Court pointed out in *Casati*,[65] the answer will vary in time and will depend on an assessment of the requirements of the common market and on an appraisal of the advantages and risks which liberalization might entail for it.[66] The obligation contained in Article 67(1) cannot be

[63] Ibid.
[64] Ibid., pp. 539–40.
[65] Case 203/80 [1981] *ECR* 2595.
[66] Ibid., p. 2614.

defined in isolation from the Council's assessment under Article 69 of the need to liberalize any particular kind of capital movement.[67] Although the Court refrained in that case from holding that Article 67(1) did not have direct effect, there can be little doubt that it has no such effect.

The answer to the question whether Article 71 (the 'standstill') had direct effect was not perhaps so obvious. However, the Court thought fit to volunteer an answer in *Casati*,[68] and it held that Article 71(1) did not have direct effect. It said:

By using the term 'shall endeavour', the wording of that provision departs notice-ably from the more imperative forms of wording employed in other similar provi-sions concerning restrictions on the free movement of goods, persons, and services. It is apparent from that wording that, in any event, the first paragraph of Article 71 does not impose on the Member States an unconditional obligation capable of being relied upon by individuals.[69]

Whether any of the provisions of the First Directive, as amended by the Second Directive[70] have direct effect is another question. That directive incorporated the political and economic judgment of the members of the Council on what was necessary in certain cases to ensure the proper func-tioning of the common market, and in so doing it supplied the precision which is lacking in Article 67. At least Article 1 of the Directive would appear to contain provisions which are reasonably good candidates for direct effect. However, the answer to this question will only become certain when the Court gives a ruling.

THIRD COUNTRIES

As a corollary to the principle of free movement of capital within the common market, it is appropriate for the Community to co-ordinate the exchange policies of member states with regard to third countries. Other-wise capital, the transfer of which has been liberalized as regards move-ments within the Community, could flow in and out of the Community as a whole at the rate allowed by the most generous member states, thus defeat-ing the policies, *vis-à-vis* third countries, of the less generous member states. Article 70 deals with this problem. Article 70(1) enables the Council, acting unanimously on a proposal of the Commission, progressively to co-ordinate the exchange policies of the member states with regard to third countries. But such co-ordination may still leave some differences between the respective policies of member states. Any resulting deflection of capital from one member state to another in order to defeat the former's policy

[67] Ibid., p. 2615.
[68] Case 203/80 [1981] *ECR* 2595.
[69] Ibid., p. 2616.
[70] *OJ*, Special Edition, 1959–62, p. 49; *OJ*, Special Edition, 1963–4, p. 5.

towards third countries may be countered by appropriate measures. Such measures may be taken by a member state in accordance with Article 70(2). The Council may, however, subsequently require that member state to amend or abolish its measures.

Article 72 also establishes some rather ineffectual controls over movements of capital to and from third countries. It does so in the following terms:

Member States shall keep the Commission informed of any movements of capital to and from third countries which come to their knowledge. The Commission may deliver to Member States any opinions which it considers appropriate on this subject.

FURTHER READING

van Ballegooijen, 'Free Movement of Capital in the European Economic Community', (1976) 2 *LIEI*.
J. Kodwa Bentil, 'Free Movement of Capital in the Common Market', (1982) 11 *New LJ* 6078, pp. 1049–50.
J.-V. Louis, 'Free Movement of Capital in the Community: the *Casati* Judgment', (1982) 3 *CML Rev*. 443.
P. Oliver, 'Free Movement of Capital Between Member States: Article 67(1) EEC and the Implementing Directives', (1984) *EL Rev*. 401.
M. Petersen, 'Capital Movements and Payments under the EEC Treaty after *Casati*', (1982) 3 *EL Rev*. 167.

PART IV

TERRITORIAL APPLICATION

IX

Territorial Application of the EEC Treaty

ALTHOUGH it would not be appropriate in a work of this kind to deal in depth with the law of treaties, it is necessary, before embarking on a study of the territorial application of the EEC Treaty, to consider in what circumstances treaties can be said to have territorial application at all. Some treaties have no such application. Examples are treaties of friendship and alliance, or treaties submitting international disputes to judicial or arbitral procedures or settling disputes by lump sum payments. In the classic case of a treaty of friendship, the treaty is intended to govern the conduct of the parties, wherever that conduct may occur. Other treaties may have a strictly territorial application, in the sense that they regulate the conduct of the parties within their respective national territories, or well-defined parts of them. An agreement conferring reciprocal rights of over-flight would be one example. In other cases the treaty may be designed to control the activities of the parties in all places in which they exercise some kind of jurisdiction, whether within their own territories or extra-territorially. The nineteenth-century treaties conferring extra-territorial jurisdiction upon one party to exercise in the territory of another have been succeeded by treaties allowing more limited extra-territorial jurisdiction, such as those which regulate safety of life at sea, fisheries, or civil aviation, to quote but a few examples. Thus a state has a measure of jurisdiction over what happens on board civil aircraft on its register, wherever those aircraft happen to be, and it may agree by treaty to exercise that jurisdiction in a particular way. Yet again a treaty may contain various provisions, falling into each of the categories described above. As will be seen, examples of each of these categories are to be found in the provisions of the EEC Treaty.

THE TREATY PROVISIONS

Provisions having no territorial application

Provisions setting up the Community institutions prima facie have no territorial application. For example, Articles 129–36 concerning the European Investment Bank do not contain anything to indicate a territorial application. By its nature an international body of this kind is metaphysical, although it may have its seat in a particular territory. In fact Article 1 of the

Protocol on the Statute of the European Investment Bank provides that the
seat shall be determined by common accord of the member states, but the
Article places no territorial restrictions on their choice of the seat. So far as
concerns the activities of the Bank, these are not confined to the four
corners of the territories of the member states. For example Article 25(3) of
the Bank's Statute enables the Bank freely to dispose of that part of its
capital which is paid up in gold or convertible currency, and of any
currency borrowed on markets outside the Community. This presupposes
that the Bank has previously engaged in borrowing transactions outside the
Community.

Similarly, the provisions setting up the Assembly (the 'European Parliament') (Articles 137–44), the Council (Articles 145–53), the Commission
(Articles 155–63), the Court of Justice (Articles 164–88), and the Economic
and Social Committee (Articles 193–8) can hardly be intended to have a
territorial application. Nor can the financial provisions of the Treaty
concerning the budget procedure and the Court of Auditors (Articles 199–
209). Article 211, according legal capacity to the Community, including the
power to acquire movable and immovable property, also surely implies
no territorial restrictions. There is no reason to suppose that the Commission, acting on behalf of the Community, may not establish a mission in a
third country to enable it to perform its functions in the field of external
trade (Article 113), or acquire all the property it needs for the purpose.
Similarly, provisions concerning professional secrecy (Article 214), liability
of the Community (Article 215), languages (Article 217), disputes (Article
219), and security (Article 223) have no territorial application. This list is
not necessarily exhaustive.

Provisions having a territorial application

It is in the field of free movement that there is the greatest need to decide
what is the scope of the territorial application of the relevant Treaty provisions. In order to know whether persons are entitled to send goods to a
Member State without attracting customs duties on imports, it is necessary, for the purposes of applying Articles 9–17, to determine whether there
is to be a movement of goods from the territory of one member state to
which the Treaty has territorial application to the territory of another
member state to which the Treaty also applies. Similarly, it is necessary to
know whether, in relation to any particular transaction, goods from third
countries are to enter the territory of a member state to which the Treaty
applies in order to decide whether the Common Customs Tariff applies.
Article 30 relates to imports 'between Member States'. Article 48(3)(*b*)
confers on workers the right to move freely 'within the territory of Member
States'. Likewise freedom of establishment (Article 52) comprises the right
of establishment of nationals of a member state in the territory of another

member state. These Articles refer only to the territory of each member state to which the Treaty applies, which, as will be seen, does not necessarily include all the territory for whose international relations the member state in question may be responsible. In the case of services (Article 59) it is necessary to interpret the phrase 'within the Community' and to decide its territorial scope in order to determine whether in any particular case the Article applies. Freedom of movement of capital (Article 67) relates only to movement 'between Member States', and again this means movement between territories of member states to which the treaty applies. In all of these cases, therefore, it is necessary to determine the territorial application of the provision in question.

The general rule of international law concerning the territorial scope of treaties has now been codified in Article 29 of the Vienna Convention on the Law of Treaties,[1] which reads:

Unless a different intention appears from the treaty or is otherwise established, a treaty is binding upon each party in respect of its entire territory.

It is probably correct to say that this provision was declaratory of the previously existing position in customary international law.

The first task therefore is to consider the provisions of the EEC Treaty itself. Article 227, as amended by Article 26 of the Act of Accession, Article 15 of the Adaptation Decision, and Article 20 of the Greek Act of Accession, reads:

1. This Treaty shall apply to the Kingdom of Belgium, the Kingdom of Denmark, the Federal Republic of Germany, the Hellenic Republic, the French Republic, Ireland, the Italian Republic, the Grand Duchy of Luxembourg, the Kingdom of the Netherlands and the United Kingdom of Great Britain and Northern Ireland.

2. With regard to Algeria and the French overseas departments, the general and particular provisions of this Treaty relating to:
— the free movement of goods;
— agriculture, save for Article 40(4);
— the liberalisation of services;
— the rules on competition;
— the protective measures provided for in Articles 108, 109 and 226;
— the institutions,
shall apply as soon as this Treaty enters into force.

The conditions under which the other provisions of this Treaty are to apply shall be determined, within two years of the entry into force of this Treaty, by decisions of the Council, acting unanimously on a proposal from the Commission.

The institutions of the Community will, within the framework of the procedures provided for in this Treaty, in particular Article 226, take care that the economic and social development of these areas is made possible.

[1] Opened for signature at Vienna on 23 May 1969, TS No. 58 (1980), Cmnd. 7964.

3. The special arrangements for association set out in Part Four of this Treaty shall apply to the overseas countries and territories listed in Annex IV to this Treaty.

This Treaty shall not apply to those overseas countries and territories having special relations with the United Kingdom of Great Britain and Northern Ireland which are not included in the aforementioned list.

4. The provisions of this Treaty shall apply to the European territories for whose external relations a Member State is responsible.

5. Notwithstanding the preceding paragraphs:

(a)   This Treaty shall not apply to the Faroe Islands. The Government of the Kingdom of Denmark may, however, give notice, by a declaration deposited by 31 December 1975 at the latest with the Government of the Italian Republic, which shall transmit a certified copy thereof to each of the Governments of the other Member States, that this Treaty shall apply to those Islands. In that event, this Treaty shall apply to those Islands from the first day of the second month following the deposit of the declaration.

(b)   This Treaty shall not apply to the Sovereign Base Areas of the United Kingdom of Great Britain and Northern Ireland in Cyprus.

(c)   This Treaty shall apply to the Channel Islands and the Isle of Man only to the extent necessary to ensure the implementation of the arrangements for those islands set out in the Treaty concerning the accession of new Member States to the European Economic Community and to the European Atomic Energy Community signed on 22 January 1972.

It is curious that Article 227(1) does not refer to the territory of the named member states. In this respect it may be contrasted with Articles 52 and 53 which make specific reference to the territories of the member states. It is submitted, however, that there is no significance in this particular omission in Article 227(1). Having regard to the terms of the Article as a whole, and its place in the Treaty, it has every appearance of being a set of territorial application provisions. The significance of paragraph 1(1), therefore, would seem to be to establish the general rule that, subject to the exceptions stated later in the Article, the Treaty applies to the entire territory of each member state. Indeed, it would be difficult to ascribe any other meaning or purpose to the paragraph. It could hardly have been inserted in the Article merely to identify the states to which the treaty applies. The latter objective is fully achieved, in a more orthodox way, by the preamble and the testimonium. To put the argument at its lowest, Article 227(1) can hardly be said to displace the presumption in Article 29 of the Vienna Convention.[2]

The next question therefore is what is meant by the entire territory of each member state. Clearly it includes as a general rule the metropolitan land territory over which the state has sovereignty and the air space over

[2] See n. 1 above.

that territory. Similarly it includes the internal waters, the territorial sea, and the air space above. The International Law Commission, in an explanatory memorandum on a text similar to the one adopted as Article 29 of the Vienna Convention, quoted above, said:

The term 'the entire territory of each party' is a comprehensive term designed to embrace all the land and the pertinent territorial waters and air space which constitute the territory of the State.[3]

This is consistent with Article 1 of the 1958 Geneva Convention on the Territorial Sea and the Contiguous Zone[4] and its successor, Article 2 of the 1982 United Nations Convention on the Law of the Sea.[5] The latter reads:

1. The sovereignty of a coastal State extends, beyond its land territory and internal waters and, in the case of an archipelagic State, its archipelagic waters, to an adjacent belt of sea, described as the territorial sea.
2. This sovereignty extends to the air space over the territorial sea as well as to its bed and subsoil.
3. The sovereignty over the territorial sea is exercised subject to this Convention and to other rules of international law.

In the field of civil aviation, Articles 1 and 2 of the 1944 Chicago Convention[6] made similar references to the air space over a state's land areas and territorial waters. It is not surprising, therefore, that Article 1(2) of Council Regulation 2151/84[7] on the customs territory of the Community provides:

The following shall be included in the customs territory of the Community:
(*a*) the territorial sea of the coastal Member States and their internal waters;
(*b*) the airspace of each Member State.

This is by no means, however, the complete picture, because it is possible to provide specifically that a treaty does not apply to a specified part of the metropolitan territory. Moreover, the entire territory of a state may include, in addition to the metropolitan territory, dependent territories for whose international relations the state is responsible. Unless a different intention appears from a treaty or is otherwise established, its territorial application extends to all such territories (and of course their internal waters, territorial sea, and air space). In the case of Belgium, Greece, Ireland, and Luxembourg no complications of this kind arise, but the other member states have each been accorded special treatment in the matter of territorial application. It is convenient to deal with each of them in turn.[8]

---

[3] Para. 3 of the International Law Commission report of its 18th session, 1966.
[4] Miscellaneous No. 15 (1958), Cmnd. 584.
[5] Miscellaneous No. 11 (1983), Cmnd. 8941, not yet in force.
[6] TS No. 8 (1953), Cmnd. 8742.
[7] *OJ* 1984, L197/1.
[8] See also the special territorial provisions in Arts. 1, 2, 4 and the Annex of Reg. 2151/84 on the customs territory of the Community, *OJ* 1984, L197/1.

Denmark

Article 227(5) provides that the Treaty shall not apply to the Faroe Islands, although it does contain an opting-in provision for them. Although, however, the Treaty does not apply to the Faroe Islands in the territorial sense, Protocol No. 2 to the Act of Accession contains special provisions relating to customs treatment for products originating in and coming from the islands into other regions of Denmark. The pre-accession customs treatment continues to apply, but the goods in question are not considered to be in free circulation in Denmark for the purpose of Articles 9 and 10 of the EEC Treaty. The Protocol also contains other provisions dealing with these islands, should Denmark decide to follow the opting-in procedure. The islands are excluded from the customs territory of the Community.[9]

Greenland has had a somewhat chequered history. Originally the ECSC Treaty, the EEC Treaty, and the EURATOM Treaty applied to Greenland, subject only to certain special provisions affecting free movement and fisheries. However, in a referendum held on 23 February 1982, Greenland opted by a small majority in favour of withdrawal from the Community. Following negotiations between Denmark and the other member states, a treaty was signed by all member states on 13 March 1984.[10] Article 6 amends the original treaties, so that the ECSC and EURATOM Treaties cease to apply to Greenland. Under the EEC Treaty, Greenland is added to Annex IV, and thus becomes one of the overseas countries and territories associated with the Community in accordance with Article 227(3) and Part IV (Articles 131-6).[11] A Protocol to the 1984 Treaty also makes special arrangements for Greenland.[12] Article 1 of the Protocol concerns free movement of goods and reads:

1. The treatment on import into the Community of products subject to the common organisation of the market in fishery products, originating in Greenland, shall, while complying with the mechanisms of the common market organization, involve exemption from customs duties and charges having equivalent effect and the absence of quantitative restrictions or measures having equivalent effect if the possibilities for access to Greenland fishing zones granted to the Community pursuant to an agreement between the Community and the authority responsible for Greenland are satisfactory to the Community.

2. All measures relating to the import arrangements for such products, including those relating to the adoption of such measures, shall be adopted in accordance with the procedure laid down in Article 43 of the Treaty establishing the European Economic Community.

[9] Ibid., Art. 1.
[10] European Communities No. 18 (1984), Cmnd. 9283: entered into force on 1 Feb. 1985, *OJ* 1985, L29/19.
[11] See p. 298 above.
[12] European Communities No. 18 (1984), Cmnd. 9283.

Germany

Berlin is in a special situation. On signing the EEC Treaty on 15 March 1957, the Government of the Federal Republic of Germany made the following declaration:

The Government of the Federal Republic of Germany reserves the right to declare, when depositing its instruments of ratification, that the Treaty establishing the European Economic Community and the Treaty establishing the European Atomic Energy Community shall equally apply to Land Berlin.[13]

The Allied Kommandatura wrote to the Governing Mayor, Berlin on 18 November 1957 in terms which included the following passage:

the Allied Kommandatura does not object to the application to Berlin of the above-named treaty insofar as is compatible with the rights and responsibilities of the Allied authorities as defined in the Declaration on Berlin of May 5, 1955, which, in the case of any conflict involving the fulfilment of the obligations set forth in that instrument, must be regarded as paramount. The extension of this treaty to Berlin, moreover, is not to be construed as implying the repeal or amendment in any way of Allied legislation.

As regards 'European regulations' issued under the authority of this treaty, the Allied Kommandatura will require that the same conditions apply in the case of these regulations as apply in the case of regulations issued under Federal legislation and that it be furnished with copies of all European regulations as soon after their publication as is practicable. Regulations issued under Federal legislation will continue to be provided in accordance with existing procedures.[14]

On ratifying the Treaty, the Federal Republic of Germany made a declaration to the effect that the EEC Treaty applied to 'Land Berlin',[15] but added: 'This statement does not affect the rights and responsibilities of France, the United Kingdom and the United States with respect to Berlin.'[16]

The Federal Republic of Germany's declarations having been tacitly accepted by all member states, it may now be taken that in Community law the EEC Treaty applies to the Western Sectors of Berlin, to the extent that such application is compatible with the rights and responsibilities of the three named Allied Powers. In the light of Part IID and Annex IV of the Quadripartite Agreement of 3 September 1971,[17] the extension of the EEC Treaty to the Western Sectors of Berlin must also be regarded as acceptable to all the Four Powers in Berlin (France, the United Kingdom, the USA, and the USSR).

The question whether the EEC Treaty, or secondary legislation adopted

---

[13] TS No. 1 (1973), Part II, Cmnd. 5179–II, p. 268.
[14] BK/L(57) 44, as quoted by R. Hütte, 'Berlin and the European Communities', (1983) 3 *YEL* 14.
[15] i.e. the Western Sectors of Berlin.
[16] UNTS vol. 28, p. 11.
[17] TS No. 111 (1972) Cmnd. 5135.

under it, may conflict with Allied rights and responsibilities is by no means academic. In connection with a Council Directive on the limitation of noise emissions from subsonic aircraft, the Federal Republic of Germany made a declaration[18] to the Council to the effect that, since civil aviation fell within the reserve powers in Berlin of France, the United Kingdom, and the USA, and following consultation with the governments of those states, the Directive did not cover Land Berlin. A similar procedure was followed in relation to another Directive concerning air services.[19]

Both before and after recognition by Western states of the German Democratic Republic (GDR), the Federal Republic of Germany (FRG) has always treated trade between the two territories as internal trade, and has allowed duty-free access for goods of GDR origin. However, this does not mean that other member states are obliged to treat GDR goods which have entered the FRG free of customs duties as in free circulation. So if such goods are re-exported to other member states they attract the Common Customs Tariff. This situation is consistent with the Protocol on German internal trade and connected problems, signed on 25 March 1957.[20] Paragraph 1 of the Protocol reads:

1. Since trade between the German territories subject to the Basic Law for the Federal Republic of Germany and the German territories in which the Basic Law does not apply is a part of German internal trade, the application of this Treaty in Germany requires no change in the treatment currently accorded this trade.

Paragraph 3 leaves the way open for member states other than the FRG to apply the Common Customs Tariff. It reads:

3. Each Member State may take appropriate measures to prevent any difficulties arising for it from trade between another Member State and the German territories in which the Basic Law for the Federal Republic of Germany does not apply.[21]

Heligoland enjoys the special status of a tax-free area to which the Common Customs Tariff does not apply. This was achieved by virtue of the provisions of Article 1 of Regulation 1496/68.[22]

Buesingen is part of the territory of the Federal Republic of Germany. But it is a small isolated enclave in Switzerland, and is treated as outside the customs territory of the Community.[23] The other member states may be taken to have accepted this pragmatic application of Article 227. It is not

---

[18] The text of the declaration, together with the Directive, is in *OJ* 1983, L117/15.

[19] *OJ* 1983, L237/19.

[20] TS No. 1 (1973), part II, Cmnd. 5179–II, p. 125.

[21] *OJ* 1968, L238/1. See also Reg. 2151/84, *OJ* 1984, L197/1.

[22] See also Case 14/74, *Norddeutsches Vieh- und Fleischkontor* v. *HZA Hamburg–Jonas* [1974] ECR 899.

[23] Art. 1 of Reg. 2151/84, *OJ* 1984, L197/1.

easy to reconcile with the wording of the Article, but the issue is in any case *de minimis*.[24]

France

Article 227(2) made special provisions for Algeria and the French overseas Departments.[25] Since Algeria's independence on 1 July 1962, the Treaty has ceased to have any territorial application to that territory. A Co-operation Agreement between the Community and the People's Democratic Republic of Algeria was signed on 26 April 1976,[26] and entered into force on 1 November 1978.[27]

The question of the extent of application of the EEC Treaty to the French overseas Departments, and in particular whether Article 95 applied to them, arose in *Hansen* v. *HZA Flensburg*.[28] Doubt had arisen as to whether Article 95 applied to spirits imported from Guadeloupe, a French overseas Department, because although Article 227(2) provided that certain stated parts of the treaty applied to the French overseas Departments the tax provisions of the treaty were not included in the list. The Court held that the tax provisions applied to goods coming from the French overseas Departments, and in particular the prohibition of discrimination laid down in Article 95.[29] In explanation the Court said:

It follows from Article 227(1) that the status of the French overseas departments within the Community is primarily defined by reference to the French constitution under which, as the French Government has stated, the overseas departments are an integral part of the Republic.

However, in order to make due allowance for the special geographic, economic and social situation of those departments, Article 227(2) made provision for the Treaty to be applied by stages, and in addition it made available the widest powers for the adoption of special provisions commensurate to the specific requirements of those parts of the French territories.

For that purpose, Article 227 precisely stated certain chapters and articles which were to apply as soon as the Treaty entered into force, while at the same time reserving a period of two years within which the Council could determine special conditions under which other groups of provisions were to apply.

Therefore after the expiry of that period, the provisions of the Treaty and of secondary law must apply automatically to the French overseas departments inasmuch as they are an integral part of the French Republic, it being understood,

---

[24] Another anomaly is that the Austrian territories of Jungholz and Mittelberg are economically integrated into the FRG. They are deemed to be part of the customs territory of the Community by Art. 2 and the Annex of Reg. 2151/84, *OJ* 1984, L197/1.

[25] Martinique, French Guyana, Guadeloupe, St Pierre et Miquelon, and Réunion.

[26] For the text of the agreement, see Reg. 2210/78, *OJ* 1978, L263/1.

[27] *OJ* 1978, L295/35.

[28] Case 148/77 [1978] *ECR* 1787.

[29] Ibid., p. 1809.

however, that it always remains possible subsequently to adopt specific measures in order to meet the needs of those territories.

It follows from these considerations that Article 95 applies to the tax treatment of products coming from the French overseas departments.[30]

Monaco is not a territory for whose external relations any member state is responsible (Article 227(4)) and the EEC Treaty does not apply to the principality. However since Monaco is in customs union with France the principality applies *de facto* the Common Customs Tariff.[31]

Equally, Andorra does not fall within the provisions of Article 227(4) and the EEC Treaty does not apply to it. Although the president of France (as successor of the king of Navarre and acting in a personal capacity) is one of the two co-princes (the Spanish bishop of Urgel being the other), Andorra is not one of the territories for which 'a Member State is responsible'.

The French overseas countries and territories to which Part IV of the Treaty applies are French Polynesia, French Southern and Antarctic Territories, New Caledonia and Dependencies, Wallis and Futuna Islands, and Mayotte.

Italy

The Italian communes of Livigno and Campione d'Italia, being small isolated enclaves in Switzerland, are treated as outside the customs territory of the Community (like the German enclave of Buesingen, to which reference has already been made).

Netherlands

In a Protocol attached to the EEC Treaty,[32] the Netherlands became entitled to ratify the treaty on behalf of the Kingdom in Europe and Netherlands New Guinea only. The position of Netherlands New Guinea is now, however, only of historical interest, because in 1963 that territory was incorporated into Indonesia under the name 'West Irian' ('Irian Jaya') and the EEC Treaty has no application to it. The Dutch overseas countries and territories to which Part IV of the Treaty applies are the Netherlands Antilles (Aruba, Bonaire, Curacao, Saba, St Eustasius, St Martin).

The United Kingdom

The EEC Treaty applies to the whole of the United Kingdom of Great Britain and Northern Ireland, i.e. the metropolitan territory. By virtue of Article 227(4) it also applies, subject to certain special limitations, to all the European territories for whose external relations the United Kingdom is responsible. The first limitation is that the Treaty has no application to the

---

[30] Ibid., p. 1805.

[31] Monaco is deemed to be part of the customs territory by Art. 2 and the Annex of Reg. 2151/84, *OJ* 1984, L197/1.   [32] TS No. 1 (1973), part II, Cmnd. 5179–II, p. 133.

Sovereign Base areas of Akrotiri and Dhekelia, in the island of Cyprus (Article 227(5)(b)). Secondly, it only applies to the Channel Islands and the Isle of Man to the extent necessary to secure the implementation of the arrangements for those islands in the Treaty of Accession (Article 227(5)(c)). The relevant provisions for the islands are in Protocol No. 3 to the Act of Accession.[33] Community rules on customs matters and quantitative restrictions apply to the islands as they apply to the United Kingdom.[34] There are special rules for agricultural products and their free movement into and out of the islands. These are to be found in Article 1(2) of Protocol No. 3 and Regulation 706/73.[35] Thirdly, Article 28 of the Act of Accession provides in effect that Community acts relating to agricultural products, rules implementing the common agricultural property, and Community acts on harmonization of legislation on turnover taxes shall not apply to Gibraltar. Moreover, in Annex 1 to the Act of Accession,[36] Regulation 1496/68[37] was amended so that, while the customs territory of the Community is defined as including the United Kingdom, the Channel Islands, and the Isle of Man, no mention is made of Gibraltar. This exclusion of Gibraltar from the customs territory of the Community is continued in Article 1 of Regulation 2151/84.[38]

The only application of the Treaty to British possessions[39] outside Europe is that the association arrangements in Part IV apply to most of them by virtue of Article 227(3) and Annex IV to the Treaty, as subsequently modified.[40] A notable omission from the list is Hong Kong, to which the Treaty has no application. The list of British overseas countries and territories to which Part IV applies has been automatically depleted by the independence of certain of those territories.[41] The list, as at 1 January 1985, is:

Anguilla	Falkland Islands
Bermuda	Falkland Islands Dependencies
British Antarctic Territory	Montserrat
British Indian Ocean Territory	Pitcairn
British Virgin Islands	St Helena and Dependencies
Cayman Islands	Turks and Caicos Islands

[33] TS No. 1 (1973), part I, Cmnd. 5179–I, p. 247.
[34] Ibid., Art. 1. See also Art. 1 of Reg. 2151/84, *OJ* 1984, L197/1.
[35] *OJ* 1973, L68/1. Measures for the protection of fish stocks seemingly apply to activities in the waters under the jurisdiction of the Isle of Man (Case 32/79, *Commission* v. *United Kingdom* [1980] *ECR* 2403, p. 2451, and Case 804/79, *Commission* v. *United Kingdom* [1981] *ECR* 1045, p. 1078), but this is not strictly a case of territorial application.
[36] TS No. 1 (1973), part I, Cmnd. 5179–I, p. 58.
[37] *OJ* 1968, L238/1. [38] *OJ* 1984, L197/1.
[39] As defined in Schedule 1 to the Interpretation Act 1978 (c. 30).
[40] Art. 24(2) of the Act of Accession.
[41] See Case 147/73, *Lensing* v. *HZA Berlin–Packhof* [1973] *ECR* 1543, in respect of the former French colony of Guinea.

Although Bermuda is still on the list, and Articles 131–5 EEC still apply in relation to it, the territory is not listed, in Annex I to Council Decision 1186/80[42] on the association of the overseas countries and territories with the EEC, as a territory to which that decision applies.

Provisions applying wherever member states have jurisdiction

It should perhaps at the outset be made clear that this part of the chapter is concerned largely with provisions of EEC law which apply in relation to situations arising in places, outside national territories, where member states lawfully exercise some kind of jurisdiction or control, or engage in some lawful activity. When Community law applies to situations arising outside the territories of the member states, it is not necessarily the case that it applies as law in the geographical areas where those situations arise. To take an analogy from private law, a national of state A who commits murder in state B may have offended against the law of state A, but this does not mean that the law of state A applies as law in state B. The law of state A does however apply to situations which have arisen in state B, and action may be taken against the offender when he turns up in state A. Similarly, it is possible for a rule of Community law to apply to situations arising in third countries, as where, for example, the representatives of a member state in that third country negotiate a trade agreement, in contravention of the Community's exclusive right under Article 113 to do so. A more normal situation, however, is where Community law applies in relation to events which occur not in third countries, but in other areas outside the territory of member states where they exercise some kind of jurisdiction. The most prominent example is the control imposed by Community law on shipping activities, both in the field of transport and fisheries. Each will be considered in turn.

Article 75(1)(*a*) EEC, concerning the common transport policy, requires the Council to lay down 'common rules applicable to international transport to or from the territory of a Member State or passing across the territory of one or more Member States'. Article 84(2) enables the Council to make appropriate decisions for sea and air transport. It might have been possible to interpret these provisions restrictively during the days of the original six member states. They had common land frontiers, and a reasonably coherent 'international' transport policy could have been worked out which related only to things done within the area consisting of the combined national territories of the member states. This approach became less convincing after the United Kingdom and Ireland joined the Community, although it would still have been possible, within its confines, to have regulated such things as uniform freight rates to be charged within a

[42] *OJ* 1980, L361/1.

member state in respect of any goods destined to travel to or from another member state. It would not have been possible, however, within a transport policy having no extra-territorial application, to have regulated what happened on board a ship while sailing the high seas between, say, Harwich and Hook of Holland. However, any claims to limit the application of the common transport policy to national territories were laid to rest in *Commission* v. *France*.[43]

That case concerned a French law which required a proportion of the crew of a French ship to be French nationals. The Court was asked to determine whether this contravened Article 48 and Regulation 1612/68[44] on the free movement of workers. The Court held that, in maintaining the French law in question as regards the nationals of other member states, France had failed to fulfil its obligations under Article 48 of the Treaty and Article 4 of the Regulation. In reaching that conclusion the Court's reasoning was:

The basic object of Part Two of the Treaty, devoted to foundations of the Community, is to establish the basis of the common market, i.e. free movement of goods (Title I) and free movement of persons, services and capital (Title III).

Conceived as being applicable to the whole complex of economic activities, these basic rules can be rendered inapplicable only as a result of express provision in the Treaty.[45]

The Court went on to say:

Far from involving a departure from these fundamental rules, therefore, the object of the rules relating to the common transport policy is to implement and complement them by means of common action.

Consequently the said general rules must be applied insofar as they can achieve these objectives.

Since transport is basically a service, it has been found necessary to provide a special system for it, taking into account the special aspects of this branch of activity.

With this object, a special exemption has been provided by Article 61(1), under which freedom to provide services in the field of transport 'shall be governed by the provisions of the Title relating to transport', thus confirming that the general rules of the Treaty must be applied insofar as they are not excluded.[46]

It is clear from this judgment that the rules on free movement of workers (e.g. the rule against discrimination on grounds of nationality) apply to their employment on ships registered in member states, wherever those ships happen to be. Freedom of establishment, however, is confined to 'the

[43] Case 167/73 [1974] *ECR* 359.
[44] *OJ*, Special Edition, 1968(II), p. 475.
[45] Case 167/73 [1974] *ECR* 359, p. 369.
[46] Ibid., p. 370.

territory of another Member State' (Article 52), and the freedom to provide services is 'within the Community' (Article 59).[47]

It is outside the scope of this book to deal in depth with the Community's fisheries policy. But that also is another illustration of the control by Community law of activities occurring outside national territories. Thus, for example, Article 2 of Regulation 101/76,[48] laying down a common structural policy for the fishing industry, prohibited the application by a member state of rules in respect of fishing which would lead to differences in treatment of other member states 'in the maritime waters coming under its sovereignty or within its jurisdiction'. Since the territorial sea is under the sovereignty of the coastal state,[49] the last four words in this quotation clearly refer to areas outside the territorial sea, and they would be wide enough to cover any exclusive fisheries zones. The Court's judgment in the *Kramer* case[50] described the position in the following terms:

It should be made clear that, although Article 5 of Regulation No 2141/70 is applicable only to a geographically limited fishing area, it none the less follows [from] Article 102 of the Act of Accession, from Article 1 of the said regulation and moreover from the very nature of things that the rule-making authority of the Community *ratione materiae* also extends—in so far as the Member States have similar authority under public international law—to fishing on the high seas.[51]

The Council has agreed that member states should act in concert to extend their fishing zones to 200 nautical miles with effect from 1 January 1977.[52] The preamble to Regulation 170/83,[53] which establishes a Community system for the conservation and management of fishery resources, refers to this extension to 200 miles and the need on that account, inter alia, for Community conservation measures.[54]

Although, as has already been seen, the main rules on free movement of goods should primarily be considered as provisions having territorial application, it is possible for ancillary rules to apply in relation to areas outside the territories of member states. One example is Article 4(2)(h) of Regulation 802/68 on the common definition of the concept of the origin of goods,[55] which provides that 'goods wholly obtained or produced in one country' (which are to be considered as originating in that country) means,

---

[47] See p. 296—7 above.
[48] *OJ* 1976, L20/19. See also Arts. 100 and 101 of the Act of Accession.
[49] See nn. 4 and 5 above.
[50] Joined Cases 3, 4, and 6/76 [1976] *ECR* 1279, referring to similar wording in an earlier regulation.
[51] Ibid., p. 1309. See also Case 61/77, *Commission* v. *Ireland* [1978] *ECR* 937; Case 88/77, *Minister for Fisheries* v. *Schonenberg* [1978] *ECR* 473; Cases 185–204/78, *van Dam* [1979] *ECR* 2345; Case 141/78, *France* v. *United Kingdom* [1979] *ECR* 2923.
[52] See Council Resolution of 3 November 1976, *OJ* 1981, C105/1.
[53] *OJ* 1983, L24/1.
[54] e.g. Reg. 3175/84, *OJ* 1984, L298/1.
[55] *OJ* 1968, L148/1.

inter alia, 'products taken from the sea-bed or beneath the sea-bed outside territorial waters, if that country has, for the purposes of exploitation, exclusive rights to such soil or sub-soil'. The effect of this appears to be that products (other than petroleum products which are excluded by Article 3) obtained from the continental shelf of one member state are deemed to have originated in the 'single territorial unit' which the member states are to be treated as constituting (Article 8 of the Regulation). Such products may therefore attract the application of other Community rules, e.g. those in Regulation 2603/69 establishing common rules for exports.[56]

To give only one other example, Regulation 3056/73[57] provided funds for 'Community projects'. If funds were provided, the recipient had to report on his activities, and in a sense therefore the Regulation regulated them. They could include work conducted outside the territories of the member states, e.g. a hydro-carbon project conducted off the west coast of Africa.

By this dynamic sort of process there is scope for extending piecemeal the application of areas of Community law, so that they regulate activities, or apply to situations, falling outside the territories of the member states. It is too early to forecast the ultimate limits to which this process could be extended.

THE CONTINENTAL SHELF

The continental shelf was defined in Article 1 of the 1958 Convention on the Continental Shelf[58] as follows:

For the purpose of these Articles, the term 'continental shelf' is used as referring (*a*) to the seabed and subsoil of the submarine areas adjacent to the coast but outside the area of the territorial sea, to a depth of 200 metres or, beyond that limit, to where the depth of the superjacent waters admits of the exploitation of the natural resources of the said areas; (*b*) to the seabed and subsoil of similar submarine areas adjacent to the coasts of islands.

Article 76(1) of the United Nations Convention on the Law of the Sea, opened for signature from 10 December 1982 to 9 December 1984,[59] contains a modified definition as follows:

1. The continental shelf of a coastal State comprises the sea-bed and subsoil of the submarine areas that extend beyond its territorial sea throughout the natural prolongation of its land territory to the outer edge of the continental shelf margin, or to a distance of 200 nautical miles from the baselines from which the breadth of the territorial sea is measured where the outer edge of the continental margin does not extend up to that distance.

[56] *OJ* 1969, L324/25, as subsequently amended.
[57] *OJ* 1973, L312/1.
[58] Misc. No. 15 (1958), Cmnd. 584.
[59] Misc. No. 11 (1983), Cmnd. 8941, not yet in force.

One common element of these definitions is that the continental shelf lies beyond the territorial sea of the coastal state. Both conventions provide in identical terms:

The coastal State exercises over the continental shelf sovereign rights for the purpose of exploring it and exploiting its natural resources.[60]

From these provisions it can be seen that the continental shelf is not part of the metropolitan territory of a member state, or indeed a territory under its sovereignty, since it only has the exercise of sovereign rights. For the reasons given earlier in this chapter it is therefore reasonable to assume that the Treaty does not, strictly speaking, have any territorial application to the continental shelf. However, it is possible for those provisions of Community law which are capable of applying in relation to activities or situations occurring outside the territories of the member states to be made to apply in relation to activities on the continental shelf. In fact, as noted earlier, Regulation 802(68) on the common definition of the concept of the origin of goods[61] applies to products taken from the continental shelf, although it excludes petroleum products. The question where petroleum products, extracted from the continental shelf, should be deemed to have originated remains to be answered. If they are regarded as originating within the Community they could, even before being landed in a member state, presumably become subject to any Community controls on exports. If they are not treated as having a Community origin they could hardly be regarded as 'coming from a third country' (Article 10(1) EEC) so as to attract the Common Customs Tariff. These questions are, however, of no practical importance at present, although it may be that one day there will be a need to answer them in secondary legislation. A hint to that effect appears in Regulation 2151/84 on the customs territory of the Community,[62] which contains the following recitals:

Whereas the customs territory of the Community is defined by Council Regulation (EEC) No 1496/68,[63] as last amended by the 1979 Act of Accession; whereas Article 4 of the abovementioned Regulation provides that it shall not affect the customs system applicable to the continental shelf or that applicable to the waters and fore-shores situated between the coast or shore and the limit of territorial waters, or the provisions applicable in accordance with Community rules to be adopted with regard to free zones;

Whereas Council Regulation (EEC) No 802/68 of 27 June 1968 on the common definition of the concept of the origin of goods[64] defined in fact the customs system applicable to products taken from the continental shelf; whereas in the current

[60] Ibid., Art. 2(1) of the 1958 Convention and Art. 77(1) of the 1982 Convention.
[61] *OJ* 1968, L148/1.
[62] *OJ* 1984, L197/1.
[63] *OJ* 1968, L238/1.
[64] *OJ* 1968, L148/1.

situation there is no reason to integrate the continental shelf adjacent to the territories of the Member States into the customs territory of the Community.

Accordingly Article 1 of the Regulation, while including in the customs territory of the Community the territorial sea, internal waters, and air space of each member state, does not include the continental shelf.

FURTHER READING

R. Hütte, 'Berlin and the European Communities', (1983) *YEL* 1.

PART V

GENERAL EXCEPTIONS

X

General Exceptions to Free Movement

THE particular exceptions to each of the basic freedoms have already been considered: Article 36 in the case of free movement of goods, Article 48(3) for workers, Article 56 for establishment (and services, by virtue of Article 66), and Article 73 for capital. There are also, however, a number of general exceptions which, on various grounds, allow member states to escape from the rull rigours of the substantive provisions of the EEC Treaty. They have not featured as prominently in the judgments of the Court as the particular exceptions have done, partly because member states have not so frequently sought to rely on them and partly because their interpretation and application involve economic and political considerations which do not lend themselves too readily to litigation. Each will be considered in turn, to the extent that it affects freedom of movement and remains in operation after the end of the transitional period.

Article 103

This Article reads:

1. Member States shall regard their conjunctural policies as a matter of common concern. They shall consult each other and the Commission on the measures to be taken in the light of the prevailing circumstances.

2. Without prejudice to any other procedures provided for in this Treaty, the Council may, acting unanimously on a proposal from the Commission, decide upon the measures appropriate to the situation.

3. Acting by a qualified majority on a proposal from the Commission, the Council shall, where required, issue directives needed to give effect to the measures decided upon under paragraph 2.

4. The procedures provided for in this Article shall also apply if any difficulty should arise in the supply of certain products.

The casual reader could be forgiven for wondering precisely what message the Article is intended to convey. His difficulty would no doubt stem from the use of the word 'conjunctural'. It is not defined, and it appears to have been adopted simply as an anglicized version of the corresponding word in the French text. In essence it means 'appertaining to the short-term economic policies of the member states'.[1] The question of the

---

[1] See Case 5/73, *Balkan* v. *HZA Berlin—Packhof* [1973] ECR 1091, p. 1122.

application of this Article in the agricultural field arose in *SADAM* v. *Comitato Interministeriale dei Prezzi*,[2] concerning an Italian rule fixing the minimum price of sugar. The UK Government maintained that, although Article 103 could not allow an exception to specific provisions contained in the rules of a common (i.e. Community) organization of a particular market (for example, sugar), it could be relied on in the general field covered by Article 30.[3] The Court agreed with the first part of the argument in the following passage:

> In so far as a maximum price unilaterally fixed by a Member State is incompatible with the provisions of the agricultural law of the Community, the State concerned cannot rely on the provisions of Article 103 of the Treaty on conjunctural policy in order to justify fixing the price, especially as Regulation No. 1009/67 comprises a framework of organisation designed in such a way as to enable the Community and Member States to meet all manner of disturbances. In this connection, it must first be stressed that it is one of the objectives of Article 39(1) of the Treaty that supplies reach consumers at reasonable prices.[4]

In essence the object of Article 103 is to allow the Council, acting unanimously, to authorize a member state to take measures to correct an urgent and serious economic situation with which it is faced, even though such measures, if taken unilaterally, would infringe other rules of the Treaty. Accordingly, although in areas already covered by the common organization of an agricultural market, a Member State cannot rely on Article 103 to justify unilateral action, *interim* measures may be authorised *by the Council* under Article 103, even in such areas, pending the taking of more appropriate steps under Articles 40 and 43: the *Balkan* case.[5]

In other cases, measures of a more permanent nature could be instituted under Article 103, for example, to control the exports between member states of crude oil and petroleum products in times of world shortage.[6] The relevance of Article 103 for that purpose was mentioned by the Court in *BP* v. *Commission*.[7] The case in essence turned on whether there had been an abuse of a dominant position contrary to Article 86, during a period of oil shortage, and the arguments of the parties and of the Advocate General, as recorded in the official report, were directed to that question. The report does not indicate whether the Court had the benefit of hearing argument about the relevance of Article 103 during the oral stage, or during any other part of the proceedings. Be that as it may, the Court seemingly castigated

---

[2] Joined Cases 88–90/75 [1976] *ECR* 323.
[3] Ibid., p. 331.
[4] Ibid., p. 338. See also Case 31/74, *Galli* [1975] *ECR* 47, p. 63.
[5] Case 5/73 [1973] *ECR* 1091.
[6] See, e.g., Dec. 186/77, *OJ* 1980, L61/23, and Dec. 879/79, *OJ* 1979, L270/58.
[7] Case 77/77 [1978] *ECR* 1513.

the member states or the Council or both in its judgment, in the following terms:

Hence, the absence of appropriate rules, based in particular on Article 103 of the Treaty, which would make it possible to adopt suitable conjunctural measures, whilst revealing a neglect of the principle of Community solidarity which is one of the foundations of the Community, and a failure to act which is all the more serious since Article 103(4) provides in terms that 'the procedures provided for in this article shall also apply if any difficulty should arise in the supply of certain products', still cannot release the Commission from its duty to ensure in all circumstances, both in normal and special market conditions, when the competitive position of traders is particularly threatened, that the prohibition in Article 86 of the Treaty is scrupulously observed.[8]

Later in the judgment the Court again referred to Article 103:

A duty on the part of the supplier to apply a similar rate of reduction in deliveries to all its customers in a period of shortage without having regard to obligations contracted towards its traditional customers could only flow from measures adopted within the framework of the Treaty, in particular Article 103, or, in default of that, by the national authorities.[9]

The reference to action being taken by national authorities in default of action taken by the Council is a reminder that Article 103, while enabling the Council to authorize measures which would otherwise infringe the Treaty, is not confined to measures of that kind. Under that Article, the member states are enjoined to regard their conjunctural policies as a matter of common concern, and the Council may decide upon appropriate measures. Such measures may or may not involve departure from some other Community rule. If an appropriate measure would do so, but the Council for whatever reason chose not to authorize it, there would seem to be nothing in the text of the Article to indicate that a member state could nevertheless take that measure unilaterally. On the other hand, if the appropriate measure would not infringe a Community rule, there seems no reason why the member states should not each act unilaterally, in the absence of a co-ordinated Community procedure authorized by the Council. It is in this latter sense that the Court's dictum, quoted above, probably ought to be read.

Article 108

Article 108 and the succeeding Article deal with the serious difficulties which can arise when a member state has a major problem with its balance of payments. Article 108 reads:

1. Where a Member State is in difficulties or is seriously threatened with difficulties as regards its balance of payments either as a result of an overall

---

[8] Ibid., p. 1525.   [9] Ibid., p. 1528.

disequilibrium in its balance of payments, or as a result of the type of currency at its disposal, and where such difficulties are liable in particular to jeopardise the functioning of the common market or the progressive implementation of the common commercial policy, the Commission shall immediately investigate the position of the State in question and the action which, making use of all the means at its disposal, that State has taken or may take in accordance with the provisions of Article 104. The Commission shall state what measures it recommends the State concerned to take.

If the action taken by a Member State and the measures suggested by the Commission do not prove sufficient to overcome the difficulties which have arisen or which threaten, the Commission shall, after consulting the Monetary Committee, recommend to the Council the granting of mutual assistance and appropriate methods therefor.

The Commission shall keep the Council regularly informed of the situation and of how it is developing.

2. The Council, acting by a qualified majority, shall grant such mutual assistance; it shall adopt directives or decisions laying down the conditions and details of such assistance, which may take such forms as:

(*a*) a concerted approach to or within any other international organisations to which Member States may have recourse;

(*b*) measures needed to avoid deflection of trade where the State which is in difficulties maintains or reintroduces quantitative restrictions against third countries;

(*c*) the granting of limited credits by other Member States, subject to their agreement.

During the transitional period, mutual assistance may also take the form of special reductions in customs duties or enlargements of quotas in order to facilitate an increase in imports from the State which is in difficulties, subject to the agreement of the States by which such measures would have to be taken.

3. If the mutual assistance recommended by the Commission is not granted by the Council or if the mutual assistance granted and the measures taken are insufficient, the Commission shall authorise the State which is in difficulties to take protective measures, the conditions and details of which the Commission shall determine.

Such authorisation may be revoked and such conditions and details may be changed by the Council acting by a qualified majority.

In so far as Article 108 enables exceptions to be made to the free movement of capital, it has already been considered in Chapter 8. However, the Article also permits measures to be taken which impede other freedoms of movement. So, for example, Commission Decision 301/68[10] permitted France to derogate from Articles 30 and 31 by restricting the imports of certain goods (notably motor vehicles) from other member states.

---

[10] *OJ* 1968, L178/15. See also Commission Dec. 287/74, *OJ* 1974, L152/18.

Article 109

Article 109 reads:

1. Where a sudden crisis in the balance of payments occurs and a decision within the meaning of Article 108(2) is not immediately taken, the Member State concerned may, as a precaution, take the necessary protective measures. Such measures must cause the least possible disturbance in the functioning of the common market and must not be wider in scope than is strictly necessary to remedy the sudden difficulties which have arisen.

2. The Commission and the other Member States shall be informed of such protective measures not later than when they enter into force. The Commission may recommend to the Council the granting of mutual assistance under Article 108.

3. After the Commission has delivered an opinion and the Monetary Committee has been consulted, the Council may, acting by a qualified majority, decide that the State concerned shall amend, suspend or abolish the protective measures referred to above.

This Article's relevance to free movement of capital has already been considered in Chapter 8. It could however, like Article 108, be used to justify exceptions to other freedoms of movement. The Article allows member states initially to take unilateral action, in order to deal with a sudden crisis which has arisen. It should be noted, however, that the Article can only apply in the most exceptional circumstances, when a member state's overall balance of payments has very quickly reached crisis point. Community decisions are thereafter required to be taken as soon as possible.

There is a heavy bias towards resorting to mutual assistance under Article 108, in that a precondition for unilateral action under Article 109 is that an immediate decision on mutual assistance has not been taken. It is thus clear that if the Council grants such mutual assistance, even with stringent conditions, unilateral action under Article 109 is thereafter impossible. What is not so clear is whether unilateral measures are possible where the Commission has, after consulting the Monetary Committee as required by Article 108, recommended mutual assistance but the Council has, by qualified majority, decided not to grant it.

A literal interpretation of Article 109 would suggest that 'a decision within the meaning of Article 108(2)' includes both a positive and negative decision. However, such an approach to a Community text can be misleading, and it may be that the Court would look at all the circumstances in which the Council refused mutual assistance, and the individual member state concerned claimed to be suffering 'a sudden crisis in the balance of payments', before deciding whether to interpret Article 109 restrictively or broadly. This potential difficulty in interpreting Article 109(1) may in practice not give rise to undue difficulty, because even if the Council decides not to grant mutual assistance, the Commission has wide powers under Article 108(3) to authorize the member state which is in difficulties to take protective measures. However, the bias towards mutual assistance, as the most appropriate Community remedy, remains, and Article 109(2) contains an additional reminder of that fact. The Court's own leaning towards mutual assistance, and away from unilateral measures, has already been noted in Chapter 8 in connection with *Commission* v. *France*.[11]

Article 115

Article 115 reads:

In order to ensure that the execution of measures of commercial policy taken in accordance with this Treaty by any Member State is not obstructed by deflection of trade, or where differences between such measures lead to economic difficulties in one or more of the Member States, the Commission shall recommend the methods for the requisite cooperation between Member States. Failing this, the Commission shall authorise Member States to take the necessary protective measures, the conditions and details of which it shall determine.

In case of urgency during the transitional period, Member States may themselves take the necessary measures and shall notify them to the other Member States and to the Commission, which may decide that the States concerned shall amend or abolish such measures.

In the selection of such measures, priority shall be given to those which cause the least disturbance to the functioning of the common market and which take into account the need to expedite, as far as possible, the introduction of the common customs tariff.

In order to understand the purpose and scope of this Article it is necessary to appreciate the Community scheme, established by Articles 9, 10, and 113, for dealing with goods which originate in third countries and then enter the Community. Leaving aside the special provisions which applied during the transitional period, the first limb of this scheme is that under Article 113 a common commercial policy is to be established. This is to be achieved through a network of agreements between the Community (as a legal person, distinct from its constituent member states) and third countries, which establish the conditions upon which goods may be exported and imported between the member states and those third countries. In a complete system, all countries of the world would be covered by this network of Community agreements. There would thus be uniform conditions, applicable throughout the Community, upon which goods could pass between the Community and those third states. The second limb of the scheme, established by Articles 9 and 10, is that once these goods from third countries have arrived in the first member state, and all import formalities and any customs duties or charges have been paid,

[11] Joined Cases 6 and 11/69 [1969] *ECR* 523, pp. 539–40.

they enter into 'free circulation', i.e. they can move freely within the Community.

In such a perfect system there would be no room for any national rules in any member state to govern the import of goods from third countries. However, the problem is that the common commercial policy is incomplete. There is, therefore, still room for a member state to impose its own restrictions on the import of any goods from a third state which are not covered by the common commercial policy, and these restrictions may not be matched by similar national restrictions in all other member states. It follows that any such national restrictions of the first member state could be undermined or defeated if goods were first imported from the third state in question into another member state, and having thus got into 'free circulation', were to be sent into the first member state.

This is the kind of deflection of trade with which Article 115 seeks to deal. It necessarily applies only where goods come from a third country to one member state, and they are then deflected to another member state which is lawfully trying to enforce its own national restrictions in the absence of any relevant provisions of the common commercial policy. The remedy under Article 115 is for the member state which is maintaining the national restrictions to seek the authority of the Commission to take protective measures to prevent goods being deflected into its territory in this way. If granted, this means that an exception is allowed to the general rule in Articles 9 and 10 that once goods from third countries get into free circulation no member state may exclude or restrict their importation into its territory. Because this is an exception to a basic rule of free movement, the rules in Article 115 are strictly interpreted and applied.

One of the leading cases on Article 115 is *Donckerwolcke* v. *Procureur de la Republique*.[12] In that case, goods originating in Syria and Lebanon were put into free circulation in Belgium. The appellants imported them into France and declared their origin to be the Belgo-Luxembourg Economic Union. The true origin was discovered, and criminal proceedings ensued against the appellants. The Court referred to the need for strict interpretation and application of Article 115 in the following terms:

Because they constitute not only an exception to the provisions of Articles 9 and 30 of the Treaty which are fundamental to the operation of the Common Market, but also an obstacle to the implementation of the common commercial policy provided for by Article 113, the derogations allowed under Article 115 must be strictly interpreted and applied.[13]

That essential conditions for the application of Article 115 are the absence of relevant rules under the Community's common commercial

[12] Case 41/76 [1976] *ECR* 1921. See also Case 29/75, *Kaufhof* v. *Commission* [1976] *ECR* 431.
[13] Ibid., p. 1937.

policy, and a consequent deflection of trade, can be seen from the following passage:

The fact that at the expiry of the transitional period the Community commercial policy was not fully achieved is one of a number of circumstances calculated to maintain in being between the Member States differences in commercial policy capable of bringing about deflections of trade or of causing economic difficulties in certain Member States. Article 115 allows difficulties of this kind to be avoided by giving to the Commission the power to authorise Member States to take protective measures particularly in the form of derogation from the principle of free circulation within the Community of products which originated in third countries and which were put into free circulation in one of the Member States.[14]

The need for there to be (i) national measures of commercial policy, which are in accordance with Community law, and (ii) authority from the Commission to take the protective measures in question, is apparent from the following quotation:

First of all it should be stressed with regard to the scope of such provisions that under Article 115 limitations may only be placed on the free movement within the Community of goods enjoying the right to free circulation by virtue of measures of commercial policy adopted by the importing Member State in accordance with the Treaty.

As full responsibility in the matter of commercial policy was transferred to the Community by means of Article 113(1) measures of commercial policy of a national character are only permissible after the end of the transitional period by virtue of specific authorisation by the Community.[15]

The Court went on to hold that, although a Member State (such as France in that case) could require an importer to state, so far as he knows or may be reasonably expected to know, the true origin of goods, e.g. to enable it to decide whether to apply to the Commission for an appropriate authority under Article 115,[16] it could not restrict the import of the goods by imposing a licensing system simply for the purpose of a possible future application to the Commission under the Article.[17] Moreover, any penalty imposed for failure to state the true origin of the goods must be proportional to the offence.[18]

The *Donckerwolcke* case[19] arose from a reference under Article 177, but the question of the admissibility of a direct application to the Court by an individual who was aggrieved by an authorization granted to a member state under Article 115 arose in *Bock* v. *Commission*.[20] The Court held the

[14] Ibid.
[15] Ibid.
[16] Ibid., p. 1938.
[17] Ibid.
[18] Ibid.
[19] Case 41/76 [1976] *ECR* 1921.
[20] Case 62/70 [1971] *ECR* 897.

individual's application to be admissible because it was of direct concern to him that the Commission had authorized Germany to exclude from Community treatment certain goods originating in China.[21] On the substance of the case the Court annulled the Commission's decision to authorize protective measures, and in doing so drew attention to the last paragraph of Article 115 which requires the Commission, when selecting such measures, to give priority to those which cause the least disturbance to the functioning of the common market.[22]

The case of *Cayrol* v. *Rivoira*[23] illustrates the point that Article 115 cannot apply in a situation in relation to which there already exists a relevant rule of the Community's common commercial policy. In that case the issue turned on whether the common organization of the market in fruit and vegetables, which pursuant to an agreement between the Community and Spain included certain provisions concerning the importation of fresh table grapes, ousted Article 115 in relation to imports of table grapes. In fact the Community provisions applied only to such imports during certain times of the year, which did not include the times of import into France of the consignments in question. The Court was asked whether Article 115 could be relied upon in such a situation. The Court's reply was that the existence of the agreement between the Community and Spain formed no obstacle to the application to imports of table grapes of Article 115.[24] By way of explanation, however, the Court referred to the fact that the Community regime only applied during certain months of the year, and went on to say:

It follows from the foregoing that during the part of the year between 1 July and 31 December table grapes were not covered by a Community import system such as to make Article 115 inapplicable to the case.[25]

Article 222

Article 222 reads:

This Treaty shall in no way prejudice the rules in Member States governing the system of property ownership.

The Court's pronouncements on this Article have been as brief and inscrutable as its text:

Article 222 provides only that the 'Treaty shall in no way prejudice the rules in Member States governing the system of property ownership'.[26]

---

[21] Ibid., pp. 907–8.
[22] Ibid., p. 909.
[23] Case 52/77 [1977] *ECR* 2261. [24] Ibid., p. 2279. [25] Ibid.
[26] Case 32/65, *Italy* v. *Council and Commission* [1966] *ECR* 389, p. 408. For similar treatment see Joined Cases 56 and 58/64, *Consten and Grundig* v. *Commission* [1966] *ECR* 299, p. 345; and for an even briefer mention, see Case 24/67, *Parke, Davis* v. *Centrafarm* [1968] *ECR* 55, p. 73.

There is a general belief that the Article was conceived in order to preserve the right of member states to nationalize undertakings.[27] It is tempting to suggest that there are clearer and more direct ways which could have been used to express that idea. Nevertheless, the objective, if that was indeed the objective, appears to have been achieved, with some consequences at least for freedom of movement of persons. It is thus of no avail to a national of one member state, who has established himself in another, to complain that he is being deprived of his rights under Article 52 if his undertaking, along with all other similar undertakings, is nationalized by the latter. It is, however, worth noting that the article refers to 'the system of property ownership'. The inclusion of the world 'system' is some indication that the Article is intended to refer to a generally applied set of rules, rather than to a particular and special application of a rule to one individual undertaking.

Article 223

Article 223(1)(*a*), which permits any member state to withhold information the disclosure of which it considers contrary to the essential interests of its security, is not directly relevant to the Community rules of free movement. Article 223(1)(*b*), however, is. It reads:

Any Member State may take such measures as it considers necessary for the protection of the essential interests of its security which are connected with the production of or trade in arms, munitions and war material; such measures shall not adversely affect the conditions of competition in the common market regarding products which are not intended for specifically military purposes.

It is thus for the member state concerned to judge what measures are necessary to protect its essential interests in this field. They could include restrictions on exports of raw materials needed for arms production, or on the supply from other member states of such materials for such purposes where, for example, it could adversely affect its security interests for non-nationals to get to know the types or quantities of materials being used. However, the member state concerned is not necessarily the sole arbiter of whether Article 223 applies in any particular situation. That some form of control by the Community's institutions is envisaged can be seen from Article 225. This requires the Commission and the member state concerned to examine together how that state's measures can be adjusted if they are having the effect of distorting conditions of competition in the common market.

Article 225 also allows the Commission or any member state to have direct recourse to the Court, free from the procedural restraints of Articles 169 and 170, if it considers that the member state is making improper use of

---

[27] See Written Question 346/80, *OJ* 1980, C213/6.

its powers under Article 223. The fact that the Court is obliged by Article 225 to give its ruling *in camera* is some indication that it may be expected to receive and impart classified information in the course of the judicial process. No doubt the Court would be reluctant to question a member state's own judgment of where its security interests lay. It might well, however, regard as justiciable any question as to whether the member state's measures were having an adverse effect on the conditions of competition regarding products not intended for specifically military purposes.[28] The answer to that question would determine whether the member state was acting in conformity with Article 223. The Court has so far, however, had little opportunity to consider the scope and effect of this Article. In *Südmilch* v. *Ugliola*[29] the Advocate General did no more than explain why the Article was irrelevant in that case.[30]

Article 224

Although expressed in 'communautaire' language which requires the member states to consult, with the object of preventing interference with the functioning of the common market, Article 224 is in fact by implication an escape clause which allows member states to disregard any rule of free movement, in the circumstances defined in the Article. It reads:

Member States shall consult each other with a view to taking together the steps needed to prevent the functioning of the common market being affected by measures which a Member State may be called upon to take in the event of serious internal disturbances affecting the maintenance of law and order, in the event of war or serious international tension constituting a threat of war, or in order to carry out obligations it has accepted for the purpose of maintaining peace and international security.

The Article applies in three types of situation:

(i)   when there are serious internal disturbances of the kind described, or
(ii) in the event of war or threat thereof, or
(iii) when a member state needs to take action to comply with an obligation it has accepted to maintain peace and international security.

An obvious example of recourse to the Article in the first type of situation would be where a member state restricted or prohibited the importation into part of its territory of offensive weapons or materials, when that part was suffering from serious rioting or other similar disturbances. With regard to the second type, it should be noted that the member state does not have to be one of the belligerents or prospective belligerents. It may

---

[28] e.g. motor tyres which fit both civilian motor cars and military vehicles, and are not specifically earmarked for either.
[29] Case 15/69 [1969] *ECR* 363.
[30] Ibid., p. 373.

need to interfere with the rules of free movement in order to comply with its obligations under international law as a neutral state. Thus a member state would be justified in refusing to allow the export of an armed vessel to another member state, if it was aware that the vessel was destined to be delivered ultimately to one of the belligerents in a conflict in respect of which it had adopted a position of neutrality.

The third type of situation is most likely to arise in the event of a conclusion being reached by the United Nations Security Council which requires members of the United Nations to take certain action—e.g. to deny weapons or strategic materials to those engaged in armed conflict.[31]

It should finally be noted that Article 225 applies the same controls by the Commission and the Court to measures taken under Article 224 as it does to measures taken under Article 223.[32]

Article 233

Article 233 reads:

The provisions of this Treaty shall not preclude the existence or completion of regional unions between Belgium and Luxembourg, or between Belgium, Luxembourg and the Netherlands, to the extent that the objectives of these regional unions are not attained by application of this Treaty.

So far as concerns freedom of movement, the effect of this Article was that the Benelux countries remained free to remove any obstacles to such freedom more rapidly than they were obliged to do under the EEC Treaty. They were able therefore to grant more favourable treatment to each other's nationals than to the nationals of other EEC countries, and the latter could not complain of the corresponding discrimination against them. But once rules are adopted for the same purpose under the EEC Treaty they supplant similar measures taken in the Benelux context.

An example of the survival of national measures preserved by Article 233 can be seen in *Keurkoop* v. *Nancy Kean Gifts*,[33] although the Court placed more emphasis on the fact that the measures in question were justified under Article 36, as an exception to the free movement of goods. Indeed, the Court made only a passing reference to Article 233, in the following passage:

On that issue the Court can only state that in the present state of Community law and in the absence of Community standardization or of a harmonization of laws the determination of the conditions and procedures under which protection of designs

[31] For a discussion of this aspect, see F. Burrows 'Division of Powers between the European Communities and their Member States in the Field of External Relations' (University of Amsterdam, Europa Institute, 1981), pp. 140–2.

[32] See p. 325 above.

[33] Case 144/81 [1982] *ECR* 2853.

is granted is a matter for national rules and, in this instance, for the common legislation established under the regional union between Belgium, Luxembourg and the Netherlands referred to in Article 233 of the Treaty.

Consequently the rules on the free movement of goods do not constitute an obstacle to the adoption of provisions of the kind contained in the Uniform Benelux Law on Designs, as described by the national court.[34]

In its 'dispositif' the Court's ruling was:

National legislation having the characteristics of the Uniform Benelux Law on Designs falls within the scope of the provisions of Article 36 of the Treaty on the protection of industrial and commercial property. In the present state of its development Community law does not prevent the adoption of national provisions of the kind contained in the Uniform Benelux Law, as described by the national court.[35]

Article 234

Article 234 deals with the problems arising from the fact that the original member states had international agreements with third countries, concluded before the entry into force of the EEC Treaty, which were inconsistent with the latter. The general principle adopted was that those agreements could continue to be honoured by the member states of the EEC, but that the latter should do what they could to escape from or modify any obligations under those agreements which conflicted with the EEC Treaty. Article 234 gave effect to that principle in the following terms:

The rights and obligations arising from agreements concluded before the entry into force of this Treaty between one or more Member States on the one hand, and one or more third countries on the other, shall not be affected by the provisions of this Treaty.

To the extent that such agreements are not compatible with this Treaty, the Member State or States concerned shall take all appropriate steps to eliminate the incompatibilities established. Member States shall, where necessary, assist each other to this end and shall, where appropriate, adopt a common attitude.

In applying the agreements referred to in the first paragraph, Member States shall take into account the fact that the advantages accorded under this Treaty by each Member State form an integral part of the establishment of the Community and are thereby inseparably linked with the creation of common institutions, the conferring of powers upon them and the granting of the same advantages by all the other Member States.

Article 5 of the Act of Accession modified Article 234 to make it apply, for the new member states, to international agreements concluded before accession. Article 5 of the Greek Act of Accession similarly preserved agreements concluded by Greece before its accession.

[34] Ibid., p. 2871.   [35] Ibid., p. 2874.

The first thing to note about Article 234 is that the rights and obligations to which it refers are those subsisting between one or more member states on the one hand, and one or more third countries on the other. In the case, therefore, of such agreements as the General Agreement on Tariffs and Trade (GATT), where both member states and third countries are parties, GATT rights and obligations prevail in dealings between any member state of the EEC and any member of the GATT. But as between member states of the EEC, rights and obligations under the EEC Treaty prevail, and not those under the GATT: see *Commission* v. *Italy*.[36]

The second point is that Article 234 relates to agreements 'concluded' before the relevant date. No problem arises in respect of agreements which entered into force before that date. However, a question of interpretation does arise when, as frequently happens in the case of many multilateral agreements such as the commodity agreements, the agreement which was concluded before the relevant date is revised, perhaps in respect of one or two details, and the revised agreement only enters into force after the relevant date. On a strictly textual interpretation of Article 234 it might have been possible to take the view that the revised agreement was not 'concluded' before the relevant date, and that Article 234 did not therefore apply. However, such an interpretation would ignore both the realities of international relations and, it is submitted, the objects and purposes of the Community. During the negotiations leading up to the revised multilateral agreement there is no doubt that it is the duty of the member states of the EEC to seek to remove from that agreement any incompatibilities with the EEC Treaty. But they may fail, particularly in the case of worldwide agreements in respect of which they do not have a sufficiently strong bargaining position. It would in such a case be unreasonable to interpret Article 234 as requiring them to refrain from becoming parties to the revised agreement, even if the amendments made to the previous edition were trivial, and even if it was in the overall economic interests of all member states of the EEC to become parties. It could even be argued that such a narrow view of Article 234 would be inconsistent with the provisions of Article 2, which refers to promoting a continuous and balanced expansion, an increase in stability, and an accelerated raising of the standard of living—all of which objectives may in some measure be achieved by participation in the agreement in question. There is clearly a distinction to be drawn between a revised multilateral agreement which is fundamentally different from the earlier version and a revised version which remains basically the same. There may also be difficulty in deciding into which of these categories a particular revised agreement falls. But it is submitted that, in principle, revised

---

[36] Case 10/61 [1962] *ECR* 1. The Court also interpreted 'rights and obligations' as referring to the rights of third countries and the obligations of member states: ibid., p. 10. See also Joined Cases 56 and 58/64, *Grundig* [1966] *ECR* 299, p. 346.

agreements which either merely prolong the life of the earlier one or introduce insignificant amendments should be regarded as falling within Article 234 if the earlier version was concluded before the relevant date.

Article 234 was considered in *R. v. Henn and Darby*.[37] The case essentially turned on whether restrictions on the import of pornographic material fell within the scope of Article 36. That aspect has already been considered in Chapter 2. One of the questions put to the Court, however, was whether a member state may prohibit imports by reference to obligations arising from the Geneva Convention, 1923, for the suppression of traffic in obscene publications and the Universal Postal Convention, bearing in mind Article 234 of the EEC Treaty. In fact the latter was renewed at Lausanne in 1974 and the renewed version entered into force on 1 January 1976, both dates being after the date of accession to the Community of the United Kingdom. The Court concentrated on Article 36, and held that it allowed national prohibitions on imports of goods which were indecent or obscene, as understood by the laws of the member state in question. Taking account of that finding, the Court concluded that observance of the two Conventions by the United Kingdom was unlikely to result in a conflict with the Community's rules on the free movement of goods.[38] The Court did not say whether the UK would have been entitled to rely on Article 234 if there had been such a conflict. Instead it ruled:

In so far as a Member State avails itself of the reservation relating to the protection of public morality provided for in Article 36 of the Treaty, the provisions of Article 234 do not preclude that State from fulfilling the obligations arising from the Geneva Convention, 1923, for the suppression of traffic in obscene publications and from the Universal Postal Convention (renewed at Lausanne in 1974, which came into force on 1 January 1976).[39]

---

[37] Case 34/79 [1979] *ECR* 3795. See also Case 812/79, *Attorney General* v. *Burgoa* [1980] *ECR* 2787.

[38] Case 34/79 [1979] *ECR* 3795, p. 3816.

[39] Ibid., p. 3818.

First and Second Directives on Free Movement of Capital

FIRST COUNCIL DIRECTIVE[1] FOR THE IMPLEMENTATION OF ARTICLE 67 OF THE TREATY

THE COUNCIL OF THE EUROPEAN ECONOMIC COMMUNITY,

Having regard to the Treaty, and in particular Articles 5, 67(1), 69, 105(2) and 106(2) thereof;

Having regard to the proposal from the Commission, which consulted the Monetary Committee for this purpose;

Having regard to the Decision of 11 May 1960 on the application to Algeria and to the French overseas departments of the provisions of the Treaty concerning capital movements;

Whereas the attainment of the objectives of the Treaty establishing the European Economic Community requires the greatest possible freedom of movement of capital between Member States and therefore the widest and most speedy liberalisation of capital movements;

HAS ADOPTED THIS DIRECTIVE:

Article 1

1. Member States shall grant all foreign exchange authorisations required for the conclusion or performance of transactions or for transfers between residents of Member States in respect of the capital movements set out in List A of Annex I to this Directive.

2. Member States shall enable such transfers of capital to be made on the basis of the exchange rate ruling for payments relating to current transactions.

Where such transfers are made on a foreign exchange market on which the fluctuations of exchange rates are not officially restricted, this obligation shall be taken to mean that the exchange rates applied must not show any appreciable and lasting differences from those ruling for payments relating to current transactions.

The Monetary Committee shall watch closely the trend of exchange rates applied to such transfers of capital, and shall report thereon to the Commission. If the Commission finds that these rates show appreciable and lasting differences from those ruling for payments relating to current transactions, it shall initiate the procedure provided for in Article 169 of the Treaty.

[1] *OJ*, Special Edition, 1959–62, p. 49.

Article 2

1. Member States shall grant general permission for the conclusion or performance of transactions and for transfers between residents of Member States in respect of the capital movements set out in List B of Annex I to this Directive.

2. Where such transfers of capital are made on a foreign exchange market on which the fluctuations of exchange rates are not officially restricted, Member States shall endeavour to ensure that transfers are made at rates which do not show appreciable and lasting differences from those ruling for payments relating to current transactions.

The Commission may, after consulting the Monetary Committee, make recommendations in this connection to the Member States.

3. [Repealed by the Second Directive].

Article 3

1. Subject to paragraph 2 of this Article,[2] Member States shall grant all foreign exchange authorisations required for the conclusion or performance of transactions and for transfers between residents of Member States in respect of the capital movements set out in List C of Annex I to this Directive.

2. When such free movement of capital might form an obstacle to the achievement of the economic policy objectives of a Member State, the latter may maintain or reintroduce the exchange restrictions on capital movement, which were operative on the date of entry into force of this Directive (*in the case of new Member states, the date of accession*).[3] It shall consult the Commission on the matter.

The Commission shall examine the measures for co-ordinating the economic policies of Member States which will enable these difficulties to be overcome and, after consulting the Monetary Committee, shall recommend their adoption by the Member States.

3. The Commission may recommend that the State in question abolish the exchange restrictions which are maintained or reintroduced.

Article 4

The Monetary Committee shall examine at least once a year the restrictions which are applied to the capital movements set out in the lists contained in Annex I to this Directive; it shall report to the Commission regarding restrictions which could be abolished.

---

[2] And to the limited derogations permitted by Art. 1 of Dir. 156/72, *OJ*, Special Edition, 1972, part I, p. 296.

[3] As amended by Act of Accession, Annex I(VII), 3.

Article 5

1. The provisions of this Directive shall not restrict the right of Member States to verify the nature and genuineness of transactions or transfers, or to take all requisite measures to prevent infringements of their laws and regulations.

2. Member States shall simplify as far as possible the authorisation and control formalities applicable to the conclusion or performance of transactions and transfers and shall where necessary consult one another with a view to such simplification.

3. The restrictions on capital movements under the rules for establishment in a Member State shall be abolished pursuant to this Directive only in so far as it is incumbent upon the Member State to grant freedom of establishment in implementation of Articles 52 to 58 of the Treaty.

Article 6

Member States shall endeavour not to introduce within the Community any new exchange restriction affecting the capital movements that were liberalised at the date of entry into force of this Directive (*in the case of new Member States, the date of accession*)[4] nor to make existing provisions more restrictive.

Article 7

Member States shall make known to the Commission, not later than three months after the entry into force of this Directive (*in the case of new Member states, three months after the date of accession*):[5]
(a) the provisions governing capital movements at the date of entry into force of this Directive which are laid down by law, regulation or administrative action;[6]
(b) the provisions adopted in pursuance of the Directive;
(c) the procedures for implementing those provisions.

They shall also make known, not later than the time of entry into force thereof, any new measures going beyond the obligations of this Directive, and any amendment of the provisions governing the capital movements set out in List D of Annex I to this Directive.

Article 8

[Deleted][7]

Article 9

This Directive shall apply without prejudice to the provisions of Articles 67(2), 68(3) and 221 of the Treaty.

4 Ibid.
5 Ibid.
6 Ibid.
7 By Act of Accession, Annex I(VII), 3.

Article 10

Lists A, B, C and D contained in Annex I, together with the Nomenclature of Captial Movements and the Explanatory Notes in Annex II, form an integral part of this Directive.[8]

Done at Luxembourg, 11 May 1960.

SECOND COUNCIL DIRECTIVE[9] OF 18 DECEMBER 1962 ADDING TO AND AMENDING THE FIRST DIRECTIVE FOR THE IMPLEMENTATION OF ARTICLE 67 OF THE TREATY

THE COUNCIL OF THE EUROPEAN ECONOMIC COMMUNITY,

Having regard to the Treaty establishing the European Economic Community, and in particular Articles 5, 67(1), 69, 105(2) and 106(2), thereof;

Having regard to the Decision of 11 May 1960 on the application to Algeria and to the French overseas departments of the provisions of the Treaty concerning the movement of capital;

Having regard to the First Directive of 11 May 1960 for the implementation of Article 67 of the Treaty;

Having regard to the proposal from the Commission, which, for that purpose, consulted the Monetary Committee;

Whereas it is appropriate to consolidate within the European Economic Community the liberalisation of capital movements to which Member States have already committed themselves within the framework of the Organisation for Economic Co-operation and Development;

Whereas the abolition of certain restrictions on the free movement of capital, closely connected with the movement of goods, persons and services, is necessary to ensure the satisfactory establishment and functioning of a common market in these fields;

HAS ADOPTED THIS DIRECTIVE:

Article 1

Article 2(3) of the First Directive of 11 May 1960 for the implementation of Article 67 of the Treaty (hereinafter called 'First Directive') is hereby repealed.

Article 2

Annexes I and II to the First Directive shall be amended as follows:

---

[8] See revised texts of Annexes I and II, pp. 334–42 below, as reproduced in Art. 2 of the Second Directive.

[9] *OJ*, Special Edition, 1963–4, p. 5.

List A: Capital movements referred to in Article 1
of the Directive

	Items of nomenclature
Direct investments	I
excluding purely financial investments made with a view only to giving the persons providing the capital indirect access to the money or capital market of another country, through the creation of an undertaking or participation in an existing undertaking in that country	
Liquidation of direct investments	II
Investments in real estate	V
Personal capital movements	
Gifts and endowments	X B
Dowries	X C
Inheritances	X D
Settlement of debts in their country of origin by immigrants	X E
Transfers of capital belonging to residents who emigrate	X F
Transfers of capital belonging to emigrants returning to their country of origin	X G
Transfers of workers' savings during their period of stay	X H
Transfers by instalment of blocked funds belonging to non-residents by the holders of such funds in case of special hardship	X I
Annual transfers of blocked funds to another Member State by a non-resident account holder, up to an amount or a percentage of the total assets, fixed uniformly by the Member State concerned for all applicants	X L
Transfers of minor amounts abroad	X M
Granting and repayment of short- and medium-term credits related to commercial transactions or to provision of services in which a resident is participating	VII I A (i) and (ii) B (i) and (ii)
Sureties, other guarantees and rights of pledge and transfers connected with them	
related to short- and medium-term credits in respect of commercial transactions or provision of services in which a resident is participating	XII A and B in conjunction with VII I A (i) and (ii) B (i) and (ii)

related to long-term loans with a view to establishing or maintaining lasting economic links	XII A and B in conjunction with I A 3 B 3
Transfers in performance of insurance contracts	XI
as and when freedom of movement in respect of services is extended to those contracts in implementation of Article 59 *et seq.* of the Treaty	
Death duties	XIV A
Damages (where these can be considered as capital)	XIV B
Refunds in the case of cancellation of contracts and refunds of uncalled-for payments (where these can be considered as capital)	XIV C
Authors' royalties. Patents, designs, trade marks and inventions (assignments and transfers arising out of such assignments)	XIV D
Transfers of the moneys required for the provision of services	XIV E

The use of the proceeds of liquidation of assets abroad belonging to residents must be permitted at least within the limits of the obligations as regards liberalisation accepted by Member States.

List B: Capital movements referred to in Article 2 of the Directive

	Items of nomenclature
Operations in securities	
Acquisition by non-residents of domestic securities dealt in on a stock exchange (excluding units of unit trusts) and repatriation of the proceeds of liquidation thereof	IV A
Acquisition by residents of foreign securities dealt in on a stock exchange and use of the proceeds of liquidation thereof	IV B
— excluding the acquisition of bonds issued on a foreign market and denominated in national currency — excluding units of unit trusts	
Physical movements of the securities mentioned above	IV E in conjunction with IV A IV B

The use of the proceeds of liquidation of assets abroad belonging to residents must be permitted at least within the limits of the obligations as regards liberalisation accepted by Member States.

List C: Capital movements referred to in Article 3 of the Directive

	Items of nomenclature
Issue and placing of securities of a domestic undertaking on a foreign capital market	III A 2
Issue and placing of securities of a foreign undertaking on the domestic capital market	III B 2
Operation in securities	
Acquisition by non-residents of domestic securities not dealt in on a stock exchange and repatriation of the proceeds of liquidation thereof	IV C
Acquisition by residents of foreign securities not dealt in on a stock exchange and use of the proceeds of liquidation thereof	IV D
Acquisition by non-residents of units in domestic unit trusts dealt in on a stock exchange and repatriation of the proceeds of liquidation thereof	IV A
Acquisition by residents of units in foreign unit trusts dealt in on a stock exchange and use of the proceeds of liquidation thereof	IV B
Acquisition by residents of foreign bonds dealt in on a stock exchange, issued on a foreign market and denominated in national currency	IV B 3 (i)
Physical movements of the securities mentioned above	IV E in conjunction with IV C, D and IV B 3 (i)
Granting and repayment of long-term credits related to commercial transactions or to the provision of services in which a resident is participating	VII I A (iii) and B (iii)
Granting and repayment of medium- and long-term credits related to commercial transactions or to the provision of services in which no resident is participating	VII 2 A (ii) and (iii) B (ii) and (iii)
Granting and repayment of medium- and long-term loans and credits not related to commercial transactions or to the provision of services	VIII A (ii) and (iii) B (iii)
Sureties, other guarantees and rights of pledge and transfers connected with them and relating to:	
long-term credits in respect of commercial transactions or provision of services in which a resident is participating	XII A and B in conjunction with VII I A (iii) B (iii)

medium- and long-term credits in respect of commercial transactions or provision of services in which no resident is participating	XII A and B in conjunction with VII 2 A (ii) and (iii) B (ii) and (iii)
medium- and long-term loans and credits not related to commercial transactions or to provision of services	XII A and B in conjunction with VIII A (ii) and (iii) B (ii) and (iii)

The use of the proceeds of liquidation of assets abroad belonging to residents must be permitted at least within the limits of the obligations as regards liberalisation accepted by Member States.

List D: Capital movements referred to in Article 4 of the Directive

	Items of nomenclature
Short-term investments in Treasury bills and other securities normally dealt in on the money market	VI
Opening and placing of funds on current or deposit accounts, repatriation or use of balances on current or deposit accounts with credit institutions	IX
Granting and repayment of short-term credits related to commercial transactions or to provision of services in which no resident is participating	VII 2 A (i) B (i)
Granting and repayment of short-term loans and credits not related to commercial transactions or to provisions of services	VIII A (i) B (i)
Personal capital movements	X A
loans	
Sureties, other guarantees and rights of pledge and transfers connected with them	
related to short-term credits in respect of commercial transactions or to provision of services in which no resident is participating	XII A and B in conjunction with VII 2 A (i) B (i)
related to short-term loans and credits not connected with commercial transactions or to provision of services	XII A and B in conjunction with VIII A (i) B (i)
related to private loans	XII A and B in conjunction with X A
Physical import and export of financial assets	XIII
Other capital movements: Miscellaneous	XIV F

ANNEX II

NOMENCLATURE OF CAPITAL MOVEMENTS

I. Direct investments*

A. *Direct investments on national territory by non-residents* *

1. Establishment and extension of branches of new undertakings belonging solely to the person providing the capital, and the acquisition in full of existing undertakings

2. Participation in new or existing undertakings with a view to establishing or maintaining lasting economic links

3. Long-term loans with a view to establishing or maintaining lasting economic links

4. Reinvestment of profits with a view to maintaining lasting economic links

B. *Direct investments abroad by residents* *

1. Establishment and extension of branches or new undertakings belonging solely to the person providing the capital, and the acquisition in full of existing undertakings

2. Participation in new or existing undertakings with a view to establishing or maintaining lasting economic links

3. Long-term loans with a view to establishing or maintaining lasting economic links

4. Reinvestment of profits with a view to maintaining lasting economic links

II. Liquidation of direct investments

A. *Repatriation of the proceeds of the liquidation* * of direct investments on national territory by non-residents*

1. Principal

2. Capital appreciation

B. *Use of the proceeds of liquidation of direct investments abroad by residents*

1. Principal

2. Capital appreciation

III. Admission of securities to the capital market

A. *Admission of securities of a domestic undertaking to a foreign capital market*

1. Introduction* on a foreign stock exchange

(a) of shares and other securities of a participating nature

(b) of bonds

   (i) denominated in national currency

   (ii) denominated in foreign currency

2. Issue and placing* on a foreign capital market

(a) of shares and other securities of a participating nature

(b) of bonds

   (i) denominated in national currency

   (ii) denominated in foreign currency

B. *Admission of securities of a foreign undertaking to a domestic capital market*

1. Introduction on a domestic stock exchange

(a) of shares and other securities of a participating nature

(b) of bonds

   (i) denominated in national currency

   (ii) denominated in foreign currency

2. Issue and placing on a domestic capital market

(a) of shares and other securities of a participating nature

(b) of bonds

   (i) denominated in national currency

   (ii) denominated in foreign currency

C. *Admission of domestic securities of the public sector to a foreign capital market pursuant to Article 68(3) of the Treaty*

1. Introduction of securities on a foreign stock exchange

* See Explanatory Notes, below.

(a) denominated in national currency

(b) denominated in foreign currency

2. Issue and placing of securities on a foreign capital market

(a) denominated in national currency

(b) denominated in foreign currency

D. *Admission of foreign securities of the public sector to a domestic capital market pursuant to Article 68(3) of the Treaty*

1. Introduction of securities on a domestic stock exchange

(a) denominated in national currency

(b) denominated in foreign currency

2. Issue and placing of securities on a domestic capital market

(a) denominated in national currency

(b) denominated in foreign currency

IV. Operations in securities*
(not included under I, II and III)

A. *Acquisition by non-residents of domestic securities* dealt in on a stock exchange* and repatriation of the proceeds of liquidation thereof*

(a) quoted*

(b) unquoted*

1. Acquisition of shares* and other securities of a participating nature

2. Repatriation of the proceeds of liquidation of shares and other securities of a participating nature

3. Acquisition of bonds*

(i) denominated in national currency

(ii) denominated in foreign currency

4. Repatriation of the proceeds of liquidation of bonds.

B. *Acquisition by residents of foreign securities* dealt in on a stock exchange and use of the proceeds of liquidation thereof*

(a) quoted

(b) unquoted

1. Acquisition of shares and other securities of a participating nature

2. Use of the proceeds of liquidation of shares and other securities of a participating nature

3. Acquisition of bonds

(i) denominated in national currency

(ii) denominated in foreign currency

4. Use of the proceeds of liquidation of bonds

C. *Acquisition by non-residents of domestic securities not dealt in on a stock exchange and repatriation of the proceeds of liquidation thereof*

1. Acquisition of shares and other securities of a participating nature

2. Repatriation of the proceeds of liquidation of shares and other securities of a participating nature

3. Acquisition of bonds

(i) denominated in national currency

(ii) denominated in foreign currency

4. Repatriation of the proceeds of liquidation of bonds

D. *Acquisition by residents of foreign securities not dealt in on a stock exchange and use of the proceeds of liquidation thereof*

1. Acquisition of shares and other securities of a participating nature

2. Use of the proceeds of liquidation of shares and other securities of a participating nature

3. Acquisition of bonds

(i) denominated in national currency

(ii) denominated in foreign currency

4. Use of the proceeds of liquidation of bonds

E. *Physical movements of securities*

1. Belonging to non-residents

(a) import

(b) export

2. Belonging to residents

(a) import

(b) export

* See Explanatory Notes, below.

V. Investments in real estate*
(not included under I and II)

A. *Investments in real estate on national territory by non-residents and repatriation of the proceeds of liquidation thereof*

1. Acquisition of real estate

2. Repatriation of the proceeds of liquidation of real estate

B. *Investments in real estate abroad by residents and use of the proceeds of liquidation thereof*

1. Acquisition of real estate

2. Use of the proceeds of liquidation of real estate

VI. Short-term investment in Treasury bills and other securities normally dealt in on the money market

1. Denominated in national currency

2. Denominated in foreign currency

A. *Short-term investments by non-residents on a domestic money market and repatriation of the proceeds of liquidation thereof*

(a) by natural persons* ⎱ other than financial
(b) by legal persons* ⎰ institutions

(c) by financial institutions*

B. *Short-term investments by residents on a foreign money market and use of the proceeds of liquidation thereof*

(a) by natural persons* ⎱ other than financial
(b) by legal persons* ⎰ institutions

(c) by financial institutions*

VII. Granting and repayment of credits related to commercial transactions or to provision of services

1. In which a resident is participating

2. In which no resident is participating

A. *Credits granted by non-residents to residents:*

(i) short-term (less than one year)
(ii) medium-term (from one to five years)
(iii) long-term (five years or more)

(a) by natural persons ⎱ other than financial
(b) by legal persons ⎰ institutions

(c) by financial institutions

B. *Credits granted by residents to non-residents:*

(i) short-term (less than one year)
(ii) medium-term (from one to five years)
(iii) long-term (five years or more)

(a) by natural persons ⎱ other than financial
(b) by legal persons ⎰ institutions

(c) by financial institutions

VIII. Granting and repayment of loans and credits not related to commercial transactions or to provision of services
(not included under I and X)

A. *Loans and credits granted by non-residents to residents:*

(i) short-term (less than one year)
(ii) medium-term (from one to five years)
(iii) long-term (five years or more)

(a) by natural persons ⎱ other than financial
(b) by legal persons ⎰ institutions

(c) by financial institutions

B. *Loans and credits granted by residents to non-residents:*

(i) short-term (less than one year)
(ii) medium-term (from one to five years)
(iii) long-term (five years or more)

(a) by natural persons ⎱ other than financial
(b) by legal persons* ⎰ institutions

(c) by financial institutions*

IX. Opening and placing of funds on current and deposit accounts, repatriation or use of balances on current or deposit accounts with credit institutions*

A. *By non-residents with domestic credit institutions*

1. Accounts and balances in national currency

2. Accounts and balances in foreign currency

(a) by natural persons ⎱ other than financial
(b) by legal persons* ⎰ institutions

(c) by financial institutions*

B. *By residents with foreign credit institutions*

1. Accounts and balances in national currency

2. Accounts and balances in foreign currency

(a) by natural persons ⎱ other than financial
(b) by legal persons* ⎰ institutions

(c) by financial institutions*

* See Explanatory Notes, below.

X. Personal capital movements
(not covered by the other sections)

A. *Loans*

1. Loans granted by non-residents to residents

2. Loans granted by residents to non-residents

B. *Gifts and endorsements*

C. *Dowries*

D. *Inheritances*

E. *Settlement of debts in their country of origin by immigrants*

F. *Transfers of capital belonging to residents who emigrate and are:*

1. Nationals of the country in question

2. Nationals of other countries

G. *Transfers of capital belonging to emigrants returning to their country of origin*

H. *Transfers of workers' savings during their period of stay*

I. *Transfers by instalment of blocked funds belonging to non-residents by the holders of such funds in case of special hardship*

L. *Annual transfers of blocked funds to another Member State by a non-resident account-holder, up to an amount or a percentage of the total assets, fixed uniformly by the Member State concerned for all applicants*

M. *Transfers of minor amounts abroad*

XI. Transfers in performance of insurance contracts

A. *Premiums and payments in respect of life assurance*

1. Contracts concluded between domestic life assurance companies and non-residents

2. Contracts concluded between foreign life assurance companies and residents

B. *Premiums and payments in respect of credit insurance*

1. Contracts concluded between domestic credit insurance companies and non-residents

2. Contracts concluded between foreign credit insurance companies and residents

C. *Other transfers of capital in respect of insurance contracts*

XII. Sureties, other guarantees and rights of pledge and transfers relating to them

A. *Granted by non-residents to residents*

B. *Granted by residents to non-residents*

XIII. Import and export of financial assets

A. *Securities (not included under IV) and means of payment of every kind*

B. *Gold*

XIV. Other capital movements

A. *Death duties*

B. *Damages (where these can be considered as capital)*

C. *Refunds in the case of cancellation of contracts and refunds of uncalled-for payments (where these can be considered as capital)*

D. *Authors' royalties*

Patents, designs, trade marks and inventions (assignments and transfers arising out of such assignments)

E. *Transfers of the moneys required for the provision of services* (not included under IX)

F. *Miscellaneous*

Explanatory notes

For the purposes of this Nomenclature, the following expressions have the meanings assigned to them respectively:

Direct investments

Investments of all kinds by natural persons or commercial, industrial or financial undertakings, and which serve to establish or to maintain lasting and direct links between the person providing the capital and the entrepreneur to whom or the undertaking to which the capital is made available in order to carry on an economic activity. This concept must therefore be understood in its widest sense.

The undertakings mentioned under 1 include legally independent undertakings (wholly-owned subsidiaries) and branches.

As regards those undertakings mentioned under 2 which have the status of companies limited by shares, there is participation in the nature of direct investment where the block of shares held by a natural person or another undertaking or any other holder enables the shareholder, either pursuant to the provisions of national laws relating to companies limited by shares or otherwise, to participate effectively in the management of the company or in its control.

Long-term loans of a participating nature, mentioned under 3, means loans for a period of more than five years which are made for the purpose of establishing or maintaining lasting economic links. The main examples which may be cited are loans granted by a company to its subsidiaries or to companies in which it has a share, and loans linked with a profit-sharing arrangement. Loans granted by financial institutions with a view to establishing or maintaining lasting economic links are also included under this heading.

Residents or non-residents

Natural and legal persons according to the definitions laid down in the exchange control regulations in force in each Member State.

Proceeds of liquidation (of investments, securities, etc.)

Proceeds of sale, amount of repayments, proceeds of execution of judgments, etc.

Introduction on a stock exchange

The admission of securities—in accordance with a specified procedure—to dealings on a stock exchange, whether controlled officially or unofficially, and their admission to public sale.

Securities dealt in on a stock exchange (quoted or unquoted)

Securities the dealings in which are controlled by regulations, the prices for which are regularly published, either by official stock exchanges (quoted securities) or by other bodies attached to a stock exchange—e.g. committees of banks (unquoted securities).

Placing of securities

The direct sale of securities by the issuer, or sale thereof by the consortium which the issuer has instructed to sell them.

Operations in securities

Any dealings in securities, including the initial sale of units by unit trusts.

Domestic or foreign securities

Securities according to the country in which the issuer has his principal place of business.

Shares

Include rights to subscribe for new issue of shares.

Bonds (under IV of the Nomenclature)

Bonds issued by public or private bodies.

Investments in real estate

Purchases of buildings and land and the construction of buildings by private persons for gain or personal use. This category does not include loans secured by mortgages, but it does include rights of usufruct, easements and building rights.

Natural or legal persons

As defined by the national rules.

Financial institutions

Banks, savings banks and institutions specialising in the provision of short-, medium- and long-term credit, and insurance companies, building societies, investment companies and other institutions of like character.

Credit institutions

Banks, savings banks and institutions specialising in the provision of short-, medium- and long-term credit.

Index